MEDIA &
PERFORMANCE

PAJ BOOKS Bonnie Marranca & Gautam Dasgupta, Series Editors

JOHANNES BIRRINGER

MEDIA &

PERFORMANCE

ALONG THE BORDER

THE JOHNS HOPKINS UNIVERSITY PRESS   **Baltimore and London**

© 1998 The Johns Hopkins University Press
All rights reserved. Published 1998
Printed in the United States of America on acid-free recycled paper
9 8 7 6 5 4 3 2 1

The Johns Hopkins University Press
2715 North Charles Street
Baltimore, Maryland 21218-4319
www.press.jhu.edu

Library of Congress Cataloging-in-Publication Data will be found
at the end of this book.
A catalog record for this book is available from the British Library.

ISBN 0-8018-5851-8
ISBN 0-8018-5852-6 (pbk.)

To my mother, Friedel Beisiegel,

to Kazuo Ohno, dancing La Argentina,

and to Imma Sarries-Zgonc,

dancing on the edge of the water

CONTENTS

List of Illustrations ix   Preface xiii   Acknowledgments xxi

List of Abbreviations xxvii

1   This Is the Theater That Was to Be Expected and Foreseen   3

1 DANCING WITH TECHNOLOGIES

2   Corporealities and Digital Bodies   27
3   Dance Screens   59

2 IMPOSSIBLE ANATOMIES

4   Lively Bodies–Lively Machines: A Workshop   105
5   Performance / Video Art   145

3 CULTURE IN ACTION

6   *Ad Mortem:* An AIDS Performance Project   189
7   Media Activism   204

4 VIRTUAL COMMUNITIES

8   Embodiment: Sharing Our Wounds   237
9   Disembodiment: The Virtual Realities   258

Notes 353   Index 375

ILLUSTRATIONS

Imma Sarries-Zgonc in *Parsifal,* opera installation/performance, Festspielhaus Hellerau, Dresden, Ninth Dresden Festival of Contemporary Music, Germany. 1995. 2

Robert Wilson's Vision, 1990. Model of set for *the CIVIL warS* (scene 1C) by Robert Wilson. 10

Théâtre du Soleil, *Les Atrides,* directed by Ariane Mnouchkine. A scene from Part 1 of *Iphigenia in Aulis,* performed at the Brooklyn Academy of Music, New York, 1992. 11

Bill T. Jones / Arnie Zane Dance Company performing in *Still / Here,* presented at the Shubert Theatre, Chicago, 1995. 14

Meg Stuart's Damaged Goods Company performing in *No One Is Watching,* presented at the Tanz im August Festival in Berlin, Hebbel Theater, 1995. 14

Guillermo Gómez-Peña and Coco Fusco performing *The New World (B)Order* at Randolph Street Gallery, Chicago, 1993. 17

Ron Athey performing his *Martyrs and Saints* at Randolph Street Gallery, Chicago, 1993. 22

A scene from Part 1 ("Personal Climate") of *Atlas,* an opera by Meredith Monk, presented at the Houston Grand Opera, 1991. 23

Molitveni stroj Noordung (Noordung Prayer Machine), created by Dragan Živadinov and performed by the Cosmokinetic Kabinet, Ljubljana, 1993. 54

Sketches of stage construction by Dragan Živadinov for the *Noordung* project, designed by Vadim Fiškin. 54

Stelarc performing in *Actuate/Rotate: Event for Virtual Body,* Obscure Gallery, Quebec, Canada. Video still, 1993. 62

Stelarc performing in *Scanning Robot, Automatic Arm & Third Hand,* MCA, Sydney, Australia, 1997. 62

Performance design by Stelarc & Merlin for *Involuntary Body/Third Hand,* a continuous performance/installation created for *Parasite: Event for Invaded and Involuntary Body,* Wood Street Galleries, Pittsburgh, Pa., 1997. 62

Betontanc performing in *Every Word a Gold Coin's Worth,* choreographed by Matjaž Pograjc, Festspielhaus Hellerau, 1994. 74

Wim Vandekeybus's Ultima Vez company performing *Mountains Made of Barking,* Tanzwerkstatt-Europa Festival, Munich, 1994. 83

x   Sankai Juku performing *Yuragi* (In a Space of Perpetual Motion),
        directed by Ushio Amagatsu, North Shore Center for the
        Performing Arts, Chicago, 1996. 89
     Pina Bausch Wuppertaler Tanztheater performing in *Palermo, Palermo,*
        presented at the Brooklyn Academy of Music, New York, 1991. 89
     LBLM, collaborative performance at Split Screen Festival, Chichester,
        England, 1996. 134
     LBLM, collaborative performance at Split Screen Festival, Chichester,
        England, 1996. 138
     Computer drawing of interactive configuration. 140
     Wolf Vostell, *Heuschrecken,* 1969–70. 160
     Peter Campus, *dor,* 1975. Installation view: Bykert Gallery, New York.
        160
     Ulrike Rosenbach, *Psyche und Eros,* 1981. 161
     Bill Viola, *Room for Saint John of the Cross,* 1983. 161
     Gretchen Bender, *Total Recall,* 1987. 161
     Nam June Paik, *TV Buddha,* 1974. 162
     Nam June Paik, *Fin de Siècle, II,* 1989. 162
     Francesc Torres, *Plus Ultra,* 1988. 162
     Street-Level Video, Block Party, 1993. 182
     Deborah Hay moving in front of the screen in her "Bad Angel" dance,
        Ad Mortem, Lawndale Art Center, Houston, 1990. 199
     Screen projection in "The Body," with Richard Nunemaker on bass
        clarinet, *Ad Mortem,* Lawndale Art Center, Houston, 1990. 199
     Deborah Hay at the head of the march of the Body Positive coalition,
        with Isabelle Ganz in a scene from *Ad Mortem,* Lawndale Art
        Center, Houston, 1990. 199
     Sammy Cucher, Video still from *CULT,* part 2 of *CORPUS,* 1990–92.
        225
     Sammy Cucher, Video still from *Meditations,* 1990. 225
     Sammy Cucher, *Blood Exile 2,* 1991. 225
     Andi Pihl, "Untitled," from "The Home Series." Chromogenic print,
        1990. Randolph Street Gallery, Chicago, 1991. 251
     Jo Spence, "Libido Uprising," part 1, with Rosy Martin, 1989.
        Randolph Street Gallery, Chicago, 1991. 252
     Kiki Smith, "Untitled" (detail), 1990; wax, wood, cheese cloth. 261
     Numerical processing of the archaeological map of the Forum of
        Pompeii. *Rediscovering Pompeii,* 1990. 264
     Liz Larner, "Body Cultures" (detail), 1991, nutrient agar, glass, food
        coloring, stainless steel. 268

Illustrations

Fantasielabor, "Dancing in the Ruins," Old power plant,　　　　　　　　　　xi
　　Eisenhüttenstadt, 1995. 335
Fantasielabor, The closed space of the Aktivist before the squatting
　　action, Eisenhüttenstadt, 1995. 342
Fantasielabor, "Squatting Action," the Aktivist, Eisenhüttenstadt, 1995.
　　343
Imma Sarries-Zgonc in *Parsifal*, opera installation/performance,
　　Festspielhaus Hellerau, Dresden, Ninth Dresden Festival of
　　Contemporary Music, Germany, 1995. 350

P R E F A C E

This preface might have been different had it been possible to publish all my video diaries, photos, sketches, and rehearsal notes, along with the dialogues, reviews, and workshop documentations of the media/performance work I encountered or participated in over the past six years. What is offered here instead is a compressed version of a body of thinking directly related to media production in and along the borders of the performing arts, the visual arts, and the new electronic arts in both the real world and the so-called virtual world of the Internet.

In terms of my investigations, a "body of thinking" here primarily implies a consciousness of performance based on physical practices and a conceptual knowledge of theater, dance, video, and performance art. It was my hope to write this book without making any unnecessary distinctions between performance media, visual media, and the new technologies of digital or immersive media, but I believe there exists a widespread uncertainty about the impact of performance art on cultural, aesthetic, and educational debates over traditional genres and newly expanding intermedia forms (including "public art") and their relations to popular culture and technology. Without always acknowledging it, many traditional disciplines of the fine and theatrical arts find themselves in an increasingly anachronistic relationship to the speed with which technological changes and electronic-information processing are transforming virtually every cultural and political activity as well as our social lives and means of communication. Basically, I believe that our exposure to mediascapes and the popular dimensions of cyberspace—for example, in the overwhelming presence of the electronic vernacular of video technology, broadcast television, MTV, digital music sampling, and computer processing—inevitably transforms our working habits, perceptions, and conceptual frameworks. Here I will neither repeat postmodern or postcolonial media theories nor dwell on academic performativities that marginalize the arts, but keep a close contact with issues and contexts of performance production.

A body of thinking about performance today is affected, in a physical and psychic way, by the rapidly changing parameters of production and transmission; the velocity of change affects our sense of embodiment or disembodiment in ways that crucially shape the responses of artists who focus on the use of media in relation to larger processes in the political culture. In my account of contemporary media possibilities for personal action and aesthetic or conceptual appropriation, I am therefore motivated, above all, by a series of questions that arise at the level of local artistic collaboration and production as well as at the level of distribution, display, and performance as modes of shifting a globally distributed set of technologies. In other words, globally distributed broadcast or satellite media or data transmissions on the Internet interest me only insofar as artists and local communities or alternative cultural producers and their collaborators in arts organizations make use of new compositional techniques and aesthetic strategies that effectively deal with technological culture in terms of self-definition and creative intervention.

Mainstream institutions such as museums and galleries have recognized the significance of the new time-based arts (video, projection, sonic, and digital), and their gradual acceptance of new parameters of display reflects back on the many site-specific and boundary-crossing experiments in performance that have shaped the history of the Western avant-garde over the past three decades. The history of performance art is, of course, much longer, and it has evolved in conjunction with popular and revolutionary cultures both inside and outside the West. Today's hybrid transcultural formations of media performance are the outcome of continuous crossovers in the political history of diaspora cultures, transmigration, and displacement.

As will become clear in these pages, my commitment is to a critical and interpretive writing practice that is inextricably linked to my own performance and production work, as well as to the work of artists and activists whose impact I have felt in many of those disciplines and diverse cultural-political contexts I have traversed. This book on media and performance near the end of the century is, in one sense, a travel book, in that I am able to view the relationships between media and performance in light of the distances I have crossed and the "movement" I have rehearsed in the workshops and contact improvisations with other dancers, performers, musicians, and media producers.

In the first half of this book I address the history of dancing in a more specific sense by recalling the movements of expressionism, abstraction, and constructivism, which take me back to revolutionary and utopian scenarios at the beginning of the century, only to travel forward in time again to the current conjunction of technology and dance in the symptomatic hyperdance of the late eighties (Wim Vandekeybus) and the new experiments of virtual choreography or digitally enhanced performance. My passion for dancing should become obvious throughout. I follow some of its historical traces in the expressionism of early German *Ausdruckstanz* and in Pina Bausch's *Tanztheater*, while paying close attention to conceptual and constructivist tendencies in eastern Europe and to movement abstraction in modern and postmodern dance in the United States. The traces of the latter conjoin with current experiments in "technography," the new interfaces between choreography and computer programming that I examine in chapter 2 and in the "workshop" chapter on Lively Bodies–Lively Machines (LBLM).

The workshop character of chapter 3 represents a deliberate attempt to highlight some of the current artistic processes involved in integrating a respect for bodily knowledge and the intelligence of dance, on the one hand, with provocative forays into "impossible anatomies" and the unseen or unimagined movement potentials generated through interactive and immersive computer technologies, on the other. The question of *interactivity* involves a range of issues that link political concerns about identity, gender, sexuality, and embodiment with an ethics of performance that includes a dynamic interplay with concepts of virtuality. It is important to consider this interplay from the points of view of artistic practitioners themselves, which have begun to inform technological development in interface design. In this context, after an excursion into the multimedia performances of Stelarc, Laurie Anderson, and Lucinda Childs, I address the "LifeForms" and CD-ROM "Improvisation Technologies" developed by Merce Cunningham and William Forsythe. Most important, I follow the exciting research and productions of the generation of young female choreographers, creators of videodance, and media artists that extend the inspiring legacy of the Judson Church.

To move from the LBLM workshop of chapter 4 to *Ad Mortem* in chapter 6 represents an unmistakable passage between larger historical trajectories in video art and video production and toward local video activism. In this passage, occurring midway in my study, I describe an aesthetics of video and performance that cannot be written as an art-historical chapter of late modernism but that illuminates the usefulness of media strategies—image/sound projections, documents, testimonial, participant education, self-empowerment—within a new cultural dynamic of performance linked to activism and community media projects, which in Chicago have come to be known as "culture-in-action." Chapter 7, which describes my involvement in gay activist struggles to alleviate the AIDS crisis, points to this space between performance and media. The vital role of alternative and activist video production, that is, the transformation of an aesthetic into a collaborative-production mode that challenges current media theories and practices, also marks a point of departure in my own transition, not only from the South to the Midwest but also from the theater to site-specific, cross-cultural performance collaboration. These transitional sections, then, anchor my personal commitment to thinking through performance media as *unstable media,* as evolving and continuously contested and contesting instruments in the negotiations between political and image space.

The *border*—concrete and material as well as virtual and imaginary—is my existential metaphor for intermediary spaces of experience and practice. And since this book ends with both a chapter on feminist and queer media practices and one on future cybernetic museums and present low-level street actions employing "virtual reality" technologies, it is necessary for me to indicate that the broader negotiation with border crossings and cross-cultural performance that represents the main thesis of this book is the subject of a companion book tentatively titled *Border-Work.* The latter and *Media & Performance* share a double emphasis on image production in media and performance along borders extended (or disappearing) between practitioners, the imagined referent of the productions, and viewers. My interest in image production and projection, linked to dance and physical theater, therefore involves both an erotics of performance that can be examined in light of the sensuous, sexual, kinetic, aural, tactile, and emphatic qualities of contemporary videosomatic work. It is self-evident that, given the contexts of actual border crossings and site-specific productions my ensemble performed in North America, Cuba, Slovenia, East Germany, Finland, Holland, and England, an ongoing negotiation with the aesthetics and politics of collaboration in this paradoxical age of globalization and reemergent nationalisms is clearly also involved. As in the "border-work," the trajectory of this book—from my initial chapter on the dislocation of theater and dance to the final speculations on "virtual communities" both within and outside the Internet—traces new and diverse media-based contexts and parameters in which intermediary spaces (and the construction of spaces) figure both in relation to the reimagining of the human body in an age of digital manipulation and, more important, with regard to the politics of imaginary identities and communities. Borders, in this sense, always imply movement and an intimacy with the sensory landscapes in which we imagine or locate our desire. Some borders demarcate differences, which are also imaginary, while others remind us of the limits of disturbance which we must perform in order to recover our unstable sense of belonging.

The idea for this book can be traced back to November 1989, when I was a distant observer of the dancing on the shattered Berlin Wall. I didn't quite trust the dancing even though I could imagine the sense of euphoria. Yet I feel that it is impossible for us to grasp "history," reflecting the passage of time and of momentous events, except emotionally, viscerally, as sometimes happens when we witness a powerful performance we don't understand except for its bodily and affective impact on us. The problem, in this case, was that I was watching the dancing on television; its virtuality became an obsession I have tried to examine, in a number of ways, in subsequent performance experiments that explore the relations between our physical movement and connection in time and space, on the one hand, and our mediated and electronically processed movement, our life as images, our monitoring of our bodies and desires, on the other.

Since the summer of 1990, I have returned regularly to Berlin and to the remains of the wall that divided the East from the West. There I began an "archaeological" video project (*Border-Land*) in the death zone, or no-man's-land, of the dismantled border, deciding to film the same locations in Berlin and along the East German–Polish border for a total of five years, seeking to create a thick description of the physical and ideological transformations in the border zones. Trying to experience and learn from the revolutionary changes in eastern Europe, in the next few years I traveled not only along the East German border but also into Poland, Hungary, the Czech Republic, and Yugoslavia at a time when the collapse of the former Soviet Union became imminent and the war between Serbia and Croatia began, followed by the Serbian attack against Bosnia. The most devastating border (re)opened in Sarajevo, as if Berlin had only been a temporary, ecstatic illusion. (I comment on this euphoria in chapter 2.)

My writing, in other words, evolved during these historical phases of the video-documentary process, and we also began to utilize the found and constructed footage in the collaborative-performance work created with ensemble members, artists, and fellow travelers. During this process, some of us founded an ensemble called AlienNation Co., whose members worked together to produce research and media/performances but which also functioned as a conceptual structure of operations for projects that did not necessarily take place in one place or needed to be identified with the same members. Our sometimes quite dispersed company recognizes "alienation" as a preface to the experience of working together, belonging, and not belonging. The pages that follow are indebted to this process of working without belonging, exploring production, political action, and personal conflicts. They are indebted to the critical experiences that arise from physical encounters, emotional relationships, and intellectual desires. Crossing the borders of familiar methods and structures of belonging requires a radical passion for improvisation, since scores and libretti keep being modified. Video functions as an unstable, changeable form of memory notation, my labanotation system.

In this type of work we practitioners do a lot of reassembling and re-mixing, and there is no foolproof series of exercises. I trust this book will not serve as a guide to performance training. But we improvise close to the limits of our imagination, and what I find so encouraging about the practice of collaboration is the necessarily constant struggle to remain receptive to the ever-widening range of the unexpected, the unpredict-able, and the transformative experience. Our creativity in performance depends on our physical awareness and critical sensitivity toward the media by means of which we translate each other's ideas, movements, and images. Although the creative process draws on what we know, there are no safeguards to protect us from the pressures of the social worlds in which we encounter the fearfulness and violence of transformation. In a sense, what I am addressing here are the limits of the aesthetic, the limits of the protection of forms.

Crossing between the political unconscious and the political con-scious, performers and cultural workers participate, by means of their embodied practices, actions, and activisms, in an ongoing social pro-cess, as well as in the production of knowledge about culture. As the boundaries between aesthetics and popular culture or between art and everyday cultural commodity production or consumption blur, media/performance itself becomes a contested concept or "property." Even though it has not been properly analyzed by contemporary theorists and philosophers, it has certainly been instrumental in promoting activism and has been celebrated in queer parades and in our "doing it together," not thinking about fucking up, not thinking about dying at a time when many already have died, remembering the link between mourning and militancy.

The blurring is necessary. Crossing the line and coming out and testing the limits of separation and rejection, which are culturally re-inforced yet always incompletely. If border relations are also property relations (whose border? whose bodyguards?), then my writing here will also emerge at the intersection of diverse genres and "techniques of the body writing," rehearsal methods, warm-up exercises, physical diaries, critical theories, reviewing habits, dinner conversations, memories, per-formance scripts, storyboards. How do I look? How do I re-view the looking?

Dancing is the movement of fantasy. It moves boundaries and touches the screens of projection. It is not contained by texts and computer memories. It thus reenacts the contested borders of scholar-ship, autobiography, fiction, and performance theory and criticism, hypothetically enjoying the fantasy of not belonging. Above all, it hopes to show that the politics of research and the politics of performance are existentially experienced, a searching for and writing about possible communities and shared borders.

ACKNOWLEDGMENTS

Initially I had planned to forgo the traditional use of the book format altogether, hoping to turn this project into an experimental video-essay. Almost all of my performance works and workshops, as well as many encounters and conversations, have been documented audiovisually. They have video lives, and my writings and reflections usually follow the practical work and the videomatic or photographic essays that are created in the diachronic process. I often feel that video and electronic postproduction have increasingly become important instruments of critical and analytical reflection on our work in different cultural locations. They are also independent and interdependent modes of creative production, infiltrating the performance work with the specific memory they record or construct of the collaborations that are the basis for these pages. Deborah Leveranz, a producer at Dallas Community Access Television during the period I resided there, taught me how to use the camera, but the integration of video and performance took time; only in the past few years have I explored the full potential of video to participate in research and its transformation.

This book should have been a documentary or a performance film, blurring even further the false distinction between memory and history, theory and practice, and thus implicating the poetic into the diffracted critical transcriptions that give form to the concepts in the chapters or scenes that follow. I am grateful to all those collaborators who helped in the construction of the images in this book, and who gave me permission to intercut some of the visual narratives of our collective memory and physical interactions into these pages. I am also grateful to the book's designer, Glen Burris, for exhibiting a willingness to experiment with the textures of video stills, computer printouts, and photographs. I am particularly grateful for the loyalty and support of series editors Bonnie Marranca and Gautam Dasgupta, who believed in this project, and to Henry Krawitz for the great care, enthusiasm, and sensitivity in his editing of the manuscript. Finally, thanks to Douglas Armato and Barbara Lamb for being the best editors any author could hope for. The photographs of other exhibitions, films, and performances are reproduced with the permission of those artists whose work I encountered and reviewed, to whom I am thankful. Several photographers, visual artists, and art galleries/museums have been very generous in allowing me to

Acknowledgments

use their photographs. In a few instances the identity of photographers was not known and I was therefore unable to credit their work.

Earlier versions of sections of this book have previously appeared in print or in my own video works. I wish to thank the editors of *Performing Arts Journal, Performance Research,* and *Theatre Topics* for their kind permission to let me reuse these materials. Some exist in languages other than English, and I have tried to translate them back into English. Several of my collaborators graciously helped me with audio/video transcriptions from Slovene, Russian, Portuguese, and Spanish. My friends in East Germany were patient and forgiving when I did not always recognize the connotations and resonances of my divided mother tongue. (Apropos of tongues my favorite painting of Orpheus is by the Cuban painter Tonel, who depicts the complex relations between language and exile in a sardonic image "del artista bilingue," which shows two long, protruding tongues emerging from a single head, one in front, the other in back. I think Paul Klee would have liked it.) So read my tongues. I should add that Kiss & Tell, the Canadian group of photographers and writers, came up with the perfect title for their collaboration: "Her Tongue on My Theory." Their photo-text essays are wonderfully inspirational.

During the six years I spent composing this book, much of my time was devoted to rehearsal workshops and productions. Finding the space to write and to think through the body of material and experience was made infinitely more pleasant thanks to the company of those who shared similar questions and concerns. We argued at length over issues we confronted in performances and cross-cultural encounters. The main metaphor for our dialogue, learned from the practice of dance, is that of contact improvisation. When I began to practice it, exercising the fullest consciousness of movement in and with my body, I realized that an alternative discourse would eventually be required to overcome the rules of conventional scholarship or theory, which refuse to be dislocated by physical experience and the processes of incorporation we live in the creative integration of the arts. New conceptualizations of/in performance are like new movement possibilities we learn by doing, and while my critical and intellectual debts will become apparent, I owe special thanks to those colleagues in both academia and the profession who have continued to encourage and support my deviations from various disciplinary streams. I would like to mention the late Robert Corrigan, Herbert Blau, Gautam Dasgupta, Josette Féral, Jeongwon Joe, George E. Marcus, Bonnie Marranca, Julian Olf, Henry M. Sayre,

Acknowledgments

Richard Schechner, Elena Siemens, Carol Simpson Stern, Nena Torres, xxiii and Heiner Weidmann.

There are many others, of course, who have made significant contributions to the errant process of my work in different locations, and who offered me opportunities to conduct artistic research or participate in cultural projects. I trust that most of them will recognize the occasions of their vital contributions in the text. This will be particularly evident in those "scenes" that recreate conversations and collaborative rehearsals or workshops/symposia. Nevertheless, I feel that I owe so much to my artistic mentors, collaborators, and students that I want to acknowledge their presence in my life. Strong and lasting friendships were forged with David Caton, Richard Stout, Melissa Noble, Diana and Carlos Glandt, Graciella Poppi, Clarissa Guidry, Isabelle Ganz, Tonya Borisov, Gabriela Villegas, Elba Baños, Malcolm Munro, the late Margie Glaser, Krista Rimple, Laura Steckler, Christopher Steele, Joanna and Allen Pasternak—all of whom provided spiritual sustenance in Houston. Susan Bianconi, Iris Carulli, Renato Miceli, Elise Kermani, Sara Chazen, Barbara Mensch, Ivor Miller, Idania Diaz Gonzáles, Donna Drewes, and the Cleary family—all generous comrades—provided shelter and inspiration in New York City, New Haven, and Boston. Juan Villegas, Lillian Manzor-Coats, Alicia del Campo, Silvia Pellarollo, and their co-conspirators in the Irvine Hispanic Theatre Research Group opened their arms and invited me into their vibrant Latin American/Latino/Chicano theater research network in southern California, allowing me to briefly escape the deadly winters in Chicago. Another way to stay warm is to rehearse in the studio, and I owe thanks to the Performance Studies and Theatre departments at Northwestern University for letting me convert teaching into experimental labs and offshore production workshops. I will always remember the students, both undergraduate and graduate, who chose to take risks and work with us in spite of the widespread, aggravating prejudice against performance art and the art process generally that informs the liberal humanism of institutions claiming to be pluralist yet anxiously defending disciplinary centeredness. A lot of decentering remains to be done.

At other times during the winter and summer months I visited performance festivals, workshops, and conferences, and I am particularly grateful for generous invitations to present my work and exchange ideas at events organized by Scott deLahunta and Ric Allsopp (Amsterdam), Janet Adshead-Lansdale (Surrey), Virve Sutinen (Helsinki), Josette Féral (Montreal), Pia Kleber (Toronto), Uschi Schmidt-Fehringer

Acknowledgments

xxiv (Saarbrücken), Chris Butler (Chichester), Uli Birringer (Eisenhütten-stadt), Attilio Caffarena (Genoa), Nils Eichberg (Berlin), Tom Mulready (Cleveland), and Tim Fiori and Mitchell Covic (Chicago). I would like to thank Kampnagel Fabrik (Hamburg), TanzWerkstatt Berlin, and Tanzwerkstatt Europa (Munich) for inviting me to their theater dance festivals; Jean Caslin and Wendy Watriss for welcoming me to the Houston Center for Photography and Houston FotoFest; Irena Štaudohar and Polona Mertelj for arranging the "Physical Theatre" workshop in Ljubljana; the Union of Democratic Communications for inviting me to their workshop at the International School of Film and TV in Cuba; and Ivor Miller for introducing me to his friends and fellow *santeros* in Havana.

During studio visits, rehearsals, group projects, and on other occasions I learned to appreciate the intensity and commitment of several artists who have left a deep impression on me, including Pina Bausch, Deborah Hay, Meredith Monk, Carolee Schneemann, Marina Abramović, Coco Fusco, Guillermo Gómez-Peña, Goran Dordević, James Luna, Tim Miller, Joachim Schlömer, Meg Stuart, Jutta Hell, and Dieter Baumann (Tanztheater Rubato), Helmut Psotta and Grupo Chaclacayo, Josefa Vaughan, Charles Boone, Barbara Hammer, Hollis Huston, Doug Ischar, Jesus Bautista Moroles, Michael Tracy, Deborah Morris, Melanie Lien Palm, Esther Parada, Bob Peters, Marlon Riggs, David Schiff, Nedko Solakov, Ela Troyano, Victor Varela, and Zoran Masirević.

The passionate generosity of those artists, researchers, cultural workers, and families I met in Cuba, Slovenia, and East Germany has had the most visceral impact on my work. The collaborations and plans that have evolved from these encounters have a certain utopian dimension that I hope to explore in future films and writings. I am deeply grateful for their hospitality and their welcome challenges to my limited comprehension of borders and transcultural processes. Special thanks are due the following: Rosa Ileana Boudet, Vivian Martínes Tabares, Nara Mansur, Magaly Muguercia, Rigoberto López, Jorge Perugorría, Víctor Varela, and Mirtha and Guillermo Diaz Gonzáles in Havana and the members of La Jaula Abierta in Alamar; Eda Čufer, Marko Peljhan, Irena Štaudohar, Marko Košnik, Emil Hrhvatin, Mojca Kumerdej, Naja Kos, Barbara Drnać, and Mateja Rebolj in Ljubljana; Anett Schauermann, Petra Schwab, and all the members of the Fantasielabor in Eisenhüttenstadt; Ute Pischtschan, Detlef Schneider, Julius Skowronek, Jo Siamon Salich and the members of RU-IN in Dresden; and Uschi

Acknowledgments

Schmidt-Fehringer, Leonie Quint, Astrid Swift, and Frank Leimbach on the western border of Germany.

Finally, this book could not have been written without the exciting, nurturing, and contentious collaborations I experienced with the composers, musicians, performers, and visual artists who journeyed and worked with me on the productions of *AD MORTEM, Orpheus / Eurydike, From the Border, Lovers Fragments, Parsifal, La lógica que se cumple,* and *LBLM.* I deeply appreciate the vitality and political commitment of those in our activist and alternative communities who have clarity of vision and are moving toward life, transforming it (as choreographer Anna Halprin would call the holistic quality of such a process). I thank you all for exploring the creative ecstasies, perversions, and pitfalls of collective work, and for sharing your erotic energies with me. Some of you have taught me more about contemporary art and social relations than I could ever learn from cultural theories. Against all odds, I trust that our AlienNation company will make it into the next century: T. Weldon Anderson, Lori Barrett, John Cook, Hilary Cooperman, Steve Ivan, Steve Lafayette, André Marquetti, Elaine Molinaro, Peter Mueller, Tara Peters, Craig Roberts, Imma Sarries-Zgonc, Patricia Sotarello, and Mariko Ventura.

In thinking of the children who enjoyed working with us (thank you Aleida, Anne, Marina, and Uwe), my appreciation also goes to those older and wiser friends who have supported our performances: Claire Berger, Barbara Davis, Martha Heimberg, Lee Masters, Lee Roloff, Hildette Rubenstein, and Ron Schenk. My brothers and their families have given me their unfailing support, and my mother, in her great wisdom, lovingly refuses to believe in experimental theater. She has never seen my work, but I dedicated my *Parsifal* performance to her, knowing that she would have been my toughest critic. This book is dedicated to her and to two other dancers who taught me movements toward life.

ABBREVIATIONS

BBS	bulletin-board system
CMC	computer-mediated communications
CT	computerized tomography
DDI	Dideoxyinosine
DSP	Digital Signal Processing
FTP	File Transfer Protocol
GMHC	Gay Men's Health Crisis
GUI	graphical user interface
HTML	Hypertext Markup Language
IRC	Internet Relay Chat
ISDN	Integrated Services Digital Network
LCD	liquid crystal display
MRI	magnetic resonance imaging
MTV	music-television
MUD	multiuser dimension
NGO	nongovernmental organization
NSK	Neue Slovenische Kunst
PLWA	person living with AIDS
PSA	public service announcement
RL	real life
S-LV	Street-Level Video
SNDO	School for New Dance Development
STEIM	Institute of Electro-Instrumental Music
TPAN	Test Positive Aware Network
VR	virtual reality
WAVE	Women's AIDS Video Enterprise
ZKM	Zentrum für Kunst und Medientechnologie

MEDIA & PERFORMANCE

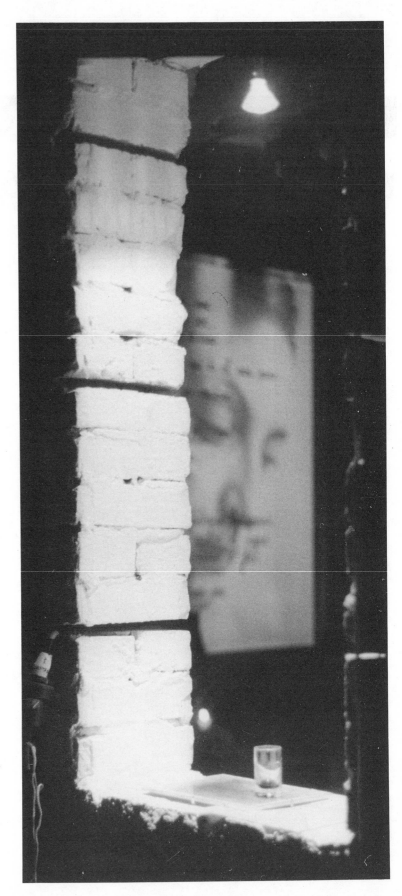

Imma Sarries-Zgonc in *Parsifal,* opera installation/performance, Festspielhaus Hellerau, Dresden, Ninth Dresden Festival of Contemporary Music, Germany, 1995. Photo: J. Birringer

ONE

THIS IS THE THEATER THAT WAS TO BE EXPECTED AND FORESEEN

Sarajevo/Tales from a City

Growing up in West Germany after World War II, I learned to understand history through the guilty silence that followed the horror of destruction. After the postwar period of economic reconstruction, school ended when rebellion took to the streets in 1968. That was my first schooling in the situationist theater of confrontation against the status quo. In the seventies my theater training consisted of reading against the grain (of textual authority and realist conventions) and studying the revisionist directors' brave struggles to demystify and politicize the classics on the stages of our highly subsidized city theaters. Modern drama (Ibsen, Strindberg, Chekhov, Pirandello, etc.) was treated as if it already belonged to the canon of classical European literature. The hope for a new theater, after Brecht and Artaud, was not fulfilled. Besides, the concrete poetry of a critical subversion of existing conditions was already taking place without actors (and without the "holy actor," as Grotowski called him at the time) in the psychedelic, music-inspired subcultures and new social movements.

The last theater productions I saw on the continent, before emigrating to the United States, were of Beckett's *Endgame* and Pina Bausch's *She takes him by the hand and leads him into the castle. The others follow*. The older dramaturgy of the absurd and the newer, emerging one of the *Tanztheater* briefly helped me adjust to the different pop-cultural climate of the United States. But I also had to learn a few new scripts over the years, since the repetitions of guilt and obsession, so overwhelmingly present in Bausch's *Macbeth* paraphrase, and the rock 'n' roll postures of angry young men or disillusioned existentialists had fallen out of currency. By the end of the cold war, my understanding of history had not improved, and I was learning to live with the "New World Order," NAFTA and Maastricht treaties, global television, and the Internet. While shuttling between the dance studio and a university seminar on poststructuralist theory, I studied the relations of the economy to law and the media, as a result of which my sense of reality suffered. Since the fall of the Berlin Wall, the revolutions in eastern Europe, the Gulf War, and the disintegration of the Soviet Union and of Yugoslavia, I've come to believe that our perception of historical change is hallucinatory and vertiginous.

To the extent that our view of the world is shaped by the media, such a belief is, of course, an effect of the expanded virtual environment manufactured by media industries. If the fall of the Berlin Wall was a simulation (in the sense in which Jean Baudrillard argued that "the Gulf War did not take place"), must we not also assume that the conversion and interchangeability of all images of war, projected onto "Sarajevo" or anywhere else, now constitute the very conditions of our technologized commodity culture, in which distinctions between sign and referent, nature and culture, human and machine, truth and falsehood, real and representation appear to be collapsing? Must we abandon our claims to know or experience existence and consciousness of life in the same manner in which we cannot presume that there is a "real world" that somehow precedes or exists outside of representation?

What does it mean, then, if Slobodan Snajder confesses, during the Bonn Theater Biennial in 1992, that "reality is changing too quickly: as playwrights we have not been able to react yet"? Referring to the trauma of political changes and the war in his country, is the Croatian playwright suggesting that theater cannot react to reality or, if it does, it will be too late? In the context of mainstream drama and comedy, Snajder's pessimism is perfectly understandable. In the United States the theater has long accepted that its familiar and generic mediocrity, fully accommodated to the status quo of the entertainment industry, continues to offer its outmoded fare to a society that has no use for it. In the context of the avant-garde, the vision of acting upon reality or integrating life into art had been pursued throughout our century. The trajectory of this vision, from futurism to cyberspace, illuminates the avant-garde's spiritual faith in technological progress. It now resonates in all the arts' inescapable dependence on the logic of the media. The science-fictions of this digital logic can be observed at the annual trade shows of *ars electronica* (Linz), for example, in the oft-repeated pathetic rituals of Stelarc hooking his body up to various computers and electrical prostheses or in the VR games that promise the user an out-of-body experience in a 3-D world that doesn't exist. Interestingly, very few theater critics have written about Stelarc's performances, but I notice he is very popular among the new theorists of cyberculture and "cybernetic body art."[1] If one acknowledges the techno-human interface as the sustaining cultural myth of our times, one could sketch the following scenario:

> Television (the prototype for the computer screen–human interface) has become our continuous, uninterrupted history; an endless flow of images, sounds, stories, and news events in living color. The technology that produces this flow, which in turn promotes itself, signals the future present in which electronic communication simultaneously channels knowledge, information, and expression on a global scale, ignoring national borders or differences of time and space.
>
> Information superhighways and computer networks, as well as corporate mergers and satellite linkups indicate the vectors of an economic logic of freely circulating media products and services. In this shift from an older industrial culture to a media-information technoculture, the economics of technology constitutes the principles of transformation that affect all ideologies, political orders, and everyday practices as they reshape audiovisual perceptions and the relations between cognition and consumption.

Hollywood movies usually capture our cultural symptoms and recycle them as entertainment. In the 1994 movie *Disclosure,* which is ostensibly about sexual harassment in the workplace, the main seduction scenes in fact feature DigiCom's new Virtual Reality products and the company's transnational cyber-business. It is the impersonal business of cyber-relations, with the old gender politics getting in the way, I suppose, for sentimental, dramaturgical reasons. However, the film implies that retrograde bodies, emotions, or sexual paranoia among white males will soon be rendered expendable in light of the new virtual economy and its applications. They will be sacrificed or phased out.

Such a movie, together with the *Jurassic Park* and *Star Wars* sequels and natural-disaster potboilers (*Twister, Volcano,* etc.), is watched by millions of spectators. Goran Stefanovski's play *Sarajevo* (*Tales from a City*), created in 1993 as a reaction against the siege of the Bosnian city and produced outside the war zones (it was rehearsed in Stockholm by an international cast and then premiered in Antwerp as part of the Cultural Capital of Europe Festival), was perhaps watched by a few hundred theatergoers. I remember the polite applause. Here is the first scene's opening monologue, spoken by a character named Sara:

> My name is Sara
> I am a researcher
> Architecture is my profession
> and music is my love.
> I am a loser
> and a refugee
> I come
> From the gloom of Europe
> From what once had dreams
> Of being united
> But is now only
> A series of lonely
> uneasy and small
> Tyrannical
> city states.[2]

Awkward, halting, stumbling words: a wounded girl searches for a vanished city, fractured memory of the promise of a thriving multicultural, pluralistic community. Her spiritual tales evoke a prayer for a life with human features; but "all these images are in fact various ways of dying" concludes the resigned and embittered playwright. The ethos of Stefanovski's spiritual struggle of resistance against the obscenity of war must be recognized; even more so, Susan Sontag and her Bosnian cast's production of *Waiting for Godot* in war-torn Sarajevo will perhaps be remembered as the twentieth-century theater's last symbolic moment. A last futile gesture?

Still/Here

This brings me to my metropolitan thesis. In the context of increasing European and North American integration, global markets, and transnational media industries, theater production as an art form now appears not contemporary but anachronistic. Compared to the central symbolic and material position of theater in premodern cultural topographies—in which performance was an integral part of the religious, mythic, and ritual expression or reflection of community beliefs—the theater of the modern industrial age gradually learned to compensate for the loss of ritual by professionalizing and commercializing its specialized production. During the historical formation of nation-states and empires, the funding of national theater, dance, and opera companies became a means of adopting the professional theater for the legitimation strategies of the state or of cultural elites. The legacy of this adoption was built into the tradition of higher education and the ideological state apparatuses that promote particular modes of representation and repertoires of national literatures and arts.

The modernist avant-garde in western Europe attempted to resist this adoption and destroy or subvert the institutionalization of dominant conventions of representation (e.g., naturalism or realism). Another side of this dialectic emerged as a result of revolutionary conditions in Russia, where the utopian constructivists sought to revolutionize the aesthetic production of a new society as such. The failure of both avant-garde movements and their accommodation to state power or to the commercial pressures of the art market can today be measured against the dystopian triumphs of capitalism in the United States, where the construction of democratic collectivities and of a national community was largely effected through the mass media and a popular culture of consumption (which, as is now known, also co-opted the rock 'n' roll protest era and the civil rights movement). The theater played no role in this construction of the political, national space.

However, as those of us working in the United States or Canada now observe the conflicts, fragmentations, and dissolutions within the social landscape of North American capitalism, the absence of a "national theater" or of any centralized cultural policy is perhaps precisely the reason for the existence of a very lively and diverse scene encompassing alternative performance and media arts. The evolution of performance art since the sixties, with its extraordinary range of phenomena (action painting, happenings, rituals, body art, land art, Fluxus, conceptual art, pop art, video art, etc.) and its rebellious, anarchic energy inspired a vigorous exploration of all aspects of the creative event and its translation of idea, image, body, self, or community. As such, time-based, process-oriented live art—with its insistence on presence; on the autobiographical, literal, and ordinary; on the sensory materiality of the body and the conceptual irritations of perception; and its experiments with new formal and informal vocabularies—decisively exploded the boundaries between the arts. After John Cage and his inclusive philosophy of composition and openness to a world of possibilities, perhaps the idea of art/performance could be rethought completely; it was certainly relocated outside the text-based, literary conventions of theater. One should recall that performance art in Europe evolved almost exclusively from within a visual-arts context, and while this was also the case in the United States, there closer associations always existed among dance, music, and video, which resulted in a livelier tendency toward intermedia and popular crossovers, as well as a constant expansion of the collaborative core of performance experiments (since the days of Black Mountain College, Fluxus, Judson Dance Theater, La Mama, etc.).

Cage's "composition as process" probably influenced postmodern dance (Cunningham and after) and new music/sound performance as much as it symbolized a commitment to the freedom of experimentation that affected a younger generation of artists, many of whom emerged from studios, art schools, and subcultures uninhibited by the increasingly theory-based university departments in the humanities and liberal arts. While no one, to my knowledge, ever taught Derrida, Foucault, Barthes, Lacan, Said, Kristeva, Cixous, Mulvey, or de Lauretis to theater students in American drama departments, I certainly remember visual and performance artists coming into town for a residency or workshop. These workshops were a core experience in furthering my understanding of interdisciplinary-arts processes, for they not only demonstrated the linked, unpredictable, generative, and transformative processes of working with mixed procedures (methods, tools, materials, techniques, conceptual frames) but also revealed the futility of integrating the arts in institutions that generally promote their separation. Performance art, being radically undisciplined art, can thus be said to create processes that cannot easily be contained by aesthetic or pedagogic theories, which themselves depend on a disciplinary paradigm. When I studied poststructuralist theory at Yale (within the English and Comparative Literature departments), there was literally no connection between its textualities and art practice. The recuperation of "the body" in theory had not yet begun, and rather than writing about imaginary bodies and tropes (Susan Leigh Foster has referred to them as "troping bodies"),[3] I wanted to move in my body and move with others.

This is how I met many of the Judson Church dancers, contact-improvisation teachers, and those body artists who had survived the ecstasies and risk-taking trials of endurance in their self-lacerating auto-performances of the sixties. Deborah Hay and Carolee Schneemann taught me to pay attention to where my body takes me and how to experience and extend my perception of being in my body. It is perhaps also indicative of the oddly intermixed spiritual and pop-cultural climates in the United States that body art, when compared to the excesses of Viennese Actionism or Art Corporel and Self-destructive Art in France or England, here saw its limits of transgression much earlier and either shifted attention to healing, therapeutic performance meditations, video/media installation performances and sculptures, or to the digital interfaces that Nam June Paik and Laurie Anderson became known for. The history of the relations and interactions between performance and video art remains one of the most underexplored areas, which is paradoxical, for I believe that it is precisely the conjunction of independent video art, performance, and activism that has most provocatively challenged the dominant hierarchies of institutional and technological ideologies. (See chapter 5 in this book.) Media art today is a steadily growing field, and interesting video sculptures are now being created by Judith Barry, Dara Birnbaum, Chila Kumari Burman, Renée Green, Gary Hill, Gretchen Bender, Toshio Iwai, Marie-Jo Lafontaine, Shirin Neshat, Marcel Odenbach, Tony Oursler, Adrian Piper, Diana Thater, Bill Viola, and Carolee Schneemann, whose kinetic sculptures/projections continue her thirty-year exploration of the spaces/images of her body-performed-painted-and-extended into film.

I alluded to the issue of teaching interdisciplinary composition or art process because I have often noticed the striking separation between vanguard performance practices presented in alternative galleries, clubs, lofts, or workshops and the evolution of poststructuralist and deconstructionist theory in the seventies and eighties. By the time postmodernist theories—especially feminist theories—began to elaborate their concerns for "the body" (or "bodies that matter"), fragmentation, sadomasochism, fetishism, pornography, cyborgs, transsexuals or other gender troubles and "the gaze," conceptual/video/performance art and photography had already explored these areas. The media arts pushed the framing and reframing of ritual bodily transformation, masquerade, and the choreographies of seduction and voyeurism to the point where the political function of performance, as a radical critique of forms and contents of representation and power, was either denounced and vilified (recall the censorship debates in the United States) or construed as a formal aesthetic ready to become reabsorbed into the art market and the museum. Poststructuralism, in fact, helped the museums and perfectly well belongs there, supplying the catalogue texts of the new exhibitions of performance history that now begin to show up in the metropolises. The Cleveland Center for Contemporary Art curated its exhibition "Outside the Frame: Performance and the Object" in 1994, and the Chicago Museum of Contemporary Art created a retrospective on "Performance Anxiety" in 1997. Since the remainder of this chapter questions strategic resistances to this reabsorption, it should be pointed out that performance theory itself, as it gradually gained acceptance in the reformed, interdisciplinary departments (performance studies, ethnography, cultural studies) in the late eighties, remained within the closed circuit of its theatrical academic scenario: its gestures at "transgressive" performance or marginalized and cultural others served as a useful supplement to subject formation in dominant academic disciplines. My own privileged position was partly included here, too, at least when it was useful for the academy to include performance art. In other words, performance theory nowadays concentrates on the performative construction of identities or genders in a wide range of practices in everyday culture, sports, science, medicine, advertising, MTV, and so on. It most often reenacts and repsychologizes an *acting theory* across the boundaries of genres, something that most of us working in performance art had specifically sought to abandon when we refused to act or represent.

If performance, video or body art, or *Tanztheater,* the music of John Cage, Meredith Monk, Steve Reich, or Diamanda Galás; and the visual performance works of Robert Wilson, Ping Chong, Squat Theatre, Bread and Puppet Theater, Jan Fabre, Achim Freyer, and the Italian *transavanguardia* failed to demonstrate the difference between being, becoming, dreaming, doing, and acting, then that fact should be of concern to us as practitioners, as long as we hope not to be subjected to or recuperated by the reproducible norms of theater. In this context of reproduction, it may also be necessary to focus critical attention on the exuberantly Eurocentric metaphysics in the borrowed metaphors of Peter Brook's *Mahabharata* adaptations or Ariane Mnouchkine's "Asian"

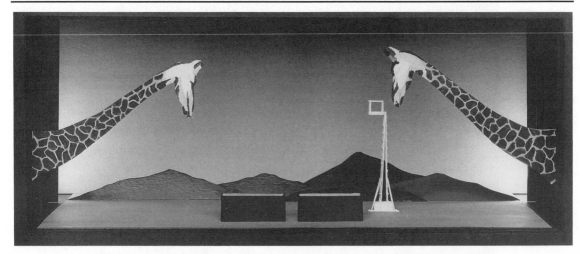

Robert Wilson's Vision, 1990 model of set for *The CIVIL warS* (scene IC) by Robert Wilson. Mixed media. Photo credit: Courtesy Byrd Hoffman Foundation. Courtesy Museum of Fine Arts, Boston.

productions of Greek tragedies, as well as on the whole international movement of syncretic, multicultural acting styles.

There was a moment in the seventies when Robert Wilson's visual scenography had created a kind of impossible freedom, an intolerable and radical hermetic openness of visual space completely removed from the parameters of literary, linear narrative or psychological drama yet densely populated with landscapes and geographies of abstract or found image-movement, unlikely constructions of time in space, colors of dreams one might dream, associations of a natural world one doesn't remember. Ironically, by the time Wilson had returned to the solemn staging of dramatic texts and opera libretti, other scenographers were pushing and accelerating different visions (e.g., the ironies of simulation, repetition, recycling and quotation) to their limits. As I suggested in my preface, I think it has become harder today not to feel overwhelmed by the relentless fragmentation of images, signs, and bodies in the landscapes of intermedia performances that have approximated the technological conditions of our late-modern perception. Yet such productions

Théâtre du Soleil, *Les Atrides,* directed by Ariane Mnouchkine. Depicted here is a scene from the first part of the cycle *Iphigenia in Aulis,* performed at the Brooklyn Academy of Music, New York, in 1992. Photo: Martine Franck/Magnum.

beg ethical questions: How can we judge the limits of human endurance, value experience (e.g., oppression and alienation), and tolerate the technological/technocratic citations in view of larger economic and political struggles for equality and self-representation (being-becoming)?

Theory owes performance a huge debt it is unlikely to repay. If it refuses to be recognized within the ruling ideology and its aesthetic criteria, performance earns the disdain of audiences wishing to be entertained or satisfied in terms of their analytic desires. When performance moves or dances across the conditions of intelligibility, when it cuts across the associations of the illusionism that surrounds the human body, it creates an economic problem. I mean to suggest that in its unaccommodated and shifting functions, performance exercises a consciousness of movement and energy potentials and an organic conscience that elude analytical languages, which seek to capture, determine, or psychoanalyze corporeal realities and cast creative sensory processes into logocentric values. The human body is not a concept. It is irreplaceable. In his critique of the avant-garde, Slovene composer Marko Košnik poignantly suggests that theater remains trapped in the dominant language of engineering as long as it is still able to afford, "amidst interminable celebrations of the decay of Western culture, to instrumentalize 'live marionettes' for the realization of ideas." Arguing that the dancer cannot be reduced to a body or a score, he also points to the limit of theory, "the mutual limitation and inseparable connection of the institutions of language and body, which are neither equal nor mutual."[4]

Given the tendency among Slovene avant-garde theater directors to utilize ballet dancers in their stage scenographies (though, contextually, differently from Wilson and Fabre), I think Košnik's argument about nonmutuality helps us to recognize how precarious the relations are between contemporary performance, media, and language, not only in the post-communist East but also in the reception of the new "physical theater" and hyperdance in the West (DV8, Wim Vandekeybus, S.O.A.P. Dance, La Fura dels Baus, Brith Gof, Carbonne 14, LaLaLa Human Steps, Dar a Luz, R.A.M.M. Theater, etc.). The argument stresses a growing emphasis in contemporary performance on nonverbal, energetic, visual-movement "languages" (beyond the outmoded actor's theater), on the one hand, and a restricted and limiting use of language-based dramaturgies and critical analyses, on the other. In other words, contemporary criticism and theory of performance often appear to cling to an aesthetic understanding of theatricality still based on dramatic and cinematic illusion, acting techniques, narratives, and representational mechanisms structured around language. Despite its tautological name

and because of its last-ditch effort to overextend the languages of dance
and theater and to (dis)integrate electronic mediation, the new "physical theater" plays precisely at the borderline of the aesthetic discourse
that would seek to constitute and commodify it. The mutual misconceptions are instructive. During the 1994 "Next Wave" Festival at the
Brooklyn Academy of Music—a festival that for years has mostly featured fashionable and established avant-garde household names, from
Wilson to Bausch—the question of critical valuation was raised precisely over the issue of whether Bill T. Jones's work *Still/Here*, was re-
viewable on aesthetic grounds. Knowing full well that the "radicalism"
of the American avant-garde is normally received in terms of formal
innovation, a well-positioned New York critic condemned Jones's performance (without having seen it) for exploiting the public's sentiments
for victims of disease and terminal illness, thus presumably putting his
choreography beyond criticism. *Still/Here* does precisely what the critic
refused to observe: it depicts (on video) the testimony of real people
fatally stricken with disease and proceeds to create a dance of compan-
ionship with those for whom death is an ever-present reality, using a
carefully, beautifully composed gestural and musical choreography (developed from the testimony) to transcend the nonmutuality between the
technical-expressive and the purely emotional or existential. What appears aesthetically pleasing to me, in other words, is not the precise
technical execution of the individual gestural languages but rather the
dancers' awareness that technical control here may function ironically
as a conscious, futile yet necessary elaboration of personal and psychologically charged experience. The very sense of control is always precariously shadowed and ghosted by the recurring video projections of
the witnesses' testimony of their struggle to maintain a sense of dignity
in the face of death.

Jones's performance, developed out of a series of workshops with
people who are fatally ill, names the "victims" that the critic refused
to watch, naming AIDS and cancer as scourges of human organisms
that our inhumane society often prefers to shun or remove from sight
before they are actually physically dead. The performers, however, are
not victims but performers. The perverse conflations of the literal and
the symbolic in the critical controversy are mind-boggling, since Jones's
ethnographic realism is, of course, transgressively political as well as
sufficiently aestheticized to be accommodated by those performance
genres that exorcize autobiographical or fictionalized-autobiographical
traumata, memories, and fantasies.

Still/Here cannot be said to be beyond criticism because it deals with

Bill T. Jones / Arnie Zane Dance
Company performing in *Still / Here,*
presented at the Shubert Theatre,
Chicago, 1995. Photo: Beatriz Schiller.

Meg Stuart's Damaged Goods Company
performing in *No One Is Watching,*
presented at the Tanz im August Festival
in Berlin, Hebbel Theater, 1995. Photo:
Joachim Hiltmann.

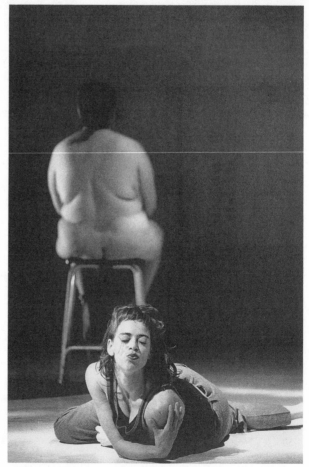

real dying people. On the contrary, it should be examined for the emotional authenticity it is capable of generating (artificially?) or marking as an ethical dilemma in our time. This is the only authenticity that the physical theater as an anachronistic medium can construct. Even if I didn't know that Jones lost his partner Arnie Zane to the disease and is HIV positive himself, I would consider his struggle to dance survival, still being here with us, both timely and vital and inspiring because it tells me something about his spirit and his bodily knowledge of the inflicted body, his consciousness of and in performance, challenging my own existing framework of still being here. His performance is rooted in bodily effect, giving me an awareness of the living and dying body (what Deborah Hay has called the "cellular body") that other forms of art cannot. Whether such an awareness is essentially useful or valid aesthetically is perhaps not an intellectual or theoretical question.

No longer readymade

The deconstruction of the real (in theory) has not removed the exclusionary constraints of a universalist and formalist aesthetic which continues to serve capitalist ideology by pretending to be indifferent to particular bodily experiences, abject conditions, and improper emotions. Paradoxically, what a choreographer subjectively shows us about real dying people may not be aesthetically meaningful to others despite his or her best intentions to make it meaningful to a larger audience. However, the privileging of the lived, real, or actual experience tells us something about the current politics of identity, not only in the theater but among communities affected by the issue of visibility or nonvisibility, inclusion or exclusion (recall ACT UP interventions during the AIDS crisis; culture-in-action projects confronting racism and violence; minority protests against mainstream media stereotyping; and the multiculturalism debate). If we observe how contemporary performance art, new dance, and physical theater derive their energy from direct, experiential knowledge of bodily sensation or privation, and how they transmit perceptions of sanctioned violence, discrimination, and social deprivation in the body politic through increased physical brutality onstage, must we not infer that such work resists or disdains critical theory's suspicion of the "truth" of emotion or personal experience? Or is its radical positing of the real a cynical gesture mimicking the outdated political rhetoric of avant-garde shock tactics? How is the "truth" of contemporary performance showing the truth about itself thinkable?

If the aggressive cultural activism of minorities—and the equally aggressive rhetoric of feminist, queer, and postcolonial theories—had not contested the exclusionary "truth" of the center and the unequal relations of center and margin, it would not be possible to think of an identity politics that could posit the visibility of racial, ethnic, and sexual others in quite the same way. In fact, it is precisely the "truth" or "identity" of dominant culture that has been attacked, reconverted, and parodied by performance and media artists/activists who insisted on expressing their rage (e.g., after the 1992 Rodney King verdict, which resulted in the Los Angeles riots), and their disgust at racist violence and economic disenfranchisement, specifically focusing on the dissemination of racial ideologies and stereotypes that denigrate people of color and contribute to the devastation of the urban social fabric. The most significant aspect of such work (by Anna Deavere Smith, Rhodessa Jones, Coco Fusco, Daniel Martínez, Robbie McCaulie, Guillermo Gómez-Peña, James Luna, Portia Cobb, the video collective "Black Planet Productions," and many of the black rappers) is not the fact that it shatters taboos but that it insistently interrogates the real asymmetrical stage of power relations in American social life, pointing to the racial classifications that constitute social interaction, as well as to gender and sexuality as regulatory regimes of constraining differences which effect the unconscious identifications with representations of "self" and "other."

A fine line distinguishes the brutality of the criticized content from the brutality of expression in the work. The abuse, violation, derealization, or erotic fetishization of bodies had been a major focus of performance art over the past decades. There is now a split between autobiographical-expressive solo performances or ritual/sacrificial enactments of pain and body manipulation (e.g., Ron Athey's *Martyrs and Saints* and *4 Scenes in a Harsh Life*), and a growing irony in the posing of bodies that parodies the very notion of authenticity and real presence. Contemporary feminist and gay and lesbian performances in the nineties are exploring multiple ways of teasing out the anxious "theatricality" of gender by overrepeating and hypersimulating (in drag) the gender norms by which masculinity and femininity are culturally sanctioned. Performances in drag have only recently emerged from the gay ghettos because the context for the questioning of identities had been created. Since the eighties a heightened awareness of the existence and significance of multicentric perspectives and hybrid cultures within the United States facilitated the enormous outpouring of work by multiracial, feminist, and queer artists that sought to explore the social construction and policing of identity, thereby posing the question of location, community, or the relation of self to context. The debates over multiculturalism are also a result of such active interventions. Latin American, African, Caribbean, and Asian perspectives inside the United States are transforming the parameters of cultural production as well as the "national" imaginary, forcing a recognition of the impact of continuing immigrations, of a constant motion of transculturation.

The politics of camp performance in the stage works of Split Britches (and the WOW artists), Spider Woman Theater, Pomo Afro Homos, Nao Bustamante, Carmelita Tropicana, Annie Sprinkle, Marga Gómez, Kate Bornstein, Tim Miller, John Fleck, and other groups ambiguously celebrates the spectacle of visibility, shifting endlessly between parodying dominant heterosexual codes (e.g., the generic, genderized codes in melodrama) and reconstructing them onto differently gendered and sexual agents. Lesbian performers, for example, have explored the wild side of butch-femme relations through deliberate appropriations of sadomasochistic imagery (whips, chains, leather, skinhead and Nazi paraphernalia) for dangerously humorous erotic play. Such reworking of symbols into different contexts ridicules the authority of the heterosexual matrix and produces a fluid arena of desire that engages the differences within and between feminist and queer communities.

If drag performances subvert the fabrication of gender norms, such subversion is more likely to be recognized and enjoyed by gay/lesbian

Guillermo Gómez-Peña and Coco Fusco performing *The New World (B) Order* at the Randolph Street Gallery, Chicago, 1993, as part of their interdisciplinary cycle of performances/installations/media works entitled *The Year of the White Bear.* Photo: Peter Taub.

audiences. That excessive representations of homosexual and cross-racial enjoyment can provoke moral panic in mainstream culture is not surprising; the significance of a specific context and reception for the production of progressive work limits any easy equation between radical sexuality and radical politics. (How radical is Tony Kushner's *Angels in America* now that it has already been canonized by Broadway and embraced by liberal mainstream criticism?) Similarly, as distinct transgressions of ideological fantasies of white homogenous culture, the work of Chicano and black artists articulating enraged expressions of subjugated forms of knowledge and lived experiences of abjection can only provoke affective responses if white audiences are led to interrogate whiteness and the ideological system that produces the cultural other as abject in the first place. I believe that in order to invigorate such interrogation and a commitment to broad-based social change, performance cannot rely on any ready-made aesthetic context of reception/consumption. Since all performances are implicated in the history of modernism (after Duchamp) and capitalism's imperative aestheticization of politics, Walter Benjamin's analysis of the conditions of reproducibility suggests that no transformation or perception is possible or reversible without altering the relations of production: "The bourgeois apparatus of production and publication can assimilate astonishing quantities of revolutionary themes, indeed, can propagate them without calling its own existence, and the existence of the class that owns it, seriously into question."[5]

It seems more urgent, therefore, to examine the way we work, our philosophies of "being together," creating the conditions of visibility, in relation to the preexisting forms of production in our time. Many of the multilingual and multiracial artists' groups I know work in between different contexts and milieus, both locally and internationally, and are deeply committed to building community relations that cut across ethnic borders and the ghettos of minority culture. The building of communities and working relationships, of performance structures for collaboration, often *is* the artwork. Such processes necessarily involve social analysis, conceptual and communications methods, and participatory models of rehearsal. They are cross-cultural experiments in the creation of alternative projects and venues, and the relational aspects of such process-art are perhaps crucial at a point in history where state institutions can no longer guarantee economic and political integration, and when fantasies/myths of a national community of culture collapse under the weight of internal contradictions: the existential crises of refugees, exiles, the homeless, the ill, the unemployed, and the disenfranchised.

Consequently, questions about aesthetic changes within the contemporary theater become pointless, because the relation between theater and its community is not a matter of style—even if queer performance contexts *do* recognize a style of being. For whom do the postmodern directors (Robert Wilson, Peter Sellars, Peter Brook, Jan Fabre, etc.) produce and design their work? Where do theater or dance companies locate themselves today? Do we actually know what is meant by "alternative" spaces and cultures?

From this dual perspective of location and context, I note the following trends in contemporary performance:

- the gradual disappearance of a national/regional theater and the dwindling of dramatic literature to a bastard art

- the cross-cultural conversion and internationalization of performance vocabularies

- the rise of transient, multicultural ensembles working in different locations and in cooperation with international festivals or producing arts organizations (especially in the migrations of new dance but also among performance artists who are "on the road")

- the parallel rise of new local alternative-culture projects and community-based performance and media collaborations.

Quotations from a Ruined City

I wish to conclude this chapter with a brief examination of this dialectic of production. On the one hand, contemporary performance approximates the transborder flow and circulation of cultural forms, ideas, images, and resources that already exist in the global distribution systems of the market. The international circuit of festivals and workshops imitates a model of diasporic communities in which dancers/choreographers in particular have become delocalized producers. I attended several European dance workshops in 1994 (Munich, Amsterdam, Berlin, Ljubljana) where the lingua franca was English but participants came from all over the world. The International Summer Theater Festival in Hamburg's Kampnagel Fabrik featured a French company (Mathilde Monnier) that had developed a new *Antigone* performance in West Africa; a Taiwanese company (Tai-Gu Tales Dance Theatre) incorporating American modern dance into the movement language of Chinese opera; and a coproduction between João Fiadeiro's Portuguese dancers (RE. AL.) and Brazilian dancers (EnDança) from Salvador de Bahia, a work sponsored by Kampnagel but created in Brazil.

Self-consciously proclaiming a "new opening" in the choreographers' awareness of the relations between cultures and continents, the Hamburg festival programmed a North-South-East-West dialogue by promoting collaborative productions or arranging the appearance of invited companies (from Belgium, Italy, Sweden, France/Burkina Faso, Germany, Spain, Portugal, Slovenia, Canada, the United States, Cuba, Brazil, China, and Japan) under the synchronous theme of "radical confrontation with reality." This synchronicity was, of course, for the festival. Some of the choreographers seem to share a similar sensibility and faith in the emotional truth of physical movement and autopoetic composition, having abandoned the technical grammar of modern dance. The contortions and distortions of bodies tormented by isolating memories in Meg Stuart's *No longer readymade* resemble the body images in João Fiadeiro's *Recentes desejos mutiladas* (Last Mutilated Desires), yet both performances make no claims about a particular contextual reality, nor do they interrogate the memories and conditions that would subjugate the bodies in this way. The cynical despair that pervades the brutally aggressive *Quotations from a Ruined City*, written by the late Iranian-American director Reza Abdoh and performed by his U.S.-based Dar a Luz company, holds up a strange mirror to the cold, futuristic engineering that controls the mechanical ballet of Dragan Živadinov's *Molitveni straj Noordung* (Noordung Prayer Machine). Both works betray a deep-seated distrust of subjectivity, intentionality, and organic wholeness, automatically presenting the human body in its most alienated condition, dislocated from any knowledge or awareness of itself.

Not surprisingly, they also completely lack or eschew the kind of sensuality and spiritual intimacy that characterize, for example, the elegiac performance of *Antigona,* by Marianela Boán's Cuban group Danza Abierta. The abrasive sadism and agonizing self-contempt in the current work of Abdoh, Fabre, and Vandekeybus, like the ironic constructivist "spirituality" of Živadinov's seemingly dehumanized biomechanical cosmokinetic apparatus, are very revealing, contrasting with the warmth, sad humor, vulnerability, and sensuous expressiveness in Boán's dance-theater, or with the mysterious, meditative inner dynamic that centers Hsiu-Wei Lin's choreography for Tai-Gu Tales.

Perhaps these contrasting moods I detect only reveal my own bias (or my awareness of the exceedingly difficult conditions under which Boán is creating her work in a spiritually and economically devastated Cuba) and the need for a common language in the encounter with others. I am groping for words that approximate the emotional color of works that do not mark their sensuousness with self-loathing or with the kind of domestic cynicism which, in my perception of Euro-American physical theater, is often sensationalist for its own sake rather than reflecting a stringent exploration of the breakdown of civil society and social behavior. If I note the absence of a spiritual sensibility in Western physical theater, I am of course assuming that there is a connection between self-loathing, dehumanization, and a disintegrated spirit of body.

What is revealing about the contrast are the different attitudes with which each group confronts its own "reality" and transforms it. The internationalized aesthetic frame of the festival makes it more difficult to determine how distinct social and cultural realities in the East and the West confront and transform the producers, since the festival stage inevitably obscures the historical contexts of specific cultural differences and the economy of the performers' relations of production. Those contexts are not accessible to the audience. Promoting a multiculturalist vision, the festival also obscures the history of its own European privileged status to showcase other "continents." While watching Fiadeiro's Salvador project, I did not get the impression that it transported a sense of cultural location and experience at all; his dance of broken, disjointed gestures perhaps symbolizes precisely the failure of incorporating and organically understanding/creating together a lived connection to the place and the people with whom he worked in Brazil. Most disconcerting, however, was Reza Abdoh's nihilistic frenzy of "quotations" and sound bites (adapted from the conflicts and bloodbaths in Sarajevo, the Middle East, Los Angeles, and American colonial history and its witch-hunts), driven by the morbid TV-style logic of disaster news he collaged for his theater—a never-ending horror/freak show that leaves me blind and indifferent to the "realities" that are quoted. The insanely campy ejaculations of this performance, which might also be considered a dark, absurdist parody of *Angels in America* (A Gay Fantasia on International Themes) and contemporary apocalyptic yearnings, signal the extent to which the political unconscious in the West has been dislocated from any utopian or humanist ethos and is perversely preoccupied by the cynicism of commodity culture.

As kinetic theater, *Quotations from a Ruined City* ultimately epitomizes the theater's failure to speed up the "frenzy of the visible" in real time, and to become a TV program or a pornographic movie. Once physical theater has exhausted itself (like body art), it will only retain its hollow quotational form, as in the case of the epigones of Bausch's *Tanztheater*. Although composed within two different transient, transnational contexts on either side of the Atlantic, Abdoh's hyperkinetics represent the cynical version of Stefanovski's impotent moral and poetic despair, displaced onto the figure (predictably enough) of the innocent young girl, Sara. The posing of the real, of the con-temporaneous, on the stage will always drag behind its virtual deconstruction in the media. The future of its pose will lie in its understanding of its own dis-location.

When I spoke with Meg Stuart in Hamburg, she explained her own sense of physical and psychic dislocation: "I now work in Brussels with my group. We call ourselves 'Damaged Goods.' Up to now New York has been my emotional home, but conditions are too difficult there. Perhaps there is no place anymore where I could feel at home, because of all the traveling. Nothing belongs to anyone anymore. You're off to another city, your friends are dispersed all over the world. Everything is mixed up, overlaps." She claims that she is addicted to this instability; yet many of the performances presented in the synchronous frames of European festivals disturbingly betray a deeper sense of loathing, of ex-

Ron Athey performing his *Martyrs and Saints* at Randolph Street Gallery, Chicago, 1993. Photo: Peter Taub.

cess (in the speed of "rave" or the slam-dancing of Vandekeybus and his imitators across eastern and western Europe), and of deliberate, abject violence against the body (epitomized as ritualized-atavistic risk-taking in La Fura dels Baus and as perverted social realism in Johan Kresnik's *Tanztheater*). As a psychic reaction, such abjection in the performances of the disjointed, tortured body indicates the phantasms of the collapsing boundaries of identity and those between the symbolic and meaninglessness.

The trend I have described above all reveals the differences in contemporary attitudes toward the body, differences in the ethics and philosophy of working with and through the bodies of actors and dancers. The question of an ethics of performance also involves the transformation of power relations as they existed at the center and in hierarchically organized institutions of art production. Displacing the center does not automatically mean that a new, democratic space of collaboration has been created. The shifting of boundaries, in fact, is always confusing, especially if our imaginary has been applied to well-defined borders or well-defined cultural and gendered roles. The abjection I have noticed, as well as the disavowal of an organic, whole body, reflect a reaction to the disturbed bodily rhythms in our Western technocultures and to the

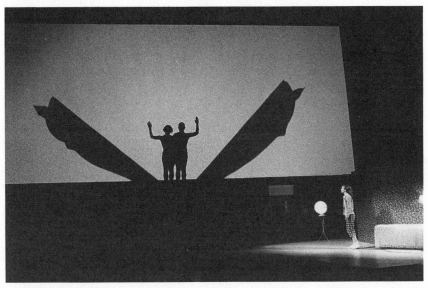

Young Alexandra Daniels (Dina Emerson) is introduced to her spiritual guides in the opening scene ("The Call") from part I ("Personal Climate") of Meredith Monk's opera *Atlas,* performed at the Houston Grand Opera, 1991. Photo: Jim Caldwell.

dislocating experience of migration. The hyperphysical theater at the close of this century rehearses its own "excorporation," so to speak.

On the positive side, I have experienced at first hand the phenomena of community-based cultural activism and art committed to a rebuilding of the fragmented social fabric at the grassroots level. I know a number of groups in Chicago whose creative activities are all neighborhood-based and instrumental in linking expressive culture (arts, crafts, media, communications) with social services and education, especially for children and young people in the barrios. With its emphasis on human services and organic processes of art making, self-realization, and self-organization, such work connects urban youth to vital issues of health, safe sex, employment, and education, as well as to the concerns of the elderly, people with disabilities, and the poor. By fostering teamwork and a spirit of cross-cultural cooperation during the building of creative cultural infrastructures, these groups help to rehearse the constitutive expression of community identities (in other words, a performing and producing community), both desired and understood as a political necessity. At the same time, these modes of production are not given but have to be created and tested in each particular set of circumstances; they therefore leave little room for the cynicism and despair we see on commoditized stages. Postmodern media philosopher Avital Ronell once said that she is "writing to the community of those who have no community," adding that writing itself is nearly obsolesced in the era of electronic culture.[6] If cynicism is a response to a widespread sense of disconnectedness, it is politically necessary to examine the media and production modes devoted to fantasies of excorporation and abandonment, and to inquire into the particular claims made on behalf of communities real or imagined. My concern throughout the following chapters will be to track the phantoms of video as well as the creativity of bodily endeavors, the contexts and relations of production in community-identified practices, and the impact of migration/dislocation on the ethos of transcultural performance.

1 DANCING WITH TECHNOLOGIES

2 IMPOSSIBLE ANATOMIES

3 CULTURE IN ACTION

4 VIRTUAL COMMUNITIES

TWO

CORPOREALITIES AND DIGITAL BODIES

Dancing on the Edges

Almost exactly ten years ago I wrote my first longer essay on Pina Bausch's Wuppertaler Tanztheater, reflecting on ways of approaching the dance and of sharing with other readers the powerful impact I had felt on my life after experiencing Bausch's company during the rehearsal process and onstage. I subtitled the essay "Dancing across Borders," and although I was also referring to the baffled and controversial reception of German *Tanztheater* in the United States during their first appearance in Los Angeles and New York City, I mainly meant to interpret the vigorous boundary crossings in the *Tanztheater*'s specific understanding of dance movement. It seemed all too obvious that Bausch's choreography—in its relentlessly consistent exposure of social relationships through the theatrical *gestus* (in the Brechtian sense) and in the dancers' unflinching parades of the habitual perversions of human interactions among gendered subjects/bodies—would create problems in terms of certain aesthetic or formal expectations in the reception of dance.

While I did not quite expect dance critics in the United States to foreground angst, fear, and self-loathing in the unbecoming German *Tanztheater* they appeared to have discovered for the first time, I realized that postmodern dance in the United States after Cunningham—having perhaps already reached the point of no return—had achieved a peculiar degree of disembodiment in its pervasive aesthetic concentration on abstract, pure movement and movement research. The pure-movement credo in itself, coming at the end of a long journey of modern and postmodern dance, might never have attained such critical dominance had both modern ballet and dance criticism in the United States (after John Martin and Lincoln Kirstein) and the structuralist "reading dancing" (as Susan Leigh Foster called the semiotic approach in 1986) kept their perspectives open to other, parallel developments in the cultures of dance. These were less burdened by the modernist aesthetic's disjunctions of form and content, formalism and expressionism, abstraction and narrative, including the homegrown social and pop-cultural dance expressions in the United States, the expressive traditions in African-American and Latin dance, and the transformational explorations of contact improvisation and meditative or healing dances that Anna Halprin has referred to as "moving towards life."[1]

In this chapter I will address the complex contradictions and intersections between Western dance practices that understand themselves as "moving toward life" and more recent performance experiments on the boundary between physical embodiment and computer-mediated, digital art. (The latter fills a kind of ghost space in here and will be discussed more fully in chapter 4.) I want to return to *Tanztheater*'s excavation of deeply sedimented social clichés, physical scars, and psychic traumata in our bodies and under our thin skins. Linking this excavation to a revision of the often misleading distinctions made in historiographies of modern dance between an aestheticist-modernist view of the body's purity or autonomy of presence (as depersonalized expression) and a romantically inflected subjectivism of the personal and emotional body, I briefly wish to retrace *Tanztheater*'s mediation of expressionist dance (*Ausdruckstanz*) and the considerable influence it has had on contemporary "physical theater." In so doing, I hope to pave the way for subsequent reflections on new movements during the late eighties and early nineties that explore the integration of dance with film/video and multimedia computers.

I wish to emphasize that, aside from the modern performance traditions of theatrical concert dance and the more marginalized experimental traditions of conceptual and performance art, contemporary dance (floor) culture has had an intimate relationship to the shifting, evolving fabric of music production and pop-cultural media. It is my contention that we can better apprehend the current interfaces between dance/choreography and electronic media if we contextualize twentieth-century dance languages, and their movement beyond the boundaries of strictly codified techniques, within the geographies of an unfolding, increasingly globalized media culture and its well-worn ideological matrix of technological imperatives. Furthermore, I believe that the new conditions of re/production in the digital age are pervasive and invasive in ways that profoundly affect—as all technologies must—our minds and bodies, our concepts of space, place, time, and movement, and thus our imaginaries and our projections of materialities (in both a corporeal and discursive sense but also in terms of visual design and spatial architecture).

Dancing matters, I wish to suggest, because our bodies' movement and movement potential are intrinsically linked to political, economic, and technological changes in the physical culture, in the public/private spaces and the spatial scales and relationships in which we participate, in the environments within which we create and derive pleasure. Dancing also illuminates a fundamental aspect of the body-in-space, namely, its inherent motivation to ascertain its existence, its being-in-the-world, by projecting itself and moving into space, by taking up space, by shaping space and touching the environment, mediating or minding the self in relation to others. Movement is production of space, so to speak, and our kinesthetic sense, based on our proprioceptive system, permits a range of different awarenesses of movement in space and time. The experience of the quality or force of a particular movement is not only the basis through which we communicate but also the ground of associations, of our concrete connections and imaginary relations with the kind of *social space* in which movement takes place.

When I think of dancing and the history of movement performance in this century, I am aware of the limited grasp I might have of the accessible traces and documents (e.g., notations, films, photographs, testimonies, reviews) of past choreographies and bodily actions. My exposure to theatrical dance and to popular, avant-garde, and alternative traditions is primarily motivated by my training and practice in the performing and media arts. My emotional connection to the stage, the cinema, music, and the visual arts has shaped the conceptual questions I direct at bodily practices and the media through which they move. These questions are also shaped by the locations and the spectatorial or rehearsal contexts within which they evolve.

Dance, I wish to argue, moves through media and moves media of representation, and since it cannot ever be fixed, saved, or recovered, it creates a particularly striking and paradoxical challenge to historians, critics, and theorists who seek to map it onto language and textuality. Like music performance, painting, sculpture, or photography, movement is extralinguistic and cannot be repeated or reconstructed in writing. One could even say that the repetition of movement (e.g., in its replay on film) is never the same movement because the momentarily present movement vanishes the moment it is enacted and perceived. It can be "recorded," yet it cannot be recorded and played back as the same, for already in the present, in the presence of the act of moving, the movement cannot be repeated. The recording creates another movement.

However, movement as a "language" does not exist on its own, nor can it be reduced to the semiotic. Phenomenologically, it is always relative to spatial relationships with the world of which it is a part and to other media it engages, even when it claims to be absorbed in its own abstract minimalism. Dancers and dance theorists may think differently about this issue, and so the problem of recording the lost moment of movement is of considerable interest to us, especially when attempting conceptually to link the *re-creation* or *reconstruction* of past movements or choreographies to the sampling, recording, and electronic-processing capabilities of the new media and, ultimately, to virtual dance and virtual choreography. After having worked with video scores and video choreography for the past six years, I feel motivated to make several claims on behalf of the memory of movement and the recording of its future.

If dance, for much of its modern history, has never been a model for writing and critical theory (excepting Hofmannsthal's "Über die Pantomime" or Mallarmé's "Crayonné au théâtre," which fascinated Derrida)—or, for that matter, for the media—and if dance studies have often been belittled as antiintellectual, this situation is now changing rapidly under the impact of a recent and rather exuberant turn toward cultural, sociological, ethnographic, and performative interpretations of dance as "corporeal writing" and "bodily discourse," fleshing out or responding to issues of gender, race, ethnicity, power, identity politics, historical embodiment, popular culture, narrativity, production, ethics, and aesthetics.[2]

The recent production of new "choreographies" of history and dance history is not surprising, since the focus in cultural studies and feminist theories on "bodies" and "corporealities" has had a considerable impact on the reevaluation of philosophical, political, and social deployments or identifications of body, organism, nature, and practically all the categories that social constructionism considers inadequate for a critical transformation of material relations of domination and subordination. In light of the current global restructuring of relations and locations of power in late capitalism, and especially in this era of immensely influential media/communications and information industries, philosophical and aesthetic speculation on "bodies that matter" may appear to be a luxury.[3] Given the economic reality of our era of reduced spending on art, culture, and education, dancing itself may be a luxury that only the most dedicated dance professionals will be able to continue to perform on their own or within the companies that survive. While dance companies are downsized or phased out of institutional support, youth cultures revolving around dance clubs, house scenes, and raves flourish. Sarah Thornton has persuasively portrayed the "media development" and promotion of contemporary subcultures, as well as the new "authenticities" of "live performance" evolving in disc cultures, that clearly "celebrate technologies that have rendered some traditional kinds of musicianship obsolete and have led to the formation of new aesthetics and judgements of value."[4]

It remains a political necessity, however, for us to retrace our steps and engage the mindful body in activities that are intimately linked to production and creativity, and thus to an understanding of how the illusions and realities of our bodily authenticities and imaginaries are affected by historical changes in the cultural geographies that influence our spatial relations and positions, mobilities and physical immersions in the world at the level of self-definition and self-capacity, which includes our capacity to remember. Dancing as a way of being in the body and being in the world has helped me to be more aware of the ways in which movement is shaped by a very volatile consciousness and memory of place, and of being placed within scales and networks of changing interrelationships that motivate or restrict my identifications with experienced reality and its discontinuities.

As I suggested in chapter 1, dance is perhaps one of the most paradigmatic artistic genres of dis-location and of an inherent dynamism that travels and exchanges places. Retracing some of the steps in the history of Bausch's *Tanztheater* may not necessarily yield greater insights into the Germanness of a particular romantic, expressionist, or Brechtian-Marxist aesthetics of performance. Nor do I want to imply that there is a certain ironic trajectory in Bausch's interest in film (e.g., her role in Fellini's *E la nave va* and her own dance film *Die Klage der Kaiserin*) and her more recent dance production about the Hollywood inside us (*Nur Du*), created during a 1996 residency in Los Angeles. Dance companies work as international, cross-cultural production ensembles—whether based in Wuppertal, New York City, London, Havana, or São Paulo—and are prone to mirror and engender cultural hybridity and heterogeneity as they are shaped by their diverse sensibilities and the susceptibilities of physical experience, despite the fact that their movement and rehearsal methods may continue a rigorous logic of technical training that we associate with (Russian) ballet schools or the Graham or Cunningham techniques, comparable to the codified in-body teaching of Asian performance traditions.

Retracing steps from within a particular choreographic vocabulary or rehearsal practice suggests a journey of learning and unlearning, and I am particularly interested here in raising a few questions about the relations between expressionism and space, between choreography and the spatial formation of kinesthetic, visual, and emotional relationships in performance. Preparing a ground for the discussion of dancing into digitized, virtual spaces, I confess that my journey is an idiosyncratic one, for I want to return to the interconnections between choreographies in the revolutionary period at the beginning of the century, claiming that it is advantageous to remember *Ausdruckstanz*, or Loïe Fuller's and Isadora Duncan's "discovery" of modern dance, for that matter, in connection with the new constructivism in revolutionary Russia as well as the various overlapping visual art and performance modernisms or vanguard movements that experimented with new conceptions of space, symbolist or geometric abstraction, machine aesthetics, the destruction of logic, the automatisms of the unconscious, spiritual mysticism, and utopian constructs (e.g., Italian and Russian futurism, dada, French surrealism, suprematism, expressionism, and the Bauhaus aesthetic).

Obviously, there are substantive and contextual differences between the diverse manifestos, exhibitions, performances, and the radical posturings of some of the vanguard artists at the beginning of the century, and audiences will have had vastly different reactions to the new works constructed on the stages of the Vakhtangov studio, Saint Petersburg's Luna Park, the Théâtre des Champs-Elysées, the Cabaret Voltaire, the Hellerau Festspielhaus, or the Weimar Bauhaus. Some practitioners of the European aesthetic revolutions, especially those who participated in actual political and social transformations (e.g., Russian Production Art, Proletkult, and the VKhUTEMAS, the Higher State Art–Technical Workshops), struggled to identify themselves and their "movements" within the contested arenas of nationalism and internationalism and the debates about elite aestheticism, primitivism, agitprop, and mass culture (a debate later subsumed under the dictates of social realism or the controlling censorship of fascist regimes). Others traveled or were forced to travel; Diaghilev's Ballets Russes, with its Russian designers, is just one example of a traveling company that had a powerful impact on stages in other countries (London and Paris). Similarly, Russian constructivist productions were seen in Berlin and Paris, and Oskar Schlemmer's Bauhaus stage-workshop experiments, including his renowned *Triadic Ballet*, toured widely after 1927. I want to look selectively at the confluences between diverse modernisms or vanguards by focusing in particular on the fashioning of the body and space, and on the formation of preferences in the accentuation of the body's presence in space. Dancing on the edges of the machine aesthetic and the productivist and constructivist ethos of the revolutionary "art and technology" workshops (such as the Moscow-based VKhUTEMAS studio or the Weimar Bauhaus), some early modern performances—in their explicit concern with the "freedom" of the body's kinetic expression of its soul (Duncan) and the "transfiguration of the human form" (Schlemmer)—illuminate something we may have forgotten. The fault lines of dance run between its celebrated and repressed histories of learned technologies that were necessary in order to develop and interpret new ones, transforming both kinesthetic experience (being in the body) and kinesthetic constructs or cultural images of the body and socially acceptable movement behavior.

Body Spaces: Between Utopian Socialism and Mechanical Ballet

Rather than choosing examples of various dance forms, genres, and historical stage productions, I prefer to concentrate on productions of space, concepts of and attitudes toward embodiment of space and toward the manipulation of spatial, temporal, and dynamic movement dimensions, and on particular contexts of such conceptualizations that have informed the "theaters" of the body. Approaching the formation of dance in and beyond the theater in this way allows for different readings of the internal movement of dance history that has been the object of aesthetic formalism.

My first site-specific visit takes me to Hellerau, located on the outskirts of Dresden, where in 1910 the recently founded Deutsche Werkbund created the first garden town in Germany based on a vision of a new utopian community dedicated to applied arts and crafts and the reform of industrial life in the spirit of nonalienated labor, communal life, social equality, and liberal and universal education. Impressed by a workshop Emile Jaques-Dalcroze held in Dresden on the new eurhythmics he had taught in Geneva, the Deutsche Werkbund invited Dalcroze to create an institute at Hellerau to teach his rhythmic exercises (involving the coordination between musical rhythm/tempo and movement, including gymnastics and dance, voice and ear training, anatomy, and improvisation), which would be open to all members of the community. In musical terms, Dalcroze taught "harmony," but eurhythmics meant that exercises were developed to integrate physical movement—the flow and energy of breathing, phrasing, stepping rhythms, patterns, and expressive body attitudes or gestures—with musical qualities, thereby connecting subjective responses to sound with conceptual pictures of a particular movement quality and performance by the body.

By 1911 Dalcroze had taught more than five hundred students—including Mary Wigman, Marie Rambert, Valeria Kratina, and others—who would become known in the modern dance movement, and by 1913 Hellerau's reputation as an artistic research community had spread so widely across Europe that Dalcroze's classes and festival productions of Gluck's *Orpheus and Eurydice* were attended by many internationally known artists, writers, and political anarchists.[5] The second festival, held in June 1913 and attended by more than five thousand visitors, inclines me to view it as a popular event (as distinct from, say, the Wagnerian opera festival held in Bayreuth) that drew its energy from the social utopianism of the Hellerau community, which projected a pragmatic philosophy of physical and spiritual regeneration for professional artisans, lay people, and children alike.

The context for this utopianism, in a larger sense, can be traced back to the immensely popular physical culture and gymnastics movement that was evolving at the turn of the century. In light of late capitalism's designer body/body building, fitness, health, new age, and human-potential cult movements, we may be inclined to smile when looking at old photographs of (mostly) girls and women in white, long dresses dancing joyfully on spacious lawns. But the image of the barefoot, Duncanesque dancer draped in a semitransparent white gown, solidly ingrained in our memories and fantasies of early modern dance created by women pioneers, could only have evolved from the physical culture of the 1880s and 1890s, with its pedagogical reforms and concern for physical and moral education. Aside from ballet, folk and ballroom dancing, physical culture in the United States became the fertile ground for new bodily expression, incorporating the imported Delsartean expressional system of gestures and postures into gymnastics and public education to further the cultivation of spirit, mind, and body and forge "an essential tie (upon which Duncan seized) between body and soul."[6] For the widely traveled Isadora Duncan, of course, recent scholarship reserves the privilege of having transformed the expressive tie between body and soul into her new art of kinesthetic dancing, mining "the body's unique capacity for displaying in its form the subtlest shades of emotion or mood. Her body referred to states and emotions by actually possessing their various shapes, rhythms, and dynamics, as she found them coded in nature . . . in art . . . and in everyday life," thereby consciously "abstracting" from the cultivated, often melodramatic posturing of the Delsartean exercises.[7]

The photos and films I have seen of Dalcroze's eurhythmics classes at Hellerau appear Duncanesque to me, and I believe the expressive idea underlying Duncan's concept of dancing "the natural language of the soul," as she calls it, implies an intrinsically idealist perspective of the spiritual, metaphysical harmony enacted through "the woman's body and the holiness of all its parts."[8] More important, Duncan's dynamic-expressive body is integrally connected to, or even originates in, music, melody, and rhythm, since the effect of her kinesthesis, which can be considered symbolist, seems to be fulfilled through her choices of romantic music and her belief in music in general as the foundation of poetic expression. In this "harmonic" integration of music and dancing, as if driven by some invisible inner necessity, Duncan seems very close to Dalcroze's efforts to make music "visible" and to find movement that is idealized in music, so to speak. Among the responses to Dalcroze's staging of Gluck's *Orpheus and Eurydice*, several commentators praise its "poetry in motion," and Upton Sinclair claims it is "music made visible."

At the same time, Dalcroze pursues a rigorous method of organizing structured improvisation to help students shape their own flow and energy of movement expression. Mary Wigman, who participates as a performer in *Orpheus and Eurydice,* neither likes Duncan's dancing nor Dalcroze's emphasis on music, preferring to dance without music or only to percussion. She feels "liberated" when she joins Rudolf von Laban at Monte Verità, another utopian community in the Swiss Alps, taking up her own movement analysis based on Laban's complex improvisations and studies, later known as his notations on the theory of spatial harmony. After the end of World War I, when she also leaves Laban and the large-scale ritualized festivals he choreographs for his group, Wigman reinvents the utopian and artistic impulses she had experienced to develop her own choreography, teaching in her own studio in Dresden and composing dances for herself and her "community of women," substituting a *Gemeinschaft* of women for the men's schools and festivals.[9]

Remarkably, many of Wigman's solos and group choreographies composed at the Laban school and her own studio in Dresden (after 1920) appear to eliminate music and musical visualization, representational framing, and narrative or archetype, seeking to disrupt the continuum between kinesthesia and the gendered body through her extensive use of masks and shape-distorting costumes. Rapidly establishing herself as a leading innovator of *Ausdruckstanz* during the restless and volatile Weimar era that follows the traumatic mass destruction of World War I, Wigman is credited with initiating modernist dance choreography in its essential focus, not on temporal/narrative dimensions of pictorial mimeticism, with its codified techniques in the ballet vocabulary, but on "absolute dance" as an autonomous language of configuring motion in space. However much aesthetic theories of modernist dance need to rely on such genealogies of dance as an autonomous, self-reflexive medium, I am more interested here in the paradox of Wigman's expressionism, both in terms of her "rediscovery of space" and her embodiment of the "ecstasy" of self-transformation in performance.[10]

DANCING WITH TECHNOLOGIES

Looking at old archival films of the Weimar era and listening to testimonies of Weimar dancers and filmmakers, I am not surprised to note the correspondences between expressionism in dance, the visual arts, and cinema. All of the surviving films of Wigman's dances imply musical (piano) or percussive accompaniment (Wigman hires a composer/accompanist in 1920), and the hyperkinetic language of silent film itself was of course generally accompanied by live piano. The kinetics of expressionist painting—especially in the distorted figures of Munch, Kirchner, Beckmann, Schiele, Nolde, and Kokoschka—draw attention to facial lines, eyes, and the torsion of upper bodies, arms, and hands. If we are persuaded to perceive a pervasive "new kinesthetic of torsion" in the physical and industrial culture at the beginning of the century, as Hillel Schwartz suggests in her wide-ranging study of gymnastics, eurhythmics, physical education, Delsartism, dance, pantomime, theater intermediated with time-and-motion studies, flashbulb photography, silent films, cubism, neurological and psychoanalytical studies of hysteria or physiological feedback mechanisms, Taylorist management of labor-time at assembly lines, technically generated kinetic patterns and effects of escalators, roller coasters, projectors, conveyor belts, phonographs and so forth—the "operative" and "transformative" functions of expression cannot be reduced to a particular aesthetic model of dancing as an autonomous language of flow and energy, or of bending the whole body to the whole music (Dalcroze) or to effort/shape movement scales (Laban).[11]

The particularity of *Ausdruckstanz*—beyond elusive notions of expression and subjective emotion, passion, or ecstasy attributed to it and considered an embarrassment to modern-dance theory—lies in the heightened awareness of space, dynamic form, and fluid rhythm it shares with other cultural-political practices intent on integrating organic embodiment with the new social, technological realities, as the constructivists understand it (and Meyerhold's biomechanics rehearse it), or with the "spiritual" in art. The spiritual in art—in the dematerializing process of abstraction and its dynamic projection beyond the objectifiable, as Kandinsky, Malevich, Klee, and many of the painters in Die Brücke or Der Blaue Reiter groups understand the utopian potential of transforming the visual languages of society—has little to do with ecstasy, mysticism, or the irrational. Kandinsky's abstracting "Improvisations" after 1910, like his "Point and Line to Plane," written in 1926 for his Bauhaus teachings on form and color and their resonant energies (their "inner sound" or "inner necessity"), point dialectically toward a concrete, not yet visible other reality. They sensuously mediate an "open feeling to freedom," and this mediation or transition from inner necessity to outward movement is crucial for the emancipatory direction of the "freie Tanz" (free dance) or *Ausdruckstanz*.[12] Post–World War II generations of artists in Europe will remember the political implications of the "freie Tanz," and Bausch specifically rephrases the approach to movement by asking why we move at all, what it is that moves people, and what it is that cannot be spoken.

In terms of the visual arts—but also including architecture, design, film, image production, and the theater (e.g., Piscator's plans for a "proletarian theater" and Gropius's or Moholy-Nagy's Bauhaus designs for a new "total theater")—a revolutionary transformation of visual languages implies a transformation of space. There is ample evidence of such transformations in the expressionist distortions of space in early German films and in the visionary architectural designs of Italian futurists and Russian constructivists, with Tatlin's Tower (the 1920 model of his *Project for the Monument to the Third International*) being the prime example of a new dynamic, kinetic architecture communicating movement as utopian aspiration based on a technological aesthetic of radical political use value. The question of the use value of constructivist and suprematist space (e.g., Malevich's nonobjective "Planits" and "Architektons," designed to project implied movement energies through floating color) has rarely been raised in connection with Western innovations in performance, scenography, and lighting, and even the obvious impact of symbolism and expressionism—especially the expressionist production of gothic bodyspace in silent film—on the actual theatrical work of Antonin Artaud or on Robert Wilson's scenography often goes unacknowledged.

In this context, the critical impulse to separate emotion (as code word for exaggerated, melodramatic acting or for the irrationalism or primitivism conventionally associated with the feminine) from motion, to desubjectify or defamiliarize bodily emotion in order to analyze or create new configurations of pure motion in space, has been at stake for aesthetic modernism in dance, yet it generally presumes that movement, evolving and continuing its own production over time, organizes the body's existence and presence in space. In other words, without movement there is no dance. My point is that the *Tanztheater* has taught us to remember differently, and my visits to Hellerau have helped me to re-envision Dalcroze's, Laban's, and Wigman's understanding of the body in space through other principles of the choreography of inner and outer realities.

If we link the school, the performance experiments, and the social reforms of the Hellerau community on site, the remarkable continuities between the space of the arts colony and the productions created there gain a new significance. Living and working there, I learn to think differently about Trotzky's impatient dismissal of Meyerhold's biomechanics as a form of "provincial dilettantism."[13] On the contrary, the economic relations between physical labor and the rhythm of machinery in Meyerhold's exercises point toward the same potential organic synthesis of kinesthetic experience (the effort/shape combinations of bodily mechanics or contrasting muscular forces) that underlies the constructivist principles of dynamic rhythm in Dziga Vertov's cinematography and the correspondences between spatial directions and dynamic qualities taught by Laban. Dalcroze's and Laban's teaching needs to take place in a "provincial" setting to allow the students of dance or of the *Bewegungschöre,* or movement choirs—most of whom were amateurs, devotees of gymnastics, or members of leftist parties, working-class organizations, unions, and church groups—to explore the premises of space harmony within the group. The provincial setting often is outdoors: parks, summer camps, communes, Laban's "dance farm" in Ascona, Switzerland. The participation in the group, emphasized in the *Bewegungschöre* created by Laban and his pupils, is as important as the individual discovery of movement scales and the improvisations with movement opposition and rhythmic counterpoint. The latter, in fact—which include opening/closing, advancing/retreating, accepting/resisting gravity, promoting stability/mobility—are kinesthetically more easily "experienceable" when practiced in a group. If Dalcroze bases his "realization" exercises on rubato/breathing, contraction/release, and measures/rhythms, Laban distinctly emphasizes awareness of the body in space even before there is movement.

According to this premise, bodies have dimensions, orientations, inclinations, weights, stances, and postural alignments, so that just by virtue of being there they occupy and produce space. Movement articulation follows from this *living in space.* Thus, Laban's objectivized movement scales, delineating the correspondences between spatial directions and dynamic qualities, follow from inner motivation and the ways in which bodies project themselves outward into space. The experience of the embodied self is felt in its approach to the space, which can be one of silence, stillness, and contraction as well as dimensional movement in space (upward, downward, forward, backward, sideward) associated with strong, bound, sustained, or direct movement qualities. Similarly, Laban's scales associate diagonal movement in space with free, light, sudden, and indirect movement qualities. The dancer's experience of mediation, however, is not just between stability and lability, effort and shape, and tension contrasts but between the two areas of experience linked by these counterplays of movement pulses: internal space (which Laban called the "land of silence") and the external world.[14]

Kurt Jooss—Laban's pupil/collaborator and, after 1927, dance director of the Folkwangschule in Essen, Germany, where Pina Bausch would later study in the 1960s—is more explicit when he treats the interdependent conditions of mental and physical tension as the reciprocal relationship between different tensions of form or of the body. As he would demonstrate in his provocative dance drama *Der Grüne Tisch* (The Green Table), hailed by the Left as a clearly political critique of the exploitative brutality of war, as well as in his teaching of "eukinetic qualities," the medium of the dance is the living human body, possessing the power to convey ideas inherent in its movements: expressive gestures cannot be autonomous but are "remembered gestures" and thus bear within their context a social meaning. Laban's kinesphere (i.e., the space around the body), and the body's three-dimensional experience in space, which is the principle of three-dimensionality itself, is also a social sphere of interaction, encompassing the associated experiential, perceptive, and receptive processes.

At Hellerau the student group often practices outdoors in the grassy courtyard, and spatial awareness of the body and of movement is inextricably implicated in the serene, nurturing, open environment of the arts colony as a whole, distanced from the more intense urban rhythms of the city nearby. The large, gently sloping open square is surrounded on one side by the small cottages of the artisans that open out onto the square and, at right angles, by the two-storey buildings housing the "workshops" for crafts and light industry. You can hear the sound of the welders hammering on pieces of metal, voices wafting in the air, the bells from the nearby church; you can smell the scent of sawdust coming from where the workers repair a roof. The green grass and leaves of the trees bordering the sides contrast with the grays and browns of the cottages.

The symmetry of the site is established in 1911, when the architect Heinrich Tessenow executes the building of the Festspielhaus on the north side, intended to house rehearsal studios, changing and shower rooms, and spaces for indoor-performance experiments. The "hall," as it was first called, is not a theater but an extraordinary kinetic sculpture, which can easily modify its functionalist spaces while maintaining a perfect harmony of symmetrically arranged rooms along a dynamic central axis. The identical front and back of the building are in the form of temple facades, each consisting of six massive rectangular pillars that support the high roof. The lower side wings run parallel to the huge main hall, which can accommodate up to eight hundred performers and spectators. Looked at from the outside, in its simplicity and harmonious proportions the hall is perfectly integrated into the colony as a whole; one barely notices it from an off-center angle.

Entering the hall, I am stunned by its immense openness, volume, and height. There is no stage, raised platform, or orchestra pit, only continuous, empty space without decoration, bare walls with a seventy-foot-high ceiling. The designs for this nontheatrical building are by Adolphe Appia, whose collaboration with Dalcroze extends the radical reconceptualizations of scenography and stage lighting he had previously explored with reference to Wagner's operas and traditional bourgeois illusionist theater. For Appia, the moment of "rediscovery" of the human body has come to haunt the flat, painted decors of old. He proposes to abolish the pictorialism of the picture-frame stage, give plastic physicality to the temporal, and create "living light" and dynamic sculptural space to heighten the three-dimensionality of bodily movement in expressive correlation to music and dramatic action. For Dalcroze's school at Hellerau's hall, which becomes the site of their collaboration on Gluck's *Orpheus and Eurydice,* he creates numerous designs he calls "Rhythmic Spaces," accentuating their plasticity with rigid, sharp lines and angles to heighten their immobility yet make them come alive in their own kinetic, architectural suggestiveness when contrasted with the softness and subtlety of bodily movement. For *Orpheus and Eurydice* he works with Russian painter/engineer Alexander von Salzmann on an elaborate lighting design hitherto unimaginable: literally thousands of lights, some of them colored, are installed behind translucent linen panels covering the walls and ceilings of the hall; in combination with movable spotlights they create a diffused, plastic light, causing Salzmann to claim that "instead of a lighted space, we have a light-producing space." [15]

The distinction between performer and audience is blurred in this continuous space, as are the differences between the forms in the total choreography of light and eurhythmic performance (dance, music, opera, visual art, sculpture). As participants at a funerary event—almost two hundred Hellerau students enacting the choral dance of mourning for Eurydice and performing the undulating, wavelike movements of the spirits in the Elysian Fields, while a female Orpheus descends on Appia's flight of steps into the "underworld," only to fail in the attempted rescue—we become collectively aware of the community that is evoked. Appia believes it to be the "transfiguration" of purely human expression into a sacred event, but in his writings on the new spatial/architectural scenography he betrays his primary concern with the formalized mise-en-scène, which integrates image, movement, light, spatial articulation, rhythm, and volume with the musicalized body of the actor figure: "[O]ur entire physical organism, if it submits to the laws of music, will thus become a work of art—and thus only."[16] The corporeality of expressive bodies, despite the focus he seems to give it, tends to be subsumed under the dynamic geometric arrangement of planes, lines, shapes, contours, silhouettes, illuminations, and effects that "transform the material reality of the actual construction of . . . movement [and] lighting: the characters share in this unreal atmosphere."[17] This view parallels the constructivism of architectonic scenographies in the work of Gordon Craig, Stanislaw Witkiewicz, Fernand Léger, Walter Gropius, Oskar Schlemmer, László Moholy-Nagy, Alexander Vesnin, Lyubov Popova, and many other early twentieth-century artists. Perhaps even more directly, it echoes the spiritualized, abstract metaphysics in Kandinsky's color-tone concerts (e.g., *Der Gelbe Klang* [The Yellow Sound]). The performer's physical body is choreographed as *performance image*, surrendered to space, to gestural figures, and to a perceptual imagism that enters a volatile dialectic between the phenomenal presence of bodied space and its projected "unreality." The boundaries of what constitutes the dance medium and corporeality are certainly widened, yet the opening up of early twentieth-century scenography mainly implies an uneasy, polar rhythm of diffusion (as in the lighting and the light/dark colors of the costumes in *Orpheus and Eurydice*) between an emphasis on sentient bodies—dancers who share their subjective and objective spatial awareness—and the design of signifying figures or life-forms. If Dalcroze rehearses with the movement choir an upsurge in consciousness of breathing and rhythm, he also choreographs the objectifying configuration of energies and gestures in the representational frame of the music drama. The nameless students become animations of the perceptual field, and Orpheus's loss ("Che farò senza Euridice . . .") is an image in flight etched in our memory. It is the image—the light spot where Eurydice stood before she disappears—become point and outline to plane, precisely as Kandinsky taught abstraction at the Bauhaus.

It is possible to understand the Hellerau context in two ways. On the one hand, I can experience the life of the school of eurhythmics and the scenographic experiments as an organic process aimed at the integration of the understanding of the body/space relationship. The exploration of music and movement in the collective festival performance allows for innovative mediations of diverse formal possibilities of choreography in the compositional field for which Hellerau's hall offers a potential that the Bauhaus designers would later dream about when they envisage their total art organisms and spatial machines. However, the Hellerau festival is site-specific, outside the state-supported theaters and professional arts institutions, and the utopian socialism that incorporates the school into the communal life of the artisans and workers holds out the possibility of freedom in collective experimentation and in the search for new forms in the life rhythms of creativity and expression. Hellerau is open to anyone, and although its utopia is not built on a return to nature, it sustains a belief in the organic wholeness of life and craft. Tragically, the vision collapses under the divisive weight of World War I and never recovers. Dalcroze resigns in protest against the war, and the "spiritual in art" opening out to freedom turns out to have been an illusion.

While Wigman continues to extend the improvisational methods of free dance and develop her own solo choreography (e.g., *Ekstatische Tänze, Hexentanz* [Ecstatic Dances, Witch Dance]) and group works for her women's dance ensemble, her commitment to formulating a new artistic dance form gradually removes her from the popular contexts of physical culture and revolutionary ideology. She keeps her distance from Weimar cabaret and revue culture, Anita Berber's and Valeska Gert's erotic and wildly satirical subversions of *Girlkultur,* and the cynical radicalism of the dadaist avant-garde in Berlin and Zurich (where George Grosz and Hans Arp are caricaturing the postwar body politic by designing puppets and puppet masks for the performers). Instead, she concentrates on a deliberate technique of abstracting from and repositioning her work with Dalcroze and Laban, completely eschewing the festival format and the Appian scenographies described earlier. Films of her concerts show her on empty stages in front of light or dark curtains. Her exploration of expressive movement, evolving and changing between 1914 and 1942, and gradually surrendering to external pressures and the reorganizations of political and cultural life under the Third Reich, initially alters the focus on the dancer's relationship to representational framing, and thus to the perspectival aspects of the embodied subject in theatrical space (i.e., the variable conditions that constitute how perceptual experience posits a body—in terms of gender, race, age, or other cultural categories). Wigman's dances of demonic "ecstasy," painstakingly reconstructed in Susan Manning's study, seem to negotiate and subvert the (predominantly male) assumptions about body, self, the expressive act, and the space invested by corporeality—those assumptions that almost invariably slide into the formalizing tendency of the scenographic revolutions of the avant-garde and, particularly, the architectonic experiments of the constructivists, stage reformers like Appia, Craig, and Piscator, and the Bauhaus design artists.

Wigman's use of costume in her dance is open to different allegorical readings, but it cannot be described as revealing or accentuating the contours of the female body. Her costume in *Hexentanz,* for example, is a close-fitting cap and a long, wide cloth attached at the neck, wrists, and thighs that "makes no reference to female dress beyond the dance. . . . In a sense, the costume functions to mask the body, to blur its female contours, its human contours. This costume-as-mask integrates the space of the body with the space of the environment, for the viewer no longer can perceive a clear boundary separating the body from the surrounding space. The costume-as-mask frames the dancer not as a persona but as a dynamic configuration of energy in space."[18]

The second approach to the context of Hellerau, then, lies in this most curious conjunction between Wigman's deliberate departure from Appian scenography and her unwitting proximity to the figural constructivism of the Bauhaus, which surfaces in her new creation of an aesthetic of dynamic expressive power in the heightened release of spatial-kinetic forms of the dance itself: the woman dancer incorporating her absence as gendered subject. In her works this release has come to be understood as her distinct and unique style of dancing as if in a metaphorical mask. Conjuring an ecstatic or sublime forcefulness (imaging chaos, anarchy, demonic power, death, endurance, survival, rebirth, self-transformation) through the sensations (or "vibrations," to use more Wigmanian technical-movement terms) she could kinesthetically evoke in the abstracting gestures and designs of pure motion in empty space, she is able to concentrate the viewer's attention on her *Gestalt.* (The original German word generally means "figure" in the sense of its contours, volume, and weight, but also includes its expressive connotations.)

Although one senses the contradictions in the concept of "pure motion," I want to propose that this dimension of *Ausdruckstanz,* generally romanticized as the achievement of body-centered independence of absolute dance (from music, other media, and the pictorialism of the mise-en-scène), in fact corresponds to the metaphysical "poetry in motion" concretized by Oskar Schlemmer's *Triadic Ballet* and dreamed about by Artaud, although the connotations are different for the male artists. Yet there is an invisible but direct connection between the failed utopia of Hellerau's organic totality and the "total theater" scenography envisioned by the Bauhaus painters and designers, whose revolutionary aesthetic claims to dismantle the old theatrical illusionism and realize a new industrial "architectonic art which, like human nature, should be all-embracing in its scope. Within that federative union of all the different 'arts' . . . every branch of design, every form of technique could be coordinated and find their appointed place."[19]

A few hundred miles north by northwest, in the provincial towns of Weimar and Dessau, we find Schlemmer's and Moholy-Nagy's stage workshops, the first experimental performance studios in an art school dedicated to the synthesis of utilitarian industrial art, design, and technology. Gropius's vision of a synthetic theater of visual effect and audience immersion in a total spectacle (developed in his plans for Piscator's epic theater of worker-actors surrounded by filmic projections, loudspeakers, revolving scenery, and action on all sides) and Schlemmer's experimentations with spatial theory derived from painting aim at a technologically enhanced and intensified experience of actors/dancers within the total environment, which, as Appia had already suggested, can be orchestrated, brought to dance, so to speak. Brecht's later idea of an epic theater that can "move" existing conditions, make them dance differently, goes back to the same fantasy of a new theater that can "de-realize" or defamiliarize the familiar ideological processes of perception and language construction. The Bauhaus designers are, of course, painters whose medium is not language but geometry. Schlemmer, in his extraordinary essay on "Man and Art Figure," draws sketches and describes (1) "the laws of the surrounding cubical space" (resulting in "ambulant architecture"); (2) "the functional laws of the human body in their relationship to space" (resulting in "the marionette"); (3) "the laws of motion of the human body in space" (resulting in "a technical organism"); and (4) "the metaphysical forms of expression" (resulting in "dematerialization"). After drawing figure models that illustrate these laws, he argues that

> the transformation of the human body, its metamorphosis, is made possible by the *costume*, the disguise. Costume and mask emphasize the body's identity or they change it; they express its nature or they are purposely misleading about it; they stress its conformity to organic or mechanical laws or they invalidate this conformity. . . .
>
> The endeavor to free man from his physical bondage and to heighten his freedom of movement beyond his native potential resulted in substituting for the organism the mechanical human figure (*Kunstfigur*): *the automaton and the marionette.* E.T.A. Hoffmann extolled the first of these, Heinrich von Kleist

the second. The English stage reformer Gordon Craig demands: "The actor must go, and in his place comes the inanimate figure—the Übermarionette we may call him."[20]

His theoretical concerns about the intersections of human and architectural space culminate in his excited proclamation of "endless perspectives," which are opening up in light of technological advancements, and, "*consequently, potentialities of constructive configuration are extraordinary on the metaphysical side as well.* The artificial human figure (*Kunstfigur*) permits any kind of movement and any kind of position for as long a time as desired."[21] In concluding his theory with a utopian vision of a new theater of the greatest possible freedom, he also includes the spectator, who needs to undergo an inner transformation to be intellectually and spiritually receptive. While he never denounces the corporeality of the *Tänzermensch,* who is "unfortunately limited by the laws of gravity," Schlemmer most certainly delights in imaging the transfiguration of form, the optical effects that can be achieved once the performer's individual corporeality is obscured or distorted, *animated* into a plastic instrument in motion which, like Kandinsky's musical poem (the sixteen moving designs he creates in his abstract dance score to Mussorgsky's *Pictures at an Exhibition*), acquires a nonrealist, abstract, metaphysical dimension.

The paradox of this technological aesthetic lies in the balance of opposites Schlemmer seems to achieve in the four-hour-long *Triadic Ballet* and in some of his other "gesture dances," or even in the cabaretlike *Figural Cabinet I:* the costumed and desubjectified dancer is experienced in the transitions from planar, two-dimensional surface image (dancer *as* costume design) to plastic figure in the larger geometry of field, from discovering music related to specific forms to finding emotional impulses to dance. Schlemmer never refers to the temporal dimension of this experience, concentrating his research on space, *Raumempfindung* (felt volume), and Laban-like directional motivation which creates the "sensation of space," the felt presence of the dance as it moves from virtual space (geometry of the plane) into depth.

If this depth of space remains indeterminate, as the *Übermarionette* alienates the viewer from kinesthetic identification with bodily expression, it nevertheless achieves what expressionist drama or silent film (of whose pathetic, lurid gesticulations Schlemmer considers his students cured) cannot, namely, to concentrate the viewer's perception, in an unfamiliar way, on the kinesthetic apprehension of movement and image. Just as Wigman dances "demon" not as self-expression or as a woman, nor as Woman/Demon or as something essentially Germanic or universal but as a distorted *Gestalt* whose release of energy affects my knowledge or sensation of such energy, so Schlemmer's ballets create a split between body/self and animated figure in the corporeal field. Kinesthetically there is a double abstraction or reorientation: the performer becomes aware of an altered, redesigned body topography (her/his perceived body), and the viewer becomes aware of the deformation of sentience, familiar physiology, and movement connotations, thus experiencing a fissure in conventionally implicit relations between inner and outer realities.

The Bauhaus experiments—however much we might see them as indebted to modernism's fascination with the machine aesthetic or the disembodying compositional abstractions of formalist scenography (as they are redeployed in Robert Wilson's operas in the 1970s after the participatory ecstasy of the Living Theater/Open Theatre generation exhausted itself)—are crucial for a proper understanding of the provocative, volatile tension between constructivism as a reconfiguration of human form and social sculpture, playing at the boundaries of self-alienation, and constructivism as a pedagogy for exploring how forms of art and industrial culture function psychologically. Kandinsky's teaching at the Bauhaus explicitly points to this interactivity of spatial form and sensation. The architectural implications for building design become clearer if one remembers that the Bauhaus, like the Moscow VKhUTEMAS or Brecht's pedagogical plays for exploited workers, addresses a need for new forms to alter existing conditions in production, crafts, and housing. Beginning in 1925, Bauhaus designs (furniture, household objects, textiles) go into mass production, and the first new workers' housing projects are built. By 1928, when Hannes Mayer succeeds Gropius as director of the Bauhaus and begins to create cooperative workshops, with workers and unions on a more pronounced Marxist premise of furthering international solidarity in industrial progress, the gap between fascist and socialist modes of envisioning cultural revolution has become too large to bridge. The Nazis close the Bauhaus school in 1933, many of the artists emigrate and continue to teach in the United States (at Black Mountain College, and in Chicago and New York City).

Bodyspaces: Between Physical Theater and Virtual Reality

When I rediscover the Hellerau colony in the fall of 1994, the script for the small international art and performance festival (Fest III) that is to take place seems written by history itself. Utopian art colony–turned Nazi military school–turned Red Army military hospital, Hellerau is being transformed again from an abandoned army base into a European cultural workshop for the performing and visual arts, whose aim is the development of artistic, sociocultural, and pedagogical projects intended to reinvent the utopian spirit of research it once harbored. When the Soviet army left the decaying buildings in 1992, Hellerau looked strikingly similar to the partially destroyed structures of Metelkova (the former Yugoslavian army headquarters and prison) in Ljubljana, where I had been working during the summer to explore Slovenian postdissident theater/dance in its relation to the new "physical theater" that has been popping up at western European dance festivals. In Ljubljana the site of the former military camp is occupied by an idiosyncratic collective of young squatters, punks, artists, and homeless people, and their appropriation of the empty buildings is now slowly being channeled into a "self-management" plan negotiated with city authorities.

In Hellerau the site has been successfully claimed by a group of independent cultural workers who founded a nonprofit organization seeking city and state support for the restoration of culturally significant historical monuments (protected by conservation laws). They hope to reconstruct Hellerau's original utopian vision, symbolized in the magnificent if completely dilapidated and decaying architecture of the enormous Festspielhaus and the workers' cottages. In fact, the buildings that housed the artists' studios and dance studios today carry all the grotesque and cruel signs of military occupation. Seldom have I seen such devastation and cynical disregard for physical property. It appeared as if the departing soldiers took everything with them that could be transported, including electrical cables, lamps and appliances ripped from the walls. The roofs are cracked; the floors of the studios are totally warped, as if moisture and rot had crept upward from below; sheets of wallpaper float off the walls; and the ceiling of Hellerau's Festspielhaus temporarily consists of a stretched canvas. It had collapsed into the hall, which for decades was used as a sports gymnasium. Russian murals depicting the battle of Berlin are flaking off the damp and mildewy walls near the entrance, and the whole scene exudes a strikingly haunting sensation, as if one had stepped into an abandoned film set, the Potemkin village of twentieth-century utopias. The festival organizers decide to dramatize this reality.

In the presence of the accumulated historical traces of violence, with layer upon layer visible in the damaged buildings, the themes "Gewalt" (violence under totalitarianism, war, military occupation) and "Gewalt in der Kunst" (violence in art) are addressed by the performances and visual exhibitions, which sparked a meditation on the instrumental function and applicability of modernist utopias in the service of state power. A public discussion following the screening of Leni Riefenstahl's 1935 film *Triumph des Willens* (Triumph of the Will) feature filmmaker Hans-Jürgen Syberberg and theater director George Tabori, who raise critical questions about the aesthetics of fascism and art's Nietzschean will to power. Tabori argues that the film's cinematic construction of "beauty" turns against itself today: contemporary viewers can only watch it as an anti-Hitler film. Responding to Tabori's ironic and polemical argument, Syberberg takes an extreme formalist and aesthetic position, defending the pathos and passion of cinematic art precisely because, as he claims, "they can unite and embody nation and art, power and beauty." The perversity of Syberberg's fascination with art's will to power is particularly obvious in the context of the festival's music and theater performances, which included *Der Kaiser von Atlantis, oder die Todverweigerung* (The Emperor from Atlantis, or The Denial of Death), an opera written by Victor Ullmann shortly before he was killed in Auschwitz in 1943, and *Ein Monat in Dachau* (A Month at Dachau), adapted from the novel by Vladimir Sorokin and directed by Carsten Ludwig.

The opera, performed by the Austrian new music–theater group ARBOS and conducted by Herbert Gantschacher, takes place in an abandoned garage next to the Festspielhaus. It represents an extraordinary document of ethical resistance to Nazi terror composed in the face of extermination. A musical allegory of Death's refusal to participate in the genocide ordered by the Kaiser, Ullmann's composition creates a highly ironic collage, mixing atonality with jazz and blues elements and liturgical hymns and chorales. Beyond its mixture of musical allusions to avant-garde, pop cultural and religious traditions, the work is at the same time profoundly humanist in its spiritual sensibility and satirical in its Weimar cabaret-style of gesture and *Sprechstimme*.

The Sorokin production, on the other hand, reflects a contemporary, much more aggressively cynical, sots-art hyperrealism which affirms ideological clichés by exaggerating them to the point where they appear both hilariously comic and darkly obscene. East German director Carsten Ludwig's staging of the novel makes spectacular use of the outdoor plaza and the festival theater, directing his large cast of twenty-five actors like a movement choir to perform a "collective" tourist vacation in a concentration camp–turned–luxury hotel which also houses the hallucinated nightmares of our century's sadistic and masochistic obsessions and pornographic traumata. The performance transforms the haunted gymnasium into a chamber of horrors, with the concentration-camp tourists being shuttled in and out of the building by a small train the actors built during rehearsals.

On each consecutive night of the festival, the Sorokin production is dialectically accompanied by the *Parsifal Prolog*–installation next door (in the Soviet army's dining hall/kitchen area), a performance sculpture created and modified by Grupo Chaclacayo in a sequence of visual-corporeal actions. Helmut Psotta, Sergio Zevallos, and Raúl Avellaneda had moved to Germany from Peru after many years of working in the Andean mountains. Their intense ritual actions create an entirely new interpretive context for *Parsifal,* subverting Wagner's mythological mysticism through highly charged emotional and physical images of suffering, torture, interrogation, and dismemberment drawn from the unredeemed, continuing experience of oppressive violence that haunts the rural population in the Andes, caught between government militias and Maoist *guerrilleros.*

The first counterpoint, or prologue, to the festival theme, however, is offered by the Slovenian industrial punk band Laibach on opening night. After two hours of technologically precise sound, light, and film production, the cool, mechanical, distanced performance of the Laibach musicians reaches its limit. Their driving industrial techno-rock creates a military facade or masquerade (in front of the facade of the Festspielhaus) that seems ironically transcendental, as if these robotic astronauts were transmitting their programmed music from a spaceship via satellite. "Perhaps we shall return to Earth one day," announces a taped voice ominously at the end. The provocation is perhaps purely conceptual, even as the band adds a public "message" for the audience, read by Peter Mlakar (a member of the Neue Slowenische Kunst [NSK] Department of Pure and Applied Philosophy) as another of his absurd "addresses to the German nation" that he had previously published. On the other hand, Laibach's role as agent provocateur within the anonymous NSK movement/organization is significant in light of the history of the underground movement of the eighties in Slovenia/Yugoslavia. The poster they composed for the 1987 Yugoslav Youth Day parade prompted a scandal and a court trial when it was later found out to have been a copy of a Nazi poster entitled "The Allegory of Heroism." The NSK practices in theater, dance, music, film, and visual art generally use such "conversions" of ideological languages (which "discipline" the body in certain ways) to examine ideologically constructed corporealities subjected to state power. The repetition of such "constructivist bodies" records the perversion, under totalitarian regimes or state-sponsored social realism, of bodily techniques that were once scripted and rehearsed to further progressive ends or emancipatory sensations (e.g., think of Meyerhold's biomechanics, Schlemmer's ballets, or Wigman's expressionism). In Dragan Živadinov's collaboration with Laibach in the mid-eighties I find the seeds for this strategy of conversion, which reminds me of the myths of early modernist and constructivist/futurist projections, and since I consider this eastern European perspective on my tracking of the dancing body very illuminating for the current context of virtual-reality technology, I want to shift locations to Ljubljana.

Ballet Utopica

In the early nineties the independent artists in Ljubljana seem already to have passed beyond the transgressive stages of their self-definition and "self-management" during the subcultural and punk/new wave movements of the "Slovene spring" of the eighties, with an extensive alternative local infrastructure fully in place (from ŠKUC Gallery, Equrna Gallery, Glej Theatre, and Radio Študent to video and design studios, print media, and fanzines). Compared to other cities in the communist East, Ljubljana had witnessed an extraordinary growth of alternative movements (feminists, gays and lesbians, peace activists, environmentalists) and artistic productions that linked new organizational forms of communication, social activities, and tactics of presentation and distribution. This complex structure of self-articulation and programmatic conceptual intervention in the public relations of art and politics resembles the polemical, performative practice of the manifesto employed by earlier twentieth-century avant-garde movements (e.g., futurism and surrealism). The historical difference is that the Slovene artists self-consciously used manifestos to *quote* aesthetic politics and polemics that had been entangled with the authoritarianism of fascist and Stalinist regimes.

Video artist Marina Gržinić, who is also one of the most important cultural critics and curators in Slovenia, has pointed out that the movement developed a particular attitude toward history insofar as it carefully documented all the cultural activities that galvanized in the clubs and underground discotheques, galleries and theaters, and especially around the performances and exhibitions of NSK, a collective that included several constituent groups (the band Laibach, the visual artists of IRWIN, the Theater of the Sisters of Scipio Nasica, Red Pilot Cosmokinetic Theater, the New Collectivism design group, and others engaged in philosophy, film, and architecture). The NSK manifestos, posters, exhibits, concerts, film, and performances are best documented in the comprehensive book *Neue Slowenische Kunst* that the collective designed and published itself.[22]

In its theater and media productions, NSK's visual-conceptual strategies adopt the state's language of politics directly or, rather, they copy or rerecord the state's representational aesthetics by refracting a constructivist aesthetic of "total art" that intermixes and compounds avant-garde styles and art/theater/ballet/music/film models ranging from the Russian Revolution (Meyerhold, Eisenstein, Malevich, Tatlin) to capitalist postmodern performance (Robert Wilson, Jan Fabre, the Italian transavanguardia) and more aggressive punk or industrial technomusical forms. Some of these deliberately provocative mixings and mimicries occur in Laibach's and New Collectivism's adaptations of Nazi and fascist iconographies for their album covers, which expose their shocking correspondence to the official aesthetics of a Stalinist-type social realism. These mimicries have been defended—most eloquently by Slavoj Žižek, Slovenia's well-known Lacanian philosopher—not as ironic imitations but as a form of *overidentification* that brings to light the obscene, fantasmatic underside of the ideological system. The state tried to label the punk-alternative culture with the fascist stigma (banning Laibach from performing in Ljubljana), but it could not answer the question: "Is it fascist?" Thus the question kept rebounding back to the state (and to those who want to know the truth).

How is one to ask this question if the tactics of NSK imply precisely the refusal to answer or decide the question for us, and if many or all of its manifestos cannot be taken at face value? In this context, the most widely remembered NSK production is the 1986 performance of *Krst pod Triglavom* (Baptism Under Triglav), created at Ljubljana's Cankarjev Center by Scipion Nasice/Laibach and directed by Dragan Živadinov. This operatic ballet constitutes the third and last phase ("retroclassicism") of Nasice's four-year experimentation with theater "as a state" and as a total cultural-national production system. The first ("illegal") phase started with the *Retro-garde Happening Hinkemann* (1983), followed by the second ("exorcist") phase and *Marija Nablocka Retro-garde Happening* (1985). The ironic references in the titles to the sixties Fluxus movement in the West are deliberate. In 1987 Nasice announced its self-destruction:

> The Theater of the Sisters of Scipio Nasica has no stage.
> The TSSN was founded with the aim of renewing theatrical art.

Renewal calls for unity. That is why the TSSN takes up the place of all
theatrical institutions. . . . Theater is not an empty space.
The theater is the State.
Each theater has a hierarchical, national, economic, and ideological
organization. . . . The TSSN is apolitical. The only truthful aesthetic
vision of the State is the vision of an impossible State.[23]

The performance—based entirely on quotations of literary, art-historical, cultural, and political motifs and themes, ostensibly revolving
around the national epic poem by Frances Prešeren ("Baptism Under
Triglav")—constructed an amazingly telescopic "device" (as Malevich
would have called it) with which it produced in accelerated, composite,
and reductive form the retrospective disappearance of the twentieth-
century avant-garde and the biomechanical body it had postulated. As
an "inauthentic retro-production" that renewed and recomposed the lost
historical avant-garde, the performance marked the Russian revolutionary avant-garde's sincere belief in its initiatory construction of a new age
of social and cosmic regeneration as a traumatic victory—a utopia that
was to become assimilated into the Stalinist state. Returning at the end
to Malevich's suprematism (the black cross), *Krst pod Triglavom* finally
staged the irony of absolute power projected by communism's belief in
itself as the final stage of a dialectical evolution, history having ended.
Yet the myth of baptizing nations (in Prešeren's poem) or traditions
shadows the syndrome of the body's incorporation into state ideology,
and Živadinov used the biomechanical body, performed by the Ljubljana opera-ballet, as the allegory of twentieth-century dance: a dance
that never liberated anything but remained trapped in successive rituals
of expression/abstraction congealed into aestheticized images, animated
in the diminishing returns of its projections.

What I'm getting at here is the post-utopian moment in NSK's
recreation of social constructive visions of abstraction (Tatlin, Malevich), as if NSK anticipated the revenge of history in the late return
of capitalism. Arriving in Ljubljana without knowing the context of the
emergence of the NSK movement in the center of Slovene urban culture, I am surprised to notice all the signs of an ultramodern visual
aesthetic in the fashion, design, and advertising now feeding the expansion of a Western-style capitalistic market economy. Many of the
references in local productions to Western pop culture, Hollywood, and
MTV suggest that Slovene art is already "inside" the Western postmodern horizon. However, the generation of performance and video artists
who lived the explosive transformations of the eighties must surely pos-

sess a double consciousness, both of their distinct history in the socialist East and of their intercultural relationship to the West's theory, art, and fashion trends. Local critics have expressed concern over the violence in the new Slovene physical dance-theater, especially as fascinated Western observers make facile equations with the violence of the Bosnian war and invite the groups to Western festivals as representatives of the convulsive eruptions in the Balkans. However, when you speak with the young physical-theater directors, they insist that the violence of the real, the pain in real bodies, is something they feel urged to explore with reference to the images of violence they have seen in the West, conveyed through the media. The dystopian reference point is an abstraction.

In Živadinov's work, the abstraction is located most immediately in the theater's history of ballet/dance and the technical, disciplinary, and scenographic deployment of bodies on the state's stages. If Wigman's "absolute dance" can be said to have been progressively absorbed into the essentializing fascist aesthetics of Nazi mass spectacle, Živadinov's retro-futuristic ballets return the biomechanical and constructivist aesthetic to the basic formal geometric features of classical ballet and its romantic association with the antigravitational ideal: the body surging up into space. Most provocatively, Živadinov's current work has pushed this ideal to the conceptual border of astrophysics and space engineering—and thus close to the preoccupations of digital artists, who proclaim the body obsolete and mediate its de-realization through computer programs.

On the tenth floor of an office building where the theater magazine *Maska* is produced, Dragan Živadinov shows me his visionary designs (executed by Russian collaborator Vadim Fiškin) for the architectonics of his ongoing *Noordung* project.[24] Each installment involves the creation of a new "space design" to be constructed inside an existing theater or public space, intended to alter the relations of stage and auditorium and of viewing public space itself (*polis:* the theater/the state). The *Noordung* project refers to Herman Potočnik Noordung (1892–1929), a Slovene scientist and the first person to deal with the problems of space travel. Potočnik's research was published in German under the title *Das Problem der Befahrung des Weltraums: Der Raketenmotor* (The Problem of Space Travel: The Rocket Engine) (1929) but did not appear in Slovene until 1986.[25] Živadinov claims that Potočnik envisioned the "future reality" in his invention of geostationary satellites and rotating space stations that generate artificial gravity through centrifugal force. Živadinov's passion for a future space theater, a *theater in space*, is tangible, as is his desire to construct public recognition of "Noordung," the belatedly resurrected myth

DANCING WITH TECHNOLOGIES

of Slovene science and universalist thinking. This new myth-making comes at a point when Slovene cultural identity itself is just taking shape and is subject to various ideological pressures from the Right and the Left. The premises of the unofficial theater of the eighties posited inside the state-controlled infrastructure, which still exists despite the disappearance of communism, have to be reexamined in the nineties.

Two of Živadinov's previous ballet-theater productions (performed by his group Cosmokinetic Kabinet) were already informed by this research: *Kapital* in 1991 and *Molitveni stroj Noordung* (Noordung Prayer Machine) in 1993. On April 20, 1995, a new "kinetic *Warttenberg*" was initiated as a fifty-year performance project devoted to the theme "Eros and

Molitveni stroj Noordung (Noordung Prayer Machine), created by Dragan Živadinov and performed by the Cosmokinetic Kabinet, Ljubljana, 1993. Courtesy of D. Živadinov.

Sketches of stage construction by Dragan Živadinov for the *Noordung* project, designed by Vadim Fiškin.

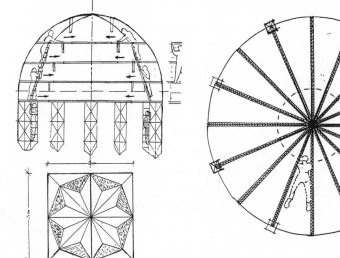
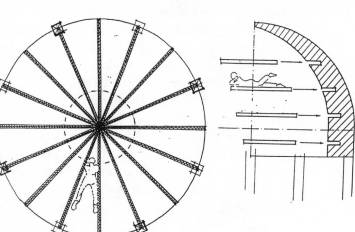

the State" and to be repeated every ten years. I have heard Živadinov's description of this "inhabited sculpture" in several versions, of which the following is one:

> On April 20, 1995, at 8:00 p.m., a premiere will be performed in Ljubljana.
> There will be 12 actors appearing in the premiere.
> The theme: William Shakespeare.
> The 12 actors live in Ljubljana.
> The premiere is to take place on April 20, 1995.
> The first reprise is due in 2005, i.e., 10 years later.
> With the same actors, same time, same place, same costumes, same
>   scenography.

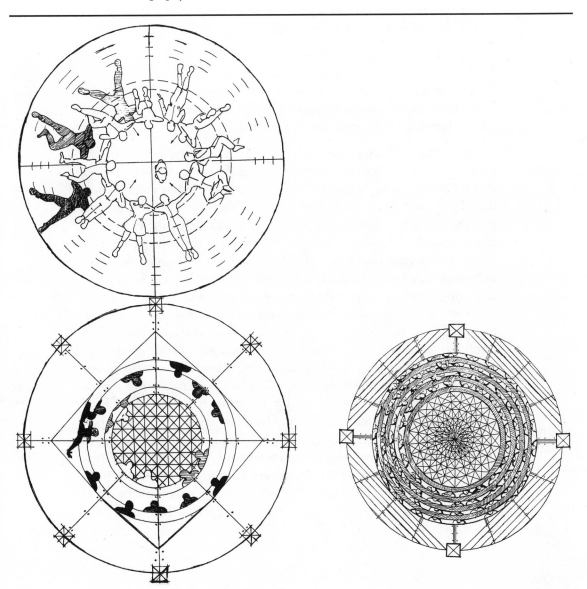

Everything is to be the same, except if someone dies.

The deceased will be replaced by a symbol.

According to the mise-en-scène, where a live actor performed, a symbol will be placed there.

Verbal parts of a deceased actor will be replaced by melody within the same timing.

Verbal parts of deceased actors will be replaced by rhythm.

The live actors will act as if the deceased ones were present.

The second reprise is due in the year 2015.

The whole action will thereby be repeated.

All the deceased ones will be replaced by symbols.

The third reprise is due in 2025, the fourth one in 2035.

The last reprise is to take place in 2045.

By that time all the actors will be dead.

I will be alive and the stage will be full of symbols.

I will then bring the symbols to Russia and from there they will be taken by a rocket to the point of zero gravity, 38,000 kilometers above the earth. There they will be given over to the cosmos.

Živadinov's drawings and sketches of a total theater hint at an aesthetic, social, and physical architecture or model of space within a space that can invade, as an "alien" or "virtual" space, the larger political state that the theater also reflects. The retro-garde premises upon which the new theater of the eighties was built in fact anticipated their own sublation, and all of Živadinov's productions explore the contradictions of an assumed autonomous space within the enforced collectivist ideologies of Yugoslavia's authoritarian brand of communism. If the theater never was autonomous, it could still function as a metapolitical space in which universal or metaphysical themes could travel, evoked by an iconography indebted to "science fiction" as well as to the original avant-garde, futurist conceptions of the temporal extension and transevaluation of spatial art. *Molitveni stroj Noordung* can also be viewed as the Slovene version/revision of the prerevolutionary futurist opera *Pobeda nad solntsem* (Victory over the Sun), created in 1913 by Aleksei Kruchenykh, Mikhail Matiushin, and Kazimir Malevich. Živadinov's visual choreography, especially his use of figurines or marionettelike astronauts who represent the "future countrymen" and women who must learn to build the new satellite *they will become,* seems to reinvent not only the de facto, revolutionary, nonobjective designs Malevich created for the futurist opera (designs to which Malevich attributed the origins of his suprematist paintings), but also the transrational thought (*zaum*) needed to inspire belief in a constructible future *after* the burnout of revolutionary horizons.[26] *Molitveni stroj Noordung* experiments with the transcendent idea of the human "satellite" floating in outer space-time, and the concept of the "prayer machine" invokes a metaphysics of communality that points to the paradoxical intersections of materiality (machine) and spirituality (cosmic faith).

The most extraordinary construction of this paradox involves the actual separation of the audience into topical spectators and u-topical observers, placing the former into separate little cubicles *underneath* the webbed stage constructed of wooden beams. The heads of the collective but separated audience are on ground level, so to speak, able to look up into the space of the theatrical action, while the observers (equipped with binoculars) are excluded, so to speak, from the corporeal experience of the spectators designed *into* the stage. The actor-astronauts, thirty-one members of the Ljubljana National Ballet, perform above the spectators' normal horizontal/perspectival vision. Judging from the exact geometric, gridlike configuration of the audience capsules, one might also think of the dancers, *en pointe*, as moving *above* the collectivized and controlled topography. If the "new formalism" of this constructivist space hints at a hyperperspectival, higher theater that must be intuited, it is no doubt ironic that Živadinov named his *Noordung* project after a Slovene space engineer whose utopian visions remained unfulfilled and whose rocket constructions (invoked by the libretto and the visual projections) are linked to the questionable "revolutions" in fashion design and classical-ballet technique displayed in the scenography.

In its double allusion to the Russian avant-garde's revolutionary constructivism and to the monumental Soviet failure to create a "scientific socialism" through social engineering, *Noordung* positions itself beyond or outside Soviet reality even as it retraces a collective memory grounded in a movement toward metaphysical horizons. Živadinov's apparent madness has a method in it, especially given the Slovene theater's peripheral relation to Russia or the West. Instead of dismantling the bankrupt belief in a transcendent utopia, he retraces the steps of a futurist art that is now, at the dystopian moment of socialism's collapse within a European civilization littered with destroyed metaphors, a vehicle for a prospective *reconstruction of another world*—and not, I presume, a return to an imaginary or mythic Slovene center or national consciousness.

At least this is my understanding of Živadinov's architectural drawings, which remind me of the compositional forms of Malevich's *Planits* and *Architektons*. The antigravity conception of his future theater implies a kind of altered state, a form of mental space travel that shifts theatrical perception of the real to a different, planetary level. The audience in this theater would become a "space shuttle," so to speak, able to sense kinesthetically what Živadinov describes as Potočnic's "Slovenian spirituality." While I am trying to follow his flight of the imagination, Živadinov suddenly interrupts himself and makes a gesture toward the window. I look out and see a placid Slovene summer sky over a peaceful city. When he speaks of the "radical evil" that has appeared in the south, traumatically close to the edge of our limited vision of ourselves (excluded outside observers?), I know he has pointed toward Sarajevo and the genocide that is happening in the midst of central Europe.

Yet Živadinov's promotion of the myth of a "Slovenian spirituality" is not so innocent either, and after experiencing the performance in 1994 and watching the rehearsals for *Warttenberg,* I feel increasingly uncomfortable with the total control that his theater's architectonic structure exerts over the audience on either side, topical and u-topical. The overcoming of the stage/audience separation in the projected rotational or orbital wheel could also be seen as the suffocating experience of being taken hostage by a master director, and his plans for the 1995–2045 project are radically exclusionary (with indoctrinary overtones), since it's apparently designed for an audience of young Slovene schoolchildren who will be the only spectator-observers of this opus for the next fifty years.

Again, this is perhaps an ironic strategy linked to the repetitive effect built into the retro-garde principle, which must invoke totalizing metaphors in order to defamiliarize our memory of balletic and biomechanical bodies constructed to idealized models of aesthetic technique in the service of the state. There never was an empty stage, as Wigman's expressionism implied, but only courts (of ballet), institutions, schools, and industries. Yet Živadinov's vision for the future zero-gravitational theater is also indirectly correlated with the telos of Western techno-aesthetics and bioengineering that simulate the redesigning of human organisms and genes to proclaim their perfectibility.

THREE

DANCE SCREENS

Enhancing the "Obsolete Body"

In the work of Australian artist Stelarc, the "obsolete body" is tested for future design applications, and in his web site on the Internet Stelarc proclaims that THE HOLLOW BODY WOULD BE A BETTER HOST FOR TECHNOLOGICAL COMPONENTS [*sic*]. Imitating, it appears, the theoretical sketches of Schlemmer's transfigured *Tänzermensch,* Stelarc's home page frames the hollowing out in the evolutionary futurism he has been testing in his own body-enhanced performances. I quote a few phrases from the "archival space" on the Web that he builds through his human/machine interfaces, extending his earlier robotics work to interactive works that "incorporate the Internet and the Web, sound, music, video, and computers."

1. ABSENT BODIES. We mostly operate as Absent Bodies. THAT'S BECAUSE A BODY IS DESIGNED TO INTERFACE WITH ITS ENVIRONMENT. The body's mobility and navigation in the world require this outward orientation.

2. OBSOLETE BODY. It is time to question whether a bipedal, breathing body with binocular vision and a 1400cc brain is an adequate biological form. It cannot cope with the quantity, complexity and quality of information it has accumulated; it is intimidated by the precision, speed and power of technology and it is biologically ill-equipped to cope with its new extra-terrestrial environment.

3. REDESIGNING THE BODY. It is no longer meaningful to see the body as a site for the psyche or the social, but rather as a structure to be monitored and modified—the body no longer as a subject but as an object—NOT AN OBJECT OF DESIRE BUT AN OBJECT FOR DESIGNING. . . . ALTERING THE ARCHITECTURE OF THE BODY RESULTS IN ADJUSTING AND EXTENDING ITS AWARENESS OF THE WORLD. As an object, the body can be amplified and accelerated, attaining planetary escape velocity. It becomes a post-evolutionary projectile, departing and diversifying in form and function.

4. THE ANAESTHETIZED BODY. The importance of technology is not simply in the pure power it generates but in the realm of abstraction it produces through its operational speed and its development of extended sense systems . . . Technology pacifies the body and the world, and disconnects

the body from many of its functions. . . . The body plugged into a machine network needs to be pacified. In fact, to function in the future and to truly achieve a hybrid symbiosis the body will need to be increasingly anaesthetized.

5. HIGH-FIDELITY ILLUSION. The experience of Telepresence becomes the high-fidelity illusion of Tele-existence. ELECTRONIC SPACE BECOMES A MEDIUM OF ACTION RATHER THAN INFORMATION. It meshes the body with its machines in ever-increasing complexity and interactiveness. The body's form is enhanced and its functions are extended. ITS PERFORMANCE PARAMETERS ARE NEITHER LIMITED BY ITS PHYSIOLOGY NOR BY THE LOCAL SPACE IT OCCUPIES. Electronic space restructures the body's architecture and multiplies its operational possibilities. The body performs by coupling the kinesthetic action of muscles and machine with the kinematic pure motion of the images it generates.

6. THE SHEDDING OF SKIN. The present organ-isation of the body is unnecessary. The solution to modifying the body is not to be found in its internal structure, but lies simply on its surface . . . The significant event in our evolutionary history was a change in the mode of locomotion. Future developments will occur with a change of skin.

7. PHANTOM BODY. Technologies are becoming better life-support systems for our images than for our bodies. IMAGES ARE IMMORTAL, BODIES ARE EPHEMERAL. The body finds it increasingly difficult to match the expectations of its images. THE BODY NOW PERFORMS BEST AS ITS IMAGE.[1]

Stelarc's script for his performance experiments is not transrational but follows the logic of a technoaesthetics that is currently celebrated in the popular books on our digital age and virtual-reality technologies. Stelarc's work can be considered a technically advanced version of the self-transgressive and self-abusive body art of the sixties and seventies. Interestingly, Stelarc's performances are practically absent in contemporary theater and dance criticism, although his experimentations and his cyborgian model of body/machine interfaces clearly echo and extend the avant-garde manifestos of the early futurists and constructivists. Whereas computer programmer Brenda Laurel never discusses performance or digital-art experiments as such in her book, mostly delineating her understanding of "theater" (based on Aristotelian poetics) as an "interface metaphor" for improving smart languages/dialogues in human-computer interactivity, Mark Dery and other contributors to *Mondo 2000, Wired,* and the ecstatic debates about virtual reality and cybernetic art on the Net have acknowledged—not without a sense of horrified, voyeuristic fascination—the McLuhanesque dance Stelarc is performing with the prosthetic devices, electrodes, and wires strapped to his naked flesh or inserted into his veins and stomach.[2]

Stelarc takes literally McLuhan's notion that technological media are extensions of the human senses, and all of his recent performances demonstrate a perverse insistence on body modification and the redesign not of the space surrounding the body's kinesphere but of the body's architecture, skin, and internal body spaces themselves—the "physiological hardware," as Stelarc calls it. The body in this conceptual theater is like the denigrated and increasingly useless "meat" in cyberpunk fiction after *Neuromancer* (William Gibson's cyber-cowboy protagonists are "jacked" into computer-generated virtual realities or are technologized with implants, biochip wetware, nerve amplifiers, neural interface plugs, and designer drugs). It is through the fictional definitions of "cyberspace" as "consensual hallucination" (Gibson) that today's playing field of on-line communication, virtual reality games, computer-generated audio/visual/tactile experiences, telepresences, and interactive digital designs has come to be popularized more generally as the cyberspace of postindustrial society.[3]

Stelarc's performances, which begin to attract attention in the 1980s, when he suspends his body high in the air with wires and cables hooked into his flesh, have increasingly objectified body/self to the point at which its agency is displaced from itself and the "fractal flesh" becomes "extruded" on the Net or other telematic, prosthetic, and medical technologies that can activate, map, and monitor the old, "obsolete" physiology. Strikingly, Stelarc's body performances display the parameter of a deterministic or post-Darwinian utopia of evolution that posit the contemporary body both as virtually disabled by the exponentially increasing complexity of information/technological support systems *and* as potentially evolving into more adaptive interface configurations. In Stelarc's view—which appears diametrically opposed to those feminist body art performances that celebrate the ecstasies of organic wholeness and female erotic power or that unearth the body's healing knowledge (as in Anna Halprin's ritual dance work)—the body will have to endure its separation from useless illusions of self, subjectivity, and organic experience. Admittedly, this may be distressing. The objectification of the body, which underlies all body art, is pushed to an extreme in Stelarc's vision of a mutating somatic and nervous system that can improve if it "opens up" to the operation of the cyborg synthesis. Successfully synthesized, one could learn to inhabit this permeable body, and while the

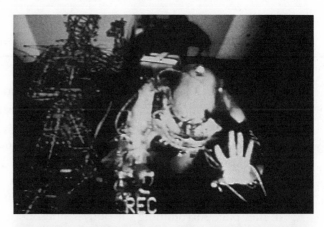

Stelarc performing in *Actuate/Rotate: Event for Virtual Body,* Obscure Gallery, Quebec, Canada. Video still, 1993. Courtesy of the artist.

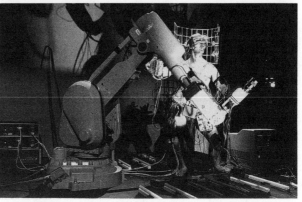

Stelarc performing in *Scanning Robot, Automatic Arm & Third Hand,* MCA, Sydney, Australia, 1997. Courtesy of the artist. Photo: Tony Figallo.

Performance design by Stelarc & Merlin for *Involuntary Body/Third Hand,* a continuous performance/installation created for *Parasite: Event for Invaded and Involuntary Body,* Wood Street Galleries, Pittsburgh, Pa., 1997. Courtesy of the artist.

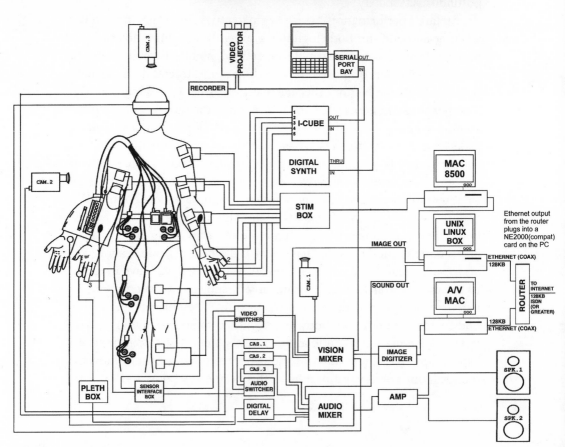

metaphor of the cyborg has by now already been adopted by feminist and postmodern cultural theorists, it is actually being choreographed in Stelarc's performances.

The prosthetic dance I remember most vividly is *Actuate/Rotate: Event for Virtual Body* (1993), in which Stelarc wears a Polhemus magnetic tracking system with sensors attached to his head, torso, and extremities, his right arm and hand doubled by a robotic arm (custom-built by a Japanese manufacturer, it has a tactile feedback system). Standing and moving in the midst of the electronic machinery that surrounds his kinesphere like a sculpture wired into his flesh (almost literally enacting Schlemmer's drawing of the "technical organism"), he interacts with his digital double, who mirrors his movements, like the "video shadows" in earlier performances, which translated his analog images onto screen projections. In *Actuate/Rotate* the live choreography transmits digitized "shadows" on video display monitors, and the magnetic tracking system converts or clones his arms into virtual arms or, alternately, animated wire-frame skeletons and "characters." While I watch this interaction, the monitor images change whenever video images of Stelarc's physical body, captured by video cameras, are mixed with the computer-generated animations. A doubling and splicing of the images occur, since the digital camera responds to his movement and triggers collages of the images of the fleshly body with those of the character animations. Stelarc's movement itself is severely reduced to gyrating arms and a tiny, hopeless tap dance on the same spot, trapped as he is in the mesh of wires, electrodes, and the ultrasonic sound transducers attached to his wrists and knees, which transmit the flow of the blood in his arteries and the bending of his knees into whooshing, fluttering, and grumbling soundscapes. While he might claim that the reconfigured future body will move (or be moved) without memory, I certainly cannot forget the haunting effect the smiling, heavy-set dancer had on me, as his extruding and emitting cyberorganism flailed and thrashed about like a trapped animal, with its industrial robot arm pointing jerkily in my direction.

Returning to the Body with Memories and Screen Lives

When Stelarc moves his outdoor suspensions to the inside, hooking his body into the computers and surrounding his performance with the conceptual space of high-tech engineering and biomedical phantasmagoria, he may be engendering another masculine mythopoeic futurism that, in the name of the quasi-scientific constructivism of his cyborg aesthetics, disclaims the profoundly antihumanist implications of the politics of extraterrestrial "bodies without memories" (THE BODY MUST BECOME IMMORTAL TO ADAPT). He believes in the necessary utopia of a technologized evolution, and his performances repeat the story of the body's limitations, which need to be overcome. His aesthetic is a classical-ballet aesthetic based on fairy-tales and pantomimes of magical resurrection, except that he always dances alone against himself in narcissistic entrapment, an Orfeo of the new cyberspace.

He is by no means the only artist, however, who has connected his body to feedback systems. Laurie Anderson worked with electronic mutations of her voice and with digital image projections and loops in *United States* (1981–83) and *Home of the Brave* (1986). West Coast new-music composers such as Pamela Z and Laetitia Sonami have performed with Data Suits and SoundGloves, and many musicians, video artists, and designers have worked for years with electronic composing, processing, editing, and remixing techniques, as well as with technologies of storage, retrieval, and modification. Stelarc's idea that the "body now performs best as its image" is a well-known fact in the film, advertising, and music-recording industries, and the image mutations of Madonna, Prince, and Michael Jackson are as strikingly familiar to us as the current "bad-ness" of the gangsta rappers in a media-saturated culture of clichés promoted by MTV. However harmful our total saturation by and immersion in media environments has turned out to be, the recording and remixing processes in the music industry and the disc and club DJ culture, for example, point to significant transformations in performer-audience feedback relations.

Writing about the "sounding image of ourselves," Simon Frith has pointed out that the relationship of visual and aural pleasures have changed since the recording and remixing technologies shifted the sound of live musical performance toward the disc—the "ideal" staging faked by the digital engineer—and toward our new sense of being ourselves *in* that sound we listen to through our headphones. Recordings and digital engineering can also effect spatiality in sound and thus construct a physical, kinesthetic experience, while contemporary sampling and multitrack recording have transformed our sense of musical time and space by fragmenting and dispersing the musical object as such, reanimating popular sound samples in so many varying sonic textures for different sonic contexts, settings, and aural spaces. Although it may tend to clean up music and separate out all the environmental noise of imperfect live-performance conditions, digital sound technology has not enforced the denial of the body in performance that Western musicology seems to take for granted in its suspicion of the physical obtruding upon pure musical ideas. Consequently, according to Frith, "we have a new socio-technological form of music, *public records:* musical events, social gatherings, discos, and clubs in which sounds on disc are the entertainment. Here, whether in terms of volume, spectacle, sociability, or emotional intensity, the private fantasies of record listening are, in a sense, enacted, felt *for real*. Dancing in public — listening in public — thus seems to be *more* expressive of how we feel about our music, more truthful, than dancing, listening, alone."[4]

This experience of ourselves in aural space is an important reminder of the kinesthetics of spatial and temporal sensation that music shares with dance. Laurie Anderson's work tends to be very self-conscious about this space (the United States, home of the brave?) of technologically fabricated or enhanced experience. Anderson's multimedia works are considered crossover performances, but, then again, so are most performances, as I have tried to demonstrate. What characterizes *United States,* however, is a particularly implosive slippage between genres and spatialities in music, voice, narrative, and image projections. Anderson becomes her own movement choir, mediator, and sound manipulator as she "travels" into and across the allegorical space of technology-as-man-made-domain of expertise and control over (feminine/unmediated) nature. Ironically, Anderson puns on the allegory of heroic man (e.g., Stelarc birthing his hyperdesigned new body) by performing, with her microphones, vocoders, sequencers, musical instruments, altered voices/audio masks and alternate personae, the "New Woman" that Russian constructivists and social realists perhaps dreamed about. However, she masks her female gender by performing a more androgenous, uncertain, and in-between body, as she does at the beginning of her film *Home of the Brave* when she enters with violin and bow, completely hidden in a white astronaut's suit. Her face is masked, her voice lowered an octave. More directly, she is punning on the paradox of narrow "closed circuits" from within the electronic circuits and loops of her own amplified voices, in the larger context of a radically diminished experience of depth in these United States that she links to the language of the future: the binary code of the computer, 0 + 1.

```
0010101000101011101001110001001001010101001010010101010
0010101110100101110101000101010101001001010101010101010
1001010101010010010001001111110101011010101010100101010
0101010101010111101001010100010101010010010010101001
```

"Not much space in between here," she jokes in her unnatural voice and in her own typical style of the interrupted or delayed speech endings, which in her half-spoken, half-sung delivery of her stories/songs attains a gestural and musical effect of attenuation. Or, rather, the spaces she puts in between her words and their uncertain meanings, like the spatial dynamics between her figure onstage and the digital images projected on the screen behind her, create a hovering or reverberating effect that continuously refuses to "resolve" the contradictory rhythmic and tonal impulses. In both musical and movement terms, her gestural dance plays ambiguously with duration and the releases of tension, thus creating an effect of incomplete or never-ending narratives. These durational antinarratives without resolution become a memorable gesture in the deterritorialized spaces of her intermedia dance. The dissonances in the spaces don't connect, and some of the strange animations on the back screen (the screen within the film screen) also hover undecidedly as if to tease our anxiety to attach meaning to them. Near the end of her story/song "Hothead / Langue d'amour," as her amplified/multiplied voice slides into an extended "La, la, la, la . . . l'amour," we see a ghostly white shirt, without a body in it, dancing jerkily on the screen, beckoning or warning us like a scarecrow.[5]

Unlike the emotional and physical aggressiveness in the hyperexpressionism and paravocal excesses of Diamanda Galás and the equally boundary-breaking but narratively more focused, race-conscious political music/video performances of black women rappers such as Queen Latifah, MC Lyte, Boss, or Salt 'N' Pepa, the *presence* in Anderson's voice creates a more uncanny effect of not seeming to belong to the voice characters and character animations on screen, almost as if the storytelling voice travels outside of a home (cf. her song "Language Is a Virus from Outer Space," quoting William Burroughs) and the homely categories of corporeal subjectivity inferred from common cultural assumptions about identity, gender, sexuality, pleasure, and authenticity. Like the progression of her titles for her concert tours (*United States, Natural History, Empty Places*) in the eighties, Anderson's "homecoming" implies a strategy of disorientation and permutation. The places (bodies) called home are becoming emptier, more virtual. Her performed androgeny with her "own" and "other" voices, simultaneously reaffirming and refuting familiar individual "body" boundaries and origins of pleasure, creates a fluidity that destabilizes audience identification with the morphologies of bodies and spaces as such. In posing the strange erotics of this fluidity, and its inauthenticity as authenticity in her electronically manipulated "system" onstage and onscreen, Anderson challenges an older expressionist system of interiority that would particularize women and men and national, natural, and cultural spaces according to origins assumed to be transparent. "This is not a story my people tell. It's something I know myself," she tells us in "Hothead," a composition that appears both in *United States* and *Home of the Brave,* and her parody of grand master narratives ("And the woman liked the snake very much because when he talked he made little noises with his tongue and his long tongue was lightly licking about his lips") underscores the tumble of animated signs on the screen that make her performance so fragmentary and allusive, resisting determined meaning and coyly hinting at fantasies of excess.

Within the expansiveness of Anderson's multimedia performance, however, she dances and voices a symptomatically North American anxiety not only over feminine excess, technological fetishism, or the excessive blankness of the surfaces of the "homeland," which only mask the racial ambivalence beneath, but also over the particular erotic intensification of surfaces and contiguities. The surfaces and skins of bodies, in the era of a killing disease that changed fantasies about sex and eros, have attracted a phobic and paranoidal gaze. In this context of postmodern obsessions over sexual identities and transgressions, Anderson's hypersemiotic performances tend to challenge a representational space in which bodies are visible and audible indices of identities, even as their deferred temporality reorients the body-subject and the troubled body-images toward another locus of the experience and perception of movement and the erotic: the body's *outside.* In "Langue d'amour" her sinuous dance suggests a movement of tongues and hands along surfaces, and her arms, covered in long-sleeve black gloves, play as if on an "unfamiliar" fantasized topography of the body's erotogenic zones and regions. This playing on surfaces liquefies the body-image and excites an almost tactile projection, a projection *across* the boundaries of her voice and what cannot be seen. It could be argued that Anderson is shifting her stories to the visual field of dissociations, which shares certain parameters with postmodern dance. The latter, initially signaled by the Judson Dance Theater's departure from the Cunningham/Cage generation of dancers and choreographers, explores an infinite variety of disruptions of formalized movement/space and aleatory composition. The impact of the collaborations of Simone Forti, Yvonne Rainer, Trisha Brown, Lucinda Childs, Deborah Hay, David Gordon, Steve Paxton and their friends was felt throughout the seventies and eighties.[6]

Although space does not permit me to trace the permutations of postmodern and new dance in the United States and their reactions to Cunningham's impersonalized choreography and the neutral, objective, task-oriented/chance-based improvisations of the early Judson Dance

Theater, I want to point out that the avoidance of expressive intentionality and the dissociations of movement, music, and setting in Cunningham's collaborations with Cage and Rauschenberg cannot be explained simply in terms of technical disjunctions of outside/inside in abstract movement. However much Cunningham may have reached for outward technical uniformity in the dance, revealing nothing about who the dancers are, it is nearly impossible to argue that dance does not affect emotion or can shift the emphasis to choreographic structure or movement energy alone. In this connection, one needs to remember that the Judson Church experiments—especially the later multimedia dance works that moved from the church and the small lofts to the bigger proscenium stages and halls—involved such a wide range of methods, approaches, and crossovers (particularly visual art, film, music and, ultimately, the whole spectrum of pop/rock culture) that it is more illuminating to see the spread of contact improvisation and the performance art, dance-theater, dance video, music-dance evolutions of the eighties and nineties on a continuum with the changing concerns and interpretations one brings to the inherent theatricalities of the dancing body.

If one thinks of the continual transformations in expressive cultures—for example, in the rich physical-spiritual history of black gospel music and its relationship to church, stage, recording studio, radio, and television—the formal concerns with "pure" abstraction betray a specifically Anglo-European blindness toward the ideological operations in the conceptual theater of the body. It is a blindness toward accumulation, the continual retheatricalizations of dance/movement, and the changes in the relationship between the visible and the nonvisible (that which cannot be spoken). It is also a blindness toward race and the social and political fact that the fluidities of "identification"—in the fetishization of surface play, body camp, and surface masquerade—are largely a white privilege. In some cases, as in the masquerading performances of Sandra Bernhard or the deliberate multiple impersonations of Anna Deavere Smith's *Fires in the Mirror* and *Twilight: Los Angeles 1992,* the complications of racial difference are acknowledged and dramatized to make the colors of "realness" visible.

Laurie Anderson and Merce Cunningham may share an interest in masking the corporeal presence of the real body; they also share, for different purposes, a desire to manipulate figure/character animation and visual space composition. Already in the mid-seventies Cunningham begins to videotape his performances and choreograph videodance, collaborating with filmmaker Charles Atlas on the rearticulation of stage space/real space and logical time in the discontinuous and unidimensional video space/time. By the late eighties, Cunningham starts to explore and design movement possibilities with his Living Sketchbook, using LifeForms—a graphic, three-dimensional computer software program—to prepare, modify, and edit choreography for the human figure or character animation.[7]

With increased demand by television producers and video festivals, videodance has emerged as a new collaborative form, supported by independent production companies and organizations such as the Moving Pictures/Dance on Film Festival in Toronto or the Vienna-based Internationales Musikzentrum. Since 1990 the IMZ has organized its annual "DanceScreen" festival in various cities, featuring more than two hundred videodances each year drawn from all over the world. Choreographers and filmmakers are encouraged to find new ways to document dance, but the emphasis is on new dance produced for the camera and on redesigning existing work or choreographing images with weight/ shape and movement dynamics specifically intended for the tenuous videospace and the language of film/television. Obviously, the awareness of the differences between performance space and film space is heightened by movement capabilities of the camera itself, introducing a host of new conceptual issues concerning the relationship between the filming process and postproduction process (editing and manipulation of the filmed images). Choreographing videodance undoubtedly reintroduces, via the analog and digital editing processes, a new constructivism and, potentially, a strong emphasis on the visuality of dance, but the compression in scale and perspective (wide shot/close-up), combined with the editing rhythms and sound textures, can also create a heightened kinesthetic intimacy with the moving body-images.

The presentation of film *as* dance, in fact, is a choreographic concept that was explored in Concert 1 of the Judson Church in 1963, when a chance-edited film by several dancers opened the evening program; similarly, Beverly Schmidt's work *The Seasons* is a solo she has performed simultaneously, in counterpoint or in unison, with the projection of *Blossoms*, a "film-stage" performance by Robert Blossom that shows earlier improvisations of the solo. The incorporation of film into dance works does not gain as much ground as the later fusions of music and film/ video in the underground film/rock and club world and on MTV would suggest, but performers such as Meredith Monk, Yvonne Rainer (who abandoned dance for filmmaking), Trisha Brown, and Lucinda Childs have certainly experimented with film projection in ways that deserve careful analysis, since the current proliferation of dance videos, video performances, and dance works incorporating video projections/monitors implies a usage of electronic images that differs from earlier 35- or 16-millimeter projection.

The technologies of film and video differ (e.g., the contrast ratios in the projection of film and video are different), and one of the most crucial aspects, in this respect, is that different technologies produce different illusions of movement. Motion-picture movement (successive stills) is produced mechanically, while video records and transmits movement electronically, which leads to a vastly different look. Video, like sound recording from which it derives technologically, produces images through a continuous scansion process, and the huge enlargement in video projection—often used in the theater or in video installations to create a more powerful, cinematic image size—tends to diminish sharpness and brightness considerably. In fact, image enlargement makes us more aware of the continuous process of electronic scanning, since the illusion of video's immediacy and directness is contradicted by our increased awareness of the pixels and the continuous construction of the pixel images (part-images, dots of information) during the projection process.[8] With its flatness and lack of depth, electronic image transmission has a more spatial character compared with the temporal character of film, which is based on its production and reassemblage process. I became especially interested in the flatness of video/projection in one of my recent productions (*Lovers Fragments*). While experimenting with spatial volume, narrative time, and spatial/temporal layering, I and my collaborators used frontal video projection onto translucent scrims downstage, mid-stage and upstage, letting two different image tracks bleed through the entire depth of the stage space. Apart from the temporal disjunctions created by the separate image tracks, we became aware of two significant problems. First, the upstage images became so thin and transparent that they seemed shadowy ghosts of the very same images downstage. Second, two of the three screens received slightly distorted or blurred image projections since the video projector had to be focused a precise distance from a particular receptor screen. Color and sharpness in the other screen images began to blur. The interrelationship of our live dance and the projected images inside the space became even more complicated once we started to project not frontally but from side angles, distorting the regular rectangular image space in ways that disturbed the geometries in the space and in our perspectival vision.

The disturbance of the perceptual terrain is one of the most important elements in postmodern dance, and I would argue that choreographers such as Childs and Brown very consciously use a cinematic approach (unlike the musical polyphony in Bausch's *Tanztheater*) in the *editing* of their asynchronic movement repetitions onstage, exploiting and disturbing the regular geometries and symmetries perceived within the visual field. Similarly, a lot of the gestural movement in Wilson's stage work is presented laterally, as if in a two-dimensional frame, and the flatness of his composition, eliminating depth perspective, creates the painterly and, ultimately, decorative design effect Appia tried to break down in his vision of organic, rhythmic space. The whole question of how we experience movement and images in the projection process remains largely unexplored in dance and performance theory, which is rather surprising in light of the attention given to multimedia performance collaborations since Wilson/Glass's *Einstein on the Beach*.

From the witty, polemical gesture-repetitions and abstract motion-variations in her early solos (*Accumulation*) to the large-scale, constantly dissolving, and reforming movement structures in group works such as *Set and Reset* (with three filmic back-projections on hanging sculptures by Rauschenberg), Trisha Brown is the only dancer in my memory who strapped a projector to her back (in her 1966 piece *Homemade*) and danced with filmed images of herself ricocheting wildly across the space. The film has survived, and thirty years later, during a retrospective at the Brooklyn Academy of Music held in 1996 ("Trisha Brown at 25: Postmodern and Beyond"), she danced with the projector again and let the celluloid images of her own younger life rebound off the edges of the room in an unforgettable recuperation of a lost memory, the loss of memory.

Lucinda Childs, who danced in the Wilson/Glass *Einstein on the Beach* in 1976, has explored the multidimensionality of dance/film stagings in her own work, *Dance* (1979), created on BAM's large proscenium at a time when large-scale intermedia productions were being promoted in its Next Wave series. *Dance* is performed to the minimalist music of Glass and uses film/setting by Sol LeWitt projected frontally and from above onto a large, translucent scrim stretched across the front of the stage, letting recorded images of the dancers' abstract movements mingle with the live dancers and bleed through the scrim onto the floor and the back screen. The resulting superimpositions of movement and projected movement primarily provoke a vertiginous effect of highly kinetic repetitions and synchronies, almost overextending the hypnotic, polyrhythmic orchestration of Childs's cool, geometric phrasings, by which I mean a sense of exhaustion I feel after being manipulated to concentrate on small differences, in the constancy of the repetition of sameness on the surface, in the dancers' relentless, rigorous, technical execution of movement. But here is a different, more metaphysical and Kandinskyan reading by Susan Sontag:

> The projection of LeWitt's film is a true setting and literal transfiguration of the dance. The synchronized ongoing of film and dance creates a double space: flat (the scrim/screen) and three-dimensional (the stage); provides a double reality, both dance and its shadow (documentation, projection), both intimacy and distance. Recording the dancers from different angles, in long shot and in close-up, LeWitt's film tracks the dancers, sometimes on the same level, sometimes above—using split screen and multiple images. Or it immobilizes them, in a freeze-frame (or series of still shots) which the live dancer passes through. . . . The film both documents and dematerializes (spiritualizes) the reality of dancing. It is a friendly, intermittent ghost that makes the dancers, seen behind the scrim, seem disembodied, too: each seems the ghost of the other. The spectacle becomes authentically polyvalent.[9]

The problem I now wish to turn to is precisely this effect of ghosting and disembodiment through *projection* in the dialectic of live dance and screened dance. Furthermore, the complex, historically evolving dialectical interdependence between movement abstraction and expressionism implies gravitations to either extreme of constructivism or physical theater. I intend to examine the contemporary paradox of the return of the real (body) at the precise moment when electronic and virtual reality technologies seem to have occupied the imaginary for good. The return to an emphasis on the phenomenal body on a predominantly spatial plane (the body/space nexus) does not necessarily privilege visuality and visual surfaces in the way in which Anderson's ironic postmodern fluidity suggests, but I feel it is important to think through her masking devices, and through Stelarc's hollowed, permeable body, in order to arrive at different understandings of the relations between choreography and history, between bodies and their (friendly?) ghosts.

Memories of the Real

There are several ways to approach the physical theater and new-dance phenomenon in Europe, and I begin again with the question of violence at Hellerau. Returning, for a moment, to the astrophysical plans Živadinov is developing in his research on the Potočnik-Noordung's spaceship-engine, which requires the construction of the future theater in the "fourth dimension," I notice a centrifugal movement away from the center of the gravitational field. This flight is perhaps a measure of experienced alienation from the terrain of the violent or repressive state. Translated into cultural terms, this means Živadinov is less interested in a new "Slovenian theater" as such than in the "cosmokinetic" energies of his metaphorical and scientific imagination (while being funded by the state-supported Mladinsko Theater). Meanwhile, manipulating the resources of the apparatus and of the corps de ballet, he becomes an engineer who constructs a new videodrome-theater in which the audience will turn around its own axis, learning a new "circumvision."

The theater spaceship as *Gesamtkunstwerk* is a crazed utopian model/ metaphor for an extraterritorial, orbital culture. It seems unavoidable that Živadinov's alienated actors become real aliens, which follows exactly the logic of what Slavoy Žižek has called the "impossible choice" in the logic of a pragmatic paradox. The same logic of a self-contradicting performance is at work in the "spaceship" itself: it is a theater that literally moves its audience. It will produce a visceral-emotional *alienation affect,* but it can only do so in a tremendously complex constructivist production economically supported by the state or the industry. When the spaceship goes on tour, as it does in its 1994 performances in Germany and Belgium, it represents "Slovenia." Even more peculiar, under the circumstances, is the cynical message with which Laibach addresses the "German nation," namely, that "death is the true and essential objective of life." It is received by a peaceful, quiet, and disinterested crowd, yet their aesthetic response can perhaps only be fully appreciated if one knows that German riot police have protectively surrounded Hellerau in anticipation of neo-Nazi violence.

Apart from the surveillance it dangerously courts, Laibach's cool, cybernetic aestheticism is disturbing not because it plays ambiguously with the iconography of fascism but because it celebrates, or pretends to celebrate, death through a poetic nihilism that refuses to take responsibility, to name itself, for its history and political effects. A Slovene answer to NSK's conceptualism is presented in Betontanc's Hellerau performance of *Za vsako besedo cekin* (Every Word a Gold Coin's Worth). Matjaž Pograjc's young and energetic troupe represents a new generation of physical-theater artists in Ljubljana (affiliated with the experimental Glej Theatre), which resists the controlling intellectual influence of NSK and seems to react immediately, on a gut level, to the pressures of political and economic transformation. Their dance at Hellerau is the only work that relies entirely on concrete bodily and emotional expression, as well as on the tensions and conflicts of physical/sexual aggression. In front of a high metal wall, a young woman sings an innocent song which sets in motion a relentless, highly visceral sequence of contests, seductions, assaults, interrogations, and defeats. First a woman then a man are raped; a coin is passed around; some try to scale and overcome the wall—all while an atmosphere of oppression ebbs and flows in a distinctly claustrophobic rhythm.

What makes the rhythm frightening and violent is the apparent lack of reflection; there is no break, no stutter in the engine of violence, and perhaps the coin is the only symbol that refers to a larger context of cynical capitalism. Interpersonal cruelty is the motor, an exchange system which propels the action and the physical risks taken but increasingly reduces and contracts the space. Unlike the expanding, deepening repetitive excavations of social aggression and paranoia in the *Tanztheater* of Pina Bausch, which create a particular space of remembrance and shame—and thus a distance for reflection—the action

Betontanc performing in *Every Word a Gold Coin's Worth,* choreographed by Matjaž Pograjc, Festspielhaus Hellerau, 1994. Courtesy of the artist.

in the work of Betontanc contracts until it reaches a standstill. Without a word being spoken in this performance, Betontanc tests the limits of physical perception in a time of reduced credibility of any and all ideological systems or moral assumptions. The hard currency of violence in the work of Betontanc adds to the disturbance of the Hellerau festival, whose ritual intention it must have been to reclaim a spirit of utopia for the aesthetic critique of civilization. The future of ritual is uncertain in a time of discredited beliefs.

Perhaps Hellerau can no longer symbolize a utopian aesthetics at the end of a century of barbarism. However, the festival tries to address the question of art's compromised role as a participant in the affirmation of death, which was written into the early proclamations of futurism at the beginning of the century. Perhaps Laibach is merely quoting Marinetti or Goebbels. If we seriously consider the possibilities of reconstruction and renewal (e.g., the attempt to rebuild Hellerau or to transform Metelkova; the new, organic dance and body-mind-centering movement; or the survival art of the "witnesses of existence" in Sarajevo), the consequences of the irony of cynical affirmation will have to be faced in the various shifting European and global contexts in order to arrive at a point where we are no longer fascinated by the seductiveness of destruction, where we no longer stare at the empty places of the homes of the brave.

Seduction is a kinesthetic element of film/video and the new technologies that seems writ large in many contemporary assessments of "immersion," of the metaphor of consciousness as computer, and of the acceleration of images and simulations to the point "where we can imagine for the future a transformation of reality into video signals stored on tape."[10] One may find this idea of transforming reality into video signals ludicrous, but the economics of technology are such that data transmission and storage, and the flow of media/information, inevitably penetrate the social imaginary and all of our infrastructures of labor, consumption, and popular culture, making these structures dependent on the instrumental potential and exchangeability of data. In their very inconsequentiality, the constant flow of media images can produce a form of historical amnesia through immersion. The concept of virtualization in VR technology promises precisely this effect: you can direct your trance-flight of the disembodied eyes and interact with nonexistent animated images in virtual space, leaving the real (body) behind.

The intensification in the speed of transmission across all contemporary media and information superhighways finds a correlative in some tendencies among young choreographers to accelerate movement speed and physical risk-taking, which is perhaps also related to the current phenomenon of house and rave parties—offering the continuous, seamless pouring out of a high-energy beat and powerfully driving rhythm, together with a low-frequency bass—for the sustained, trance-inducing dancing and its psychedelic effects on the body. (DJs tell me that raves often use up to two hundred beats per minute and a steady 4/4 rhythm; drum machine, volume distortion, and boosting of the bass are also typical of house and rap music, but rap producers use multiple rhythms and breaks in the loop more frequently because the lyrics require them.) The acceleration of speed in dance choreography has reached distinct levels both of emotional abandon—as in the work of Lloyd Newson's DV8 Physical Theatre, with its emphasis on gay masculinities and relationships—and of the kind of athletic brinkmanship and daredevil movement I tend to refer to as "hyperdance" in my exhausted and disbelieving response.

My first exposure to Edouard Lock's Canadian group LaLaLa Human Steps and Flemish choreographer Wim Vandekeybus's Ultima Vez company provokes kinesthetic excitement and exhilaration, I feel swept, drained, and hypnotized, and after I cool down I have forgotten everything except a lingering sense of physical overextension. This can be a very emotional experience, yet it doesn't register in my consciousness—there are no afterimages. Then I begin to realize, after attending a number of dance festivals in the late eighties and early nineties, that there is a rapidly growing scene of younger companies in France, Belgium, Holland, Portugal, England, Germany, Scandinavia, and Canada which seem to celebrate vigorously the sense of risk, danger, and physical abandon proffered by movement aggression and a furious use of energy. Are these dancing bodies furiously resisting the hollowing out, the dreaded yet expected future of the cyborg and its computerized memory? What kind of memory will "it" have?

One of the most interesting aspects of this new athletic aesthetic is the fact that many of the choreographers also shoot and direct their own videodances or collaborate on video production of dance as a new art form, exploring, in particular, the rhythmic and kinesthetic potential of motion specific to dance. Many of the dance films and videodances I saw at Moving Pictures and IMZ screenings clearly emphasized an experimental attitude toward the combination of the two media in terms of the use of digital editing techniques, effects, and overall production values as well as in the composition of the dances' abstract, linear, or nonlinear narrative content. The videodances of Anne Teresa de Keersmaeker, Alison Murray, Lisa Cochrane, Edouard Lock, Lloyd Newson, and Jean-

Claude Gallotta are outstanding examples of this compositional playing with filmic choreography and sound. Vandekeybus has collaborated with Walter Verdin on the videodance productions of *Roseland* (1991) and *La Mentira* (1992); the first is a video that places the three dances Vandekeybus has created since 1987 (*What the Body Does Not Remember, Les porteuses de mauvaises nouvelles* [The Bringers of Bad News], *The Weight of a Hand*) into a new location setting—an old Brussels movie theater that had been abandoned for more than twenty years. *La Mentira* is a complete reworking of the 1991 stage performance of *Immer das Selbe gelogen* (Always the Same Lies) and elaborates, in a more dialogical, narrative way, the portrait of an elderly German outsider artist whom Vandekeybus had befriended. The twelve-member company, which includes composer/architect Peter Vermeersch, has also released the music for *Immer das Selbe gelogen* on CD—a new practice that is gaining ground among other dance companies who distribute videos and CDs of their multimedia works. In 1994 I see one of the more recent Ultima Vez productions at the Tanzwerkstatt-Europa Festival in Munich. *Mountains Made of Barking* integrates the stage choreography—including blind dancer/actor Saïd Gharbi—with 16-millimeter films written and directed by Vandekeybus during the company's initial rehearsals in Morocco.

I now wish to offer a careful rereading of my earlier reaction to hyperdance—taking into account my far-reaching response in the seventies, to the *Tanztheater*—and then complicating both responses by presenting an outline for a theory of dance-memory in the age of digital interfaces. When I say that I feel put off by the relentless, athletic speed-dancing in some of the new dance works (while admitting the kinesthetic effect the movement has on my body), I am responding to a more complex issue that seems to lie behind the critical approaches I have taken to the visual (re)construction of dance, formal-movement composition, and spatiality. My impulse not to separate form and content—and to explain expressionist dance through constructivism with regard to the Anglo-European obsession with dance as an autonomous language—leads me back to an initial discomfort with references to Mary Wigman's "ecstasy." It is quite likely that the notion of ecstasy, in its association with the mystical and the spiritual, constitutes a taboo I learned to incorporate during my rebellious adolescence in the sixties, which for my generation in Germany meant a head-on confrontation with the Nazi horrors and the Holocaust to which our parents had willingly contributed. The time of reflection and critical analysis is a time of distancing, or separation, and in my generation's intellectual upbringing it included what Brecht had called "learning plays," namely, rehearsals of critical subversion that separated certain myths and ideologies from the historical and material content they masked by producing questions about the masking. It included questioning the story my people told me and the story they didn't tell.

The *Tanztheater* opened my eyes and ears to stories openly hidden in bodies and to bodily behaviors, costumes, social customs, and barely contained emotions in the land of silence. If all theatricalities and techniques of deploying aesthetic forms (whether expressionist, constructivist, realist, or epic) are ideological, then the interpretation of movements and of corporealities in the dance needs to be analytic without avoiding the paradox of encountering the emotional, irrational, and spiritual in art, especially if the spiritual in art can be understood or sensed in different ways, including radical and transformative as well as pacifying and harmonizing—which may not always be a contradiction in terms. The *Tanztheater*'s distancing devices, including distancing the dance from the dance, also address the physical spirit and politics of memory. Distancing, in this respect, means precisely *not forgetting*.

In approaching dance through analytic frames, one risks the danger of reducing bodies and corporealities to mere functions within the descriptions we make of theatrical constructions, compositions, designs, movement languages, shapes, and patterns. These descriptive constructions also tend to map and spatialize dance description as such, drawing attention to figures and movements through space instead of through time; we tend to make these analytic distinctions, although we know that bodily expression exists inseparably in both space and time. The evidence in the history of modern dance seems to encourage this analytic of construction. What it obscures is how the expressive body of the dancer, the subject of the dance, shifts the borders between the Anglo-European obsession with visuality, surface, form, or abstraction and that which cannot be spoken or seen. Unlike the self-referential and autarchic movement promoted by modernist dance theory, the separation between dance and music—and the stories both tell simultaneously about the spirit-inhabiting body—would be virtually unintelligible in other (non-Western) cultural contexts since dance expression (e.g., in African, Caribbean, Indian, Native American, Latin American, and Polynesian traditions) is always intrinsically connected to music. In contexts of sacred performance, ritual, and worship, as well as in community and artistic festivals, dance depends on the integration of particular, embodied rhythms in the spiritual, devotional, joyful, and ecstatic experience. The joy and the *jouissance* in the embrace of the spirituality of the body (in union with ancestors, spirits, deities, god) have magical,

sexual, erotic, and social dimensions that are tied to the consciousness of
community, especially since they hold significance as embodied, shared
memory. They can have a healing effect; they can reconstruct continuity
and tradition; they can be politically resistant to external domination
and influence; they can teach and reassemble community identity; they
can nurture respect for the body and its ages; and they can certainly remind participants and witnesses of the intersubjectivity of the dance as
embodied memory. Without memory there is no dance. This suggests
that the investment of meaning in the dance—and in the *images* of dancing—and what I draw from the experience cannot be reduced to the
form. In the present context, therefore, the investment of meaning into
its filmed images and reproductions cannot be reduced to the technological medium either. If the kinesthetic and, perhaps, ecstatic experience—the emotional, physical, and spiritual union in the body-soul—
cannot be properly spoken because it is in excess of conscious language
and rational symbolic systems, then it becomes more problematic to
evaluate the different kinds of decentering that occur, for example, in
the economy of the relations between dance images and the viewer.

If I admit to having been thrown off balance by the hyperdance of
Ultima Vez, it is perhaps contradictory to argue that I have forgotten
everything, that there are no afterimages. I am aware that the phenomenon of physical rapture, as it is experienced in rave dancing, grounds its
authenticity in the liminal, psychedelic ambience of forgetting or dropping out of time: the sustained hyperrhythmic trance-dancing seeks and
implies a loss of (self-)consciousness. It is not a staged performance, however, even though the rave party creates a theatrical/ritual context and
an "outside" space for itself. In a dance performance for viewers, however, I am invited to feel, with all my senses, the imagined kinetic effect
of such a loss of (self-)consciousness, and in Ultima Vez's early dances I
am invited to identify with the speed and risk-taking as such. It is the
only content of the action. And this may very well be the cause for my
dissatisfaction, and the video of the dance works heightens my ambivalence toward such imputed authenticity.

In *The Power of Dance* (1993), the first installment of a PBS-produced
ethnographic series on dance in diverse cultures, there is an interesting short interview with Vandekeybus spliced into footage from *Roseland*
and from the company's rehearsals with cameras. The excerpts from the
dances are edited with typically high-kinetic speed, making the moving
dancers almost jump out of the frame and into your eyes, taking your
breath away. Vandekeybus then reassures us that his dance is a high-
speed language that can move *quicker* than the eye.

> It's not lying, we never lie with the video, it just gives a possibility to show something in a different way; and for the speed, in performance it's completely another time. I don't like at all performers when they go and make a video and say, please don't destroy the choreography, please don't destroy it. On TV it's nothing, even the light, you have to change it, you have to change the light, it doesn't fit at all for the eye. And the speed, yes, you look at TV, well, while you open the fridge to get a beer, you take a sandwich, and the TV is always on there, it's like this, mostly.

The narrator then claims that the explosive works of the choreographer tap into the spontaneous movement of the body's instinct to survive; it is "raw" dance. Vandekeybus explains:

> What interest me especially are movements that have to happen; it's the same, when I throw this chair at you, you would catch it or try to avoid it, it's like a self-protection, as soon as you see, your eye makes you do the thing before you really think about it. This feeling that you do something before you are conscious, it's the same when you fall in love, for example, you are in love before you know it, the intensity of the moment is more important than the sense you get from it.

As I watch the excerpts from the stage rehearsals for *What the Body Does Not Remember,* a voice-over tells me that out of the basic elements of running, leaping, dodging, catching, dropping, and falling, Vandekeybus is forging a new dance language.

> I am very physical in this way, I like to sweat, when I sweat the performance for me is good. It's not a sprint, or something in one tempo, it has many rhythms, and you know you can recuperate here because just in this moment you say, *now* I get the energy, it's like jumping and trying to stay in the air as long as you can, it's this kind of feeling for me, and if you don't have a little sympathy for it, or this excitement, you can't do it. It's like people who go to dance in the discotheque, they dance until six in the morning, it's a trip. I think dance is something that can transform the state of people who do it or the state of people who look at it. I think dance is seduction, and it is used in religion, in ritual, or it's just for fun, people dance when they are sad, too, but it has to do with something really inside.[11]

If I take Vandekeybus at his word—including his live performances, videos, and CDs—I can understand his emphasis on the instantaneous and the raw, but he is working with dancers' bodies and media that are unforgiving. What, exactly, is it the body does *not* remember? And what is it the media versions of the dance remember? Surely after countless Pavlovian rehearsals the dancers will remember how to dodge, fall, leap, and catch someone jumping at them. Their awareness will be heightened as our potential seduction is extended through the electronic screen and the acoustic mirror of the CD music. Do we remember a dance when we hear the soundtrack again? Does the music put us back into the space and the sound of bodies whacking into each other? Do I ever share the same space with the viewed? Do my eyes, knees, joints, and muscles react when the dancers leap in my direction? The work is imbued with exhilaration and the sexual energy of getting high through physical risk-taking, yet it also denies rational thought as a result of this self-abandonment.

Here the intimate connection between new dance and electronic media becomes more clearly focused, insofar as dancers dance to get high, and they shoot their dance while running into the space with the camera. In fact, having danced with the camera while shooting, I remember the sense of exhilaration I felt as I imagined becoming one with the dance itself. In fact, I was dancing, dodging, and swirling myself. Yet while watching the videotape the connection is not quite so obvious, and the image cannot control the process of watching or of kinesthetic empathy. The "seduction" is a screen. As a viewer, I am invited to project myself into the kinetic action of the dancers, but a direct experience is not possible since my own body may not necessarily remember the reactions or the dancers, or it may project different meanings onto them. Do I become aware of my own impulses to react? Can images affect my kinesthetic sense of myself, as horror films might frighten me or make me sweat? Do the images arouse me?

If I follow the idea that dance is sexually expressive, then my consumption of dance images can be as gratifying as the use I or other people might make of watching erotic or pornographic media. If dance is an acceptable cultural expression, compared to the stigmatized pornographic media, does hyperdance (or any other dance genre) cut across the specious distinctions between good, healthy, sensual erotica and dangerous, forbidden, shameful pornography? It is commonly known that sweaty bodies, leather, or high-heeled shoes can be deeply arousing for some men and women, and I should think that athletic, leaping men can be also deeply arousing for some men and women. But, again, there is no predetermined relation between dance images and arousal, and my reaction or fantasy projection will depend on the context and my individual circumstances, especially on how I read the "violence" in the leaping men and women. The electronic image of dancing can affect but not literally transform me; its interactive potential is provisional and thus limited despite the videodance creator's assumption that the image is transparent or blurs the distinction between video images of movement and those in my body-mind.

Applied to the larger context of contemporary technological experiments with digital processes and interactive video/computer configurations, Vandekeybus's notion of the truth of seduction ("we never lie with the video") implies psychosexual parameters impregnated by the eye (voyeurism, fetishism, scopophilia) as well as a kinetic dimension of high-intensity energy that does not correspond to the media's privileging of objects of sight, since dancers' bodies remember with their muscles, nerve tissue, bones, skin—their visceral and tactile feedback system and injuries. It is a sad truth that the turnover in companies such as Ultima Vez is rather high since dancers often drop out because of injuries, whereas many of Bausch's dancers in the Wuppertaler Tanztheater have, in fact, been with her for nearly twenty years.

The transition from dance to video image or digitized/manipulated image is not fluid; whatever dynamic movement video and computer can simulate in "real time," they cannot capture the full spatial context, movement pathways, and relative positions of all dancers through time, nor can they adequately compensate for body heat, sweat, breath, and visceral and tactile feedback. New digital multimedia software is trying to offer increasingly complex options for breaking down the dance (capturing the movements from all angles and allowing for overlay and see-through manipulations, mappings, animations, etc.) to get "into the dance." But the "living page" or "living sketchbook" remains a visual photoshop of layouts and montages; the relationship to the screen, via computer, remains an external one of postproduction. There is no temporal collapse or loss of spatial differentiation (as in VR systems) that would fuse the (un)conscious with the screen of the monitor. The fantasy of identification with the movement image may exist in the heightened awareness of the dancer/videomaker confronting the (un)consciousness of the dance, but the transfer to the viewer is more complicated, since the screen images are *enclosed memories*. They cannot "recuperate here . . . in this moment" whatever high the dancer feels in the leap; the viewer will have to project something.

This "something," I now believe, has actually become the source of inspiration for Vandekeybus's *Mountains Made of Barking,* a considerably more challenging work in terms of its content and level of reflection on the very invisibility in the visible. One of the meanings of recuperation, of course, means resting or taking a break from the exhaustion of constant leaping. The other sense in which I am using the term refers to

the recovering of something that is lost or lacking or ungraspable. There
are many sequences in *Mountains Made of Barking*, both in the dance
and the projected 16-millimeter films, when I am drawn to linger and
meditate on a physical gesture, a sound, and a mysterious, troubling
image that recurs, such as the milky, blind eyes of a stray wolf in the
desert mountains of Morocco. Or perhaps I am imagining the alienating effect the surreal film had on my reception of the choreography. The
movements on stage generally alternate between striking visual compositions—women wearing sheepskin masks dance behind the blind Saïd
Gharbi, who, wrapped into a woolen carpet, sits quietly at the edge of
the stage; one dancer, half human, half animal, floats through the air,
while another lies precariously atop a pile of long, thin broomsticks—
and frantic physical-athletic movements underscored by the driving rock
rhythms of the composer. The dancer who floats through the air also
doubles as a German-speaking emcee who constantly shrieks incoherent
bits of information on the darkened stage. In front of the upstage screen,
also made out of sheepskin, the performance increasingly delves into
the inexplicable metamorphoses of humans into beasts of prey and then
victims, wolves and sheep, some dancers darting into the hollow space
like projectiles, others colliding and rolling into each other as if driven
by the frenzy of primal survival instincts.

Wim Vandekeybus's Ultima Vez company performing *Mountains Made of Barking*,
Tanzwerkstatt-Europa Festival, Munich, 1994. Photo: Octavio Iturbe.

Two performers stand out. One, the British dancer Mary Herbert, seems like an innocent, childlike Alice caught in an unending, labyrinthian effort to whisper a love story into the mike. She is repeatedly and aggressively interrupted in her recitation by the others, who attack and try to bite her. Downstage, almost as if lost in his own inner world, Gharbi carefully seeks to orient himself without actually seeing the chaos that has erupted behind him. He can sense the chaos but needs to localize the space and the others through his kinetic and aural awareness. The whole production hinges on the precarious balance or ambivalence created between the blind movements of Gharbi—the intensity of his inner calm versus his increasing outward uncertainty—and the reckless, nightmarish madness that exists around him. The madness sometimes has hallucinatory power, especially when the hypnotic rhythms suddenly cease and for several silent minutes, we are allowed to watch how three men undress and wash themselves. But they obsessively continue to scrub and rub themselves down to the bone; the cleaning attains a frenzied level and ends when huge amounts of dirt inexplicably fall on them from the sky.

The work gains its provocative kinetic and psychological impact less from the brutality of the stage action or the seeming irrationality of the madness than from the distinct frailty of the one blind dancer in his human craving for touch, warmth, reassurance, and love, the very story that the woman is not allowed to tell us. Moreover, I feel that the intensity of this recognition is produced—and complicated—by the very poetic, surrealist, and mystic images of the film sequences Vandekeybus shot in Gharbi's Moroccan village, located at the edge of the ocean, and in the mountains. The large-scale projection of the film (covering the entire upstage woolen screen) repeatedly shows Buñuel-like glimpses of animals' eyes; the ocean is shot as a refracted image in the pupil of a horse, and men are seen wrapped in sheepskin singing a song that merges with the galloping of the horses' feet. In the village at night, a chicken is slaughtered for the meal, and the woman who cannot tell the love story cuts herself with the knife. The blind wolf stares at me, the soul of the dark night shimmering in his pupils. The symbolism of the mystic images in the film give a depth to the dance that Vandekeybus cannot achieve in the repetitively violent movement vocabularies, even though I imagine that he is himself becoming troubled by the intensity of being carried away by hallucination or mad aggression. When I ask him about the relationship between stage and film, he suggests that the stage generally has a concrete and direct quality that allows us to experience the intensity of the moment, and for him these intensities are moments of danger, when we are willing to give up security.

> Again and again, you lose the certainty and security of the ordinary, as in a dream. Now, what you see on screen is less momentary, it belongs more firmly to the realm of timelessness and imagination. But then, a few seconds later, it's the other way round. It is crucial to juxtapose stage and screen; there is a certain magic, an opportunity that neither film nor theater can open up by themselves. Both worlds exist in themselves, and even though the same characters appear in both, they appear in a different context and under different circumstances. When they come together, borders are blurred and new perspectives open up.

Although I agree with Vandekeybus's assumptions about the differences and conjunctions of dance and film in the time-space of the theater, it is troubling to reflect on the unrecuperated (inexhaustible) violence of the seeing dancers who are blind to their own "intensity" of aggression. The film does provide another context, although imagination is hardly timeless and ahistorical. I would argue that the film creates a space of the mystical that is more deeply affective and manipulative than the less focused, sprawling repetitiveness of the dance, but a necessary return to the reality of the stage, beyond the exotic film, is perhaps meant to remind us of the fantasy or illusory power we might attribute to the image. The senseless violence onstage might undercut the "magic" of the film, contrary to what Vandekeybus seems to hope for. At least my distance from the dancers, with whom I do not identify and don't want to change places, affects my resistance to the lure of the film images and the projection: I am not blindly attracted to the animistic fatalism embodied in this work.

It could be argued that the concern with the intensity and magic of the inexplicable moment is a form of autointoxication that might prevent one from seeing the image dissolve. The current technological impact of video images on production clarifies, at least in my experience, the inevitable break in the relation between eye and body. As the enlarged video projection of images fades, so does the fantasy/memory it can form. The memory of the fantasy cannot be upheld by the technological medium since the physical and intersubjective quality of memory is in the body and not on the screen. The presence of the image on the screen—for example, in the scene of the woman cutting herself with the knife—is only as strong as the physical memory I confer upon it. In the editing suite, when I assemble and insert such images, they run forward and backward; slow, fast, or not at all; depending on how I manipulate the frames. But the magic dissolves in the construct-edness of the memory on file in the computer. In the dance-theater the image projections largely depend on the physical context created for, not through, them.

Tanztheater, Experiential Memory, Computer Memory

In raising the question of fantasy and memory, I am returning to Pina Bausch and the recuperation of the silence of the land inside that can-not be spoken. In comparing *Tanztheater* to the current waves of physi-cal theater, new dance, and videodance, I would like to suggest that some of the virulent energies expanded in contemporary hyperdance to the instantaneous experience of present moments relay a symptomatic difficulty of coping with the immense acceleration of media/data trans-mission speed, with fleeting time, with other times, the time of others, and elapsed time. However much dance travels, it seems to have ar-rived ahead of itself, breathless and too late, barely looking back to give pause and ask: Why dance at all? The utopian space for dance seems to have disappeared; in the severely diminished horizons of the West's belief in the progress of (its) rationality, the time of dance has been com-pressed into spectacularly transient moments of intensity or has fallen outside the economic laws of the market. The new temporalities of im-material data flows, computations, the Internet, satellite TV, and video games render the older physical laws of performance theater anachro-nistic. Hyperdance perhaps reflects a last-ditch effort on behalf of the physiologically slow real-time arts to be as fast as the eye catching the flickering images on the screen. Vandekeybus seems to have admitted as much when he says the time of the theater is different: it no longer adequately correlates to the digital time in virtual dimensionalities. The artificial, immaterial construction of virtual realities no longer requires a bodily subject in real time-space since its "movement-time" is itself no longer analog. Perhaps without intending it, Vandekeybus's dance has confirmed the limits of analog media. In cyberspace, we are told, such limits don't exist.

The exception to the acceleration of dance, of course, is the margin-alized presence of butoh dance in the West and its deliberately glacial pace, which briefly made itself felt in the eighties without leaving many traces, except perhaps in the subconscious of some practitioners of con-tact improvisation and the transformational dance works of Anna Hal-prin and her students. A critical observer of the New York dance scene has described how stunned he was when he attended a contact impro-visation festival in 1993 and noticed a pervasive atmosphere of loss and sorrow, expressing itself in the dancers' stillness and the manner in which their "quiet exposure over-stated the frailty of the body and questioned the purpose of moving."[12] The spiritual affinities between Japanese bu-toh dance and *Ausdruckstanz* seem quite striking to me, and I have always wanted to see Kazuo Ohno onstage with Bausch's dancers. I have al-most no words for Ohno's dance. It transforms, in more than one sense, and it exposes itself in a way that throws Western analogies between violence and art into sharp relief. In the very frailty of his aged body, Ohno can gently express and impress on us sensuous reminiscences, as if moving through one life or several lives, with the subtle lifting of a hand or the curling of a finger, slowing presence down to a point where our minimal comprehension of the land within, like our anxiety over the impermanence of our organism, might unravel.

There is another affinity between *anokoku butoh* (dance of darkness), as Tatsumi Hijikata named it, and the repressed side of early German *Ausdruckstanz* in its more outrageously grotesque or politically challeng-ing satirical form (e.g., in the work of Harald Kreutzberg, Valeska Gert, or Jean Weidt). The transgressively contorted dance of naked, grotesque, and convulsive bodies, created by Hijikata and Min Tanaka in Japan and brought to the United States and Europe by companies such as Sankai Juku, represents a dangerous displacement of the classical and the organic body ideal in most if not all of our dance traditions. Even taking into account the Buddhist cosmology and post-Hiroshima sensi-bility inherent in butoh, one must admit that the ascetic commitment to practicing the unsublimated living excess of this dance broke taboos in Japan; it also encompasses a difference in expressionism that was rarely broached by Western practitioners of grotesque realism. The existential-ist side of the latter, however—in bringing out the hideous aspects of the fleshly, vulgar, mortal, hysterical, and hurting body—underscores the emotional vulnerability of the dancer that we see acknowledged in *Tanztheater* and physical theater. After moving to Paris and settling there, Sankai Juku seemed to have toned down and stylistically smoothed out the dangerous side of the unrecuperated, monstrous otherness of the body. However, younger choreographers like Lloyd Newson or Meg Stuart, along with performance or body artists and queer performers of camp and drag, have turned to the "anachronistic" relationship of the body to the time in the theater or, in other words, to the dissolu-tion of identity. The fear of dissolution, which hyperdance has no time to acknowledge, is confronted in DV8 Physical Theater's morbid obsession with homosexual despair and self-loathing (e.g., *Dead Dreams of Monochrome Men*) or in Meg Stuart's "disfigure studies." In her work *No One Is Watching*, a naked, very obese woman is silently present upstage throughout the performance, her back to the audience, while much of the dance occurs near the sidelines, often pushed to a point where spoken words are inaudible and movement slows down to nearly invisible gestures. There is not a trace of camp in this dance, and yet the presence of the woman's fleshy excess, the unmoved stillness of the "female grotesque"—which may signify exuberant power, voluptuous pregnancy, or bulging, protuberant irregularity—haunts the dance's intimate and emotional exploration of abjection.[13] Stuart undercuts the camp laughter at the unbridled, "unnatural" body by eschewing the codes of parody that frame physical excess or excessive femininity. Her dance is out of step with any morbid fascination over external decay or outmodedness. It is resigned to listen to an inner pain that is barely articulated. It waits to be articulated again (while no one has the time to be watching?).

If hyperdance has now superseded butoh and *Tanztheater*, one may want to look back on the sixties and seventies as a period filled with a different restlessness, promise, and radical excitement propelling political questions about the past, the future, and the status quo. No longer set up in representative national institutions, as was and still is the case for ballet companies at opera houses, Bausch's Wuppertaler Tanztheater was able to build its repertoire between/outside canonical opera and drama at a time in Germany when a rampant postwar conservatism sought to normalize and stabilize sudden economic prosperity in a fledgeling democracy. The emerging generation of choreographers— including Pina Bausch, Susanne Linke, Reinhild Hoffmann, Christine Brunel, Mitsuru Sasaki, Rosamund Gilmore (all from Kurt Jooss's Folkwangschule), along with Johann Kresnik and Gerhard Bohner—did not renounce the prominent cultural role of neoclassical ballet. Instead of seeing the rise of *Tanztheater* in critical opposition to ballet and the conservative political restoration in the country, I wish to suggest that Bausch's choreography after 1975 (the year she completed *Orpheus und Eurydike* and *Le Sacre du Printemps*) questioned the traditions of dance altogether. Those traditions were readily available; she had studied ballet, the Jooss-Laban school of dance-theater and improvisation-composition, and modern dance (in the United States). The Folkwangschule in particular encouraged an open, Bauhaus-like atmosphere of intermedia creativity and international collaboration. Although *Ausdruckstanz* seemed to have disappeared from the public stage after Mary Wigman's retirement under the Nazis, and although her few choreogra-

Sankai Juku performing *Yuragi* (In a Space of Perpetual Motion), directed by Ushio Amagatsu, North Shore Center for the Performing Arts, Chicago, 1996. Photo: Delahaye.

Pina Bausch Wuppertaler Tanztheater performing in *Palermo, Palermo,* presented at the Brooklyn Academy of Music, New York, 1991. Photo: Detlef Erler.

phies and private teaching in Berlin during the fifties and sixties seemed anachronistic, that tradition has also been kept alive; Susanne Linke has honored it in her danced reconstructions and homage to Wigman's pupil Dore Hoyer.

The questioning of historical traditions and continuities I have in mind refers to a radical self-examination of embodied techniques and memories in their intersection with culture and consciousness as such. Bausch and her dancers are all trained in these traditions, and the company has been international from the start, a fact usually overlooked by the critics. In her widely toured 1978 piece *Café Müller*, for example, Bausch initially danced with Malou Airaudo, Meryl Tankard, Dominique Mercy, Jan Minarik, and her designer Rolf Borzik, and in *1980* only four out of nineteen dancers were German. What is not forgotten, however, is Bausch's abandonment of available traditional or modern-movement choreography. Her rehearsals do not begin with movement and, as she explains, the steps always come from "somewhere else, never from the legs." There may not even be steps in the sense in which this is understood in dance. Her rehearsals start with questions that can refer to any small, intimate, or not so intimate aspect of the dancers' lives, her own life, and the life and history that exist between them and behind them, reaching back to childhood or family memories as well as to other memories, imagined or real. These questions also address the space in which they can be asked: none of Bausch's performances take place on an empty, neutral dance stage but are located inside highly constructed "natural" environments, landscapes, cluttered rooms, private mansions, and public cafés. The work of exploration that is built over weeks and months of rehearsal grows "from the inside out" and often remains fragmentary, absorbed into the memory process of the life of working together. The answers that the dancers demonstrate or try out imply a "movement" through diverse recollections—familiar, unfamiliar, idiosyncratic markings of the times that can be expressed, regressed into, or remembered differently in a reciprocal imagining within the group.

> It is simply a question of when is it dance, when is it not. Where does it start? When do we call it dance? It does in fact have something to do with consciousness, with bodily consciousness, and the way we form things. But then it needn't have this aesthetic form. It can have a quite different form and still be dance. Basically one wants to say something which cannot be said, so what one has done is to make a poem where one can feel what is meant.[14]

The answers to something that cannot be spoken are rehearsed and developed, small poems germinate, and Bausch's extraordinary musical sensibility enters into the process of shaping the structural principles of the emerging work, with its poignant and absurd stories, ambivalent behavior, and strange, unfulfilled desires. The poignancy is achieved not through poetic effusion but precise, literal gestures of everyday-ness. The emerging work in rehearsal deals with every kind of phenomenon; nothing seems to be excluded that can be thought or remembered. Thirty dancers and their diverse personalities constitute the dynamics of the improvisations. Their social and emotional intercourse, through bodily consciousness, cannot rely on "dance techniques," and if social or gendered techniques manifest themselves, they will be repeated and recollected until they begin to distort their typical patterns and promptings. The gradual deconstruction of body languages also arrives with the pressure to produce and search for answers, with the failure to produce within the framework of the theatrical machine, the time machine. Things fall apart, bodies fall apart. But if the questions go beyond the technical boundaries of dance languages, they also leave the frame of the theater itself. The failure to conform and confirm becomes a necessary part of a choreography of personal history within the larger context: the *Tanztheater* can only develop its dynamic through transgressing the limits of movement performance and the spatial confinements and limits of cultural acceptability. At the time (1975–77), that also meant producing questions precisely at a point when mainstream postwar Germany was at its most volatile and paranoid ("Germany in Autumn"— the time of the Red Army Faction's challenge to the system). The angst and the masochism that some critics discovered in the work were projections that may very well betray the truth of the limits and the terrifying ambivalences and risks of identification, of recognizing the self in the other and the other in the self.

Bausch's choreography, indebted to Laban and Jooss but growing out of her own politically incorrect feminism and sense of independence, strives for a polyphonic dramaturgy that composes the associations, overlappings, variations, counterpoints, and dissonances in a musical and cinematic manner reminiscent of montage, but all compositional metaphors (poetry, music, cinema, and nonlinear narrative) are merely references to an extended process of relocating the concrete, distinct times of physical comprehension. I want to suggest that Bausch's dance works are dislocating experiences primarily because they take up time and move carefully and patiently. They appear to last too long, and some silences or gestural repetitions are repeated so often that looking at them or through them becomes unbearable. The polyphonic "spacing" of time in *Tanztheater,* however, draws attention to the mundane, the embarrassingly everyday banalities, compulsions, obsessions, beginnings and end-ings, little failures, and hysterical compensations. Rhythms and tones in the work seem completely distant from the ecstasies and transfigurations in Wigman's dancing, and if Bausch's expansive, arm-swinging move-ment in *Café Müller* may remind us of Wigman's *Ausdruckstanz,* it does so in a painfully jolting way.

Repeatedly, as if sleepwalking, Bausch's arms and body bump into the wall; she slides down, falls, crawls along the wall. Two other dancers who are self-absorbed and unaware of each other, their eyes closed and their movement restricted by dozens of chairs and coffee tables, run their hands over their bodies as if trying to feel themselves out. When one of them suddenly moves sideways, a male figure (the stage designer) frantically pushes the chairs or tables out of the path, creating a bit of free space, then repositioning them. Throughout *Café Müller* no word is spoken, but the accidental contact between the two dancers (Malou Airaudo, Dominique Mercy) turns into a scene I find paradigmatic of Bausch's work. The scene stages the implicit or explicit yearning for human contact, touch, and tenderness, for an embrace that speaks to an overwhelmingly felt sense of alienation in the midst of a public, social space. In the background, a woman in a red wig and coat (Maryl Tankard) enters repeatedly, nervously paces around, and watches the "couple" before exiting. The couple has bumped into each other now, yet a large man (Jan Minarik) enters and tears them apart. Airaudo and Mercy resume their self-absorption, their movements turning inward. Later the yearning for the other is rekindled; she finds him and leans on him, but he is unable to respond. Minarik enters and pushes them together, but she slides down on Mercy's body. Although this is repeated numerous times, both of their gestures remain ineffectual and incapaci-tated. Minarik carefully reunites them and rearranges their gestures in such a way that he reconfigures the embrace back into the cliché of the man carrying the woman, supporting her weight. Mercy is too weak, however, and Airaudo falls down from his outstretched arms. Minarik's repeated reconstruction of the couple's gestural attitudes grows more urgent and more determined; he needs to increase his effort to shape and "construct" them, but each time Airaudo drops to the floor. After what seems like an infinite number of repetitions, Minarik suddenly leaves; he is no longer needed. After he is gone, the couple automatically reenacts the scene according to the same pattern, as if they had accommodated the external pressure even though the gestures as such make no sense, nor do they fulfill the initial yearning for touch or affection. Instead, they become repulsive and begin to look inherently violent and abusive.

There are other times in the performance when the sense of existential futility in the café relents, when small, literal gestures are juxtaposed against Bausch's own evocation of internal space, and when Tankard's amazed reactions to the failed "couple" offer a humorous commentary on yearning, desire, and on the dissolution of intimacy. Many of the later works—from *Kontakthof, Arien, 1980, Bandoneon, Walzer,* and *Nelken* to the more recent *Viktor, Palermo, Palermo* and *Nur Du*—reinforce the mutual dissolution and reconstruction of dancers' bodies and spaces through the intensified interdependence Bausch creates between self-absorbed intimacy, confessional exhibitionism, aggression and shame in the body (with the many nuances of hiding and acting out, compulsion and repression), and the texture of the space (water, earth, grass, trees, flowers, leaves, sand, rocks, a broken ship, an aquarium, etc.). The texture of environment influences the space of remembering, but the dancers are also seen (re)producing the real, material landscape of their desire and their propensities. The constructedness of "nature" in the space often begins to resemble a junkyard full of debris, remnants of objects and clothes, discarded toys and scrapped illusions. Beginning with *Bluebeard* (1977), Bausch used music only as citation; songs from the thirties, forties, and fifties alternated with citations from classical or popular music, and the range of questions listening to what is written in the bodies extended to all manner of voices, impulses, and intuitions, including the compulsion to talk too much or to hide and avoid performing altogether. When I first saw *1980* and *Walzer,* I felt so touched by the inherently terrifying absence caused by the disruption of time (the order of performance) the dancers created that I became aware, as if for the first time, of my own compulsive faith in movement, moving forward, returning, marking time. The movement of political revolt in the sixties had such faith in its forward attack and its claim to uncover the truth after years of silent repression and the gaudy kitsch of respectable, middle-class prosperity. What we thought of as our political and sexual liberation could not easily acknowledge the slowed-down rhythm of disillusionment and the guilt-provoking tension between radical fantasy and actual performance. The rhythm of time in Bausch's work is not merely about this rhythm or movement, the phenomenal or real body and its history; nor does the polyphony of times in the *Tanztheater* literally refer to the historical times evoked by the songs, childhood games, social games, sexual and emotional conflicts, and victimizations.

And yet the deconstruction of phrases (thousands of true little stories and proverbial nonsense the dancers tell) and social role-playing in and through the body, especially as they purport to mark sexual and emotional identities, carries a force that touches upon the very space of anxiety in which our identifications and misidentifications are composed. If audiences in the United States were appalled by the gritty, messy, and disturbing reality of Bausch's *Tanztheater* ("But is it dance?" was probably the most disingenuous question), so, initially, were German and European, Asian, Australian, and Latin American audiences, before the shocked surprise or recognition settled in, and the disruption of dance could be reconsidered in its various context-specific sociocultural and ethical resonances. Unlike the biographical portraits of German fascist male fantasies in the shrill, agit-prop "Choreographic Theater" of Johann Kresnik, and unlike the more analytic examination of abject, distorted, and forsaken bodies in the new dance of younger choreographers in Europe and North America, Bausch's *Tanztheater* never explicitly marks the body as if it could reveal an inescapable identity or disfiguring memory. Rather, it is marking the subjective time it takes to insistently explore the fear of intimacy with the "land of silence."

This process of dancing and not being able to dance embodied knowledge and fantasy takes a lifetime. In an interview with filmmaker Kay Kirchmann Bausch suggested that she would be very happy if the scenes in *Café Müller, 1980,* or *Walzer* could be reenacted again and again by the same dancers now having grown old: "There are always different ways of looking, and it will be most interesting to see these scenes in thirty or forty years from now."[15] There is a provocative logic in this vision since, on one level, it completely runs counter to a standard dance-career practice based on substitution of the dancer after a short-term "filling out" of a movement role. On another level it raises the very question of repetition and recollection, of moving dance's ephemeral transience yet very real accumulated, organic body consciousness forward to a future, through the future in which it can be remembered. Since the performances are created by particular dancers, they cannot exist outside them. If these performances are testimonials of a particular process of creation, then the fundamental idea of the *Übermarionette,* namely, of "filling in" and providing a more perfect "copy," is untenable.

In the context of *Tanztheater,* there can be no hollowed-out, obsolete bodies, only repeated and ongoing performance creation that raises the question, over time, as to how the dancers (and their audiences) will remember and experience not the disappearance of the dance but the (im)possible identifications with the always changing bodily memory.

The *Übermarionette* is the conceptual ghost in the machine garden of our new interactive, digital software. I want to end this section by referring to a very different attempt, undertaken by Frankfurt Ballet director William Forsythe, to create a CD-ROM–formatted computer memory of his company's movement choreography, with a little help from the programmers and engineers at ZKM (Zentrum für Kunst und Medientechnologie) in Karlsruhe, Germany. The implications of this attempt are more far-reaching than, say, Cunningham's movement sketches with the help of LifeForms, even though both choreographers have begun to conceive of their more recent stage works as analogous to computer operations (e.g., Cunningham's *Enter* and *Crwdspcr* and Forsythe's *ALIEN/A(C)TION* and *Eidos: Telos*). But while Cunningham is interested in LifeForms as a way of discovering "unthinkable" movement, Forsythe seems more fascinated by the underlying mathematical and algorithmic systems of information processing themselves.

Forsythe's project may have significant repercussions for our understanding of intermedia art of the future since it places itself in the context of advanced video, audio, and multimedia computer technologies designed to improve interactivity and, indeed, physical interplay across the virtual divide. Not surprisingly, Forsythe has also consistently worked with an electronic composer (Thom Willems) since taking over the directorship of the Frankfurt Ballet in 1984, and both in *ALIEN/A(C)TION* (1992) and *Eidos: Telos* (1995) the dancers perform to visual electronic icons and signals (projected into the wings), while Willems uses either computer-processed and manipulated samples (found music) or live DSP (Digital Signal Processing) devices in which actual live music is additionally computer-processed to generate new output in the moment. The new CD-ROM, first issued in a limited, private edition under the title "Improvisation Technologies," is only one part of the larger four-gigabyte archive of the Frankfurt Ballet's movement systems that are being constructed. It points the way towards a reevaluation of popular depictions of cyberspace as a disembodied medium. While I want to discuss the notion of "embodied virtuality," I also wish to point out the treacherous side of reconfigured digital memory. It is perhaps a fitting irony, in light of my scanning of constructivist tendencies in this century, that the first kind of dance choreography to appear on CD-ROM, apart from technopop animation, was postmodern abstract ballet. The positive side of the irony is that the work of Pina Bausch's company, or that of butoh dance, is not transferable to computer memory.

As computer artists and VR designers have begun to point out, the body cannot be left behind or abandoned in actual immersive VR environments since that would imply ignoring the technical and sensory interface connecting real and virtual realities. Consequently VR interfaces are to be designed in light of the body and the speed with which human eyes can read CRT screens.[16] It is also true that the immersion effect—once one "enters" the screen and interacts with three-dimensional images, virtual objects, and sounds—affects one's sense of being grounded in physical space, and this is the sense of disembodiment or motion sickness many users have experienced. VR environments effectively confuse the experience of bodily sensation and bodily boundaries, and this disturbance of bodily kinesthesia and proprioception should be of concern not only to dancers but to all those entertaining the idea that psychological and proprioceptive remappings of our bodies are a logical consequence of information technologies crossing over into our physical practices.

In the case of Forsythe's "Improvisation Technologies," the interplay between dancers' bodies and the computer stops short of such remapping since the CD-ROM is not an immersive VR environment but only approximates the capturing, transmitting, processing, and memorizing of physical movement for computer storage and redeployment. The actual recording for the storage is done by videotaping. At the same time, the screen user is invited to open the windows and menus of the CD-ROM to explore the hypergraphic interface in order to learn about the movement research and rehearsal "systems" of Forsythe's dancers; the information space certainly has an algorithmic quality. Forsythe's approach to movement composition employs the language of systems analysis. The windows are set up in such a way that the user can browse through a wide range of pathways laid out around a diagrammatic "video stage" (a box with four icons in the four corners—"t" for theory, "e" for example, "r" for rehearsal, "p" for performance—with Forsythe demonstrating all examples of "t"). The general home page is laid out like a Laban kinesphere, allowing the user to click into various directions such as "writing," "reorganizing space and time," and other chapters of body-based knowledge systems that have been developed in Frankfurt (isometries, anatomical exercises, lines, rotating-inscriptions, etc.).

In the center of the home page is the face of a clock, with letters replacing the usual numbers; it is an image/stage object from the 1994 piece *Self Meant to Govern*, and if you click on it you can see the actual thirty-minute performance (with soundtrack) videotaped from four different camera angles. This already explains why the project requires enormous amounts of gigabyte memory, since the user is invited to view the movement alternately from four (preselected) angles, requiring that all four camera angles be loaded from memory to run simultaneously. There is a lot more visual data, including a hundred short video lessons by Forsythe, as well as rehearsal footage. There is no contextual information about the life of the dance or the dancers apart from the technical and aesthetic data.

When Heidi Gilpin, a longtime dramaturge with Forsythe's company, explained the project and its raison d'être at the "Connecting Bodies" conference in Amsterdam, she pointed out that "a lot of the information the Frankfurt Ballet works with is based on a whole slew of theoretical material, scientific information, mathematical theory, literary and linguistic theory, and since *Enemy in the Figure* and *Limb's Theorem* (1989) we worked very much with architectural models, drawings, and principles as a way of imaging the body in space, and ways to embody ideas, literally, to manifest them in some way." The computer-storage project was actually intended to function as an archive and information data bank for the dancers themselves, which they began to utilize in rehearsal.

> It came out of a requirement we had in Frankfurt for accessing information more quickly. We are working with video constantly, in rehearsal, every day there are at least 3 videos made, so you can imagine, over 10 years, how many videos that is and how slow the access rate is for, you know, what happened at that particular day when we needed that moment that nobody can remember. In some sense we needed a quick, digital database; that is what it meant to me as a conceptual worker with the company; it meant a resource for the company, but also for researchers looking in from the outside. We also realized, while we were thinking about it, well, we don't just want to build some kind of archive. First of all, you can't archivalize 10 years of information; CD-ROMs can't handle that amount of information; it's also not viable financially. But we wanted to record a more accurate picture of the systems of movement composition used in Frankfurt, and there is not just one system but many different systems Forsythe and the company developed over all these years. It's like access to a mind-set, it's not a training tool; a little access point to the kind of work that happens there and how the research proceeds: What is movement research? How can it empower us? [17]

Gilpin has here expressed her firm belief—which I share—that dancers can use technology for their own ends, and in a political sense she was appealing to dancers to take charge of the further development of new technological media and structures and to utilize their highly developed sense of proprioception and embodied knowledge to deal with these media and "give them a sense of proprioception." This call for empowerment is absolutely to the point, and it is noteworthy that only through such projects do we get an idea of the flexibility of interactive media. For the first time the team of programmers and media artists at

DANCING WITH TECHNOLOGIES

ZKM seemed to take notice of physical movement, gesture, and bodily expression in real space, and they became so enthusiastic about the CD-ROM that they hailed it as a new "digital dance school" that could initiate further projects of this kind, providing future generations access to the work of important contemporary choreographers.

But "Improvisation Technologies" is, of course, not a dance school, and it is not clear to me what I could actually learn from the CD-ROM even if I tried to reintegrate its "information" into daily physical and organic practice. As a documentary archive, it represents a first and very valuable attempt at storing information about a particular rehearsal system and its theoretical premises, although the latter remain largely obscure and hermetic. Having seen many of Forsythe's works in live performance, I very much understand the excitement he has generated in his company and among his cult followers. The work is tremendously difficult and challenging, and over the years it has evolved its own distinct deconstructivist ballet aesthetic, which Forsythe himself describes as "postclassical analysis." It is easy to see that he is as much a rebellious son of Balanchine as he is fascinated by the postmodern architecture of decomposition (Libeskind, Eisenmann) and Wittgenstein's or Derrida's philosophy of language. The program books of the Frankfurt Ballet always look like essays from a poststructuralist seminar, and there is an alluring parallel between Forsythe's obsession with deconstruction and his current embrace of digital algorithms and computer codes.

The problem, however, lies in the unquestioned or apparently seamless commutation of physical creation and embodied knowledge into computer memory and its graphic user interfaces. The transformation of the dance experience—the training, rehearsal, creative process, performance, and reception—into *information* needs to be fundamentally challenged and examined if we seriously wish to influence the development of new technological systems and their interaction with organic, cultural, and site-specific experience.

What strikes me about "Improvisation Technologies" is the completely untheorized acceptance of digital media as an archive and as a direct interface, especially in light of Forsythe's poststructuralist attitude toward master-language codes. His deconstruction of classical ballet can be raucously beautiful (as in *Artifact* or *Impressing the Czar*) and thought provoking on many levels, especially when he urges the viewer to consider the dance in terms of a highly complex, almost philosophical logic of composition (as in *Eidos: Telos*). In subverting the very logos and telos of classical ballet vocabulary, in his own movement research with the dancers he draws upon intellectual sources that would be perplexing to many dance communities dedicated to organic, body-affirming, and integrative working processes. His distance from expressionism and *Tanztheater* is as obvious as his distaste for utopianism and the spiritual in art. The "postclassical analysis" he practices is mostly informed by eclectic scientific theories ranging from chaos theory, theoretical mathematics, fractal geometry, linguistics (alphabet structures, language games) to theoretical architecture and to *drawings* of lines, planes, polygons, and volumes. Gilpin has actually referred to the "structures" in performance as complex, self-organizing systems.

In *Eidos: Telos* groups of dancers within the ensemble perform complicated equations they devise instantaneously by themselves according to three-dimensional computer animations they glimpse on the wing monitors. On these monitors (not "accessible" to the audience!) the dancers read word-icons that are linked to a data bank comprising more than 150 words and sentences from the alphabets the company invented; the dancers then improvise with the movement inscriptions they have rehearsed in the various systems. Thus, Gilpin has argued that "the dancers become agents of their own compositional strategies," adding that the interfaces between the various ongoing algorithms in the space can no longer be controlled or even understood by the choreographer since they are "sometimes organized like these computer games, like the Game of Life."

The different rule-systems functioning side by side apparently can only be predicted by whatever limit theorem or "entropic" parameters the company agrees upon, and if one were to continue to describe the work in this way, one would have to switch to mathematical languages or models of distributed processing, computation, and arithmetic operations. In other words, one would switch to formal models of cyberspace, matrix, navigation data, and so forth. Perhaps it is fair to say that the Frankfurt Ballet now works in both directions, storing their movement systems on computer banks and redeploying randomized information signaled to them onstage in their live, spontaneous dancing. They dance interface, they dance across the virtual divide, but only at a loss. It seems to me that the unacknowledged bias of the work is toward playing compositional games with visual surfaces, with visual perception in the information space. At no point in the formalist memory bank do I find any reference to expression, content, meaning, or audience, except in Gilpin's enthusiastic claim that the dancers' enormous "states of concentration" onstage have an emotional affect:

It comes from the total dedication to the task at hand, the very total dedication of the dancers, as if nothing else exists, literally nothing else exists; that kind of state is insanely beautiful. I think that's the affect we are getting, when you realize you are witnessing something and you don't know: How did this happen? These lines, well, you cannot animate lines. It's like with language and dictionaries; you can learn them, but you then literally have to make them your own. So, too, in the dance; you have to incorporate them, embody them, incorporate them in your proprioception, and that is a very different kind of embodied knowledge.

It is here that the contradictory, affirmative side of Forsythe's deconstructivism becomes apparent. Considering Gilpin's claim in light of the dancers' leaping "with the vertiginous thrill of exactitude" in front of a "sky-blue background" (projected as words onto the back screen in Forsythe's *Six Counter Points*), a background that looks like chroma-key, I can't help feeling that the insistence on the stunning virtuosity of the performer betrays a strong investment in the memory of neoclassical ballet at the very moment of its apparent disappearance into digitized memory. As Forsythe has written,

> The more you can let go of your control, and give it over to a kind of transparency in the body, a feeling of disappearance, the more you will be able to grasp differentiated form, and differentiated dynamics. You can move very very fast in this state, and it will not give the same impression—it won't give the impression of violence. You can also move with tremendous acceleration provided you know where to leave the movement—not where you put the movement, but where you leave it. You try to divest your body of movement, as opposed to thinking that you are producing movement. So it would not be like pushing forward into space and invading space—it would be like leaving your body in space. Dissolution, letting yourself evaporate. Movement is a factor of the fact that you are actually evaporating.[18]

He has put forth the same idea, standing Laban on his head, in the CD-ROM–recorded theory of his dance, where he advises the dancer to "use the surface of the body with your imagination; the less substantial your body becomes—in your own sense of your body; in other words, if you think of your body as very transparent, as permeable—the more sensitive you will be to very complex shape." What might remain after this reduction is an idea of the kinesphere as "memory," a ghost of the desire to have a physical, sexual, sentient body that remembers more than spiritually disenchanted abstractions of line, point, plane. The sensing of the body's "evaporation" is, of course, an embodied sensing, and the dancers in Frankfurt are rehearsing it in their bodies. Yet the emphasis on dance as language system in Forsythe's work perhaps makes it an ideal candidate for digital processing, and the example of "disappearance" on the CD-ROM is Forsythe's video clip fading him out. That, however, is a digital editing effect used to illuminate a theory of movement trace. According to this theory, movement expression can be sampled and processed, in all of its various rotating inscriptions, without any loss of depth because there is very little of it under the virtual skin. The cyberspatial dismissal of psychological depth, narrative, and subjectivity strikes me as one of the unacknowledged dangers of the dynamics proposed by the synthesis of virtual realities and artificial languages. Not much space left to think about, here.

DANCING WITH TECHNOLOGIES **1**

IMPOSSIBLE ANATOMIES **2**

CULTURE IN ACTION **3**

VIRTUAL COMMUNITIES **4**

FOUR

LIVELY BODIES – LIVELY MACHINES: A WORKSHOP

Other Parameters

LBLM is now the filename for a workshop entitled "Lively Bodies–Lively Machines" that originated at the Split Screen Festival held at the Chichester Institute of Higher Education, England, in the summer of 1996. I had met Chris Butler, director of the Chichester Institute's Related Arts Program, during a dance workshop in Amsterdam, and when she invited me to teach a dance-based workshop on new-media technologies, I designed the project in collaboration with another member of AlienNation Co., choreographer-dancer Imma Sarries-Zgonc, who would play a vital role in helping me to facilitate the physical rehearsals. The workshop is sequential; being set up to enter further experimental stages and encompass other local contexts of collaboration. Our rehearsals focus on developing an integrated method of experimentation connecting organic physical performance and dance research with digital arts processes. In the following section, I want to describe the context and conception of the first workshop, its process, and the practical issues that have evolved in our experiments. In sharing some of these concerns, I hope to contribute to the critical feedback that will prove vital to all the diverse communities of cultural workers who straddle the performing and visual arts and new digital audio/video or VR technologies.

Someone recently said that the territory between the performing or desiring body and digital projective space is a contested no-man's-land. While I admit that it's contested, I don't think it's a no-man's-land at all. On the contrary, techniques and technologies involved in making art have existed for many centuries, and modern processes of composition, choreography, and scenography have become accustomed to using and manipulating media within the specific production apparatus of a given work process. The hierarchical and gender relations within production have undergone considerable changes, although the body-based time arts and their training systems, often connected to schools and theater institutions, have retained some old-fashioned or reactionary habits of specialization that need to change in the era of "shareware." Modes of production in the arts may differ, as do the assumptions and choices made and the principles by which training and creative process are conducted. What may be qualitatively new today is the impact of increasingly complex computer technologies on the human side of the production relation, that is, on the psychology and perception of the performers themselves, on our physical experience and cognitive accommodation of multiple environments of work. Again, these impacts may play out differently in different social, cultural, and gendered contexts. If some of these environments now are virtual or immaterial, how do we incorporate digital tools of composition in our creative process? How do immersive and projective computer-generated temporality and space (digitized form, content, movement, image, sound) affect the kinesthetic and psychological experience in our lived body? In a very mundane, pragmatic sense, I'd like to ask whether our work habits have been fundamentally altered. Although I'm sure many of us will not necessarily ever have access to high-tech science or computer laboratories in the way Forsythe did during his CD-ROM project ("Improvisation Technologies"), I am confident that we can test technological improvisations in any space that we ordinarily use to rehearse and to work together. The main impetus for the exploration, in a basic political sense, is to work against the grain of the privatizing tendency of our era of PCs and to publicize collaborative creative work by extending our diverse knowledge of low-end or high-end equipment that is raising the stakes for our own interaction with technical systems.

I also frankly admit that I didn't know where the work with digital media would take us, although I have been interested in mixed-media art for quite some time, at least since the mid-eighties, when I decided to abandon text-based theater and begin a series of collaborative projects focused on the exploration of "social movement" (performance, travel, immigration, urban living) and the mediation of image/sound movements. The most constructive dimension of this shift in my work was learning to dance and to understand choreographies and scenographies of movement in an expanded sense of their relationships to the images, projections, and imaginings of the subjective, physical body. At the same time, I became increasingly interested in video/film, photography, music, and the visual arts; I can trace almost all of my work back to the conceptual influence of these media on my experience of physi-

cal movement and the rhythms and motions of the stories we tell with
our bodies in specific environments or constructed spaces. Although the
visual sensibility may appear to be dominant in such multimedia performance work, it is important to remember that physical rehearsal involves all our kinesthetic and synesthetic senses; the experience of space,
time, energy, balance/imbalance, weight, scale, texture, color, sound,
and touch gain a crucial significance if we construct fully mediated environments. I have also come to value "touch" in a very concrete way,
insofar as much of my work involves cross-cultural collaboration with
people I get to know intimately during the process of creation. Touching in rehearsal is a fundamental basis of performing together and of
getting to know the distance or proximity of space between our bodies,
the weight of our bodies, and the boundaries of our imagination. In recent years artists in the dance and performance communities have been
forced or, rather, have wanted to respond to the increasing presence of
imaging/recording and electronic technologies in the cultural and exhibition contexts in which we work; a wide range of responses or negotiations could be observed by the mid-nineties.

The Connected Body

In 1994 an international workshop entitled "The Connected Body?"
convened at the School for New Dance Development (SNDO) in Amsterdam to examine the practice and holistic body-mind philosophy
of the "new dance" then spreading across Europe and linked to the
network of contact improvisation and Body-Mind Centering in North
America.[1] At SNDO "new dance" is defined as exploration/experimen-
tation in movement art not bound to strictly aesthetic forms but open
to a wide variety of means of body-mind experience. The intensive
workshop brought together over a hundred participants from different
countries, and we felt there was a huge investment among everyone in
creative, spiritual, and existential approaches to movement and bodily
experience that depart from the technique-based rigors of ballet/mod-
ern dance training, on the one hand, and that appear to be antagonistic
to the technological imperatives in media culture and the new hype of
cyberspace and virtuality, on the other. To the practitioners of Body-
Mind Centering, these hyped theories of escape velocity, mindspace, and
dematerialization seem especially alienating and distorting to dancers,
who need to work with and rely on their intimate knowledge of the concrete body-organism in phenomenological reality and real time.

I must have been the only participant who brought a camera to the workshop, but this instrument was hardly inappropriate since I also produce videos and films in and through the dance or performance work I create with my ensemble. Video sequences—or video memories, as I prefer to call them—are used as independent and interdependent projections within the performances we create, but they also function as a documentary tool, rehearsal graft, and as conceptual sketches that, in some cases, become temporal scores for the sequencing of the dance and music performances onstage or in an installation/environment. I have a logical interest in integrating movement research and physical expression with image/soundscapes in electronically processed media. The new catchphrase in many current debates (not about older multimedia performance in real space but about the new multimedia software) is "interactivity," and here is where the problem resides. At the Amsterdam workshop, however, we never talked about the potential challenges of such interactivities but focused instead on collaborative processes of physiological, anatomical, and psychological awareness in corporeal work and movement creation. The camera was of little use, and I used it only to film the context/site and the interactions in the shared spaces. The intensive work, conducted in five groups, ended with small work demonstrations, performances, and site-specific actuations, followed by a two-day conference with additional guests (artists, writers, scholars) during which the workshop's premise—the body-as-site for re-integration—was reframed by participants whose various approaches to the very discourses and metaphors of the "fragmented" body within our disciplinary and commodifying societies would seem to marginalize or deny the experienced body and its authenticity.

I want to emphasize that I have rarely attended a physical/intellectual workshop that was simultaneously so balanced, harmonious, and yet concentrated, in such a physically and spiritually uplifting way. These harmonic convergences were facilitated, to a great extent, by the organizers' sensitive and selfless thoughtfulness in providing intimate rehearsal space, nourishing food, and housing for us—in a literal sense, making us feel at home. During the parallel work studios, younger and older performers gathered to form a temporary community committed to an experiential rediscovery of the major body systems—skeletal, muscular, fluid, organ, neuroendrocrine, and evolutionary developmental patterns that underlie human movement—as well as of the potential of body-mind integration for our perceptual consciousness and the physical changes in our social relation to the world. The most important learning experience for me resulted from the noncompetitive relations among the workshop groups. The program was not production or training-oriented, focusing instead on a shared attentiveness to communication through our bodies and through the careful development of our sensory perceptions, waking up memories in the body or stretching the inter-actions between body and mind toward heightened self-awareness and awareness of being connected to others. As Deborah Hay explained in her group work involving "intrinsically appropriate dancing," we are using our dancing life always and constantly as choices of *being*. Moving thus involves a constant listening, inviting being seen, being awake to in-finite possibilities of experience of the totality of life/death. Understood in this sense, dance or physical movement cannot be reduced to a "tech-nique" or style of expression, to a cultural or aesthetic influence, but is an evolving, organic process of being in "communion with all there is." With her group she explored what she has called "cellular conscious-ness," allowing performance to become physicalized meditation rather than structured movement or choreography.[2] In the shared environ-ment of SNDO—meditating, living, eating, and working together with people (both trained and untrained dancers) from many different coun-tries—the process of learning based on being well in the body generated a climate of shared responsibility and awareness of our coming (back) to the body as our most familiar and most forgotten country or "house," as Marina Abramović described it in her workshop entitled "Cleaning the House."

After many years of body-art/performance work testing the limits of endurance and the bodily unconscious, for her, the current practice is like a bridge that can enable people to experience their inner selves more fully. She never uses the term "spiritual" in any deliberate way, yet her workshop was unique in setting highly focused and stringent conditions (fasting, other forms of abstention, blindfolded tasks, yoga, physical exercises) in order to inspire participants to experience a deeper connection with the mental and physical self. As in the other workshops, the attention given to physical states, small and large energy levels, inner- and outer-directedness, and the various implicated states of men-tal discipline evolved and changed over the course of a week. On the third day it became impossible not to notice the particular way in which Abramović's group moved, blindfolded and in slow motion, through the house (including the rooftop), sensing their way while orienting them-selves acoustically and exploring the space in terms of its tactile reso-nance. I could kinesthetically grasp their sense of a recomposed sensory landscape in which the body functions and redefines the boundaries of its interior and exterior spaces. I spent several hours on the rooftop filming the group's movements, offering help if someone needed it. The dangerous rooftop became a particular boundary-space for me.

The process heightened our sense of interconnection even as—or precisely because—we would notice differences among our energies, expressions, and reactions to the work demonstrations we shared later on. This sharing is another example of what I mean by "recollection" (memory): it is possible to practice openness to others through listening and observing, and through recognizing the movement within. Perhaps the heightened attention to body-self is the opposite of narcissism; it is a precondition for being better prepared to perceive the physical presence of others. Coming back is thus also a moving outward, toward recognition of social textures in the alienated, technocentric world of consumption and distraction, based on a specific ethos of bodily connection to the world. Not surprisingly, the final group discussion on "disconnection" centered on the complex and difficult issue of *healing* the damaged body and spirit.

Reconstructions

A darkened dance studio, empty except for a blackboard freshly painted and lying on the floor in the middle of the room, left there by Alastair MacLennan after his action-performance the previous night. On one side of the rectangular room the workshop participants/audience gather; the other side is empty. The long and short walls are used for video and slide projections. Two small video monitors display silent image tracks: one is raw footage from the war zone in Bosnia; the other is an edited version of the dance piece AlienNation.

In my own audiovisual dance presentation at SNDO I speak about collaborative work as "reconstruction," simultaneously moving across the space of projected images from my ensemble's cross-cultural work on location in the United States, Cuba, Slovenia, and East Germany, where we meet with other artists and cultural workers to build relationships, exchange ideas, and perform together. In a sense, all of the photos or film tracks are rehearsal images, propositions for action or rememberings of actions. Not all of them are my own, whatever that means. Some of them I produced, while others were given to me or produced jointly under conditions that were not as peaceful or harmonious as they are at SNDO.

I have been haunted for some time by a photo taken in Sarajevo during the siege of the city. It shows the sculptor Zoran Bogdanović standing in the empty door frame of a bombed-out building, the former Obala Gallery, one of the first cultural sites to be shelled by the attacking army. On the exterior walls of the ruined building one can see large white banners, on which is written "Destrukcija–Duhovnost–Rematerijalizacija" (Destruction–Spirituality–Rematerialization).

As with other genocides that haunt our memory in the twentieth century, we will have to learn to listen to the witnesses and survivors of this horror. Such a confrontation with firsthand testimony doesn't come easily. On the other hand, the normalization of war through daily television coverage ought to be unacceptable, even as we have begun to take the global presence of media and its power to manipulate for granted. The first act of manipulation is our willingness to become passive spectators viewing events from a safe distance.

When I met with Bogdanović I realized he was too tired to express the emotional "evidence" of destruction that befell his city and culture. Yet the work he and his friends created as a "permanent" installation (*Witnesses of Existence*, October 1992–April 1993) in the bombed-out gallery speaks powerfully of a creative human spirit that reconstructs its will to survive from within the ruins of reason and the annihilation of being. *Witnesses of Existence*, like the ongoing video production about life in wartime created by the SAGA collective in Sarajevo, or the theater, dance, and music created under sniper fire, testifies to spiritual acts of resistance while also demonstrating the human need to document the traumatized existence, building or composing imaginative portraits out of what is left. Bogdanović has called one of his installations: "Memory of People," and like other artists he is using and transforming available materials (old newspapers, bricks, glass, burnt logs, sand, ashes, found objects).

As I dance I speak about recorded images as testimony and as a creative way of inventing joint narratives or movement scenarios. As with any other visual or sound media, video production is able to transform available materials, found objects, sites, and our bodily imagination. Video listens. For me, working with the camera creates a physical connection, a tracking connection to material culture, and this is one of the aspects I want to add to the body of workshop research.

Several times over the past few years I have worked in situations where such memories and the transformations of material were crucial aspects of our rehearsals and physical encounters with the pressures of reality. In Cuba working conditions were permanently overshadowed by scarcity and the disillusionment of a faded revolutionary society trapped on an island and cut off from the rest of the world. Our physical work, and the experience of being in our bodies, was always subject to elementary questions (Would there be water, food, medicine, electricity?). At the same time, such questions gave way to other rhythms and a free flow of energies not encumbered by technical or aesthetic concerns. The imagination of our bodily being on the island was both existentialist and fantastic, informed by a deep-seated tradition of Yoruba spiritualism and a musicality that mobilized and inspired every movement and every perceptual capability. And when there was no electricity, we could always rehearse outdoors, in front of the house or on the shore. During the last joint project, we used a camera to shoot a film based on a poem by one our Cuban collaborators. It was a silent film about the logic of disillusionment, carefully focused on different body languages of the actors as they enacted seven dreams on the shore near the uncompleted, roofless houses of a small workers' town.

The images projected on the other side of the wall are inserts from the performance of *AlienNation,* a dance-film work first created during a cross-cultural workshop in Chicago and then recreated in Eisenhüttenstadt on the East German/Polish border in 1994. Some of the film footage comes from an earlier documentary film I shot after the fall of the Berlin Wall and the subsequent historical transformations in Germany. Other parts of the projections reflect our fantasies and imaginative responses to the process of "unification," the uniting of two distinct social bodies and nations that had been separated not only by an ideological borderline but by a completely different social/political construction of reality. Our rehearsals for *AlienNation* started with the idea that our bodies, like the countries where we were raised, are imaginary homes — containers or frames that have grown to be our sensory and psychic boundaries to the environment in which our biographies are played out. *AlienNation* tells three different stories from three different, gendered perspectives, and the documentary film projections of the breaking down of the Berlin Wall create another frame (historical/fictional) against which the physical movements onstage establish themselves as internal monologues, so to speak. These internal movements do not come together since they are neither parallel nor synchronic or unifiable into a single narrative. The three performers' bodies remain interconnected yet radically distinct: their connectedness is based on their distinction. On another level the performance reflects a series of obsessions inhabiting these bodies — one could call them fantasies or traumas — which are developed from personal bodily memory and thus help us to reconnect to who we are becoming.

For me the production of this work revolves around my ambivalent relationship to my former West German identity and, more precisely, to my split sense of self, which is the result of physical and cultural dislocation and emigration, and to the intensified sense of distance from "home," which is an experience shared by many migrant workers, immigrants, exiles, and refugees. This experience is also coupled with the political awareness that changing, transforming, and fluid identities are not always a matter of choice but are conditioned by economic, educational, class, and racial privileges or disadvantages. In fact, the conscious choice of working in cross-cultural and multilingual contexts immediately brings the distinct positions of cultural difference and the controlling forces and images that affect our identities to the foreground.

The video projections on the wall change from AlienNation *to* From the Border, *a cross-cultural production workshop conducted in Chicago in 1993. The images display rehearsal scenes and interviews with Indian, Korean, African-American, Japanese-American, Latin American and Anglo-European performers/visual artists engaged in a process of addressing their expressive means and motivations as well as the emotional process of collaboration. Some of the young artists who participated in the project comment on the difficulties of sharing a common rehearsal method or language; they also speak about the gender and power relations in such a production context, involving technical and design decisions as well as the question of how to represent different performance vocabularies, centered on different cultural content, on the same proscenium stage of an arts institution that caters mostly to white, middle-class audiences.*

The political struggle over identity in the realm of the arts, media, and education in the United States reflects the embattled relationships between culture, making art and self-representation—especially the relationship between artists and powerful institutions that can delimit or exploit their work. Even, or particularly, on the level of physical practice and training, we are constantly reminded of the sanctioned borders of legitimate work, methods, genres, technologies, and parameters of public presentation. Physical performance rehearsals (including the audio-video technologies of recording and edited representation) that seek to explore new ground of collaborative experimentation, or to transgress familiar habits of directorial or hierarchized production, tend to challenge basic assumptions about cultural technique and practical procedure. In a sense, each rehearsal *process*, given the context of its location and the composition of the participating group, must (re)construct its own mode of interaction and creation.

In the case of the *From the Border* workshop, this turned out to be particularly difficult since we could not agree on a common language or perception and therefore split into parallel groups, each dedicating its performance research to the theme of "borders" and "boundaries." We learned to understand our differences and distinct cultural biorhythms and creative sensibilities by allowing the unbridgeable gaps to exist; at no point did we assume that we could find a unifying aesthetic for our diverse experiences of our perceptions. It could not be projected. This realization, however, does not imply that we cannot interact or share these different perceptions. On the contrary, we can learn to comprehend our bodies as a *movement of boundaries* that brings our fluid selves into contact. We become researchers of distance and proximity, of our movement across and between spaces of perception, blindness, hurt emotions, aborted fantasies, suppressed arrogance, and hard-won patience, learning to listen without judging.

This also implies that we become researchers of our own inner bodies, of our organic being and becoming, and of the boundaries we may perceive within ourselves and toward others. The physical work of creation inevitably involves some mode of translation when we work with others whose physical parameters, accents, steps, and languages differ from ours. We slowly learn to listen to the different sounds we make and the different images we compose with our bodies. In the work I am involved in, we speak a lot about the *images* we make or have of ourselves and others. Perhaps this is a result of the fairly constant use we make of video and photography: we document and develop image-ideas, and we explore the movement of our living bodies in relation to the still/moving images created by our cameras. Video production, in this sense, is another mode of border-crossing since video rehearsals are performative encounters. One cannot use media, shoot and edit footage, or manipulate visual languages without exploring power relationships and the conditions of production. In my experience, video and computerized editing technologies have not so much changed the modes of production in the performing arts as they have foregrounded the reorganization of visual cultures and complicated the processes of interaction. To initiate cross-cultural production means to acknowledge the precarious gender and race relations that need to be negotiated in the process of finding a structure for the mediation of different languages, experiences, and sensibilities. The image/sound technology itself, highly fluid and capable of instant and extensive reprocessing of recorded or generated signals, affords the producers an immediate experience of the constructibility of imagery and image relations, and of decision-making and selection processes. Participatory video production is therefore an organizational process that moves the creative operations across social relationships. As in performance, it rehearses interdependence.

This becomes particularly evident when you shift a work process from one context to another, as we did when we performed *AlienNation* together with other artists in Cuba and East Germany. It is in such new constellations, when we approach our physical rehearsals with the camera or link our live work with prerecorded images, that the question of our consciousness of our bodily relations and our projections of physical culture are posited anew. Again, I would speak of *reconstruction* if we agree that such work is based primarily on the compositional process of finding images and editing them into those image-movements that we discover, looking or looked at in turn, imagining, remembering, anticipating. My body is a medium that is itself constructed by my ideas, sensations, experiences, habits, idiosyncrasies, and dispositions. When I perform it and simultaneously record it with the camera, I become more aware of my production and of the particular subject positions I assume in taking up my body. As a reflexive strategy, filming my bodily movement also helps me to reconnect or deconstruct what I could not see moving. Others film my movement with their point of view, and I can again look at it through other eyes. In other words, I do not make dance videos or videodances, nor am I preoccupied with film or media as such. Rather, my performance work is always interconnected with media because I believe that our lives and creative explorations are acts of comparison and recomposition; the camera work allows me to reconfigure the evidence from one practice where meaning is generated into another where it perhaps has only been latent or constituted differently. It allows me to speculate on different time levels and in different spaces of bodily "identity."

When we rehearsed *AlienNation* in Havana and Eisenhüttenstadt, our collaborators were not familiar with the conjunctions of performance and film in our danced dialogue. Seeing the performance, of course, can be different from doing it on stage. I am moving in my body. You will be seeing me at least twice, two dancing images that never seem to become one and the same. For our Cuban friends this was perfectly acceptable as long as we agreed to participate in a spiritual invocation of the *oricha*s asking for their divine healing powers to assuage our schizophrenia. The rehearsals in East Germany were first greeted with silence, and the subsequent public performance was met with outrage because my portrayal of a self-deluded, masochistic angel with broken wings stammering revolutionary slogans about "one people" was interpreted as a sinister parody of recent historical events. I hope that both responses—the wish to heal and the angry denial—helped to close slightly the distance between the images. Imma Sarries-Zgonc, in fact, worked for six months with young, amateur dancers and students in Eisenhüttenstadt, creating a dance work that specifically addressed the young East Germans' experience of their homeland before the collapse of socialism and the move toward unification. This work, *Ewige Seelen, Ewiges Land,* was shown together with *AlienNation* and helped to establish more intimate relations between us. Since 1993 we have continued to collaborate with young artists and cultural workers in Eisenhüttenstadt. In the future we hope to carry out an urban-art project devoted to the city's future during a time of tremendous uncertainty, caused by the layoffs at the local steel plant and the transformation of the entire social and economic infrastructure.

As with so many experiences we believe to be immediate or direct, bodies are also subject to experience because they are symbolic systems or, if you prefer, organisms. We believe we understand them—if, in fact, we do—because they are representable organisms within the larger symbolic systems and institutions that have been built. Bodies and minds, our images of ourselves and others, are derived from such symbolic representations, histories, conventions, and myths, from choreographies that derive their authority from the symbolic, which, politically speaking, is a mechanism of dominance. I am interested in how states, nations, or institutions maintain their power (or lose it), for such maintenance involves both the social body or various communal bodies and a body politic that governs (internally and externally) the relations between the individual and the collective, between majorities and minorities, between various energies and desires and their control/containment or fulfillment.

To speak of relations (or bodily exchanges) means to speak of *images* (or the imaginary). And I am not just saying this because I work with video or perform before film/slide projections but because I assumed that all participants at "The Connected Body" workshop have already formed images of the work we did in our minds—and we brought these expectations and desires with us to Amsterdam. We are at this moment already disconnected from ourselves and each other by the differences we felt or saw or imagined, while we continue—I trust, to place demands on these images of a connected, whole, knowable, or reconstructible body to which this workshop addresses itself.

In other words, we pose questions relating to that very symbolic notion or concept of a *whole, connected, integrated,* or *organic body* upon which the philosophy of the workshop is founded. In another sense, the notion of wholeness or holism is also part of a New Age cultural discourse, and as such includes a utopian dimension and carries ideological inflections that oppose it to the widespread cynicism which permeates our crisis-ridden cultures and much of our postmodern art, as well as to the enthusiasm of new digital art that wants to transcend bodies entirely or remap them.

The question hovering over the workshop points to changes we may expect or welcome in the future. Perhaps a future is possible for our evolving civilization if we make the right choices. Yet the choices of becoming, as positions to take on, are impossible to occupy simultaneously. Should I stop speaking about the various performance experiences and exchanges that have taken place or have shaped my life's itinerary? I am full of conflicting but complementary impressions and can only pretend to "connect" them. Choices and commitments are crucial, however, in the social and political sense in which I understand our practices as explorers, manipulators, and editors of images.

Our bodily practice, our performance research, involves the *disorientation of the senses,* and seeing how degraded and brutalized our social conditions are, this is probably a very positive and necessary procedure. Eva Schmale, who taught the workshop ("Written in the Body") in which I participated, would probably disagree with my formulation; she might speak of the reorientation and uncovering of our senses and our consciousness toward all those underestimated somatic possibilities that are naturally invested in our bodies. All those possibilities that are *verschollen,* lost or forgotten in memory. After working with her and the other members of the group, and after observing the climate of creative investigation here among us, I realize that reconstructive bodily research, body-mind centering, experiential anatomy, and the holistic exploration of movement capabilities have opened up new avenues to the *witnessing of existence,* and a new approach to returning home (to the body) to rebuild the destroyed houses. I am probably predisposed to suspect any claims on behalf of a natural or "authentic" body, and I know that even after such an intense week of listening to my body I may not have discovered many of its lost memories, even as I felt a deeper contact with my mental and physical self. Quite aside from the question of the body's authenticity, I have become aware of a new range of sensations, and I wish to thank all the other collaborators for helping me to gain a new awareness of how sensory perceptions can be communicated, without words, in a group. I experienced an ethics of collaboration that week which I imagine to be fundamentally vital for any political project of reconstructing our damaged existence.

A short, silent film is projected which is composed of sequences of imaginary and observed workshop activities, moments of action and interaction, pauses, sudden and unexpected encounters and disappearances, shadows and memories, rooftops, traces collected in this building over a few days.

Connecting Bodies

When I am invited back to Amsterdam in 1996, we gather for a second workshop entitled "Connecting Bodies" and foregrounding the return of the repressed: *technology*. Remarkably, the technological workshop is made part of a two-week international forum, "Bodies of Influence," organized to permit professional experimental dance artists—working in a wide variety of movement, sound, improvisation, meditation, body-awareness, and release techniques—to come together and exchange ideas about making and presenting their work in today's cultural climate.[3] Open to the public, more than thirty-five dance makers teach workshops, give performances, and discuss their individualized approach to training, practical strategies, and aesthetics. The actual technological workshop thus inserts itself into the nodes of a wider space of practices, including SNDO's hosting of specific dance-related "networking activities," such as a video-collection project, an audio installation, an internet-access room, a special project on cooperative networking, the development of an "improvisation performance" event, and the temporary opening of the Stamina Choreographic Computer Atelier, exhibited for hands-on training by its founders, Bianca van Dillen and Mari-Jan Boer.

Participating in "Connecting Bodies" thus means shifting the focus to another side of bodily praxis, namely, the sharing of bodies of information that "originate" in what the Canadian installation artist David Rokeby has called the "very nervous system" of technological interfaces. We look at Thecla Schiphorst's LifeForms software program written for Cunningham, her interactive installation *Bodymaps*, which is activated by the viewer's touch, and other digital animation software while sitting in front of terminals in the Stamina Choreographic Computer Atelier. We watch a performance with STEIM's "Big Eye" computer program involving video cameras that convert a live dancer's movements to MIDI messages controlling lights, image projection, and sound onstage. STEIM is Amsterdam's well-known Institute of Electro-Acoustic Music, and electronic composer Joel Ryan drops in to demonstrate some of his live sound-processing work for William Forsythe. Amanda Steggell and Pier Platou give a hilariously funny video lecture on their *M@aggie's Love*

Bytes concert, which combines media dance performances and music in real and virtual spaces, allowing dancers in actual space to interact with multilayered sound, text, and real-time video images beamed through online Internet facilities. Motion-capture technology and character animation are introduced as an "extension" or simulation of human body motion, while virtual-studio producer Peter Mulder patiently explains the most arcane features of his NOB-Interactive Laboratory: the operations of "Kinemation" (motion capture integrating forward and inverse kinematics); "Digital Doll" (animated skeletons that can be connected to each other in any configuration); and "Smart Skin" (character animation that can be taught to behave according to skeletal position or time). Heidi Gilpin demonstrates segments from Forsythe's CD-ROM–formatted "Improvisation Technologies"; Andrea Zapp introduces new theories of the interactive viewer and the confusion of the senses in the *Telematic Dreaming* project by Paul Sermon; and Kitsou Dubois, a researcher at the National Center of French Spatial Studies, demonstrates new dance ideas derived from experiments in microgravity and weightlessness. The symposium begins with a theoretical exposition of "Choreography, Women, and the Gift of Dance" by André Lepecki and ends with Diana Theodores's comprehensive inventory of new perspectives on "technography," followed by a breathless plenary discussion involving everyone.

Indeed, women choreographers and their gifts of dancing have shaped much of twentieth-century dance history, but it is perhaps even more remarkable and poignant to realize how many women have entered the technological realm of programming and redesigning interface systems that can incorporate movement ideas and choreographies. There are different angles from which to approach such incorporations and the nature of the interface, and we must bear in mind that the computer as a medium is strongly biased since it operates purely logically and in very tiny playing fields of integrated circuits. Even if it is patched up with other media (video cameras, projectors, image processors, synthesizers, MIDI managers, sound systems, etc.), it remains a mechanical device operating on programmed code, treating everything quantitatively as information based on cybernetic models of positive/negative feedback loops and pattern recognition. The quantity of information it processes is mathematically defined, and the kind of information it processes depends on the way the program is coded to read pattern and randomness. All operations revolve around binary code. Since so much energy in cultural theory and criticism is spent on decentering the dualisms of Cartesian rationality (including the mind/body binary), the persistence of binary logic in computer technology effectively shifts attention to the quality and the activation of the interface configuration and the artistic and social practices that mobilize the interface, including the unresolved contradiction that the computer may not be concerned about Cartesian mind/body or gender distinctions when it reads bodies or physical actions, like everything else, *as information.*

Schiphorst argues that it remains vital, of course, to write code, as in the LifeForms software, that applies an understanding of anatomy and body movement while allowing the user to modify predefined movement possibilities. On the other hand, most participants at the conference approaching the issue from the side of dance practice and performance express an interest in the points of contact between what takes place in the human-scaled physical space and the information systems. As Gilpin suggests, we need not wait for digital technology or think of it as a device for body representation but should empower ourselves as informers for technological interface design. We may not yet possess an influential language to impress corporeal aesthetics upon network and graphical user interface (GUI) design. Gilpin is demanding "a discourse that can actually deal in articulate ways with movement and dynamism of any kind, not just moving bodies." But dance surely has articulated its operational, conceptual, and aesthetic systems, and since they already exist in the same media environment as digital technologies, their physicalities necessarily interact with virtuality. The question is, rather, how the interaction changes the images and sounds in cyberspace, the virtual geography of potentially infinite computational possibilities in a "place" that is not a place, or how the interaction can generate new kinds of "places," either *between* dance and multimedia activities or *along* and *within* real-time multisensory immersion environments.

Furthermore, interaction with virtuality potentially or actually modifies human proprioception, as Dubois's research on weightlessness confirms. She points out that the dynamic conditions of movement are altered when "the sources of information provided by inertia-gravitational force disappear. The absence of gravity is lived as an aggression from sensorial origin." The new sensorial images are unusual and conflictual, and they effect space sickness, "a sort of disease of adaptation." In weightlessness or free floating, every movement can induce a totally unexpected displacement. In approaching new possibilities of being in this space, one has to concentrate on the internal space of one's body (organs are reorganized, blurring the references to internal space) and the interaction with external space, as well as on the imagination as it is stimulated by the new environment. Dubois became committed to exploring the exchange between space techniques and dance after she realized, during parabolic flights, that in a fluid universe of weightlessness the body needs to construct a subjective referential or inner vertical in order to apprehend external space and react to it. "The inner vertical can be felt as an infinite spiral; on the outside everything is relative and one experiences an extraordinary fluidity of movement." Her dance research has been influenced by her interest in the "space in-between" internal body space and external space. She tells us that in her choreography she searches for a "quality of movement where the dancers are always in a situation of experimentation, a state of unstable balance . . . an interactivity between that movement quality and systems of scenographic apparitions that blur habitual references to the gravity axis of the spectators themselves, thus creating a phenomenon of resonance in their own bodies."

This notion of "scenographic apparition" can be linked to the role "video ghosts" might play in interactive designs of movement. In terms of the nodes, or zones of turbulance, we currently have at least four models of interaction in digital art. First, the basic point-and-click or touch-screen interactivity of computer-based multimedia projects, either encoded in CD-ROM formats or left on a hard drive, is confined to a site-specific installation and is thus comparable to video installations or intermedia exhibitions that may include user access to the Net. The screen/monitor or its projection remains the primary surface of information, although hypertext or hypermedia formats imply a nonlinear, nonsequential information structure that is unlike the performance experience in real time, especially since hypermedia is digitized information allowing the user to manipulate it in ways that are not possible for the viewer of a performance in real space.

Second, the potential extension into the Net implies distance and spatial separation. The circuitry of telemedia can link locations and thus an interactivity that is not a one-way communication (as in broadcast media) but an engagement involving reciprocity and feedback. Reciprocity opens the possibility of altering and transforming the terms of reference of the exchange; multiple connections between sites create greater turbulence and dynamism among the connected surfaces.

In the case of Paul Sermon's *Telematic Dreaming*, two separate interfaces are installed in separate locations connected via an ISDN digital telephone network. The two separate installations in themselves are dynamic installations that function as customized videoconferencing systems inviting interaction with users. The success of the "performance" depends on the creative input of the audiences at both ends. Screen or video projection surface is replaced by rooms with a bed or sofa, a television, and carpeting. The rooms come alive when the user steps inside and acts. The bed in each location has a camera situated directly above it, sending a live video image of the bed, and a person ("A") on it, to a video projector located above the other bed in the other location. The live video image is projected down on the bed with another person ("B") on it. A second camera, positioned next to the video projector, sends a live video image of the projection of "A" with "B" acting upon it back to a TV monitor positioned next to the bed containing "A." The telematic image functions like a mirror that reflects one person interacting with another person's reflection.

Andrea Zapp describes this scenario as a dynamic system with a considerable psychological complexity since the viewer actually becomes a physical user able to experience theatrical roles or spontaneous, playful behavior, like acting, pantomime, and visceral movement or choreographic possibilities. The physical bed, with its social meanings, can provoke emotional responses heightened by the telematic experience, since geographical distance is dissolved in the interaction with another person. The ability to exist outside of the user's own space and time is created by the real sense of touch (the bed), enhanced by an acute shift of senses in the telematic space, which Zapp (who has worked with Sermon in Japan) explains as a conversion of sight and touch. The two users in distant places exchange their tactile senses and touch each other by replacing their hands with their eyes. While it might be difficult emotionally to interact with a stranger on a bed in a public installation, the bed interface actually creates a new level of virtual consciousness and immersion affect. The participants act in real space but manipulate themselves in virtual space, the projection field of interaction. Zapp goes so far as to claim that although the image representation is analog—reaching out with the hand or touching and reacting is shown in a physical, visible form—the telematic performance affects consciousness of body and self in such a way that the user's attention, initially focused on the real bed, gradually no longer concentrates on the immediate environment but on the distant telematic one and the virtual movement. The cause-and-effect interactions of the body extend through a fiber-optic network, and the shift in sensory perception may dislocate the awareness of where the body movement resides. Zapp argues persuasively that such a shift, which implies controlling and "feeling" virtual touch with the eyes, often leads users to explore different sensitivities, and a perhaps unfamiliar playfulness, in the contact and emotional exchange with the other. However, I feel that such visual "controlling" of tactile sensibility forecloses the most intimate sense we possess, while shifting attention to the screen/projection-as-skin.

The intermixing of analog and telematic media in this installation project suggests that interactive electronic art does not depend on a particular technological mode (analog, digital, radio, video, modem, satellite) but on the quality or conceptual structure of the meeting points and conduits of interactive levels. As a third example, *M@aggie's Love Bytes* opens up the possibility—which has also been explored in spatially separate music concerts linked up via satellite or Internet—of staging a dance concert in one location to a real-time audience while inviting the input of other artists, connected via modem and Internet, so that externally transmitted video images (from quicktime cameras), sound-samples, voices, and texts can be integrated instantaneously and layered onto the closed-circuit video projection and soundmix in the real space. The choreographer becomes a virtuality-DJ. The real-space performance is also filmed with digital cameras and projected to the virtual site on the Net, and since the dancers are moving in front of the local video projection (hooked to the Mac) that is already a projection of the integrative virtual concert, Steggell could be seen as "choreographing" a live mix both for local audiences and for Web collaborators. Her work with present and absent collaborators utilizes the Web playfully for what she calls the "postmodemism" of "time warping and space bending," and this warping indeed functions as an aesthetic of chance events in which the dance between pattern and randomness replaces all known, stable contours of unitary time-space theatricality. When she first "staged" the event in a discotheque in Copenhagen, Web browsers from as far away as Tokyo and San Francisco tuned in to drop off sound and video samples, turning the dance-music concert into a kind of electronic quilt pieced together by the multiple-site collaborations. The quilt-concert migrating across the Net intimates an idea of collaborative performance that has largely gone unexplored in its effects on content, structure, and reception. We would have to substitute more familiar principles of the rehearsed and structured collaboration process with the defining features of the digital and distributed medium, where such "information pieces" may not belong to anyone any longer and where the completely unpredictable "dance" may be electrifying or senseless. Moreover, the live Internet switching demands such an amount of high-tech equipment, lines, and cable connections to work properly that the smallest bug in the system could bring it all down, which has to be considered part of the unpredictability pattern.

Finally, a fourth model of digital art would remove the intersection of actual and virtual performance and place interactivity inside immersive virtual environments. I don't know of any examples where full immersion has been tested without the hitherto existing limitations of strapping the viewer/user to body suit, headphones, and dataglove, which implies wiring the body to the computer and shifting the kinesthetic experience to the simulated spatiality produced for eyes and ears inside the headphones. At present, the wiring is still necessary, which obviously reduces the number of users who can actively move into virtual performance spaces at one time. Some large-scale immersive environments were built during a research project at the Banff Center in Canada, and the photo and video documentations of Diane J. Gromola and Yacov Sharir's *Dancing with the Virtual Dervish: Virtual Bodies* (1994) display it as an ongoing project consisting of cyberspace "chambers" constructed as a fully connected lattice.[4] Sound and VR artist Marcos Novak, who works with Gromola and Sharir, has called them "Worlds in Progress"; the chamber he programmed presents a space of abstracted forms, lines of light, and geometric constructs. Sharir, however, is seen dancing in the "Virtual Body" chamber, rendered as a three-dimensional simulation of an enormous virtual body configuring the immersive environment out of visualizations of X-rays, sonograms, and other medical and MRI data of Gromola's real body. Her virtualized body becomes an architecture that can be "inhabited"; for Sharir it is the performance space for an interactive dance that engages both the three-dimensional simulation of Gromola's hollow body and the digitized images (video feedback) of himself dancing within these layers of virtual images. The tracking devices in his headphones and Dataglove give him the illusion of multiple-body experiences at high navigational speed, causing a sensation of disembodiment and disconnection since his point of view, which can change at a flick of the wrist, doesn't establish a full perceptional grasp of the interior body landscape as a coherent body. Rather, the interior body tends to dissolve into an inchoate environment of giant organs, endless strips of tissue, cavernous bones, curves, lines, and shapes. The virtual-body environment, in other words, doesn't pretend to be realistic; it is a reconceptualized space mapped by numbers of codes.

Gromola is aware of the disembodiment effect caused by disorientation, but she designed the space in this way to explore transcendent spiritual states of pain, since for her the "dervish" effect (in Sufi dancing) enables her to link a function of virtuality with her experience of medical treatment of chronic illness. While her conceptual relocation of her body as a virtual stage is truly astounding, what is more difficult to understand is Sharir's relationship to it and his assumptions about choreographing his movements and video images in response to his distressed, disoriented body-experience. Is his internal experience translated into conscious movement choices or do we see him react to a state of disconnection from himself? In the documentation accompanying the experiment he expresses considerable uncertainty, wondering how agency and self are altered by immersion, and how a virtual environment and the possibilities of "distributed performance" can redefine performance venues. This raises another question, namely, how an audience without headphones would watch the dance of the VR performer.

As Theodores points out in her exposé on "technography," interactive immersive computer technologies extend and transform the shape of movement and choreography, and if digital media can penetrate the materiality of the body, then our perceptual and ontological notions of embodiment are profoundly affected.

> We can challenge and/or confuse all existing senses we have of order and of norms, spatially, biomechanically, kinesthetically, and aesthetically. Classical frameworks of symmetry, specific body architecture, notions of sequence, and even the way we recognize our own sensory responses and faculties—all of these are challenged and reordered radically and perhaps liberatingly. As we shed the ingrained ideas of what the body ought to do, we enter into a new aesthetic and experiential order.

While it is true that the collaboration between digital technology and choreography potentially expands the concept of nonphenomenological information and virtuality as much as it expands the concept of what the body is, it is much less clear how the audience is integrated and transformed into interactive users, since most of the practical experiments to date have been undertaken by the artists/programmers and designers themselves.

For example, the acclaimed Electronic Visualization Laboratory at the University of Illinois has constructed "The Cave," a ten-foot cubical "theater" with synchronized, wall-size video projections that potentially allow interaction with VR environments without the intermediary of headphones and gloves.[5] But "The Cave" is not open to the public, and when I was allowed to see interactive, animated VR artworks by graduating computer science students, I was given stereoscopic glasses and told exactly what I could and could not do in the VR theater. The exhibit was structured as a four-part "tour," beginning with an introduction to the system at a computer terminal. I was then given a hands-on training session at a larger ImmersaDesk (a rear-screen video desk with stereo capability), where a young computer artist showed me how to move a pencil that permits drawing in virtual space with an electromagnetic tracking system. Finally, I was ushered into "The Cave," where I was shown how to draw in four differently programmed modes, scribbling yellow, red, blue, and green lines into a digitized, moving landscape of abstract mathematical visualizations. Almost as if I were following Forsythe's movement instructions for "lines" and "inscriptions," I wildly drew lines of color in the virtual space of a relatively poorly simulated four-dimensional "reality" that remained meaningless to me. My scribbled, hieroglyphic algorithms would hover in virtual air for a few seconds, then congeal and fade out. Upon leaving "The Cave," I was taken to a computer surveillance room where the vanished drawing-movements I had made were tracked down and printed out on small postcards showing the abstract mathematical landscapes as background. Alan Millman, who created the interface, explained that he was interested in the aesthetic quality of the live interaction with the simulation program that was running on Silicon Graphics "Infinite Reality Engines," as the computers were called.

To build full-scale theaters for larger audience interactivity of this kind is as yet technically unimaginable, and the experience of "The Cave" left one with a feeling of insignificant, childish playfulness, decidedly bereft of content and kinesthetic or psychological affect. My input role as user was quite minimal, and my drawing with the "wand" did not change or transform the terms set up by the program. In this sense, the body's intelligence doesn't get involved in informing the virtual configuration; as in *Dancing with the Virtual Dervish,* the question of the reconstitution of limits or borderlines between the interior and the exterior is not adequately addressed. On the "mirror stage" of such environments, the constitution of specific kinds of distances between self and the digital surface, the "other," seems crucial for the exploration of physical and psychic confusion or disorganization of the senses. One way to investigate these boundaries, I think, is to challenge the biological organism or organic movement in relation to surface intensities and in the tactile meeting of surfaces.

Telematic Dreaming challenges our assumptions about the merger or connection between vision and touch, and my idea of "scanning" dancing, in fact, is precisely related to this phenomenal interface between movement (and movement copy) and digital video projection as a performative projection of another moving skin or tactile surface. My ideas for LBLM evolved from this thinking about deep contact between organic and nonorganic surfaces or projections. Before turning to this videosomatic research, let me conclude the Amsterdam workshop by pointing to a few aspects of Theodores's concepts.

A decisive issue in our thinking about technology and choreography is the question of commensurability. Theodores quotes Susan Kozel's prediction that "if technology is regarded as abstract, logical and mechanical and bodies are seen as organic matter only, then the two will be mutually hostile. But if technology and bodies are seen additionally in terms of flows of energy or intensity or as fluid dynamics, then there is ground for collaboration." If, indeed, the technology in our performance experiments were driven by the experience of the body itself, then the knowledge of the body can inform ways of connecting with nonphenomenological structures in digital art, or it can influence visual or sonic digital environments in such a way that they transmit information sensually or heighten the physicality experienced in the electronic interface, as is the case in David Rokeby's "very nervous systems" (interactive sound installations), where the spatial sound events triggered by persons moving inside the interface can create a phantasmagoric aura and affect their acoustic behavior both inside the space and after leaving it. Theodores posits that the notion of "disembodiment" in technological immersion is resisted here for its perpetuation of the transcendent metaphysics of mind-space over body intelligence. Indeed, the thinking and sensing body empowered by technology offers up, in reverse, visceral languages of bones, organs, fluids, and even of seeing inside a movement. This would lead us, in choreographic terms, to the notion of "impossible anatomies," or the "impossible body," as I suggested earlier in reference to Cunningham's experiments with LifeForms. Zapp, Dubois, and Schiphorst would add that new systems of behavior can be informed by the absent presence of electronic bodies in telematic media, while unstable/weightless bodies or the animated models of LifeForms both hint at giving more materiality to "spaces in-between," to nonsolid or vanished presences, to unlikely gestures (for trained movement behavior), and to possibilities of movements as yet unseen, which Schiphorst joyfully compares to the "shock of freedom."

Furthermore, technology as a compositional tool, as opposed to its recording and archival functions, assumes as a starting point such crossovers to an impossible body aesthetic. Theodores is correct in reminding us that the "thrill of the unnatural is reaffirmed by technology in much the same way that aesthetic pleasure was derived originally from classical ballet in terms of virtuoso technique and 'unnatural' acts. The technologically possible anti-gravitational body, the multi-layered, extended, enlarged, the vanishing, the inside-out bodies of the virtual and the immersed invite us to a new definition of artifice, of the extra-ordinary, and thus to new desires for the performing body."

This idea of the unnatural, desiring body offers a fascinating, erotic, and deeply politicized ground for performance/media practice, since it also reminds us of a whole range of contemporary performance-art experiments that have focused on the production of the "other," the foreign, the abnormal and dysfunctional, the diseased, and the abject body. As a political site, the body thus already performs a potentially dysfunctional role vis-à-vis technological abstraction and recuperation/dispersion. Theodores claims that the concept of "instantaneity" needs to be carefully examined as an effect of technology's affording us access to instant transactions, transformations, and morphings. Technological composition or technography, in this sense, "can disappear before it has ever fully appeared," raising the issue of both a "radical forgetting and a radical remembering as perhaps two emerging ideologies of technography." Linking this to my critical description of Vandekeybus's hyperdance, I feel that the notion of instantaneity forces us to reflect on the contemporary experience of saturation and image/data transmission speed; if all art is speeding up, the very speed and intensity of technological advances are in themselves an informing agent of choreography, which also implies that the notion of an "aura" of the instantaneous loses its mystique. We would simply have to relearn how to operate or function without the familiar integrity of an older physics of space, time, and mass. According to the new parameters of digitally enhanced performance, compositional strategies, hierarchical structures, or linear movement/narrative are replaced by templates of varying intensities, screen spaces, and lattice structures. In such noncentric spaces there is no stable point of view, and body forms and movement forms can be transformed and "disappeared" in many unforeseeable ways. In new performance research, such technological and bodily contingencies need to be tested in order to create physical platforms or stages on which such work can be exchanged with audiences.

Regrettably, there are no black, Latino American, or Asian dancers/choreographers at the SNDO workshop who might have expressed their reservations about disappearing bodies, and no one addresses "radical dismembering" or "remembering" from the point of view of queer or camp performance and its specific investment in denaturing the "natural," normalizing conventions of gender and identity. Indeed, perhaps with the exception of Steggell's pseudonymous "M@ggie," practically all the dancers present experiment with technology while remaining essentially invested in somatic and organic notions of the body's interior, which distinguishes them from body camp's emphatic recourse to surfaces, textiles, fabrics, and deviant excess. No one mentions Stelarc's horrific and grotesque body, although his prosthetic performances are deeply preoccupied with obsolescence and morbidity. Anyone who has heard Stelarc's guttural laughter during his explanations of "fractal flesh" or the outmoded "distraught body" will inevitably be reminded of the grotesque. But it is not a comforting reminder, since he stages the very inappropriate, abhorred, and disunified body that all ballet and modern-dance traditions—supporting the humanist ideology of the singular, autonomous, classical body—have denied. As an example of the denial of the subcultural "lower instincts," outrageously demonstrated in the gay community's camp toying with venerated icons, it is rather ironic to learn from New York's *Village Voice* (Michael Musto's gossip column) that Martha Graham's estate had sent the owners of the downtown club Mother a letter demanding that they cease and desist from unlawful use of the name "Martha" for their regular Martha dance revues. The masquerades in clubland, of course, may change as quickly as Calvin Klein's latest fashion models, and "radical forgetting" is a function of the market-driven profitability of newer excesses in the arousal of desire. The disconcerting side of the mainstreaming of camp's drag aesthetic is the further denial and dislocation of the real psychic and social anxieties written into the male-as-female crying games and, more ambiguously and sadistically, into the excessive male-as-male and female-as-female masquerades. As I implied earlier in my reference to Meg Stuart's *No One Is Watching*, there is a limit to parody and the "othering" of the grotesque. When do we turn away from the screen? When does the laughter stop?

If unnatural acts and impossible bodies have become the playing field of technography, or if bodies-without-organs are already playing games as electronic avatars in Internet relay chat rooms or dance floors, then Steggell's "M@ggie" is perhaps an interesting test of sending up a real cliché (Steggell's women dancers are dressed as riot grrrls/cleaning maids equipped with toilet plungers) into the Net, cleaning up the drainage system of multiuser simulation environments. Watching the riot grrrls dance their "love bytes" (which reminded me of the "organically-techno-pagan funk" shows of the band D'Cückoo), I am amazed at their vivacious playfulness with the digital eye of the camera, yet I also sensed a barely disguised uncertainty about their own artistic process and the unknown, physically absent, interactive audience in cyberspace. When feedback set in, the dance continues to be directed at the digital eye and their own superimposed video projections on the screen. In the real space they are caught between the eye and the screen, measuring the distance.

Reflecting on the experience, I feel positively surprised by the new willingness among dance artists to organize studios or create independent collaborations among performers, musicians, engineers, and computer artists in order to work in parallel frames (performance rehearsal and computer/Internet platforms). Until very recently many dancers and actors I know were reticent and suspicious. But we are only at the beginning of a process of subversion that will reverse the software multimedia "applications" and bring our own performance knowledge to bear on the machinery and codes that act according to their programmed logic. "Liveliness" or human-movement creativity can't be programmed in terms of numbers, nor can we physically dance like "life forms." However, we can perhaps stage the processes of incorporation and our unconscious resistance to or desire for different, unfamiliar kinds of "liveliness." I am particularly interested in the question of the "liveliness" of the technologically dominated/informed interfaces between human organisms and intelligent machines, for I find it equally crucial to investigate the politics of computational possibilities in our cultural environments now that there is a growing fascination with cyberspace and VR not only in the commercial industries that sell information and market the software but also among the writers and critics who speculate on the progressive aspects of "being digital."

LBLM was conceptually planned as an intensive laboratory for artists from different fields to test the feasibility of cyborg parameters for creative processes.[6] Together with my collaborator, choreographer/dancer Imma Sarries-Zgonc, I prepared to ground our potential encounters with technomedia and digital processes in the physical work with/through our bodies and sensory experiences, and one of the most fundamental aspects of this grounding was the quality of the space we would construct or occupy.

Workshop Description

The performance/multimedia workshop LBLM is offered to provide a laboratory for the organic integration of performance and digital arts, and for the development of new interdisciplinary methods of composition. The workshop is open to students/ artists of every age and every artistic/technical background or experience. Required is a commitment to intensive work and experimentation and to the shared process of intermedia research, composition, and theoretical reflection. We are particularly interested in collaborations between dancers, performance and visual artists, actors, musicians, videomakers, computer engineers, and designers.

"Lively Bodies–Lively Machines" presents a nine-day intensive workshop that is conceptually based on autobiographical stories, science fiction, and fantasies/projections of physical bodies and virtual realities. As a brief introduction, we will examine Marie-Françoise Plissart's photo-scenario Droit de regards, *William Gibson's* Neuromancer, *Margaret Morse's essay "What Do Cyborgs Eat? Oral Logic in an Information Society," Chris Marker's film-novel* La Jetée, *Bill T. Jones's* Still/Here, *as well as other examples of choreographers working with film/ video in order to create a theoretical framework for our focus on "incorporations."*

Our day and evening rehearsals will explore the relationships between performance/writing and photography/film, image-time and movement-time, music and movement, the grain of the voice and the grain of the body's image, analog and digital processes, samplings and conversions, as well as between movements of the body, the unconscious, and the erotic fantasies of "consensual hallucination" (as they are depicted in cyberpunk). The workshop is based not on a theater or dance technique but entirely on the imagination and on our physical-mental practice, self-awareness, movement, and creativity. Our process will explore the limits of technology and gender in our fictions of identity and memory.

We will also work with onscreen/offscreen reversals and with the double-space of stage/screen, exploring digitally enhanced performance spaces. All participants will be invited to work compositionally/choreographically as well as with camera, camera movement, electronic sampling, mixing and editing techniques, and possible computer interfaces. PC and Mac software and multimedia applications will be tested to investigate new electronic interferences with physical space-time. The workshop is open to anybody interested in contemporary cultural paranoias about borders and border crossings.

The Process

Fortunately, we discover already on our first day that the Chichester Institute's quiet campus environment and the large dance studio we are given allows us to concentrate and focus our energies in a single communal space that we are able to modify and transform over the course of the workshop. The decision to stay inside the dance studio and work on and off the dance floor becomes crucial for our sensory experience of collaborative work during the physical training, contact improvisations, and scene rehearsals (morning and afternoon), as well as during the afternoon and evening projects that evolve in and around the multimedia workstations we gradually set up in the studio (video-editing deck, video-mixing board, video projectors, cameras, sound-recording deck, three Macintosh stations, scanner, lighting and sound-mixing board, etc.). The dance studio, which functions as a black box that is highly flexible and accommodating, also gives us a sense of intimacy and control over our space, permitting the air and natural light to stream through it yet also, within seconds, darkening and transforming the space into a film/sound stage or recording studio. It is a logical step for the group to become so comfortable that some of us could have stayed overnight; it is our creative space and our dressing room, our recording suite, cinema, and computer center. We do our brainstorming here, and we laugh as we dance to Tim's jungle music mix.

The group, consisting of nineteen participants—Rachel Arnold, Tim Charles, Tessa Elliott, Melanie Fowke, Jools Gilson-Ellis, Jim Grover, Guy J. Hilton, Joel R. Johnson, Adèle Levi, Karen MacBride, Joumana Mourad, Beth Partridge, Robyn Proctor, Justine Reeves, Dominique Rivoal, Olivia Stevens, Chris van den Bosch, Imma Sarries-Zgonc, and myself—is graciously treated by the institute's dance studio and media staff, while also being observed by an independent filmmaker and her crew there to document the workshop. Such documentation of performance/digital art research cannot be valued too highly; most of us work with cameras and recording devices anyhow, yet such concentrated group work has a temporal dimension and an unpredictability that sometimes makes it difficult to monitor our recording cameras, and it is perhaps more interesting to let observers interact with our environment and find their own perspectives on the work we create.

After a few days, the daily ritual of our early-morning training and physical work on the dance floor has created a sense of rhythm and cohesiveness, and the creative ideas that emerge over time are attributable, to a large extent, to the energy that is generated here, ebbing and flowing through the group. I cannot overemphasize the spirit of this energy, because the actual sharing of ideas and inspiration, experience, and practical technical knowledge could not have been structured into a rehearsal plan or imposed by the project directors. On the contrary, I feel we are able to allow for an open structure that evolves naturally, so to speak, according to the flow of energy and motivation. Participants choose to follow an idea or work together on specific projects, regardless of whether they involve choreography, video shoots and editing, sound recording, image grabbing and processing on the Macs, hooking a hoop dress to a car battery, or building a triangular tent on wheels. Each of us individually wants to contribute to this process of exploration and development, and yet the personal input is always channeled into the larger group and the shared moments of discovery. Many of the individual "scenes" we work on, in fact, require collaboration both on the artistic/ creative and the technical production levels, and since most of us come from different backgrounds (some arrive with either a very basic or no acquaintance with cameras, editing facilities, computers, and software), it becomes necessary to share and exchange what we know or don't know, and to support each other.

What Do Cyborgs Eat?

Food and nutrition are important during such intensive, nonstop work, and the dance studio itself becomes a little more cluttered as we drag more things into it, try out more costumes and machines, bring more laptops, cables, and water bottles. Warming up for a technomedia-performance workshop in a studio filled with machines raises questions we might not be prepared to answer. In a very fundamental and concrete sense, our bodies and physical senses may not be completely compatible with the emerging world of electronic multimedia. We stumble over the clutter of cables; some input/output connections malfunction and things break down or unwanted results show up suddenly. Our training and artistic process need to be rethought if we aim at integrating the live arts with such concepts as interactivity, virtual realities, sampling and digital processing as they exist in the culture of computer technologies.

LBLM represents an attempt to create such a laboratory for interdisciplinary synergies among artists of all ages and backgrounds who profess a commitment to shared explorations. As in any science lab, our trial-and-error experiments lead us in different, sometimes unexpected directions, but they combine to open up a new perceptual structure for our creativity. Many of us are perhaps more familiar with the synergies of dance, theater, and film production, the creation of music in concerts, or with synthesizer keyboards. We may have less experience constructing a studio that can also be transformed into virtual environments or link our more familiar analog world to the digital "space." I don't think I know all the implications of linking our bodies to cyberspace, but our dance studio provides us with a wide range of advanced technical equipment, and we adapt them to our needs. Placing (shifting around) these machines in the dance studio enables us to develop our own work rhythms and to build an unusual and rather sensual environment in which daily physical practice—generally intended as physical and mental preparation for such performance media as dance, theater, music— is transformed into something else.

This other side—our experimentation with cameras, camera movement, screen projections, closed circuits, scanners, electronic sampling, mixing and image-processing techniques, and computer interfaces— creates challenges to our understanding not merely of the functioning of the new hardware and software but of our acceptance of machines that are perhaps becoming more lively and competent, more flexible and attractive, than our fantasies about computers had envisioned. The intelligent machines, then, are our partners; we learn to cope with their idiosyncrasies. We still stumble over cables, the connections malfunction again, and we grow impatient with the stubborn machines. We laugh a lot, too, or, rather, we sensibly adjust to the logic of cables (knowing the right adapters and compatibles), information processing, and the night-life at the terminals.

On the other hand, our workshop group becomes aware of several meanings of "interface" and of the incorporation of multimedia computers into the artistic process. Image-making attains a certain "screen" life that cannot be readily translated back into the phenomenal realm of objects and human sensations, movements, and actions that we used to know in the corporeal theater of consciousness. "Electronic presences," like our video ghosts, seemingly begin to exist in real space, and our individual physical actions are no longer needed, for example, if we wanted to stage the postproduction. You could come and look at the files we saved for you, installed in a computer or on the Net. (Joel and Guy are busy feeding some of our findings into the web site arranged for the Split Screen Festival.)

After a few days it dawns on us that we are meant to show our workshop "results" to the public audience that will attend the Split Screen Festival. We have to decide whether we should build an installation, a virtual environment, or whether we should perform in the flesh. Most of us want to remain present and perform, so the second week of the workshop includes "technical rehearsals" for a kind of workshop production

based upon a collage of various scenes and images we are creating. The **135** main leitmotif for us is the idea of movement: as long as we are movers and create with our physical languages of the body, we continue to want to move through the mediascape we construct around us.

Our proposition is to explore the continuum of human-machine interfaces in a live performance that tries to raise a few small questions about the insecurity of cyborgs, which lack an organic memory or sense of self, have trouble eating the right stuff, and whose erotic fantasies are all mixed up. The metaphor of eating introduces orality and a whole "tropology" of food, communion, passages, orifices, permeable boundaries, tactile surfaces, skins, membranes, viscera, deep cavities, dark spaces, the inside body, biopsy, endoscopy, colonoscopy, the ill/medicalized and anorexic body, the phantasmic body, the sexual body, and memory. We are becoming very lively in our performance experiments, and ideas begin to move toward and beyond the natural/unnatural divide. And, yet, perhaps at some point we are slowly forgetting how to dance, for I notice many of us huddled around the Macs in the dark, faces illuminated by screen light; then I realize we are just continuing to choreograph and edit our own images. We donate some images to the frame-grabbing computer, we store our images, and then we manipulate them in the "Photoshop" or the "Director" programs. The programs are not as flexible as we would like.

We are also interested in the experience of virtual spaces and the peculiar fascination with fabricated images and virtual connectedness (interactivity) that is being promoted in the technoculture. Warming up to a new kind of dance, therefore, means examining the images of the (cyborg) body with which we pretend to connect with others. Above all, each of the participants in the workshop has been willing to explore and exchange personal responses to this question of *connectedness*, which is ultimately a political question about our care and love for bodies—not screens—we can touch.

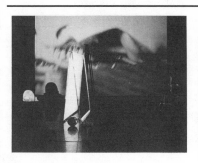 

LBLM, collaborative performance at Split Screen Festival, Chichester, England, 1996. Photo: J. Birringer.

IMPOSSIBLE ANATOMIES

The Performance/Postproduction of LBLM

As we prepare to invite an audience to visit our studio, I propose a score to the group consisting of the various scenes or images that have been developed. After the first run-through of this collage, some participants feel that the sequencing could have been different. They are right. We discuss issues of a/synchrony, linear movement, nonlinear narrative, juxtaposition, montage, flow, and time. We are not only enmeshed in a choreographic and compositional debate; we also trust the strength of our scenes as much as one can after only a short period of experimentation and rehearsal. We are rehearsing with quite a few scenes that are not edited yet or even completed; working in an open-ended composition.

While Imma is already programming the computer for the lighting design, Tim is needed by almost everyone to help out with sound recording and musical sampling. Joel is working on his complex architectural sci-fi scenario of the "Church of Artificial Intelligence Version 2.0," and Jim seems to have lost some of his video footage at the editing deck. Justine feels sick as a result of a cold, and Beth's car has broken down, preventing her from rehearsing for two days. Melanie, who has to leave a day early, is busy producing "shareware" for others. Jools is writing and inventing scenarios incessantly, contributing her great poetic gift and her jubilant laughter to the group. Karen, Joumana, and Adele are plotting some surprises, and during the last few days Adele is seen taking measurements to determine the feasibility of flying through the projection of her film on a bungee rope. Tim has become the resident composer, while Rachel, Chris, and Robyn seem to enjoy spending endless hours redesigning their bodies in the Mac's Photoshop. Tessa and Dominique are working on a complex choreographic interface with a program code Tessa has written. Guy is helping everyone while rehearsing a scene with a little robot. Olivia is shooting photography and writing/recording a cyberpoem.

As the scenes gradually take shape, we realize that the production will become a theatrical event, involving a certain duration and evolution over time, which excludes other parameters of experience or interaction. Toward the end of the rehearsals, I also become intensely aware of the unusual amount of video/computer projections we will be using, and it seems as if we don't have the time to reflect and analyze the evolution of this focus on screen projection (of various types, angles, shapes; on screens, walls, and bodies). The zoning and distancing of the screen surfaces have not been decided since we are too busy with other things.

Perhaps we need to reflect on this immersion in real-time screen projection. In fact, video projections tend to create flat, cinematic surface spaces; they don't really envelop as much as they build (retrogressively) two-dimensional surfaces of light. Since they increase image scale dramatically (compared to video or computer monitors), they tend to be interpreted, in the evolving video-art practices, as "installations," with an aesthetic dimension related to painting (still images), photography (billboards), cinema (motion-picture projection), and sculpture (projection environments).

On the other hand, their theatrical emplacement in a dance space creates another important dimension that reflects on the crucial aspect of video, namely, its manipulation of time and duration (through the mixing of real time/nonreal time, slow motion, freeze-frame, repetition, fragmentation/recombination, etc.). In many contemporary video-projection works, the depictions of movements, light, or color in space can create a sculptural or architectural experience, and often such work is non-narrative. For us it seems more important to connect the projection to the ideas we developed in the contact improvisations and dance rehearsals, and these ideas tend to be narrative.

The performance could be justly criticized for lapsing back into a more conventional theatrical parameter, while the screen projections themselves could be understood in a different light. Since we are beginning to move them inside/alongside the movement choreography, they tend to hide, sculpt, or silhouette the human figure dancing in their illumination, while emitting the particular quality of pixilated textures that, in huge close-ups, can blur and dissolve fixed-image configurations so that the light projection in real space begins to hover and float like sound movement or vibrations. These vibrations and light pulses provide access to the video projections in a manner of a physiopsychological interface, a tactile quality of translucency that turns opaque when touching the body of a dancer. The vibrating light is part of the telling, the recapturing of the images with the physical bodies that serve as the support, receptacle, envelope, the repelling and shifting skin of unstable images.

On the other hand, we base our exploration on movement, and although some of the movement motivations in our group are narrative, others are not. The performance primarily reflects our physical process and our group's careful connection to technological media, derived from a specific effort to understand why we use machines and how we experience our lives in relationship or interaction with technological partners. We are particularly interested in the gestures of our machines, yet one of our early meditations was based on Margaret Morse's essay "What Do Cyborgs Eat?"—and almost everyone in the group had an individual response motivated by her question and her concern about the "oral logic" of incorporation/excorporation, body and food loathing, repudiation, denial, disavowal, identification, immersion, and the dialectic of inside and outside. We observe ourselves performing organic, physical work and grow more intensely aware of our skin, of membranes, of fantasies/fears of transitions, transmissions, fluids. We become interested in exploring our bodies' reactions to the demands made by an electronic culture seemingly obsessed with new virtual realities and technical images or substitutes for the human organism. We have a disturbing discussion one morning about prostheses, abandoned body parts, surgery, decomposition, dying. We remember that we are living and dying. We remember love and erotic obsession, the ghosts of our lovers coming back to haunt us.

Perhaps our performance of LBLM does not have a clear narrative leitmotif after all, being a latticework. We connect the scenes in a manner involving association and intensification, retracing our steps and our image compositions as they evolved over time, placing the projection into the three-dimensional architecture of our physical "real life" (RL) space. The unspoken problem, alluded to in many of the screen projections, is the haunting presence of a lost connection, or the felt disparity between organic and virtual bodies. We cannot live in disembodied virtual space, and we are foolish not to acknowledge the cartoon world of our computer animations. What, then, is the attraction of virtual worlds, and why have we become so obsessed with interactivity, with our specters and the substituted/recorded images we love to manipulate on the computer screen? Have we become attuned to the "redesigning" of our "increasingly obsolete bodies"—or, as the Australian artist Stelarc calls them in his own performance efforts to reconfigure the body in the electronic realm of images, "phantom bodies"?

 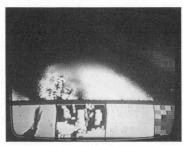 

From Analog to Digital Choreography

LBLM is only the first phase of an ongoing search to answer or locate some of the questions that will challenge us as we develop further contexts of movement-connection to the computer codes. In the work we created at the Split Screen Festival, the movement ideas were all generated from our personal motivation and desire. None of us changed the primary reliance on the weight and gravity of our physical bodies and emotions, although we posed the screen projections as "screens" for the new parameter of questions about virtual movement or movement extended into virtual space. I wish to conclude this chapter by describing the one experiment we made in exploring this extrusion of awareness to the ungraspable, immaterial process of random code-switching within the computer program. The experiment was initiated and carried out by Tessa, Dominique, and Imma, and I have great respect for Tessa's research and programming, which she shared with us. Since we are only just confronting a choreographic, conceptual, and aesthetic challenge, I want to describe the experiment as concretely as I can. It concerned one of the scenes in LBLM (Choreographing Memory, scene 11) that was virtually unintelligible (in terms of its construction) and also largely invisible, since the dance studio was completely dark at that point in the performance, and the red, yellow, and white pixels projected on Tessa's sculptural wire-fence screen were not easy to decipher. The compositional image tended to be very clear on the small computer screen, but it blurred as a result of the enlarged scale of the projection.

Wanting to work toward a stronger, more challenging interconnection of the analog and the digital, we shifted our choreographic experimentation closer to the conceptual and physical/digital possibilities *in* the interface, and thus to the conceptual level of VR and cyberspace. This concerned the relations between two types of "movement" and two kinds of "space" (and what the movements project as movement and as

LBLM, collaborative performance at Split Screen Festival, Chichester, England, 1996. Photo: J. Birringer.

projected image within the screen space). Tessa's work with Dominique and Imma set up this conceptual challenge.

According to this configuration, there was a live performer, a digital camera, a Mac connected to a video beam and the projection (onto screen or other structure), and a special software program. Tessa had written the code for this program and had stored information on files (sound sources and what she calls "image-objects" from the camera's recording; these consist of other image sources that can show up in the field at the lower level of the screen composition created by the Mac/program). Her program permitted the manipulation and digital processing of the recorded movements (grabbed from Imma's performance), which was accomplished through editing of an animation film sequence. The gestures or movement-images recorded with the digital camera were recomposed, reconstituted, and stored. The stored image sequences/samples could be "cleaned up" via Photoshop. The program's framework then installed an interface, linked through code that responded to the closed-circuit digital camera.

In the live performance situation, this special camera responded to motion in space and to light (or color). Tessa proposed using darkness in the scene, and Dominique performed her dance illuminated only by a flashlight, which she held in her hands, directed at her body surfaces. As she pointed the light at her body, she danced with/the light. The camera picked up motion and light, and interfaced with the program, which was done in such a way that the computer reacted randomly and spontaneously to the motion/light capture and triggered the recorded/stored memory (i.e., the sound samples, image samples, and animated

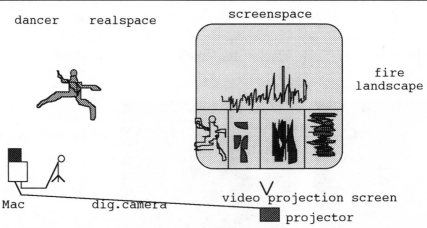

Computer drawing of the interactive configuration.

movies within the framework that was created—in this case a landscape
of algorithmically generated fiery flames). The "framework" was composed of regions, and the regions became active through movement. The
largest region appeared as a black landscape into which the fire moved;
this movement of the fire was a composite, unpredictable, semiabstract,
fragile image-motion.

You therefore saw not a closed-circuit video projection but an actual
interactive video–computer–sound interface. The human dancer's motion in real (physical) space triggered the "memories" encoded in the
computer, in the virtual space (e.g., cowbell sound, clock-ticking sound,
electronic sound landscapes, flame images, body images, fragments of
recorded/animated materials—all of this creating a painting-collage-
in-motion). These memories or severed tokens slowly emerged on the
screen projection—phantasmagorically, eerily, unpredictably—before
dissolving again. And you didn't know what would emerge or how precisely the dancer's motion triggered a particular shape, sound, color.
Thus, one could say the physical motion composed the color-field onscreen. In other words, if you produced and programmed the motion
paths in the whole parameter, and then collaborated with a dancer,
the resulting dance would be a new composite (chance event); it would
be unfolding, immediate, and yet would interlink present/presence and
storage (past/memory) in a way that appeared to well up as if from the
unconscious, from someplace other than the self, in some indeterminate
and unforeseeable way.

As an electronic interface, this configuration opened up a new dimension of dance (the parallel dance on screen) that left behind physical
motor-muscle memory in choreography, as we know it, and the analog
projection-relation. Or, rather, the dance/choreography entered dialectically into a new parameter, co-generated with the computer and the
computer-reactions and sensings of the motion-capture camera eye. The
dancer in real space *had* her own movement motivation or choreography,
and she could experience it kinesthetically, but this movement (caught
by the digital camera eye) "choreographed," so to speak, the memory of
the recorded movement, sound, image sequences. Those virtual movements (from storage) appeared on the projection screen.

Tessa's objective in the interactive constellation was to achieve a
greater fluidity of the digital, to move the pixilated, stored digital-image
repertoire across the screen regions within the intermingling of the
framework–image space (fire landscape or other image). This implied
"moving" the animation or the stored images (memory) in a new way,
making images appear that could dance, making the image dance. When

I suggested to her that the real dancer in physical space can attain the full potential of human movement (a potentially infinite range), whereas the stored image movement was "fixed" (in the animation sequences) and thus limited, Tessa responded that this was not quite true since the virtual image had a certain "weight" to it, and therefore the virtual image that was triggered could move in different ways. Quick motions by the RL dancer could send an image swiftly across the screen space, whereas a slower motion deanimated the screen movement and almost immobilized it. I realized that I needed to familiarize myself with the habits of algorithms. To speak of the weight of an image is to adapt dance language to electronic movement; indeed, there may be many possible associations between Laban-inspired movement grammars and the geometries of algorithms. But how do we "read" or perceive the virtual movement (the projected images) if we look at the interface from an aesthetic point of view and not a technical one? How do we respond kinesthetically to the rhythm of images and the emotional texture of flames, the fires of consumption?

How does the RL dancer "choreograph" memory when the dancer has no conscious or understandable influence or impact (based on movement knowledge) on the stored image movement? Is the interactive relationship determined by the program? To what extent is the computer program constituting a (pre)programmed randomness, and how are to we analyze such purely random modes of selection (as in chance events, for example, in John Cage's philosophy of music as weather)? In other words, what is the meaningfulness and effect of this *interactivity between dancer and memory storage?* Is this a relation of strict choreography (shaped and constructed movement choreography) to programmed randomness? Or is the dancer in RL improvising, responding, moving without pattern or choreography, making arbitrary choices (like the user in computer/media installations who pushes buttons and clicks the mouse)? Are there differences or similarities in the user randomness and the pre-programmed randomness of the stored motion-path functions? How interactive is the interface if human choice or the creative motivation (choreography) of the dancer (user) is another means of triggering/ achieving random juxtapositions or superpositions (between RL stage/ space and screen space)? Why is this fluidity of randomness so valuable or interesting? Why is it desirable to move with/along/against the memory in the program? For Tessa, clearly, the performance was triangular, involving the actual dance, the predetermined virtual forms, and the re-configuring, interactive dance. Are the digital interfaces that make us look at the unpredictable and perhaps unknowable image movement occurring onscreen a retreat/escape from constructed meaning in choreography, or is it enriching, adding a depth or dimension that the real dance alone cannot achieve? Can we call the conjunction of the three planes of choreography a doubling, not in the sense of mirroring the live dancer but constructing new composite asynchronies?

In visual terms, the screen movement appears like an abstract expressionist field, yet within this field gestural "bodies" or bodily gestures can emerge. How does the RL dancer's physical movement relate to (and signify in itself) the screen imagery? Is there a concrete-abstract relationship, a dominance of abstract form over content, a correspondence between figural movement and abstract image movement, or do we read the screen movement in figural terms if we assume that the shapes we see are body shapes? Is the interactivity that is taking place creating the illusion of participation/collaboration between real dancer and virtual body/image, or is this an illusion that essentially boils down to motion, motion selecting *from a set of predetermined choices?* What is this "set" and why does it appear as if we don't know the set and see the images flash up as mysterious, connected on a deeper level of association, or in a specific relationship that is dependent on the *quality of the movement in RL?* Does the RL dancer's movement choreography overdetermine the way we "read" the abstract image field? Do we tend to read a narrative into the projected space/screen space, since we are also reminded of the cinematic framework and larger context of the performance? Does the fire, along with the dancer's skin, evoke a region of erogenous zones on fire, a burning delight, a powerful, incandescent, female all-consuming desire that threatens stable, clear, fixed boundaries?

The relationship among the women in this experiment creates a complex scenario, for in rehearsal we ask both Imma and Dominique to create movement derived from specific personal memories, and the internal emotional subtexts are not exchanged but respected as separate. What we do not know is how Dominique is watching or feeling the screen *and dancing with the screen movements* sampled and reconstructed from Imma's body. What is the skin/membrane of desire and how do we interject our shattered and reassembled ghosts? How is the sound (triggered from the computer memory) impacting or accompanying the live dance and the virtual-image movement and what "space" is created by the sound events? If the sound creates an ambient environment, are we regressively wishing to be immersed, fantasizing a locomotion that remembers infancy, or are we living out other complex fantasies in the landscapes of flames? Do specific sonic samples trigger specific memory associations in the acoustic chamber that heightens our tactile relations?

There are many unresolved issues, but I think the scene was created on a level of technological experimentation that succeeded in constructing the interface effectively, even if we did not find the time to analyze all the implications of the interactivity we had set in motion. I leave these questions intact since they may not be easily resolvable. Their analysis will lead us to the next level of our work and to a deeper engagement with the quality and emotional or spiritual resonance of *fluidity* that is intimated by Tessa's rich and intensely associative parameters for the dance among three women and a computer code. There is a political dimension in the experiment that underlies the choreography as well as the poems Jools wrote for the performance of LBLM, namely, the intricate connection between fluidity and cultural assumptions about femininity and sexuality. We suspected an obvious homoerotic economy of looking and moving/passing between the live dance and the imagined dance of the screen images, but the identifications of analogy, the real consonances between the live female body and the scanned female body, occurred in the movement relationship established among them and inside each of them. These consonances evoked a vertiginous memory of shared bodily space not bounded by social rules and norms but smeared, splayed out, and intensified by different pleasures. Performance—dancing with and across patterns—is one avenue to contest rigid or aggressively masculine formulations of virtual technology handed down to us. The emergence of bodily intelligence and tactile pleasure helps us to unravel the grids and pixilated monotonies of the computer's inscriptive power and its systems of violence.

FIVE

PERFORMANCE/ VIDEO ART

On the Border

Although I will here attempt to think through the history of video and speculate on the roles it might play in the future, my present understanding of video-making is such a complicated mixture of crossover experiences that I hardly know where to start. In the worldwide context of video's economic and technological development (the production and sale of domestic VCRs, tapes, and hand-held cameras; the constant upgrading of recording and editing equipment) as an electronic medium operating across all commercial, public, and private domains, I can't separate my interest in the new aesthetic experience of "video art" from the cultural and social applications I infer from the medium's highly flexible and multiple identities. I would even argue that video as a creative medium is not "medium-specific" but always and inevitably interdisciplinary, a production mode that interfaces with all image and sound media—especially film and broadcast television—and communications systems, while gradually being assimilated into the widest range of institutional and domestic practices, and ultimately into the constructions of our collective memory/history.

We thus face the first theoretical paradox in the definition of a postmodern electronic medium that does not extend modern traditions, techniques, or genres in spite of its obvious relation to film and photography, nor does it respect the conceptions and cognitive orders upon which modernist categories of art/art objects were based. The video age is no longer an age of artworks, and we have been slow in recognizing that the lack of a theory of video art is an effect of the increasing effacement of the referent (the real) in our postindustrial culture of information-processing and sampling. An aesthetic theory of video art would have no object of study commensurate with the analytical and referential constructs of autonomy, authority, authorship, genre, style, and intellectual property through which subject/object boundaries of knowledge and representation were drawn in modern, literate culture.

Even if we could accurately trace the technological history of video over the past three decades, video-making in the current context of transnational multimedia transmissions cannot be adequately captured, documented, or explained in a single language since the information on video is always a process potentially intermingling a plurality of image/sound repertoires which can be infinitely reprocessed and re-sited. It is worth restating the complex relationship between video creation and its technology. The latter's technical range of image/sound manipulation, modification, and recomposition is almost limitless, while the materiality of video (invisible electro/magnetic charges on magnetic tape) is elusive. Video is literal and actual in its immediate recording of surfaces; its computerized control systems simultaneously permit distortions and synthetic effects. The video maker has no literal access to the medium, but the electronic editing process (postproduction) permits a multiplicity of interventions and manipulations of the video signal (computer-generated special effects). In spite of the technological interventions made possible by the electronic-processing system, video remains a "personal" medium since camera work, recording, and editing effects are within the total control of the video maker. The recording and editing process makes video creation an abstract, conceptual activity, and yet here we reach another paradoxical conclusion, namely, that the specificity of video as a creative expression is contradicted by its function as a medium designed for reproducibility.

Its technology can effectively reproduce and rework any given camera or VCR source, but it can also reproduce any particular systems of signification, styles, and modes of address of film and television and, in turn, can be appropriated by other tape media (music), performance media (dance, theater, music), and promotional, educational, and instructional industries. In today's televisual culture of ubiquitous and instantaneous information, video has emerged as the most paradigmatic operational venue for the exchange of images from medium to medium. As a mode of operation, video technology, with its implications for visual representation and image-making, thus performs a strategically crucial role in the transformation of the entire ecology of art and culture, and in the mediation of cultural experiences, values, and perceptions under the new paradigm of the communications revolution.

It is with respect to this social context of video that I propose to discuss several of its modes and artistic *sitings* not as an isolated genre of works but as conceptual operations and interventions into institutional structures or locales, which implies that I am less concerned with its technical and formal characteristics than with the ethos of its "borderness," its continual crossing of all kinds of cultural and political boundaries. I deliberately use the metaphor of the border in reference to video's intercultural variability and transferability as a dynamic practice that can traverse any site of cultural expression.

A Postmodern Pedagogy

Let me begin with an example of artistic creativity and critical thinking which places video both in relationship to popular culture and to the classroom. During a visit to Houston in 1989, Roberto Aparici presented a bilingual, visual lecture-demonstration of the research project "Reading Images and Mass-Media Productions" he directs at the Universidad Nacional de Educación a Distancia in Madrid. A professor of educational technologies and a video maker, Aparici has produced several textbooks and videotapes (including a series for Spanish television) which introduce a new pedagogy of mass-media literacy designed to teach educators how to instruct children in the reading and interpreting of images.[1] Aparici presented selections from a video entitled *La imagen* which demonstrated that just as children are taught to write at the same time they are taught to read, they can be taught to read images by making them. In one of the typical sequences of the tape, a whole class of Spanish fifth graders were shown going through the stages of scripting and producing a video after having learned how to use photography and the video camera. More important, the children were taught how to analyze the technical means of creating images (focus, distortion, cropping, color, composition, framing, lighting, camera angle, movement, sound, graphics, etc.) and their ideological functions in the enframing and staging of reality, or in the construction of temporal and visual narratives. In the process of deconstructing the impression of reality conveyed by television and advertising (but also by comics, newspaper photographs, photo-novellas, etc.), the young video makers learned to grasp the ways in which visual technologies can be used both for the promulgation of stereotypes and as a means of articulating their needs and experimenting with their understanding of reality.

While Aparici took the children's exposure to the mass media for granted (including some of the highly popular American TV series and soap operas that have completely saturated European programming), he directed their analytical attention to the constructedness of the images and to the connotations on the surface. Learning to "see through" the actual production and fabrication of meaning, the children were next encouraged to invent their own stories countering the stereotypic model and to perform the process of scripting, shooting, and editing them. The composition and creation of a collective video which brings together diverse stories drawn from the children's archives of personal and pop-cultural experience can thus perform a double function: they learn not only to examine critically the icons, clichés, and mythologies of mass-mediated everyday life but also to rediscover a sense of individual and original articulation of self and community. Although Aparici's notion of "originality" may evoke the memory of modernist aesthetics, it is here obviously not juxtaposed with mass culture but intersects with hetero-geneous cultural expressions and materials in a pedagogical sense. The project, on the whole, is aesthetic, political, and ethical in intent, func-tioning for the young video makers the way Brecht's "learning plays" were conceived as a praxis by which actors could learn how to judge and intervene in their historical situation. Remembering Brecht's search for a revolutionary theater praxis, I am also reminded of Walter Benjamin's historical critique of capitalism's increasingly universal commodifica-tion of visual experience and the image. Commenting on his own peda-gogical effort to contest and disrupt the consumption of surface mean-ings, Benjamin insisted upon the power of historical remembering as a motivation for present action, collectively and individually, advising us to "educate the image-creating medium within us to see dimensionally, stereoscopically, into the depths of the historical shade."[2]

In light of Benjamin's interest in surrealism and in cinema's poten-tial for generating the shock effect of dialectical images (as an effect of the montage of historical citations ripped out of their original context), which could, in turn, provoke a radical interpretation of the commodi-fied "dreamworld," it is tempting to think of video as our paradoxical, contemporary Medusa, an invisible machine with the infinite potential of rearranging, recontextualizing, and reconfiguring images and social documents for our allegorical reading. But whereas Benjamin still relied on the perception of a critical distance between image and its referent (the real), the postmodern electronic media leave no traces behind since they continually simulate and reduplicate citations as such. The dialec-tical tension between history and the image seems to have disappeared.

For Aparici the pedagogical struggle to be waged in the postmodern era takes place in the image sphere. From his Marxist European per-spective, influenced by the demystificatory political critique developed by the Frankfurt School, the shift in emphasis from speaking/writing (oral/recorded culture) to video/mass-media research implies a direct attempt to utilize audiovisual media for the reinvention of a critical praxis that can cope with the overbearing impact of a global "culture in-dustry"—the transnational merger of entertainment, information, and advertising technologies based on the American model.[3] Aparici's bilingual video lecture simultaneously translates and disrupts the ideological terms of the ongoing commodification of the image in a predominantly visual culture. His disruption is also aimed at the quotational vogue that seems to dominate the self-reflexive aesthetics of postmodernist art. If *La imagen* implies the universalizing tendencies of visual consumerism and the final incorporation of all aesthetic and artistic strategies into a vast media database available for recycling and recombination, it also points to the particular ways in which video can reposition subjective experience against the dominant parameters and channels of consumption. In its inherent relationship both to televised mass culture and to postmodern art's mass-cultural aesthetic of appropriation, video's self-representation unfolds in terms of the social and political questions that are confronted by video production itself.

"Vogue": The Madonna Model

It was one of the perplexing ironies of Aparici's lecture on the politics of the medium that he felt misunderstood when a young Asian-American high school student from Houston got up during the discussion period and presented a five-minute music video entitled "Vogue," that he had collectively created with his classmates. Unnerved by its excellent production qualities and its slick adaptation of the seductive surface of Madonna's latest promotional vehicle on MTV, Aparici saw the tape as an uncritical reproduction of a stereotypical pop-culture format that not only paraded its cult objects of desire but also reflected an entire visual and temporal organization, a discipline of cultural consumption which structures ideas, values, bodies, and lifestyle fashions.

At the same time, one could view the student's version of "Vogue" differently, and I want to comment on its symptomatic reference to the communication of visual culture and television/pop music stars as icons, in light of my subsequent examples of crosscurrent video art/performance. These examples, like "Vogue" (the original and the copy), also communicate the fundamental ambivalence of postmodern-art practices which pose as critiques of representation and media images but share the same space of public promotion (print media, television, the art market) with producers (such as Madonna) who have already demystified their own false consciousness through the obvious and cynical manipulation of poses, fantasies, fetishes. "Strike a pose, there's nothing to it," raps Madonna in one of her dance hits, mocking the gender conventions and image stereotypes of the woman as spectacle that she herself had flaunted in her previous incarnations. Her sold-out "Blind Ambition" tour, launched in Houston in April 1990, followed the international release of her "Vogue" music video and preceded the film (her gender-bending role of Breathless Mahoney in *Dick Tracy*) and triple-set release of albums/CDs with music from and/or inspired by the film. Since then much has been written about the self-promotional aspects of her concert tour, and especially about the choreography of her stage show, a retrospective of the evolution of the shifting and contradictory personae and fetishes she has embodied throughout the eighties. (More contradictions and cynical provocations would later show up in her behind-the-scenes film *Truth or Dare*, and yet another level of self-fetishization was reached with the publication of her book *Sex* in 1992.) Obviously "Vogue" promotes and markets a new stage in the ongoing "Madonna" production (from Lower East Side club kid to sexy virgin with bared navel, from material girl to lapsed Catholic, from femme fatale to devoted lover and businesswoman, and on to bisexual, soft-core porn star, pregnant mother, etc.), continuing her constantly changing, outrageous, and titillating role-playing on the border of sexual and moral taboos. But the colossal success and prodigious power of her multimedia performance are also a function of popular culture's ongoing integration with advertising and mass communication, and with the generalized exchange of images and commodities in a vast system of inner references. Madonna's floating self-images follow the accelerated rhythms of fashion/lifestyle changes (the voguish becomes outmoded and is then resurrected as high camp and parody, soon to be degraded as retro), as well as the temporal-programming flow of MTV itself, which shapes its endless repetitions into an ever-shifting mosaic of disparate, glamorous bits.

Until I saw her at the live concert in Houston, it had not occurred to me how pervasively her stage performance would be copied in the visual style of MTV. Together with the severe makeup and the Jean-Pierre Gaultier–designed costumes, her athletic dancing and lascivious posing foregrounded the rhetoric of the images. Early on in the concert she freely admitted—speaking in a deliberately fake accent—that she was going to lip-sync to the (canned) music. Each movement, each gesture, each pose became a prerecorded video scene replayed to the knowing audience in a ritualistic celebration of the power of the fetishistic image. She was live onstage but was reduced to a simulation of prerecorded images. The live simulation itself was duplicated: the computer-controlled double was beamed onto the large video screens that were suspended from the ceiling. Madonna's mimicry of Marilyn Monroe, Marlene Dietrich, or Greta Garbo was a continuous game of staged appearances, which was provocatively allied with the sexual and religious transgressions edited onto the gospel-inspired "Like a Prayer." (Fundamentalist viewers took the special effects of the video clip literally and pressured the soft-drink sponsor into withdrawing its worldwide Madonna TV commercial.) There is, of course, nothing real about the transgressions, except that the calculated publicity effect of the protest sold and absorbed the image of transgression, thus reproducing the essential model of promotional culture based not on unity and stability of meaning but on simultaneity and interchangeability.

As if mocking the vacuity of their content, Madonna's images always define themselves with reference to something else, to another image or fantasy that can be disavowed *and* used to reassert the actual power of image-making. The stylized artificiality of her stage performance neutralizes her physical presence as much as her music videos dematerialize her identity in an ongoing series of metamorphoses. The desirable identification she offers the viewer in "Vogue" is not with her but with the numerous poses she borrows from Hollywood stars. She is a clever and equally cynical disciple of Andy Warhol, and I await the intervention of another Valerie Solanas. In naming and copying her (female and male) sources, Madonna's self-parodic message proposes her own *video model of appropriation* itself, for her image track refers us simultaneously to the nostalgic aura of black-and-white Hollywood film and to the dance style of "voguing," a black and Latino gay-club phenomenon in which dancers imitate the gestures of movie stars and runway models. If we add the borrowed music and choreography (performed by black, Latino, and white dancers) to this list, the video in fact mediates a complex social relation between producer and spectator by suggesting, both naively and ironically, that all images are available to everyone.

This ambivalent unification of producer/spectator may be the paradoxical aspect of a new theory of video, since it suggests that the spectator-as-passive-voyeur—the normal position of the consumer—is here repositioned as appropriator and producer. However, this is precisely the proposition which I believe motivated Joseph Kahn, the young Houston student, to undertake his reshooting of "Vogue." He and his classmates did not literally copy the "Vogue" music video. Rather, they appropriated the soundtrack for their own lip-syncing experiment, resulting in an entirely new performance, which they scripted, designed, choreographed, and performed, with Kahn shooting and editing the visual track using a special lens filter that created a more grainy, photographic image. The result was highly ambivalent since the dance choreography in Kahn's "Vogue" seems to mirror the style and rapid editing of Madonna's video. It is the same image yet different since it is produced by the receivers and communicates a playful and self-conscious gesture of vandalism, which at the same time exposes the fetish character, the "cover up" of Madonna's modeling. His "Vogue" is a form of mimicry that does not attempt to reveal anything underneath or beyond the fetish, since the students know that there is nothing. If their appropriation is a form of reception, it is not a critique or an opposition to the Madonna model but a necessarily ambivalent and ghostly simulacrum that responds to the corporate power of Madonna's mass-mediated performance by showing how viewers can dislocate the border between sender/receiver and ironically control the "found images" they are supposed to merely consume. Appropriation cannot create resistance or change on the level of actual power relations, yet these students in a predominantly Asian and Latino neighborhood in Houston created a videotape that produces and reflects their knowledge of alienation and their mastery over the codes of the master, the mass-media industry which sells them a cynical video goddess "like a model."

Video and Its "Other"

If we look at the dominant role of television and music as mass cultural-entertainment media, their convergence (music video/MTV) reminds us that in its beginnings in the sixties video was not considered an art form but remained either excluded from the privileged system of high art or defined itself in opposition to the aesthetic canons of modernism. The genealogy of the medium, including early experiments with the conceptual, formal image transmission and the closed-circuit feedback loop, can only be understood if we recognize that the language, form, and function of video did not emerge independently from other object- or process-oriented art forms (visual art, film, dance, theater, and what came to be called "performance art"). Nor could video develop a "language" that was not already shadowed by its inevitable "other," the television screen and its omnipresence as an icon of mass culture. As with the interpenetration of pop art and mass culture, which initiated the final breakdown of high art and its historical avant-garde traditions, the U.S. and European movements of the sixties—Fluxus events, action events, happenings, performances—provided the context for the cross-currents of postmodernism which have emerged in direct relation to mass-media cultural forms and technologies.

Video (or "electronic television," as Nam June Paik called it) as a nonmaterial medium featured all the attributes that distinguished it from the autonomy of modernist work: it was dispersible, reproducible, ephemeral, theatrical, and interdisciplinary. But if the history of video is concurrent with the history of politicized postmodernism (i.e., the more recent history of new social and countercultural movements arising in the sixties), it also shares the unfulfilled promise of a radical transformation of art and society. The realization of its destiny (e.g., its gradual incorporation into the art institutions during the eighties or its frustrated and enfeebled relationship to broadcast television) returns us to the early attempts by Nam June Paik and Wolf Vostell to use the medium creatively against itself, against the institutions of art, and against commercial culture. Representing a first stage in the history of video, these early attempts did not focus on the immateriality of the medium but rather on the physical and iconic function of the TV monitor. Paik had studied music in Japan and Germany before meeting Stockhausen and Cage and experimenting with sound-tape collages and electronic music. He was known by his aggressive "action music" performances before he created his first exhibition, "Exposition of Music-Electronic Television," at the Galerie Parnasse in Wuppertal in 1963, in which he assembled twelve TV sets with altered scanning components and electronic signals. Each of the sets displayed a distorted image, and Paik's technical interferences created different kinds of white noise that appeared random and indeterminate. Much like his performances in the provocative Fluxus events of the early sixties (organized by George Maciunas, Allan Kaprow, Dick Higgins, George Brecht and influenced by John Cage and Marcel Duchamp), Paik's TV assemblages not only subverted the normal function of commercial television but suggested the technological constructibility of a kind of visual/optical music of the flickering image.

Compared to Vostell's "dé-coll/age" works (consisting of manipulated and partially demolished TV sets which he exhibited at New York's Smolin Gallery in 1963) and destructive action events (*TV Begräbnis,* a "funeral" happening during which he buried a demolished monitor wrapped in barbed wire), Paik's intimate knowledge of electronic technology led him to concentrate more on the abstract and conceptual potential of the image transmission and the physical, optical, and temporal architecture within which it is placed. The extraordinary body of work created by Paik since 1963—including electronic TV assemblages, videotapes, projections, performances, robots, closed-circuit installations, multimonitor installations—reflects the trajectory of video art from its subversive, dadaist beginnings, coupled with a Duchampian challenge to the status, value, and authenticity of the art object, to its gradually accepted versatility as a techno-aesthetic practice operating in a yet undetermined space between the established arts, popular culture, and social documentary.

Paik's video works are now exhibited in museums, galleries, and public sites all over the world; they have stimulated the many-faceted development of video and legitimized the so-called media arts. But they have also abandoned the radical premise of the Fluxus performances, which had contradicted the institutional power and logic of television as the common denominator for the congruency of culture, consumption, and ideology. The Fluxus events were not merely "concerts of everyday living," as the poet Dick Higgins once called them, nor did they identify life and commodity society as one in the manner in which Andy Warhol adopted and copied the logic of mass production. Rather, Vostell's idea of "dé-coll/age-aktionen, um die umgebung zu verändern" (dé-coll/age actions to change the social environment) was politically closer to Joseph Beuys's conception of "social sculptures" as dynamic processes, or transformations of (in)organic material and consciousness, *in order to* peel away the ideological surface of organized and structured everyday experiences, which are pre-mediated by a centralized power and determining force such as television.[4]

To invoke Warhol and Beuys in this context implies that a comprehensive analysis of the evolution of video art would have to differentiate between the social and historical conditions in Europe, the United States, and other cultures that do not share the same economies of perception or political avant-garde trajectories. Contrary to all theories of transnational mass culture, individual works often betray highly differentiated and gender-specific relations to the other media and the homogenizing pressures of commodity culture. They also reformulate a logic of self-expression, of identity (beyond the question of national or ethnic identity), made possible by art but here critically endangered, in a political sense, by the very video technology which tends to dissolve identity, physical presence, time, place, continuity, history, and so on, in the flow of electrons. Video art redraws the boundaries of what we mean by identity and dissolution since it is not a perpetual program (TV) but must always rebuild new temporal and spatial relations of production.

Double Performance

The realization of these relations of production has direct implications for the separation and/or inclusion of the viewers. In this sense the history of early video can be said to overlap with the performance art and dance experiments of the sixties and seventies, especially with their participatory ideals and their overriding emphasis on the physical body, on real-life presence in real time, and on the breakup of theatrical illusion. Carolee Schneemann, commenting on her *Meat Joy* performance in 1964, explained that the active physicality of her body could reintroduce smell, taste, and touch to art and "at the same time transform and integrate any action or gesture of performers and audience: an enlarged 'collage,' to break up solid forms, frames, fixed conventions or comprehensible planes, the proscenium stage and the separation of audience and performer." [5]

Practically all artists belonging to the first generation (after the first video camera/recorder was released by Sony in 1965) who were attracted to video as an interactive and immediate recording device began to extend their original practices in sculpture, painting, music, performance, or conceptual art by using video feedback as a new collage or décollage technique for performance events and installations. Apart from the innumerable videotapes and video documentaries that are available today through museum or gallery collections and independent distribution systems, a significant body of work has also been exhibited in video installations and video sculptures. We are reminded that such exhibitions are a direct outgrowth of earlier assemblage and collage works, in which the relations between live performance and installation were fluid and formally inseparable. Since no editing and digital image-processing equipment was available until the mid-seventies, many of the first-generation performers—and, increasingly, women artists among them—concentrated on real-time closed-circuit projects in the studio and the gallery, or they directed the camera at themselves to record performances or body-art events and to explore questions of individual and social identity through the simultaneous projection and reception of the video "mirror"-image. The tautological aspects of these performance videos, rendered problematic by the *technological gap* (there is a minimal time delay in the reproduced subject/image which effectively appears to be simultaneously reproduced *in real time,* thus operating according to an illusionistic principle), opened up a whole range of complex interrogations into the conditions of representation, of self and other, of time-space-movement-image-relationships, and the fluctuations of an ahistorical perceptual present.

In fact, I would go so far as to claim that video became the catalyst for a new stage in the radical critique of representation which exhausted the Dionysian energies of the rebellious sixties and led to a dead end in most of the antitheatrical experiments, the narcissistic and self-lacerating autoperformances and body works by such performance artists as Rudolf Schwarzkogler, Chris Burden, Gina Pane, Vito Acconci, Günter Brus, Stuart Brisley, Stelarc, and Marina Abramović. In some cases the performers tested the limits of their bodies and then transplanted their ideas about participatory performance or ritualistic action into a closed-circuit environment in which the camera interacted with the performers/viewers, placing them within the production process or, rather, inside the doubled process of viewing and being viewed (monitored). The demonstrative presentation of physical presence became provisional, a function of an interlocked gaze and a continuous dislocation between "real" and "live."

In *Centers* (1971) Vito Acconci placed his body between camera and monitor and pointed to the center of the monitor. Following the artist's sight line, the viewers could include themselves in his field of vision and obtain an equivalent relation to the screen and the transmitted doubles on the monitor. But the relationship implied a construction both of equivalence and of difference, since the recognition of the double provoked questions about the inversion of roles and the "real subject" of this performance/image, this encounter. Or was it an installation? In his 1974 work *Command Performance* Acconci himself was no longer present but addressed viewers, who had gathered in an empty room, via live-monitor transmission, a "closed circuit" within which Acconci spoke from the outside and demanded from the viewers inside that they develop their own performances. After this piece Acconci withdrew and began to create "virtual" performances, which was similar to Dennis Oppenheim's decision, in 1972, to withdraw from live performance and to design installations for self-performing video sculptures. Joan Jonas, who had been one of the dancers at the Judson Church, stopped performing in the mid-seventies but continued to exhibit installations about earlier or fictive performances, such as *State Sets* (1976) and *Upside Down and Backwards* (1979–82).

Valie Export's video installations *Split Reality/Zeit und Gegenzeit/Interrupted Movement* (1973) and *Die Praxis des Lebens* (The Practice of Living) (1983) are complex ensembles of materials and images which also refer back to her earlier performances, body works, and films. In *Die Praxis des Lebens* she constructed a triangular container filled with oil and floating photographs of people who had died or suffered from severe injuries and deformations caused by electrocution. A monitor loop surrounding these images showed "live" footage from *Hyperbulie* (1973), a dangerous body work she had performed inside an electrically charged wire cage, and a self-repeating tape contained the fictional suicide scene from her film *Menschenfrauen* (1980). These harrowing images were interlocked in a "closed circuit" that thematized the electrical current which ran through it as a political metaphor for the psychic and physical deformation of human bodies. Marina Abramović had become known in the seventies for her intense performances with Uwe Laysiepen (Ulay), in which the couple subjected various forms of gender behavior and social interaction to extreme tests of physical endurance and pain. In their ninety-day performance of *Nightsea Crossing* (1980), they pushed the feminine/masculine dichotomy to the edge of absurdity by remaining completely passive and immobile for the entire duration. After traveling through Asia and India, they transferred their experiences of other cultures into such video installations as *City of Angels* (1983), *Terra degli Dea Madre* (1984), and *Continental Video Series* (1989), in which their earlier performance dialectic was meditatively repositioned in image/sound/object collages that superimposed gender and intercultural relations.

From Closed Circuit to Multimonitor Theater

As more recent and increasingly complex video art illustrates, there is a new emphasis on content, narrative, and the mediation of personal and social experience, reflectively fractured through the combinatory arrangements of electronic images and physical/sculptural materials and other media. On the one hand, video art has gradually been replacing the earlier closed-circuit installations and their fixed camera/real-time transmission while, on the other, counterbalancing the abstract-formalist trend among experimental video makers who concentrate on digitized and synthetic image compositions.

One can note several important aspects of this transition from the late sixties to the eighties. First, performance-oriented videos and installations have gradually come to redefine the problematics of the physical presence of the body in performance art: the body disappears or is replaced by its double. The physical absence of the performer often becomes a crucial, indirect element for the interpretation of installations, which dramatize the gap between subject and image in ways comparable to earlier minimalist sculptures, which elicited the viewer's participation in a perceptual process wholly dependent upon the temporal/spatial conditions of viewing. The contradictions in the electronic process of reproducing reality have led Acconci to argue that video "is a rehearsal for the time when human beings no longer need to have bodies." But even in Paik's cybernetic experimentations with electronic distortions and "fractalizations" of the image, we still perceive a fundamentally humanist concern to reconcile technological abstraction with the physical and kinesthetic experience of time. In 1977 Paik wrote, "In video art space is a function of time" (i.e., the time of the image), but in his own early work (e.g., *Magnet TV, Participation TV*) the viewer is also an actor. Even in his closed-circuit installations of the seventies (e.g., *TV Buddha, Stone Buddha, Real Plant/Live Plant*), the site or material source of the video feedback is never identical with the image and remains in a contradictory or ironic relationship. The Buddha's meditative gaze is not subsumed by the monitor image it produces.

Second, it is significant that most of the important closed-circuit installations by Les Levine, Bruce Nauman, Ira Schneider, Frank Gillette, Peter Campus, and Dan Graham remain indebted to formal modernist concerns about the interplay of space and time, perception and illusion. A typical example of the many video installations of the early seventies that focused on the self-reflexive formal codes generated by the continuous "real time" and time-delay feedback modes of the medium itself is Frank Gillette and Ira Schneider's *Wipe Cycle* (1969), which confronts the viewer with nine monitors displaying live camera images mixed with prerecorded tape, a TV program, delay loops, and a gray wipe that sweeps counterclockwise every few seconds. The images move cyclically from monitor to monitor and manipulate the viewer's space/time orientation since the viewers identify themselves as part of the fraudulent "live" closed circuit. Bruce Nauman's *Live/Taped Video Corridor* (1969) is different insofar as its physical construction of a long, narrow corridor that becomes a passageway for the viewer—who walks toward two monitors (one image revealing an empty room, the other a reversed closed-circuit image)—reintroduces architectural and theatrical conceptions of illusionary space into the "real-time" video medium. Nauman's work anticipated some of the later video sculptures that became popular sites attracting crowds at such large exhibition events as the documenta in Kassel, Germany, or the Venice Biennial. (Gary Hill's illusionistic video corridor *Tall Ships* was one of the most popular sites at the 1992 documenta, and one had to wait in line to get to see it.) After Paik's creation of such multimonitor sculptural environments as *TV Garden* (1974), *Fish Flies on Sky* (1975), the largest architectonic structure was the 1984 *TV Trichter*, with ninety-nine monitors suspended from the ceiling in widening concentric circles—perhaps a video pun on the architecture of the Guggenheim Museum. It had become clear that the speed of technological advances in computerized editing systems, digital image/sound processors, and synthesizers had overtaken "real-time" video.[6]

Gretchen Bender's *Total Recall* (1987), a completely computer-controlled multiple-monitor/screen installation (eight video channels, three film loops) which she describes as "electronic theater," represents a new metalevel of total media fusions feeding off every available sign, logo, and image that can be appropriated from television and absorbed into the digital-processing apparatus. Her "theater" copies the viewing condition of the movie theater, but the assemblage of fragmented screens is only perceivable as a swirl of flickering images that multiply and run amok in the frantically speeded-up editing effects, creating an overwhelming spectacle of technological representation which finally implodes. The seemingly autonomous movement of this image machine has an almost fascist quality in its overwhelming reduction of all the controlled and manipulated particles to a flat surface or totality that leaves no access for human intervention. Bender's "theater" simulates the speed and abstract power of technology itself; the apparatus functions automatically and inevitably through its own vectors of technological speed, which eliminate the space of participation as such.

It is remarkable how many contemporary video artists, however much they install such work as "exposures" of our contemporary technosystems, seem to have surrendered the idea of a participatory space. Antonio Muntadas's *Board Room* (1987), for example, is basically the mise-en-scène of a symbolic conference room with tables, chairs, and red carpet, a vacuum contained in the coercive, self-repeating movement of mass-mediated propaganda. The messages are the media: recorded speeches of political and religious leaders are the "talking heads" of the portraits hanging on the walls of this room representing corporate power. Having reached a point where many multimonitor installations use appropriated and recycled footage, it has become more difficult not to reproduce the seamless circulation of signs which reinforce the power relations structured into the apparatus. Likewise, it has become more difficult to recover and relocate, historically and critically, the unresolved ideological crisis of the fragmented subject which motivated the early performance/video events and still haunts the current experimental multimedia theater in its continuing rehearsals of the deconstructed and disappearing actor (Wooster Group, Richard Foreman, Robert Wilson, John Jesurun, Squat Theatre, Laura Farabough, etc.).

Finally, having noted the tendency of video installations to abandon a dialectical approach to the subject and its relation to history (narrative, causality), it is uncertain whether one must gradually assume, as Margot Lovejoy has suggested in her important and wide-ranging book on the electronic era, that "the major aesthetic impetus of the eighties [was] to comment on the influence of mass media by reacting to it, quoting from it, and seeing everything in relation to its perspectives."[7]

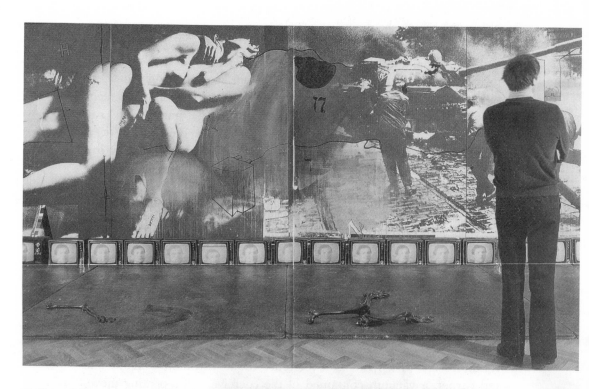

Wolf Vostell, *Heuschrecken,* 1969–70.
Courtesy Museum moderne Kunst,
Vienna.

Peter Campus, *dor,* 1975. Installation
view: Bykert Gallery, New York. Photo:
Bevan Davis.

Ulrike Rosenbach, *Psyche und Eros,* 1981. Courtesy of the artist.

Bill Viola, *Room for Saint John of the Cross,* 1983. Photo: Kira Perov.

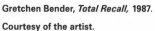

Gretchen Bender, *Total Recall,* 1987. Courtesy of the artist.

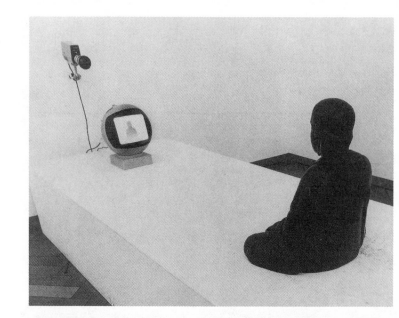

Nam June Paik, *TV Buddha,* 1974.
Courtesy of Stedelijk Museum,
Amsterdam.

Nam June Paik, *Fin de Siècle, II,* 1989.
Courtesy of the Whitney Museum of
American Art, New York.

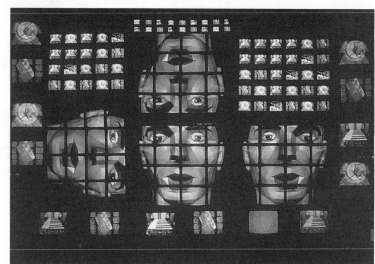

Francesc Torres, *Plus Ultra,* 1988.
Courtesy of the artist.

I have already implied that technological advances have indeed created the condition for video art to reprocess and manipulate any medium and cultural material, but this also makes it rather more difficult to speak of postmodern "independent video" and to distinguish video installations such as *Total Recall* from video sculptures, displays, tapes, or performances that do not necessarily take place in relation to art-world or mass-media perspectives. We are only beginning to understand the implications of the "aesthetic impetus of the eighties," and our boundaries are extended constantly if we investigate the diverse cultural and economic contexts of production, distribution, and reception that were addressed, for example, at the 1989 multiscreen video festival "In Visible Colors," held in Vancouver. Dedicated to the work of third world women and women of color, the festival demonstrated the enormous difficulty in specifying technical, aesthetic, and political criteria to measure our understanding and expectations. The historical trajectory from closed-circuit to multimonitor installations that I have attempted to sketch is only one measure of both the logical and the incomplete displacement of performance by installations and sculptures. Here it becomes necessary to distinguish between the trajectory of abstract-formalist and self-reflexive work and an alternative trajectory that extends the politicized, adversarial impetus of the sixties. The latter, I believe, constitutes the most flexible and indeterminate gauge to measure reception since it is connected to local and specific grassroots activities, and reformulates its "aesthetic" in terms of political or social documentary critiques or creative-activist objectives.

Before returning to this last point in the final section, I want to speculate further on the relationship between performance and installation. The most notable aspect of Nam June Paik's and Gretchen Bender's recent multimonitor installations is their strictly formal, geometrical matrix configuration, as well as the calculated temporal and visual fragmentation of the video images. Sometimes the computer-processing effects can be so extreme that the swirling colors, the digital painting and matrixing of disjunctive forms, create a purely abstract, contentless "mood art" not unlike Brian Eno's ambient video paintings. Devoid of semantic structures, such visual music creates an immaterial architectonic or luminous space even as it remains physically dependent on the monitor frames. This architectonic is descended from the constructivist tradition of kinetic sculpture (Bauhaus, Naum Gabo, Lázló Moholy-Nagy, Otto Piene), for it can only imply performance in terms of the rhythm and motion of the light/images.

If one now thinks of Vostell's décollage-installation *Heuschrecken* (1969)—which depicts two huge photomontages of a lesbian couple and a Russian tank (Prague Spring, 1968) overpainted with acid, a row of twenty closed-circuit monitors below them and animal bones, hair, shoes, and other objects in front of them—one is faced with an entirely different parameter that provokes critical interpretations of the historical and material references and the "real-time" process, in which viewers of the sexual and political images simultaneously see themselves as voyeurs who are complicitous in the production. The viewers are subjective and operational in this site, caught within the dialectic of historical and gender-specific relationships involving sexual liberation and political oppression, standing both inside and outside this "installation" yet faced with the question of moral value and personal responsibility.

Vostell's décollage works, as well as the many action events and pedagogical demonstrations Joseph Beuys created around the same time in Europe, had a considerable impact on the younger generation of German artists, which included Rebecca Horn, Ulrike Rosenbach, Astrid Klein, Jochen Gerz, Klaus vom Bruch, Rosemarie Trockel, and Marcel Odenbach. The young installation artists of the eighties in England, who tended to resist the spectacular use of video technology, remained largely indebted to the anarchist, subcultural energies of the British Live Art movement and often worked to transform specific sites and site-contexts. I admittedly cannot discuss all the different conceptual influences of action and Fluxus events on artists worldwide, though it would be a most significant contribution to our historical awareness of video art if one could trace these differences and their contextual conditions of production (e.g., the lack of support, space, or access to production), especially in eastern regions then under communism. The early performances of these artists always stood in an interactive relationship to organic materials (similar to the body and land art experiments in England and Ireland) or constructed objects, and their video works evolved parallel to their body and performance sculptures. Some of these artists explored the repressed materiality and subjects dealing with contemporary life in performance modes which incorporated universal symbols of ritual and personal action in a live/video dialectic that dramatized the postmodern schizophrenic subjectivity.

Ulrike Rosenbach's installations are emblematic of the feminist point of view that entered into this dialectic. *Meine Macht ist Meine Ohnmacht* (1978) ritualizes her individual experience in a performance that sets her physical entrapment and her struggle to free herself in counterpoint to a large overhead mirror and a miniaturized video stage where tapes replay traditionally powerless women "objectified" into art-historical or pop-cultural icons. As in her later *Or-phelia* (1987), Rosenbach actively engages the position of the "feminine," passive protagonist in order to overturn the mythical stereotypes and expose them as oscillating signs within an information environment (video) whose codes she can scramble. Both the altered video images and the performance/installation thus become mutually dependent and immediate frames that do not create a synthesis of site and medium but rather sustain the contradictions. These material contradictions are set in motion. The work's unresolved movement narrative, or *gestus*—to draw an analogy to Brechtian theater and the contemporary European *Tanztheater*—opens out onto a series of altered views of the social circumstances and behavioral roles we inhabit and repeat. The political edge of Rosenbach's work connects it to a growing body of independent videotapes, some of which are performance-based. (Many French, Belgian, Dutch, Scandinavian, Slovene, and Japanese dancers are currently choreographing directly for video production in the context of a growing interest in videodance, supported by annual "DanceScreen" festivals organized by the Vienna-based Internationales Musikzentrum and similar organizations in Italy, France, England, and Canada.) Others are narrative or documentary in nature, and they are being produced all over the world, testifying to the empowerment that the medium can bestow on alternative voices wishing to construct a self-defining history against institutional and cultural stereotypes.

At the "In Visible Colors" festival held in Vancouver, Trinh T. Minh-ha presented her *Surname: Viët, Given Name: Nam* (1989), a disturbing and difficult filmic interrogation of her native country, in which she simultaneously questions and mocks the objectivity and truth value of ethnographic documentary. Her video is a performance in the sense that it completely undermines a "monologic" or authoritative narrative, instead choreographing a polyphonic, discontinuous collage of voices, images, sounds, and rhythms with which she reconstructs a historical and a changing Vietnam. Asking actors to reenact scripted monologues transcribed from recorded conversations with a number of Vietnamese women, Trinh interweaves these scenes with archival footage of women interacting in the resistance movement and in folk-cultural activities. At the same time, the video recording of these oral histories is interactive in another sense since it reconstructs the process of the transcriptions (subtitles, translations, often out of sync) and Trinh's voice-over reflections on the process (voice track). Her comments intimate that she respects the separate identities of the sources and subjects of her video. The work provokes the viewer's recognition of the *movement* between media, of the gap between then and now, between the various stages of history.

Image World

Moving to another locale, the museum, I want to comment on the new role video art has come to play now that several major exhibitions in Europe and the United States have testified to the degree to which the museum/gallery system (and art-historical discourse) has begun to mythologize video and recuperate it as part of the established art world. To acknowledge video was not a self-evident step since the temporal and technological arts had never played a role in the exclusive hierarchical system (painting, sculpture) of museums and private collections. But the increasingly frequent exhibition of video installations and sculptures may indicate not only the popular acceptance of video art but also the slow recognition among curators and art historians that video, as an art form and a technology, is contemporaneous with the pervasive influence mass-media technologies have come to exert over all visual languages in a world which considers itself "global" because of the transnational flow of images produced and marketed by its industries.

While the idea of a global culture is as yet undefined and largely a neocolonial projection of capitalist expansion, the museum as a regulated market system can now affirm the strategically crucial role video art may embody as a paradigm of postmodern aesthetics in a culture of reproduction. Video has thus supplanted photography vis-à-vis the traditional fine arts. This affirmation is not without consequence if it leads to the incorporation of video art into the hierarchical history of Western art. The fluid and intermediary role of video, and its particular relationship to performance, is obscured when the museum chooses to foreground the formal and aesthetic achievements of "master artists," as happened with Nam June Paik's 1982 retrospective at the Whitney Museum or the 1987–88 Bill Viola retrospective at MoMA. I think that the more hesitant presentation of video at larger, internationally significant exhibitions (such as Dara Birnbaum's *Damnation of Faust* at the 1985 Whitney Biennial and Marie-Jo Lafontaine's *Les Larmes d'Acier* [Tears of Steel] at documenta 8 in 1987) should have more sharply delineated the contradictory role of a medium utilized by a younger generation of artists, both with explicit reference to mass culture and to complex relationships to the feminist and political critique of representation in the early eighties.

This double relationship finds an uneasy expression in the current practice of polychannel video sculptures in which the three-dimensional, kinetic presence of the screens-as-objects and the physical context of viewing are as important as the critique of culture which is staged through them. Since I have already called video a transitional medium, the distinction between installation and sculpture may not prove helpful. At the documenta 8 exhibition, for example, all the large-scale video sites were referred to as "sculptural installations." But in terms of the political content of later work, we can see a significant shift in the viewing situation itself: from the frontal presentation of surfaces (screens) to more complex configurations in which the spatial dialectic between material objects and images remains an intrinsic part of the work's meditation on the apparatus of representation.

A good demonstration of this shift was provided by two major exhibitions mounted in 1989: *Video Sculpture* (curated by Wulf Herzogenrath for the Cologne Kunstverein and shown in Cologne, Zurich, and Berlin) and *Image World: Art and Media Culture* (curated for the Whitney Museum by John G. Hanhardt, the resident curator of film and video at the Whitney, who has also made the video selections for the last ten Whitney biennials, thus holding one of the most influential positions of affirmation/exclusion for video art in the museum world). While both shows constructed a narrative of art-historical influences showing present-day postmodernists as the children of sixties pop and conceptual art movements, the Cologne retrospective began with Paik but tried to generate a critical discourse by differentiating between the aims of each work. The New York show, however, seemed to begin and end with Paik's *Fin de Siècle II* (1989), a monstrous installation wall that faced viewers as they stepped out of the elevators to be crushed by the flashing onslaught of its weightless image world. Paik's position at the entrance was not an unfortunate irony, of course, since the museum and the sponsors of the show had jointly declared that "our contemporary corporate culture" is completely penetrated by media and that the realities of our world are experienced through powerful image-making technologies and techniques. What I found so revolting about Paik's spectacular wall was the suggestion that its mosaic of recycled and relentlessly grinding image "bytes" could say anything about the realities of the world outside, except that Paik's electronic machine had access to the entire data bank of the twentieth century and could mix it all up in a promotional program of aestheticized entertainment.

The program, lasting twenty minutes, was distributed via digital and analog computers into three hundred monitors. The multichannel program was looped and thus insinuated the infinite continuity of the televisual flow. Its cool and impassioned visual seduction was accompanied by the droning beat of disco rhythms, a digitally produced sound which interfaced with the pulsating rhythms of the computerized abstract graphics on the monitor borders of the wall. The central images consisted of visual quotations culled from various contexts (a David Bowie music video, a dance concert by LaLaLa Human Steps, a Joseph Beuys performance in Japan, an image of a female nude, etc.) that were fused into a single iconographic image, the nowhere space of titillating techno-pop art. I admit that Paik's sardonic humor could be interpreted in other ways, and as a commentary on the end of (art) history his electronic painting was rather clever. But I doubt very much that the power of this technological apparatus, which he seemed to enjoy and affirm, was meant to encourage interpretation, and that the installation succeeded, as Bonnie Marranca has suggested, in addressing the philosophical faith of modernism in technology as cosmopolitan, liberal politics.[8] The audience—at least the one I saw in the elevator on my way out—seemed disinterested in Paik's faith, probably because they had seen such monitor walls before at the Palladium or other fashionable discotheques.

The "placelessness" of the image surface of Paik's video wall stands in direct contrast to the contemplative resonance which instilled the *Room for Saint John of the Cross* (1983) that Bill Viola rebuilt for the Cologne exhibition. Viola's work expressed a metaphysical yearning and a personal vision that is rare among his contemporaries. There was also a sense of poetic anachronism in the way in which he sought to touch an inner core and spiritual perception in the viewer. His room sculpture created a metaphorical space for a flight of fantasy (a hand-held camera shot that seemed to be flying through the air toward a distant mountain range) and a literal contradiction between the large projected image of the landscape and the miniaturized reconstruction of the cell in which the mystic poet was imprisoned for his subversive beliefs. If one stepped closer to the tiny cell one heard a recording of the Spanish monk's poetry, while a tiny monitor within the prison cell showed a still image of the mountain next to a water jar. The gap in this "closed circuit" lies between the poetic metaphor and its projection beyond the confines of the torture chamber. As prisoners of history, we remain in our enclosures, and the experience of such a room as Viola's refers us to the crucial question of where we stand as viewers when the circle is closed.

It is challenging, in this respect, to note the difference between Dara Birnbaum's *PM Magazine* (1982–84) at the Whitney Museum and her *Damnation of Faust* (1986), recreated for the *Video Sculpture* exhibition in Cologne. The former installation, fusing five-channel video, six-channel sound, and framing panels of greatly enlarged still shots from the video, explored the juxtaposition between appropriated footage from TV commercials and popular-entertainment programs on the monitors and their architectural "frames," which were here constructed out of the blown-up still images from the mass media themselves. The loop was self-referential, and its hypnotic effect was largely produced by the music-driven repetition of the densely layered monitor images. For *Damnation of Faust*, on the other hand, Birnbaum did not use found TV images but shot her own footage in a children's playground. Her edited and altered images of the children playing, shown on several monitors set into the walls of a room painted red, created a quiet, elusive, poetic quality that grew deeper in resonance when the physical language of the young bodies (the children sat on benches and waited or flew through the air on swings) was perceived as specific, contextualized *movement* and as *communication*. This movement of expression, contained in the gendered, behavioral modes of "playing" on the swings and enclosed by the fenced-in urban playground, was juxtaposed with the sculptural construction of large photo stills (in the shape of a folding fan or arch) that depicted close-up details of the body language through which cultural codes of sexual, social, and racial difference are inscribed onto the children. Avoiding the tautologies of media-based critiques of the media, this sculptural installation permitted a more profound view of political culture by treating it not as a ready-made but by dissecting a microcosmic process in an innocent playground where the "disciplinary society" (Foucault) exerts its invisible power to train children and to exploit the loss of their innocence.

Interestingly, Belgian artist Marie-Jo Lafontaine's *Les Larmes d'Acier* (1985–86), shown at the documenta 8 exhibition, also focused on the social rituals of body training, but the frontal display of her twenty-seven-monitor wall installation had a considerably more abrasive and aggressive effect since the flickering, time-programmed images of the bulging chests and distorted faces of male body builders created a perversely ecstatic scene of narcissism, punctuated by a soundtrack ranging from Maria Callas to emergency sirens (announcing air strikes) and bombardments. Lafontaine's close-ups were an unambiguous indictment of male fantasies, ritualized as obsessional competition against their own bodies, and linked to associations of "hardening" (steeling) the body in preparation for warfare. Between her circular sculpture *A las cinco de la tarde* (At Five in the Afternoon) (1984) whose images alternated between a bullfight and a Spanish dance, and the later *Victoria* (1988), her contribution to the Cologne show, where she built a spiral of nineteen black columns with embedded black-and-white video monitors, the physical effect on the viewer was remarkably different. While *Les Larmes d'Acier*, not unlike Paik's *Fin de Siècle II*, tended to fragment and disperse any focused perception of the image content, the sculptural configuration of the obelisk-like spiral in *Victoria* did not create a spectacular surface but rather a more complex, intimate arena into which the viewer was forced to enter. The images on the inside were identical, depicting a seductive, erotic, and violent encounter between two men. They encircled the viewer, and since they were shown with a split-second time lag between each monitor, they seemed to move around the spiral and create a dancelike motion. But the dance became one of sexual aggression, and the encirclement of the viewer created a highly visceral experience of claustrophobia, which inverted the panoptic structure of Lafontaine's sculpture and actually turned the central position of the viewer into a spatial metaphor for captivity. The watcher was imprisoned in the apparatus of a cultural ritual that was both seductive and dangerous. The circle of homoerotic/homosocial love, so to speak, enclosed the inside viewer, becoming the circumference of a social relation.

My final reference is to a video sculpture by Marcel Odenbach entitled *Eine Faust in der Tasche machen* (Make a Fist in the Pocket), first created in Madrid before being shown at MoMA's *Video Spaces* exhibition in 1995. It could be said to constitute a critical examination of the "global village" ideology celebrated in the earlier Whitney show, but its (self-)critical intention, which cannot be doubted, needs to be measured against its own formulaic aestheticism and its minimalist spatial arrangement. I found the arrangement simplistic and trite, exercising a model of juxtaposition that became all the more questionable if it meant to create a dialectic of historical and political "spaces."

Odenbach's eight-channel video/sound installation placed a seven-minute program projected onto a huge wall against a row of seven nineteen-inch monitors hung at eye level, on which three-minute programs consisting of news clips from the 1968 "revolution" were intercut with archival footage from the Nazi book burnings and with a recurring inset image of a hand striking the keys of a typewriter. Interestingly, the monitors displayed news coverage from different countries (Germany, France, Italy, England, the former Czechoslovakia, Mexico, the United States) and their respective police or government treatment of the rebelling or striking revolutionaries. This assemblage of news clips from the world of politics reminded me of Terry Berkowitz's similar mise-en-scène for her installation *When the World Was Flat* (shown at the Houston

Contemporary Arts Museum in 1990), which also had mixed images extracted from international newscasts and programmed into a loop that simulated a global simultaneity of violence, fundamentalism, nationalism, and commodity consumption. Odenbach evoked the archival footage of Nazi Germany and the 1968 rebellion (which was stifled by police aggression against the demonstrators and antiwar protesters) as a deeply ingrained historical memory, hoping that the monochromatic, slightly faded history "tracks" would resonate in our personal recollection of the political protest of the youthful generation that had grown up after the fascist terror. Yet these images rolled by on the small monitors, accompanied by the staccato rhythm of the typewriter, as if the urgency of their political content could expose the repressive channels through which "order" and democracy are upheld. The synchronicity of protest and repression, however, was here mostly an effect of the televisual history footage, culled from very different geopolitical and ideological contexts, and unexamined as *media information* and manipulated coverage of the actual events in these countries.

Juxtaposed against this reductive assemblage of history-as-image, the large screen projection showed Odenbach's personal footage from his travels in Thailand. Here the spatial representation of the dialectic became truly twisted, since the travelogue implied an outsider's look at local customs (beautiful if grainy images of shrines and robed monks chanting at religious ceremonies) and landscapes. The exoticized images of beautiful Thai prostitutes soliciting customers in the street were disturbing even without being intercut by the image of the naked body of a Caucasian man being stepped on during a massage. I had trouble making sense of the whole juxtaposition of contexts until I noticed a scene in which a Thai kick boxer was seen watching CNN coverage of German neo-Nazi skinheads attacking and firebombing an asylum for refugees. Suddenly one noticed on the "screen" containing the video from Thailand the frightened faces of African and Asian refugees framed by the windows of their burning homes or shelters in Germany.

Odenbach is trying to raise the ghosts of repressed memory and to illuminate the contemporary, self-distracting complicity with the violence against the "other" that has become the stuff of daily news coverage in racially divided, prejudiced, and bigoted Western societies. The violence against foreigners in Germany is watched elsewhere, as the Germans watch their own internal eruptions of neofascist violence, with "a fist in the pocket," that is, with thwarted and inexpressed anger that remains hidden in the privacy of one's own fantasies of protest. Fantasies of intervention or revenge? It is, of course, the forgotten history that

presumably is revenging itself, and it is most provocative that Odenbach had written a sentence on the wall of his video space quoted from
the Austrian poet and activist Ingeborg Bachmann: "I am writing with
my burnt hand about the nature of fire." If this statement is applied to
the static and formalistic juxtaposition of the video loops itself, it begs
the question that Odenbach cannot answer, namely, whether it makes
much sense to present his mediascapes (which display the fires of violence and the muted violence of forgetting and self-repression) without
dismantling the role (the fire) of the medium itself and the nature of
its collaboration with the existing condition of amnesia, its reinforce-
ment of the law of forgetting. Paradoxically, Odenbach's constructed
loops of televised history challenge the "media massage" of which Marshall McLuhan once spoke, but the video phantoms of traumatic history
remain uninterruptedly vacant in their own neutrality vis-à-vis the violence we may not want to remember. Television is exposed by the violence, and violence is posed by television, and in the museum we stand
there, somehow suspended in the middle of a cool arrangement. Perhaps the museum, reflecting on "image worlds," cannot be a test site for
video's capacity to interrupt the aesthetic arrangements and to bear witness to the fire that burns the bodies of foreigners in our midst.

Future History

I don't feel it is my task to speculate on the predictable advances in video
technology, computer animation, digitized simulation, high-definition
TV projection, interfaces with multimedia computer and cyberspace
networks, and all the other interpolations and editing techniques that lie
ahead of us. I'm more interested in video's interface with the social and
historical realities that are excluded, repressed, or aestheticized by the
"image worlds" in the museum or the mass media. I'm more inclined to
wonder what remains, a question Christa Wolf posed in her book, which
appeared—with some very unpleasant consequences for its author—at
the very moment when the country which published it had ceased to
exist, only to become absorbed by the West German economy and the
imperatives of "our corporate culture." I will conclude this chapter by
drawing attention to practices which can help to tear down the walls
and facades of ideology without canceling or editing out the historical
formations and the private and public memory that lie buried in the unconscious as well as in the architecture and installations of culture.

Francesc Torres's video sculptures offer some of the most encouraging contemporary examples of a conceptual and poetic methodology

that brings found objects (from various areas of everyday life or from historical sites) into concrete and living symbolic relationships with the video medium in order to create the analytical ground (not a "video space") for an archaeology of social and political conditions. After spending 1987 in Berlin (two years before the "revolutionary" collapse of the GDR), Torres literally constructed the event-specific installation *Plus Ultra* (1988) out of the remains he discovered from the partly collapsed and abandoned Spanish embassy used during World War II. "Plus Ultra," the words inscribed in the Spanish imperial emblem, signifies the desire of the state to reach beyond its historical destiny. Torres wanted us to look at the tomb, the deliberately abandoned ruin hiding the forgotten expression of the hyperbolic myths of fascism. Since the building itself could not be used for safety reasons, he built a site with reassembled "building blocks" from the embassy, together with twelve monitors whose separate tape channels displayed images and sounds from the interior of the embassy and from the fall and reconstruction of Berlin. They also reconstructed stages in the common political and ideological trajectory of both Germany and Spain, linking the archive of a ghostly fascism with the archive of the unequal postwar development in the two countries. The accelerated capitalist rejuvenation of West Germany was symbolized by a merry-go-round Torres placed in the center of the installation. The found and constructed materials mutually informed each other and remained locked in a tense embrace; the video images, having no aesthetic function, provided an immediate surgical dissection of the silent, physical material of history. These images, our memory bank, looked at the ruins.

Torres's *Oikonomos* project, a multimedia installation for the 1989 Whitney Biennial, ran into institutional obstacles when its initial plan to create a video décollage of the gold-colored copy of a classical Greek sculpture (an oversized Zeus figure) was halted by the Metropolitan Museum of Art, which owned the replica and had loaned it to the Queens Museum, where Torres discovered it. He had wanted to explore the collision between the powerful and powerless by attaching a small video monitor to the god's genitals (displaying images from the stock exchange) and making the sculpture face a video projection screen showing scenes of the homeless and destitute washing cars and panhandling in lower Manhattan. He explained that he wanted to display the two extremes of the economic spectrum (and the class relations between downtown/uptown) through the "appropriation" and "reconstruction" of the classical sculpture, an obvious symbol of patriarchal high culture. The ensuing controversy between Torres and the museum generated some fascinating postmodern ironies. The Met filed its injunction against Torres's "trappings" (especially the monitor attached to the god's penis) based on the argument that the "original image" of the masterpiece (the god) was not to be altered even though the museum only owned a replica. The politics of Torres's reediting of the copy of an "image"—the most common video operation and one that is often copied by postmodernist artists who show their work in the museum—put him squarely on the side of the powerless, who are denied access to institutionally controlled or monopolized images and media. The intervention, in any case, had taken place and was not without consequence.

It is to be expected, for example, that the current censorship movement in the United States and the policing of image production and reproduction will only exacerbate the already existing economic and social contradictions and inequalities. The immediate historical pressures will create even more flexible and unexpected appropriations of images on the part of subcultures, disenfranchised communities, multicultural minorities, immigrants, disgruntled antigovernment groups and militias on the right, religious fundamentalists and tele-evangelists, members of the New Age and self-help movements, the poor and disadvantaged, the ill, the elderly, the jobless young, and probably many others in the mainstream as well who have experienced the collective social loss of identities.

Video has the potential to traverse the borderlines that are still being policed, and I expect it will be used more frequently to reframe countermemories and to dispute overdetermined images. In his study of the official, mainstream cultural agenda concerning AIDS during the first decade of the epidemic's appearance, Simon Watney has analyzed its limited set of heavily overdetermined words and images, stressing the need to intervene and interrupt an agenda—and the social-policy decisions it covers up—which at this point in time is only being actively challenged by those whom it already has effectively delegitimatized, namely, people with AIDS.[9] It is also obvious that television only promotes an illusion of control over the health crisis caused by the epidemic. This crisis has, in fact, taught us ways to construct new political alliances and identities within and between marginalized groups. Some of these politically active groups—such as Gran Fury, People With AIDS Coalition and ACT UP—have been supported by a steadily growing number of video works, performances, and interventions. (I discuss them in the next chapter.) In view of the image of fatality which dominates AIDS coverage in the mass media and many public institutions, the alternative production of independent videos that show people speaking up for themselves and wanting to live offers perhaps the most concrete example of a practice committed to the historical present and a possible future.

To take another example of such countermemory production, shifting the focus more resolutely outside the video art and art-world contexts, one could think of several arenas in which video production is used for activist purposes, say, in the women's health movement (e.g., the "Health Care and Gerontology Video Collection" distributed by Fanlight Productions), or in environmental, human rights, pro-choice, pro-life, immigration, labor, social work, religious, and other community service–oriented organizations. There is a growing sector of new social documentaries produced by independent and amateur video makers whose work operates neither within the commercial nor the art world and is therefore not dependent on the institutional discourse and ideological agendas underpinning the marketplace (e.g., print media or art press coverage; museum, gallery, or university curatorships). Much of the independent work—including personal video diaries, home videos, music videos, experimental and underground videos, or erotic tapes (e.g., the "Femme Fatales" productions available at some women's and lesbian bookstores, or the soft-core porn videos circulating in gay bars and videotheques)—functions outside mainstream distribution networks and is complementary to educational and politically committed documentaries only insofar as it operates in a closely defined relationship to its audience. One would have to examine a wide range of different tapes and modes of production before drawing any conclusions about effective distinctions among video productions and their tactical employment for sociocultural, political, and entertainment responses. One might assume, for example, that content-based alternative work uses formal/technical codes and collective production methods that intrinsically or implicitly resist dominant cultural production in mainstream television, commercial video, and fine art/video art.

In connection with such oppositional positions vis-à-vis mainstream culture, one should mention the work of the Chicago-based Street-Level Video collective (S-LV), which offers a tremendously interesting and inspiring "model" of production on a level of social and critical representation quite different from my initial example of the Houston student's "Vogue." I don't want to claim that S-LV's videos position themselves in opposition to art and art spaces. Rather, their videos originate in a particular urban, working-class Latino neighborhood (Chicago's West Town) and address issues and social experiences of urban youth in and for the community. Their sitings, however, function tactically and can shift the mode of address and the location of display, depending on specific occasions and projects. Their politics of video production can perhaps be sketched in terms of three major concepts: *collective agency/ autonomy, territorial tactics,* and *community negotiation/healing.*

Street Gangs and Video Gangs

I found out about S-LV when I met media artist Iñigo Manglano-Ovalle during a cross-cultural radio workshop taught by Guillermo Gómez-Peña in late 1992.[10] During our collaboration on the radio works, Iñigo told me that he was involved, as a facilitator and teacher, in one of eight community-based "Culture in Action" projects initiated by Sculpture Chicago.[11] An independent organization that sponsors public art projects, Sculpture Chicago incited the community-based projects by suggesting that local artists connect with their communities in order to examine the *territory* of public interaction and participation and to discover how such projects would evolve as processes of artistic and political activism, and as engagements with "community audiences" in culturally diverse, hybrid neighborhoods. Together with high school teacher Nilda Ruiz Pauley and video maker Paul Teruel, Iñigo met with various West Town social service agencies, cultural workers, and high school students to discuss a physical/conceptual project, "Sereno/Tertulia," meant to rekindle social gatherings and dialogue on the street by providing public seating and better street lighting in a neighborhood that was considered a fearful environment because of gang violence and turf wars. *Sereno* is the traditional word for "lamplighter," and *tertulia* in Latin cultures means outside gathering for a bit of socializing in the evening. Iñigo's main suggestion was to reclaim a safe space for social and intergenerational gatherings, thereby counteracting the cycle of crime and fear by involving young and old—even the gang members themselves—in a process of defining a sense of community.

With the energetic help of high school teacher and youth-at-risk coordinator Ruiz Pauly, plus further negotiations with social service advocates, community leaders, and Denise Zaccardi's Community Televison Network (an agency that teaches media literacy to economically disadvantaged minority, inner-city youth and provides job training), Iñigo facilitated the formation of alliances that eventually led to the creation of a new coalition of youth organizations. It called itself Westtown Vecinos Video Channel (WVVC), using the symbolic logo of a TV channel to indicate that the initiative was shifting to the young people themselves and their production of images and self-definitions.

What could be called a thoroughly situational *détournement,* the process was gaining its own dynamic, and *tertulia* was converted into visual/ video interventions into the definitions of public space and neighborhood territory, soon to be called Tele-Vecindario (Tele-Neighborhood). An open-ended group initially consisting of fifteen Latino youths from West Town formed a "street-level" video collective (a kind of alternative "gang") that would be trained in video production and editing by Iñigo and Paul, acquire equipment and a studio through Sculpture Chicago, and receive encouragement to devise its own projects and take responsibility for its actions. By the end of 1993, S-LV had collaborated on a "video map" (a description of the neighborhood, including various opinions on who represents it, who belongs to it, who is inside/outside, and how a community asserts its power or authority over its territory) and on more than fifty video tapes which articulate the video makers' views and experiences as well as those of the *vecinos* they filmed and interviewed. Lamplighting became video-making, and Iñigo has asserted that "the intention of the project is not to organize but to channel and illuminate the vitality of the community's own organizational structures."

Since video was already familiar to most of the youth through popular culture and the mass media, it took only a small step to encourage workshop participation and dialogue about the camera as an active tool in the creative resituating of images of urban youth or minority cultures. Alfonso Soto, one of the members of S-LV, has related that the first tape they made was called "This is my Stuff," which was shown continuously in the front window of Emerson House Community Center for four months during the summer of 1993. When I saw it I was struck by the self-assertiveness of the young men and women speaking on the tape. Many of the tapes I saw later displayed an extraordinary motion-texture of spontaneity, funky angles, quick shifts, streetwise humor, and unusual relationships—for lack of a better word—between camera operator and subject. The video makers sought out particular locations in the neighborhood and spoke to neighbors, elders, community heads, and gang leaders on front porches, in cars, on the street, and on the thresholds of private and public spaces. Edith Pauley, another member of the collective, has argued that they are not kids anymore but young adults: "We don't consider ourselves punks or gangbangers; we are grown up and we may know more than you." Ronnie Pauley and Alfonso Soto added that many of the members in S-LV, although considered "at risk" in their schools, in fact stayed in school longer because of the opportunity to work in video production. Working on their own video projects also gave them an incentive to redefine what it means to be considered "at risk" in our society.

Listening to them, I realized that most adults may not comprehend how young people who have grown up with media and popular-culture styles incorporate and transform what they like about them in their own unique ways. When asked to talk about the unconventional camera-motion angles, close-ups, and editing choices in their work, Soto explained that he had been making videos since eighth grade, and after he had learned the basic rules of videotaping, he and his friends thought they could break them, especially since they had no intention of imitating mainstream television. Furthermore, producing videos on the street about life in the street brought up a number of difficult issues they had had to confront in their planning, brainstorming, and scripting sessions. As they continued to produce "neighborhood television," they had to face the deep-seated alienation and dysfunctionality in the social fabric of Chicago's low-income Latino/Chicano community, both in themselves and in their families, as well as their own experience of cultural and class restrictions, housing conditions, street violence and gang affiliation, joblessness, drugs, alcoholism, domestic violence, homophobia, cruising, and sexism. Soto has pointed out that for their video production to be effective, they had to take on some of the immediate power relations on the street and negotiate with groups: "We got started as a way of getting different people from different streets talking. We work with gangbangers and others, young and old. We use video as a way to work with others on and off the streets."

One of the most dramatic differences between mainstream television, or the formalist aesthetics of much contemporary video art/sculpture for that matter, and street-level television is, of course, the radical dialectic at work in the latter's critical constellations. S-LV's image of itself and its dialogues reflect a personal language and lifestyle, revealing the discontinuities and fault lines in the community and giving voice to the young people's perceptions of their class consciousness and their territories and colors, all the while fulfilling its fundamental social mission by portraying such negotiations with its peers. (Immediate territorial questions are alluded to by means of the colors of the gangs, dress codes, hand signals, street signs, murals, choice of music/soundtrack, and the "languages" of the graffiti writers.) The dense, volatile texture of these encodings could not be produced by the formatted styles of top-down television broadcasting and the mainstream apparatus's mythic function of self-perpetuating/commodifying its constant form of betrayal. S-LV television neither advertises nor buys time, nor promises the eternal return of the same. S-LV's tapes—sited temporarily in the neighborhood looking outside to the street or changing along its itinerary of

"getting different people from different streets talking"—create dialectical images that are catalysts for change from the past: exchanging a gun
for a video camera or food and friendship for images; trading places; developing community ownership of a "neutral zone" or a mural project;
diminishing risk and fear; learning the history of houses and monitoring
signals of gentrification; questioning property and economic relations;
talking openly about gender and sexual relations; examining rivalries;
and creating new colors and signs that spell a street semiotics of survival.

"Cul-de-Sac"

By the end of its first year of operation, S-LV had created an "ex-
territorial" work-in-progress installation at the downtown Museum of
Contemporary Arts (a version of their "Cul-de-Sac" project), completed
nine outdoor video installations in spaces reflecting the local economy
(ranging from schools to grocery stores, hot dog stands, and video arcades), and mounted a huge block party/installation. The ex-territorial
act of installing a pilot project, following an unexpected invitation by
the mainstream art museum, proved an effective tactic for drawing attention to the planned outdoor event in West Town (for downtown
art patrons who might not be familiar with or feel inclined to visit
the neighborhood), especially in its subversive logic of "detourning"
Mayor Daley's newly announced city "cul-de-sac" policy of blocking
off streets to inhibit drive-by shooting. The appearance at the museum
was also clearly a symbolic, empowering moment for the young "unknown" video makers, who realized they could now see their tapes in
their neighborhood *and* in the high-cultural venue on the other side of
town. Shortly thereafter they were invited to show one of their tapes on
CTVN's "Hard Cover" program, a series produced by teens. "Cul-de-
Sac," coproduced with Iñigo, was set up as a fourteen-monitor installation behind chain-link fencing, running eleven S-LV video programs
simultaneously in a darkened space illuminated only by an eerie yellow
glow. The choreography of the installation had a very powerful effect
on the viewer, showing head-on the faces and scenes of the young and
old people of West Town being fenced in, trapped, and isolated behind
a cage—a political critique unmistakably directed at law-enforcement
strategies of containment. In S-LV's positioning of its neighborhood/
television in such a manner one must read "cul-de-sac" as an entrapment
that blocks the residents in their physical mobility and, under the guise
of a crime-prevention program which does not address the economic,
social, and historical context, reinforces social and racial borders. As

something imposed from the outside and not negotiated, the city policy defined the neighborhood as crime-ridden and "at risk" instead of seeking other ways of supporting the community in its own programs for improvement, growth, and social interaction.

Negotiating Power

The block party on a warm summer night in late August transformed one residential street and, in my view, the entire notion of "video installation," expanding further the site-specific and contingent radicalism of situationism, or what Joseph Beuys has called "social sculpture." This fiesta embodied the quite miraculous dimension of a healing ritual that relied on hard work and unwavering commitment in its preparation, and it organically used the traditions of street art to unleash the multifaceted dynamism of social interaction and channel the energies toward a kind of initiation.

But perhaps one should ask oneself how one reviews or remembers a block party: the smells and sounds; the colors of the crowd milling about; the laughter of children; the intense interest in the videos; astonished and cheerful reactions coupled with the relaxed attitude of Sunday-afternoon baseball spectators who know the pratfalls of their home team; the movement of hips, legs, arms, and the erotic gyrations while dancing to salsa music; chatting and meeting friends; the palpable pride of a neighborhood in touch with itself; the powerful recognition of something shared, which can be called spirit. The food was good, the beer tasted better than ever. There was the unfamiliar look of a street turned into a huge experimental video arcade slowly turning into something else, the flow of time and the bustle of voices, noise, music, something resembling a celebration of local pride in the creativity of the folk who had taken control of their hood.

The aesthetic rules of the museum or the gallery don't apply; in fact, they are irrelevant to the realities on the street and the interactions among those who made this particular "Culture in Action" event take place. At the same time, I felt very comfortable calling the process of building the communal relations for the event an artistic process, especially since the creativity of S-LV and its collaborators exceeded the material process of video production itself and took greater risks. While the six-hour block party showed West Town the video productions of the collective and invited neighbors to celebrate its achievements, it was an ephemeral and transient event that cannot be identified with the underlying duration of the collective's efforts, negotiations, plans, or as-yet-unrealized hopes. In fact, if one calls the event a healing ritual, one needs to recognize the organism as a whole, the interdependent homeopathic elements of its nervous ecology, the sources of its energy and replenishment, and the ongoing attendance to needs, desires, setbacks, and environmental pressures on its fragile immune system.

During the weeks and months of preparation, Iñigo and S-LV had to deflect suspicion and seek cooperation, devise concepts for the "installation," yet also take chances in arranging a public party that would bring more than a thousand people to the festivities. After completing the editing of scores of videos portraying themselves, their friends, and *vecinos* in terms of their daily troubles and aspirations, S-LV realized it had come a long way in the process of adapting certain rhythms of video representation, gradually devoting more time to its subjects' responses or life circumstances, as well as to economic and political issues in the West Town ecology. Furthermore, the arrangement of seventy-five video monitors on Eerie Street, playing close to fifty different tapes in various configurations all evening, involved more than the technical design of an open-air video installation. Rather, it called for a performance design directed at the transformative, integrative ritualization of lived and bodied space. The party was planned to reconvert the cul-de-sac metaphor and literally use different spatial tactics for the deployment of monitors (behind chain-link fences in vacant lots, stacked on milk crates in the street, on high front stoops, or placed in cars and on the sidewalk) and the "barricading" of the neighborhood, creating a temporary, autonomous zone that juxtaposed its "entrapment" with the fluid openings for visitors coming in from the cross street. The group obtained the city's permission to hold the event and use the "barricades" (stacks of monitors), and in order to guarantee a peaceful coordination of the event, Iñigo and S-LV met with four rival gangs to negotiate an agreement for Eerie Street to become a neutral zone. This symbolic truce was heightened by another collaborative effort for the block party, namely, the joint composition of the "Westtown Respect" mural whose negotiated painting design pulled together S-LV, members of the local gangs, neighbors, and the Spray Brigade graffiti writers who carried out the design incorporating hybrid styles. During the party itself, thirty members of the four gangs volunteered to protect the safety of the monitors and the people enjoying the event, which included a concert by a local Chicano salsa band. Monitoring the monitors, the gang members contributed to the safe atmosphere of the neighborhood the night of the video party, making the presence of Chicago police officers unnecessary. With a wonderful sense of irony and empowering self-consciousness, the people made sure that their party was successful and that enough "juice" was supplied. In a brilliant imaginative stroke S-LV had set up the various monitor installations by asking the neighbors to lend their yellow extension cords to hook up the monitor-VCRs to the power in the houses along the block. Nearly a hundred extension cords were lowered from apartment windows or wound their way from the domestic interiors to the outdoor television world of Tele-Vecindario, thus composing another concrete sculptural metaphor of the distribution and circulation of shared power in the communal event.

Many impressions of the block party remain in my memory. On one side of the street a monitor barricade was erected in front of a sign alluding to the planned construction of four new luxury condominiums (each priced at $234,000), while one of the monitors "demonstrated" against the investors: "Our community is not for sale." At another location a vacant lot was transformed into a temporary commemorative cemetery. Entitled "Rest in Peace" and consisting of eleven monitors stacked randomly all over the grass plot amid a tangle of yellow cords, this video graveyard showed testimonies and still images of flowers dedicated to those youths who had died as a result of gang violence. Someone placed candles on the grass, and in the waning light of the evening this lot, with its tombstone-like video monitors and flickering candles, became a haunting scene of the deaths that are part of the life of community, as well as providing incriminating evidence of the social violence that

Street-Level Video, Block Party, 1993. Courtesy of Sculpture Chicago. Photo: Antonio Pérez.

hurts the communal body. The vacant lot itself perhaps functioned as a spatial metaphor in the staged allegory of social space inhabited by urban populations in ethnic neighborhoods often divided from the rich enclaves of the suburbs and fragmented internally by the interests of the land-owning classes.

S-LV's video testimonials play out the history-making claims of local production aimed at healing the rifts and bridging the gaps between people and generations. The block party makes history because it testifies and appeals to the human potential in collective and communal action, and the incorporation of video production as a vital tool of community-building similarly testifies to modes of creative innovation not accounted for in the art-world discourse. Video maker Guillermo Arcos, who once showed me a documentary he made in 1992 on the activities of the Near Northwest Arts Council (an alliance of artists and cultural workers in Chicago's Wicker Park neighborhood), confirmed the political meanings of communal activism when he told me that artists in the Wicker Park area had become tired of being considered "cheap labor" or treated as idiosyncratic bohemians who bring innovative ideas to the neighborhood. The problem, he said, is that artists often don't get any respect for what they do because a lot of people think artists enjoy being poor and make art out of a private passion or obsession. As happens so often, artists have an impact on neighborhoods: they fix up decaying houses or apartments; paint murals and "beautify" the neighborhood; open cafés, small bookstores, galleries, and music venues. But when real estate investors pick up on the trend and launch their upscale projects, these same artists get kicked out because they can't afford the higher rents. Arcos's video showed the formation of the Near Northwest Arts Council as a response to such local economic developments, and it was illuminating to see how strongly the artists in the video expressed their vision of participating in the microeconomics by claiming space and struggling for ownership of their studios and houses, for ownership raises the stakes of one's commitment to the health of the neighborhood.

It could be argued that S-LV's video block party externalized, in a neighborhood event of considerable magnitude, the stakes of innovative community involvement on the part of the young, who are often considered the weakest, most endangered strain in our troubled urban social fabric. Racial, class, and age discrimination needs to be fought in a concerted effort to enforce fair housing and equal-opportunity policies and to provide better education, jobs, public services, and incentives for communities' cultural enhancement. The persistent cycle of discrimination and poverty among black and Latino minority populations in the inner city needs to be broken, and local effort and a moral commitment to residential desegregation in Chicago can take a lesson from S-LV's self-administered creative contribution toward fighting crime and drugs, especially since the young people's video productions helped to make visible their community's often hidden and heterogeneous concerns.

It is appropriate in this respect, to recall the long tradition of mural art, stretching from Mexico's muralists, who participated in the early revolutionary ideals of public education, to the more recent tradition of political-protest murals during the Chicano movement of the sixties and seventies. Many inner-city murals in the United States reflect the "outsider" status of displaced minority cultures and youth rebellions, but the existence (since 1970) of the Chicago Mural Group and today's joint efforts between Urban Gateways (an art outreach program) and Chicago's inner-city schools have helped to shape a new conception of community-based mural art that depends on collaborative design and performance. In the process of planning and composing a neighborhood mural and of finding a theme that addresses the local audience and a specific site that communicates with its surrounding architectural and living environment, the creative dimensions of community art are tested and negotiations with institutions, city administrations, or property owners are played out. Such negotiations constitute a vital learning process, and they generate dialogue among partners in a commonly stratified system of unequal power relations. Muralists and graffiti writers have always understood the significance of territory and spatial relations in their invention of visual messages, and just as New York City's subway cars became transient, mobile signifiers of graffiti messages, so S-LV's videos participate in an economy of visual culture that is highly flexible, transient, and paradoxically connected to principles of ownership.

As I argued at the beginning of this chapter, the medium is clearly transient and ephemeral since it does not function as an object or physical structure that adheres to a fixed place. Video does not have the relative visual permanence of a mural. On the other hand, S-LV took responsibility and ownership of its "neighborhood television," making it an evolving and continuing instrument of communication and education, and finding ways to place it inside and outside its immediate production sites. Moreover, the young adolescents' sense of responsibility toward maintaining their studio equipment (the grants were used to purchase camcorders, monitors, and editing decks), training their younger peers, developing new projects, and creating a certain permanence of media production in and for the community will surely increase. Although it is hard to predict the future of community-based video, S-LV's historical contribution will be its immense creativity in channeling its energies and making its videos a public vehicle in an ongoing dialogue about life in the city. In demonstrating its artistic productivity, it will also encourage others and justify further funding of educational or neighborhood arts projects.

In the two years that have elapsed since the block party, S-LV has demonstrated its resilience and creative energy by securing a permanent studio space, coordinating a second block event, and upholding an ambitious instruction, shooting, and screening schedule. In the fall of 1995 S-LV merged with Live Wire Youth Media, a similar collective founded by artists and youth in the black community. The joint group now shares a coordinating staff, a board and advisory committee (for fund-raising and organizational purposes as well as to fulfill the regulations for nonprofit status), and a web site (<http://www.iit.edu/~livewire/>). As formulated in the home page of the web site, it is committed to putting "the latest communication technology in the hands of urban kids" and, through innovative courses in documentary production, computer art, and the Internet, to giving young people "the opportunity to address issues and share their dreams with a global audience." The home page displays a picture of a young black from a local high school, smiling broadly as he rests a camcorder on his shoulder. One eye looks at the viewer, while the other is hidden behind the viewfinder. Without a doubt, new generations of youth will find media production empowering for their self-expression, looking with critical eyes at reality and perhaps taking the fluid relations between education, community development, art and activism in stride. As one S-LV tape of a street interview plainly states, "Is this my reality or your reality?"

1 DANCING WITH TECHNOLOGIES

2 IMPOSSIBLE ANATOMIES

3 CULTURE IN ACTION

4 VIRTUAL COMMUNITIES

SIX

A D   M O R T E M :

AN AIDS PERFORMANCE

P R O J E C T

The Idea of Community

The AIDS crisis has challenged our understanding of death and our ways of living at every level of experience. In the face of confusion over the representation of AIDS in social service, educational, and popular discourses, and a government that was and still is slow to act, the impetus for confronting the disease has come from the people most directly affected by it. Given that AIDS hits hardest among the arts communities, new work is being created every day that gives voice to a shared sense of loss and anger. But it is also clear that not everyone in our society shares this sense of loss, and when a widespread lack of compassion is coupled with a conservative backlash against free expression, the stakes are raised and each "voice" testifying to the experience of living with AIDS becomes a means of survival—and a political act. What is at stake, to my mind, is the idea of community itself.

If the AIDS epidemic has produced a radical challenge to cultural perceptions of sexuality, dying, mourning, and healing, a performance that confronts taboos and political conflicts over the definition of AIDS will have to address the creators' knowledge of AIDS and their relationship to the affected communities. Dedicating a work to the struggle against AIDS involves testing one's own personal and political choices and resistances and, perhaps more important, examining one's own perceptions of community.

Foreground

Ad Mortem, whose Latin name can be translated as to, toward, or against death, was originally conceived as a benefit concert and a contribution to the annual "Day without Art" (December 1), nationally promoted as a day of mourning and action in recognition of the toll AIDS has taken.[1] After witnessing the silence and the grieving that attended this day of nonaction in Houston in 1989, I met with mezzo-soprano Isabelle Ganz and composer Paul English to plan a concert exhibition of music, film, and dance that would address the silence, fear, and paranoia in the social reaction to AIDS. We also wanted to explore the meanings of the proposition "Silence = Death," a rallying cry that had become widely known within and beyond the gay community, both as a challenge to the official discourses of "public health" and to those who bear the burden of the diagnosis. The defense against silence requires public acts of intervention. As a public work of cultural production for the community, we wanted *Ad Mortem* to celebrate and reinforce the self-empowering practices and spiritual or political activism of the people most affected by HIV and AIDS.

After a twelve-month process covering conceptual workshops and composing the video footage and music score (a process of filming, recording, and postproduction that involved no joint rehearsals but a constant dialogue about strategies and the immediate concerns of those members of our communities or neighborhoods with whom we worked), we were eventually joined by two other musicians (Richard Nunemaker on bass clarinet and Brian Green on synthesizer) and dancer/choreographer Deborah Hay for the live performances of *Ad Mortem* held during December 1990.[2] The creative relationships and processes of composition for this collaborative work require some commentary in order to pinpoint the stumbling blocks we faced. In addressing some of the shortcomings—we were unable to reconcile the differences in our own production processes and failed to build a broader audience community support base—I hope to contribute to an exchange of ideas that is a vital aspect of the growing body of alternative-media activities seeking to contest mainstream representations and repressions of the issues.[3]

Staging Communion?

The main purpose of *Ad Mortem* was to break the silence and widespread indifference surrounding the AIDS crisis in Houston, a city that in 1990 ranked fourth nationally in reported cases and was estimated to have thirty-five thousand area residents infected with HIV. In drawing attention to the racist and homophobic climate of the city, we knew the work was going to find itself on the margins of a fledgling performance art scene that had tried for years to locate its audience. The musicians in our group suggested that we address the broadest possible audience by using the spiritual force of music to appeal for a sense of community and compassion. Based on our belief that AIDS affects all of us, the performance would cut across barriers of gender, sexual orientation, race, and class.

As we began to develop the images and leitmotifs for the musical score, I argued that video as a medium would not support the vision of a transcendent spirituality. Reality in film can never be objective, for each aesthetic choice, each framing of the reality or experience of AIDS, is subjective and political. Our claim, then, that AIDS affects all of us created the first paradox: who this "us" is could only be answered by showing how HIV transmission is translated into differing cultural practices and experiences. None of the white, heterosexual/bisexual members of our group were infected, and our solidarity with those struggling to survive reflected our differences from them as well as the ideological roles of our performance media. As a partial answer to this dilemma, I was asked to produce a poetic video that would evoke the subconscious patterns through which disease has historically been construed and used for purposes of exclusion and stigmatization, and thereby to address our contemporary, fragmented, secular, and religious community inscribed by such manipulative practices. Since we had decided not to suppress the paradoxes and complexities of our positions vis-à-vis our subject, I planned to disrupt the more allusive poetic video images with documentary footage referring "us" directly to people in Houston living with AIDS and their personal accounts. After we had created the structure and thematic leitmotifs for the performance, it was decided to work separately from then on. My own documentary approach created a further contradiction involving the second purpose of *Ad Mortem,* namely, to address individual reactions to illness and death as well as the consequences of being identified as HIV positive in a society where sexuality, disease, and death are either invisible or spectacularized.

I knew I could not speak for others about the experience of AIDS, yet I wanted to break the silence which was also my silence, my unawareness of the painful experience of being ill and stigmatized. The necessity of abandoning intentionality, authority, and the directing of the camera generated a process that allowed the video performance to evolve from my encounters with affected individuals and their support groups. In these recordings, some of the people hit hardest by AIDS—gay men, people of color, women, the poor—spoke about their desire to live and the much-needed and appreciated support of volunteer workers, community organizers, and lovers. Some frequently referred to these groups as their "chosen family." In the staging of *Ad Mortem,* I had hoped to recreate a sense of community-based art that could be politically meaningful at the very moment when such a functioning community was absent or questionable. In speaking for themselves and the love and understanding they require in the face of approaching death, people living with AIDS don't simply address a specific dilemma, they also invoke a collective mode of reflection on how "community" can be mobilized. At the same time, their "family" is a politically constituted collectivity based on an identity (seropositivity) that is life-threatening. Identity conflicts abound (here I am speaking as a nonresident alien and will address the issue of AIDS and immigration later in this chapter) once we pursue the question of our putative community and recognize the different levels of professional or personal relations by means of which we express ourselves. In theory, the work I wanted to help create was not tied to any essentialist idea of racial, ethnic, or sexual identity but to the diverse needs and experiences of communities affected by AIDS discrimination. It seemed vital to find a shared language in which the community's fear about sexuality and about death could be explored. In practice, our work sought to promote a shared reality between the so-called general public and the affected communities. However, this meant that we were simultaneously speaking from several subject positions, and the visibility of the gay position in our minds was privileged insofar as it represented the most outspoken and effective mobilization of this community in Houston.

Since the documentary portions of the video for *Ad Mortem* had been developed over several months in close collaboration with community support groups and AIDS organizations in my Montrose neighborhood, we were prepared neither for the divisive reactions among audiences nor for the lack of response from the multicultural and gay/lesbian communities in Houston. Our attempt to straddle the existing social and racial barriers seemed to have landed us in a void, yet the unease of the arts community and the media critics with our treatment of the subject reflected the central ambivalence of the work. We had created a performance artwork that explored the social memory of disease and the stigmatized body in history, one that presented a spiritual vision of community. In shifting its focus to a community-based documentary showing the isolation and fragility of such a group within the political process, the work lost its aesthetic and theatrical framing device—the leitmotif of disease—and became divided against itself. The audience was invited to witness this shift from a general, historical perspective on public conscience to the very concrete, immediate, and local struggle for survival expressed by people living with AIDS. The vulnerability of real people speaking about their lives presented a litmus test for an audience willing to let the protective aesthetic boundaries drop and to acknowledge the painful losses being experienced in the communities.

In offering to drop, even temporarily, the pretense of art or the fiction of art's cathartic or consciousness-raising effect, the video documentary raised the issue of AIDS as a fact of everyday life. It showed a fractured community and its possible recovery. To speak of this knowledge is a precondition *for* a sense of community. Since not everyone in our audience could accept this proposition, I must assume that the communication of AIDS knowledge is dependent on a number of conscious and unconscious assumptions about the legitimacy of information and, more important, about what may be said. When the musicians in our ensemble began to raise their own objections to the gay political activism represented in the documentary, gaps which could not be bridged by the music or the dance opened up in the very fabric of the production.

Aesthetic closure was also prevented through the silent, intermittent dance by Deborah Hay. Playing across the unstable boundaries of self and other, and across the video's juxtaposition of historical images of scapegoating with the present stigma of exclusion enforced by society for people living with HIV/AIDS, Deborah's solos offered no comforting meaning or spirtually gratifying emotion. Rather, her "identities" as performed in the solos only made sense in relation to what the audience wanted to see.

Masked by costume and facial paint, she first appeared as if in another body, her shadow refracted on the video projection screen. Later, during her gradual movement from the screen toward and into the audience, Hay discreetly articulated her awareness of the bodily self; in extreme proximity to the viewers *she invited being seen.* What she has referred to as "practicing dying" in her training and creative process—an exploration of the organic and cellular consciousness of the ever-changing, vulnerable body—here became a performance process during which the heightened self-awareness of the body could be shared in the context of a work that showed the painful distancing effect of the AIDS crisis on the inflicted body. The intimacy of this sharing, however, created some of the strongest signs of resistance among audience members, who could not bear to see or be seen.

Perhaps some audience members left the auditorium because they feared to be touched. Hay's caressing arm movements and gestures, performed within the audience as a series of seductive, alluring "close-ups," provoked an awareness of the sensual, erotic body through the immediacy of touch and smell. Her/their only "protection" was the gauzelike veil she wore, made of the same transparent plastic material used for dental dams (and other safe-sex practices). Ironically, her very gentle, unthreatening, and almost reassuring presence generated an unbearable tension among some members of the audience and seemed to arouse the very homophobic and antierotic reactions she wanted to exorcise.

The Performance

Performances of *Ad Mortem* were held in two different sites, first in the more intimate theater gallery at DiverseWorks and then in the cavernous exhibition space of the Lawndale Art Center, an old warehouse now closed. Since no sets were used, audience attention was directed toward the large screen images and their relationship to the musicians and the dancer. Countering the segregation of space in the movie theater, our use of the auditorium, including live performances of music and dance, was intended to turn the filmic images into a chorus whose movements would neither converge with the music nor create its own fictitious narrative space, instead remaining simultaneously and ideologically present.

The structure we evolved was based on the oratorio form, and we designed three movements for solo "voices" (mezzo-soprano, bass clarinet, dance, the interview speakers on video), "chorus" (silent video images), and "orchestra" (synthesized and live, improvised music). The impetus for this structure derived from Isabelle Ganz's idea to incorporate the music of the *Llibre Vermell* as a counterpoint. A powerful document of fourteenth-century society's understanding of death and communal healing, the *Llibre Vermell* is a manuscript consisting of festive songs and dances rediscovered in Montserrat (Spain) in the nineteenth century. Folk and ecclesiastical traditions in Spain, France, and Italy influenced the polyphonic and monodic songs of the *Llibre Vermell*. A direct outgrowth of the period of the Black Death, which ravaged Europe from 1347 to 1348, "Ad mortem festinamus" is the oldest known surviving example containing music for a "dance of death." It has been speculated that the form of this musical dance expressed the communal acknowledgment or embrace of dying.

The delirious dimensions of this embrace may seem foreign to Western society today, but as a counterpoint to the postmodern disavowal of aging and death and the stigmatization of disease, the medieval leitmotif served at least two functions in our performance. First, in Paul's music for the opening prologue, during which the still image of a boarded-up house and two brief texts were projected onto the screen, a leitmotif from the *Llibre Vermell* introduced a historical sequence of images drawn from the Middle Ages. This leitmotif is later echoed in the choral passages, which mingle past and present iconic constructions of the body, of sickness, isolation, and venereal disease ending in death. Second, the recurring leitmotif paved the way for the accelerating, marchlike rhythms of the last movement, which resonated with images of spiritual healing and communion, the vocal repetition of "Ad mortem festinamus," and the quiet, circular dance performed by Deborah. The interweaving of medieval and contemporary musical modes, with their sacred and secular connotations, corresponded to the image-movement of the video montage. Using a disjunctive technique of image-time (static, fixed-shots and mobile camera editing), the montage presented a slow, meditative continuity or, conversely, an intense discontinuity achieved through the crosscutting of chronologically and logically disparate footage.

The parallel structuring of the music and the visual track followed the progression of three main metaphors: "The Ghetto," "The Body," and "Communion." These metaphors were mediated by a central, dialectical section entitled "body politic" in which the contradictory logic of identity—HIV positive/HIV negative—was explored through images of both local and national political activism and community mobilization. The bulk of the video was silent and constructed a lyrical mode of visual allusions abstracted from different contexts: ghettoization; the Holocaust; the Crucifixion and the Eucharist; medieval iconography of the body and of damnation; contemporary art and pornography; the medicalized body; *los desaparecidos;* and the Names Project Memorial Quilt. In addition to these predominantly silent allusions, a documentary plane articulated a double narrative. On the one hand, the narrative examined the cultural pathology of fear and its manipulation by the mass media. On the other hand, several people directly affected by AIDS told of a whole range of positive avenues they had pursued in order to live their lives in dignity.

From my work with AIDS support groups and in AIDS clinics and day care centers I had learned that it was necessary to focus not on dying but on living with AIDS and on challenging the image of people with AIDS as victims. One of my most memorable experiences occurred during the first support-group meeting I attended at Bering Church Day Care Center in my neighborhood. At the end of the meeting a gay priest suggested that we adopt a eucharistic ceremony for our own purpose of establishing communion among ourselves. A young HIV-positive man who had just told me the story of his diagnosis smiled as he handed me a piece of bread, saying, "This is the body broken for you." When we kissed, I remember being completely aroused by feelings of joy, compassion, anxiety, and shame, and it took me a while to make the necessary and deeper connection to a ritual meaning of communion that I was once taught during the religious upbringing of my childhood. Our gesture of sharing compassion and acknowledging each other was perfectly simple, but it meant so much more than the empty repetitions of ceremonies I remembered from the days I'd attend Catholic mass. The communion of ritual and activism no longer seems such a paradox to me.

In this sense, the video's double narrative also challenged the historical analogy between the Middle Ages and postmodern society by giving new meaning to the spiritual in political activism. Following a clearly noticeable trajectory, the music of the oratorio began with an elegiac opening, proceeded to a very tense, conflicted middle section, finally reaching an inspirational, celebratory ending. This ending, symbolized in the screen images of "communion" (a secular meal, the breaking of bread and sharing of wine, crosscut with a candlelight march organized by Body Positive in Houston), remained tentative because it projected the kind of integrative, compassionate community that I could locate only in isolated instances among the by no means equally well-organized affected groups in the barrio, the black neighborhoods, and the gay white neighborhood. The diversity of experiences shown in the documentary sections *posed* the very question of community and placed the ritual significance of communion or solidarity in direct relationship to the symbolic transsubstantiation of the body.

Ad Mortem thus staged communion as a positive and hopeful gesture to counter the pressures of isolation that are the social consequences of deep-seated fears of and medievalized moralizations about the diseased body. As Simon Watney and other activist writers have pointed out, AIDS commentary either involuntarily or deliberately reproduces a racist and homophobic imagery of contamination wrought by depravity and deviance, thus returning to a "premodern vision of the body, according to which heresy and sin are held to be scorned in the features of their voluntary subjects by punitive and admonitory manifestations of disease."[4]

Movement 1: The Ghetto

The communion evoked in *Ad Mortem* had no religious or redemptive function. It referred instead to a social space in which a "shared body" is a contradiction in terms as long as we don't recognize scapegoating and the violence of censoring enjoyment as symptoms of our variously imagined and displaced fears. This reference to a symptomatic displace-

ment was conjured up in the first movement's slow panning shots of
the fifteenth-century Jewish cemetery in Prague, and was framed by the
later images of the Body Positive candlelight march across a deserted
urban center of downtown Houston.

Deborah Hay's solo "The Bad Angel" initiated the opening movement. As the cunning title of this first of her three "Dying Plays" suggests, her dance created the figure of a symptomatic body. Dressed in
a flowing red gown, her feet and teeth painted black and face white,
Deborah emerged from behind the screen and slowly advanced toward
the audience, gazing at them and letting herself be gazed at and imagined as a devilish monstrum that, from one moment to the next, looked
like a pitiful, grotesque clown or child, someone both haunting and
haunted.

The subsequent sequence of images from "The Ghetto" introduced
the medieval leitmotif, as the performance shifted to an elegiac mood
that involved projected remembrances of persecution, segregation, and
genocide. In the introduction's concluding moments, Isabelle extended
the Latin song from the *Llibre Vermell* into a traditional Hebrew prayer
hymn to the dead ("el Maleh Rachamim"), her voice gradually rising
and reverberating throughout the space.

Richard Nunemaker's bass clarinet, with its deep, throbbing voice,
accentuated the musical setting during "The Body," a video segment
that cut from the medieval iconography of disease and divine punishment to contemporary images of the objectified, abandoned, pornographic body and, finally, to the testimonies of two men infected with
AIDS. In breaking with the decontextualized anonymity of "victims" of
AIDS, the interview section intruded into the cinematic space created
up to this point by showing the two men at work in real time. Travis
Christopher Pfeiffer, a gay artist, explained the installation he had built,
depicting the paraphernalia of the hospital room in which his lover
had died. David Webb, a biologist working on a cell-transformation experiment in his lab, warned against the potentially murderous political
reactions to a disease that would remain a homosexual disease in the
public consciousness. It was David who actually made the allusion to
the abhorrent Nazi policies of euthanasia and genocide explicit.

Counterbalancing David's pessimistic references, the last section of
the first movement, "Remembering," affirmed the necessity to document
the losses publicly and to prevent a regime of silence that would treat
people with AIDS in our society as disposable constituencies ("Silence
= Death"). The symbolic weight of "Remembering" rested on the easily
recognizable images of the Names Project Memorial Quilt exhibited in

Houston in the fall of 1990. The images and the music, however, did not so much evoke a ritual of communal grieving as insist upon the *visibility* of these people and these deaths: their names were called out repeatedly. The chorus of voices and names stood as a testimony against disappearance.

Movement 2: Body Politic

Using a fast-paced montage of images from a wide spectrum of local and national sites of protest and repression, this section depicted more explicitly the social and political repercussions of the phantasmagoria of AIDS. Paul's powerfully driven and conflicted music heightened the unreleased tension that had been built up and, at one point, almost literally threatened to break the frame of the screen when the extreme close-up of David Wojnarowicz's face appeared, contorted by anger and screaming against our "diseased society": "My rage is really about the fact that when I was told I'd contracted this virus it didn't take me long to realize that I'd contracted a diseased society as well. . . . [A]ll I can feel is the pressure . . . and the need for release."[5]

Wojnarowicz's rage and activist stance, which had been exacerbated by the scapegoating of his art by the NEA during the 1989 exhibition *Witnesses Against Our Vanishing* at Artists Space in New York City as well as by Donald Wildmon's American Family Association, marked only one, albeit an important, facet of the video's wide-ranging exploration of the disunity in the social body. In contrast to the rage and frustration found among affected communities, the video also showed the more sobering side of ineffective, overburdened, and underfunded health care.[6] It revealed the many efforts that have been made (mostly from within the affected communities) to remedy these dysfunctions in the public health system and to draw political attention to AIDS as a local and worldwide crisis that demands new definitions of community and communion. David Fowler, one of the community workers who helped organize a large coalition of local groups that staged a march and demonstration during the Economic Summit in Houston, expressed the purpose of this action in a brief and simple manner: "We are trying to save our lives. Which is more than our Government is doing."

The final image of this section was a single long shot of a large group of marchers from the candlelight demonstration in downtown Houston, which was organized by the Body Positive coalition. They were seen slowly approaching the viewer and holding up the light of hope against

Deborah Hay moving in front of the screen in her "Bad Angel" dance, *Ad Mortem,* Lawndale Art Center, Houston, 1990. Photo: Birringer/Lakes.

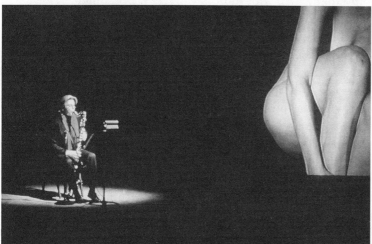

Screen projection in "The Body," with Richard Nunemaker on bass clarinet, *Ad Mortem,* Lawndale Art Center, Houston, 1990. Photo: Birringer/Lakes.

Deborah Hay at the head of the march of the Body Positive coalition, with Isabelle Ganz (*at right*) in a scene from *Ad Mortem,* Lawndale Art Center, Houston, 1990. Photo: Birringer/deSoto.

the shadows of indifference reflecting back from the cool glass-and-steel towers of corporate America.

Movement 3: Communion

During the documentary first half of "Communion," several caregivers and people living with AIDS spoke frankly about the dramatic impact of the illness on their lives and the choices they had to make in order to be able to live *and* to accept death. Most of the speakers—the previously mentioned Travis Pfeiffer and David Webb; Kaci Fannin, a student who had developed an educational outreach project in her black community; Tootsie Smith, a mother who had just lost her son; Mary Lou Galantino, a physiotherapist who serves as a volunteer at the only Houston AIDS outpatient clinic; Joey Marz and Aldon Wisdom, two unemployed gay men with full-blown AIDS; Bob Singleton, a schoolteacher and support-group counselor—explained how their attitudes had changed from denial to acceptance and how they reevaluated their lifestyle choices, seeking new relationships in their "chosen families." David Webb was the only speaker who rationalized his HIV-positive status and acceptance of mortality in a highly individualistic, philosophical-scientific way; the others addressed specific experiences in a diverse community of men and women, including black, Latino, white, gay, lesbian, and heterosexual. What each of them shared was the expressed need and the courage to draw on the particular strengths, nurturance, caring, openness, and emotional bonding they found in support groups and peer-counseling networks. By the end of the documentary, the picture of the body politic had been redrawn as the body-positive, pointing to the increasingly important role that community-based action has played in offering people a practical and spiritual means of struggling with the specter of death; by contrast, the official neglect of the failing health system and the existing economic, political, and medical inequalities among the communities were also evident.

Building upon this perception of a "new" community born out of crisis and out of an awareness of a limited future, the concert/exhibition ended with the musical evocation of a communal dance. Deborah's circular movement linked the projected community of the candlelight march (screen image) with the live audience. Some members of the audience who had participated in the march were seen on screen; others were invited to see—if they were willing to look—that the dialectical terms of "communion" and of *Ad Mortem* as a whole posited the absence of community as the culturally rooted, negative form of that which might come to pass. However, once we are willing to embrace and not to blame those affected by the disease, the positive form of a virtually present community is within our grasp. It is in these terms that our work ultimately recognized the space of the performance itself as one of the many testing grounds on which the struggle as/for a community is acted out.

After leaving Houston in the spring of 1991, I decided that instead of dwelling on the disagreements we might have had while working on *Ad Mortem,* I would direct my efforts toward developing new links among AIDS service organizations, community groups, educators, and artist-activists. At my workplace, Northwestern University, I began to teach a workshop on the representations of AIDS and, together with an international group of students, artists, and researchers, to shape a production concept for an exhibition entitled *AIDS Interfacings.*[7]

AIDS Interfacings

This event was organized like an "open house," where we displayed our resources and research materials, including books and articles on AIDS, a listing of the local network of support groups and health care providers, information on the impact of AIDS in Africa and Latin America, as well as practical information on drug use, safe sex, and physical and creative therapeutic methods that had been explored by a member of our team in his own support group. We provided demonstrations of this knowledge, showed AIDS education videos, and exhibited some conceptual images (slides, posters, maps, audioworks, text-collages) in the installation. We also intercepted the daily TV soap-opera broadcast piped into the student center lunchrooms and substituted our own AIDS education videos. Later that day we were joined by local activists from Chicago's ACT UP chapter, who contributed performances and skits.

The action took place at Northwestern's Block Gallery, adjacent to the student center, on 14 March 1991. Structured as a continuous, day-long performance, it included discussions, exhibitions, and demonstrations on homophobia, sexism, and racism (organized by Richard Geer); support group and therapy work (Deryl Johnson); the cultural politics of AIDS education in Africa (Mbala Nkanga); safer sex education (Amy Ludwig); installations on victimization (Moe Meyer) and virology/immunology (Terri Kapsalis/Shannon Jackson); narrative performances on individual and community experiences (Stephen Wroblewski); interactive and documentary videos on people living with AIDS (Gabriel Gómez); the local Bonaventura House (Mara Adelman/Howard Motyl); image formation and AIDS awareness (John Wat); and body politics, activism, and spiritualism based on a collage of materials from *Ad Mortem* (myself).

Targeted at the young student population, educators, and university employees, the performance focused on prevention and on an informed response to the AIDS epidemic, examining existing AIDS discourses and, in particular, challenging the false inside/outside structure of mainstream representations and their mythic construction of a "general public" somehow safely above the infected, "anti-body" populations (linking the so-called dangers of homosexual lifestyles with drug use, prostitution, and the plight of impoverished minorities, immigrants, or third world peoples). Challenging mainstream misinformation, paranoia, and sensationalism while appealing to the politicized consciousness of young people—who already seem to have shifted from a sense of anxiety to a more lethargic indifference to the dangers of transmission—is an enormous task that requires patience and constancy. We suggested that such participatory workshops be made a regular component of the curriculum, and that the work could only be sustained if grassroots campus groups interacted with community-based health care workers and AIDS service organizations, since information about treatment and other aspects of the epidemic is constantly evolving and changing.[8]

By the time we staged the exhibition-performance, I had come to realize that the mediation of AIDS awareness cannot be contained within a single artwork or concert. I recalled our long discussions in Houston about the length of *Ad Mortem* (originally lasting ninety minutes, but later cut to seventy-four) and about why we failed to achieve a "unified" work of art that could speak to everybody. I had assumed that we could only speak to those willing to listen and respond. We remained onstage each night and invited feedback from the audience— an effort that largely failed because most of the people seemed either too moved and embarrassed or simply unwilling to speak openly about their feelings and reactions. We also heard some negative comments about portions of the video documentary, especially in connection with David's allusions to the Holocaust and his own atheistic allegory of scientific Darwinism. Others described their discomfort during Deborah's close-up dance within the audience. My disillusionment about the lack of communion with the audience may very well be a nonrecognition of the vulnerability and denial of the spectators themselves. This denial surfaced in the press reviews we received in Houston. The unwillingness of art reviewers to enter into a serious dialogue over the question of the absent community was exacerbated by the chronic unease Houston editors feel about performance art and alternative media. This led to reviews by music and film critics who never even acknowledged the vital symbolic role of Deborah Hay's presence as a mediator between the music and the video. The reviews effectively diminished the work's ethical and political thrust by silencing the question that was unmistakably raised by the mixed-media performance: What constitutes a significant cultural or aesthetic response to the AIDS crisis?

SEVEN

MEDIA ACTIVISM

Alternative Communications

During my work on the *AIDS Interfacings* workshop/installation and my identification with the activist practices and strategies of ACT UP and the in-your-face video work of collective groups such as Testing the Limits, Gran Fury, Women's AIDS Video Enterprise (WAVE), the Audio-Video Department at Gay Men's Health Crisis (GMHC), or the "Seeing Through AIDS" media workshops, I have come to believe that the answer to the question posed at the end of the preceding chapter lies in the ongoing *process* of intervention and the building up of self-empowering practices that cross the boundaries of different cultural communities. Such crossover work requires an exchange of knowledge and experience, as well as a growing understanding of how different life experiences and health issues are interpreted. Beginning with our action in March 1991, *AIDS Interfacings* has been defined not as an art project, nor primarily as an exhibition/discussion project modeled after the "Democracy" town meetings organized by Group Material in 1988–89 (which included the important forum on "AIDS and Democracy: A Case Study"), but as a continuous media project with the goal of testing the potential of video production as the most flexible, instantaneous medium with which to engage the evolving experiences and shifting discourses of the social crisis surrounding HIV/AIDS. With the help and participation of individuals and groups from within and without affected communities, our group began to develop a media outreach project that offered to document the self-representations of people living with AIDS, activists, care providers, community workers, and support networks as an ongoing process.

At the same time, our focus during the development of the media project, as with the preparation for the *AIDS Interfacings* action we staged at the university, was on the open and participatory form of production itself—on the mediating production of *communication*. What are possible visual/verbal representations of ways in which individuals and communities themselves can define or create forms of information? What styles of learning are most useful to them, and how do we work as facilitators or affiliated media producers? How are the modes of production, facilitation, distribution, and feedback exchanged, and what are the channels that can be used to reach community centers, hospitals, churches, schools, campuses, public-access stations, and other local groups and networks that share an interest in obtaining information on health care, drug protocol and prevention, and the creative production or representation of survival and self-help strategies? What are the processes of reception, criticism, discussion, and utilization of tapes or strategies connected to media?

I have already tried to answer some of these questions in chapter 5, ("Performance/Video Art"). The issues of the relations of power/control in production and the ethos of collaboration/participation apply both to the rehearsal process or site-specific situationism in performance and to the shared production of images and voices from within a group or community, since the latter always involves a critical evaluation of the construction of form and content based on the structuring of the interactions and boundaries among the group members.

It should be clear that activist video is product-oriented since it wants its message or its intervention to get out; it wants to act quickly and efficiently in order to reach its constituency or inform other audiences of its concerns. For example, I arrived in Chicago during the week when the Gulf War broke out—or, more correctly, when UN (for which read U.S. and U.K.) armed forces initiated their devastating air strikes against Iraq. We were out on the streets starting with the second night of the nationally televised air strikes, and over the next few days a growing number of antiwar protesters—including women's groups, unions, and ACT UP members—demonstrated in front of the Federal Building. I videotaped the demonstrations and the protest speeches and also interviewed some of the people participating or watching. By the third day it was becoming obvious that the mainstream U.S. media were transmitting the war and reporting on its progress with an evident bias in favor of Operation Desert Storm, thus siding with state policy and editing out/silencing any images/voices of dissent. I tried to submit my tapes to the local broadcast media and radio stations but was rebuffed; prowar sentiments had gained such force and public momentum that dissident viewpoints remained excluded for quite some time. It was only outside the mainstream that a growing number of pamphlets, posters, and videos were being circulated to mobilize a coalition against the war machine, which proved difficult since no broad-based peace movement or labor-union movement currently exists in the United States. Nevertheless, some of us continued to document and exchange critical diagnoses, assuming that the history of this protest had to be recorded in order to ensure its existence at a later stage of public debate over the politics and imperial interests of this U.S. intervention, and over the Pentagon's media management, the spectacle of televised war coverage, and the blackouts and distortions of minority public opinion.

The impotence of alternative media and of the spellbound public intellectuals in the face of an elaborate, integrated corporate/military engineering of the tactical operations of Operation Desert Storm (both in the Gulf and back home) had depressing effects on some of us, but we already knew that the so-called New World Order also signified the nearly total dominance of the West's information channels/media monopoly in terms of the use of satellites, airwaves, and broadcast, telecommunications, and computer-related transmission capacities. The dominant commercial media also can choose their own commentators or experts.

As an integrated system of media information management, this New World Order needs to be resisted through equally interactive and horizontally integrated local counterdiscourses on a large scale (internationally) in order to continue to develop independent methods for gathering and distributing information and processing it for the purpose of active interventions. Such interventions, as has been the case during the years of government silence regarding the spread of the AIDS epidemic—can only be effective if local "dissident" or oppositional groups establish modes of cooperation, exchange, and solidarity, while making use of all available technologies of communication (video, phone, fax, photocopy, Internet). More important, these cooperatives need to develop their own organizational strategies for creatively interfacing with the population and with institutions, so as to better communicate what a particular demonstration or direct action is intended to accomplish— as has been successfully practiced as far back as the anti-Vietnam protests, the civil rights and Chicano movements, and the post–Stonewall gay and lesbian liberation movement and, more recently, by women's pro-choice groups, ACT UP, or the Greenpeace choreographies of dramatized conflict (intended to focus media attention on an ecological problem).

The role of ACT UP in the current wave of alternative video productions cannot be overestimated, for it was the theatrical and graphic creativity of the early ACT UP interventions, poster and ad campaigns, and strategically staged protests (i.e., for the soliciting of media coverage) that, since its inception in 1987, sparked a broader involvement of artists and cultural workers in the production of our own media documents, which could be distributed and shown in the alternative network even if the mainstream media decided to remain silent.

Toward the end of the eighties, activist and AIDS-related videos began to appear more frequently at video events and gay/lesbian film festivals, and since many of the video makers also worked in schools, universities, and community centers, the development of a different media landscape became tangible. I cannot even begin to describe the complex, slow evolution of a production history and infrastructure for radical activist media, but it is a task that needs to be undertaken if we want to understand the role and function of alternative video in the larger force field of what Jane Gaines has called "contested culture," referring to today's increasingly embattled relations between communications technologies and the political, legal, and cultural issues of rights, property, freedom of speech, access, images, and values.

The contestation I am pursuing here is based on my assumption that our articulation of free, critical, productive, and oppositional (to dominant regimes of signification, to the corporate-controlled, profit-oriented media) opinion involves the dual practice of social/political diagnosis and direct action. I consider video production a form of direct action that involves conceptual and experiential processes. These processes are deeply affective, often involving the core of our emotional experiences, and they are also nurturing, pleasurable, and full of expenditures that cannot be recuperated; yet even our losses contribute to the visible affirmation of our politicized efforts to change the conditions we are subjected to.

Activist video very often is a collective process, especially if it involves partners (workshop, group) or subjects (documentary, interview) who need to speak for and name themselves. In many situations, shared video production begins by introducing the video technology to the partners. It is therefore also an educational or instructional process that requires time, especially when it comes to decision-making during the montage of the editing, where choices have to be made about what is left out and what image and sound rhythms are preferable. The process of shared production necessarily involves the locating of funding resources and facilitators to provide the equipment and demonstrate the use of camera, microphone, and editing controls.

In order to accomplish the difficult work of self-expression and of framing an issue and creating an effective compositional form, the process of production necessarily hinges upon the conditions of cooperation, trust, and commitment that are built up from within the group. Individual sensibilities, lack of experience, good intentions, and time-consuming negotiations all enter into the process and the repositioning of power relations (i.e., distributing the control or authority of the director-function among the members of the group or finding a working model of parallel/equal responsibilities) that shape the creative outcome of the production. The excitement of finding a collaborative mode that results in a shared video created and owned by the group can be very uplifting, and I have often experienced how fulfilling such work becomes when the group members realize they have taken their representation into their own hands and self-consciously politicized their positions, languages, and images.

It can also happen that a sense of frustration may occur once the video is out and distributed, since we often don't have control over what happens to the images when they are presented in different contexts and under different conditions, or when they are copied and appropriated for other purposes (by mainstream media, curators, organizations, or other video makers). I always emphasize the instability of the medium in my collaborative work; I have adapted and revised my own performance-video work repeatedly over the years because I tend to think of video not as a completed object but as a transitional, open-ended medium that is "processual" and contingent on contextual use. I also believe that this special nature of video destabilizes its function as a documentary medium, since its alternative production code—as opposed to mainstream news media, public television's political-interest stories, or so-called archival footage—often wavers between "testimonial" and "ironic" or subversive/countercultural strategies. Its critical, deconstructive employment of the conventional realism of TV documentaries aligns it more closely to the fictional and the performative, to video art and to what Gregg Bordowitz has described as activist video's "queer structure of feeling," especially if the producers "identify the work as queer, . . . claim the work has significance to queers, [and] if the work is censored or criticized for being queer."[1]

I believe that the crossovers between the testimonial and poetic, experimental, and activist imaginary can produce very powerful work. Marlon Riggs's *Tongues Untied* (1989), which I consider a collaborative work, is a splendid example of a video filled with anger that is simultaneously also a poetic manifesto, elegy, testimonial, meditation, and revolutionary call for love among black men ("brother to brother"). It is impossible to categorize the work in terms of form and genre. I was working in Houston at the time it was supposed to be aired on the local PBS station, but somehow the station director was afraid of its "queer structure of feeling" and cancelled it despite our protests. It has since been made widely available through alternative video rental stores and outlets, and I've seen images taken from it, as well as from Isaac Julien's

Looking for Langston (1989), which have been appropriated and quoted in other videos.

Activist video, in other words, creates its own models, textures, and influences on other activist video. It is perhaps interesting to determine to what extent complex and more elaborately post-produced videos—whether by a single author or a collective—will inevitably alter or diffuse the testimonial content by drawing on fictional/experimental filmic styles associated with avant-garde cinematic history or with video art. Can one speak of an "activist aesthetic"? Are there particular formal techniques or modes of camera work (hand-held, camera-edited, disparate camera styles filmed by different people) or enframing that make such videos recognizably amateur or activist? What distinguishes them from home movies or chance documentary footage, such as the tape made of the Rodney King beating? Would one consider big-budget alternative video work with high production values no longer activist, even if such a video created an incisive and penetrating AIDS documentary, advocated greater environmental concern, or demanded more freedom of speech? Must distinctions between conventional and alternative forms be retained if an independently produced activist video opts for the prevailing realist style or adopts a mainstream television or MTV format, such as the talk show? What happens to the existing types of alternative and experimental video practice when Hollywood filmmakers such as Steven Spielberg, Oliver Stone, or Spike Lee "quote" these styles or incorporate them into their narratives as "special effects?"[2]

Perhaps none of the conceptual borders we delineate will stand up to the pressures of reality (e.g., the market and mainstreaming forces) except for the ultimately determining factor of the video's political position on the side of the AIDS-affected communities, gay/lesbian/bisexual and feminist communities, or disenfranchised minority or immigrant communities—and thus squarely in the not-for-profit sector that has created its own reception and distribution circuits outside or parallel to the commercial, profit-driven market. At the same time, activist video production is often intended to question media constructions of reality and must raise issues of representation in its own formal construction, quoting filmic techniques as well as resituating mainstream television discourse or Hollywood's commercial realism. If it embodies quotations and parodies of dominant ideologies, it will necessarily operate within the dominant ideological form while creating incongruencies and internal tensions. Its style being eclectic, it is unpredictable as to how the "structures of feeling" will be read by diverse audiences, and what types of responses videos about AIDS will elicit from audiences, whose composition may vary considerably, depending on their knowledge of AIDS, their identification with affected individuals or communities, and on public attitudes ranging from fear to tolerance. Many of the videos by gay and lesbian activists included in the compilation *Video Against AIDS* were shown to an enthusiastic and supportive audience at the Montreal AIDS Conference; yet numerous community health organizations and health educators, traditionally considered straight, proceeded to order the videos because of their content. Actually, a growing number of straight viewers have seen the videos in schools, universities, and community centers, since the material most often is more interestingly presented and provides more up-to-date information than mainstream media treatments. Other viewers will have seen excepts of the videos compiled by conservative fundamentalists (e.g., *The Gay Agenda*), who want to warn their constituencies, which may not be all that bad, since I always hope that my work is seen and discussed by the opposition.

As I implied earlier in my critique of inside/outside, us/them structures, AIDS video production has sought to undermine the discriminatory binary power relations between "general" and "high-risk" populations constructed by scientific and government discourse and mainstream commercial media, yet it often finds itself reacting to the structure by assuming a position at the margin, which expresses its actual social and economic relationship to corporate America as well as its strategic position of difference from oppressive, heteronormative regimes of knowledge and power (the industrial, educational, military, judicial, and medical regimens described in Foucault's critical genealogies). Gay/lesbian liberation after Stonewall, together with the new social movements that fought for civil rights, were based on the minoritizing discourse of ethnic, sexual, or other identities and successfully invoked an affirmative ethos of "marginality" to build community and self-identification in the seventies and eighties. But the intensity of the antigay and anti–affirmative action backlash has also exposed the internal divisions and class differences within the marginal communities, thus reflecting the limitations of a radical social activism that grounds its identity politics in mutually exclusive subjects (homosexual/heterosexual) or ethnicities and social worlds.

With the growing realization that there is no consensus—not even in the Queer Nation movement—as to what constitutes social, sexual, or national identities, and as the new queer theory celebrates social differences beyond the normalizing (assimilationist) politics of mainstream straight *and* gay America, I am reminded of remarks made by John Greyson at a gay/lesbian video film festival, poking fun at the self-righteousness and seriousness of some AIDS activist "professionals" and complaining about the constricting realist consensus prevailing among educators concerning the production of safer-sex videos or the use of sexually explicit images. In his own video *The Pink Pimpernel* (1989), Greyson produced an amazingly hybrid collage of stylistic effects by intermixing three different levels of narrative form: documentary interviews with AIDS activists intercut with "Pink Panther" cartoons; an updated, dramatic retelling of the melodramatic film *The Scarlet Pimpernel* (1935) involving two gay lovers, one of whom is depicted as a Canadian dandy who smuggles DDI across the border for people with AIDS in Toronto; and, finally, four interruptive safer-sex ads performed by famous dead gay artists (remakes of miniscenes from Fassbinder's *Querelle*, Genet's *Un Chant d'Amour*, Warhol's *Blow Job*, and Jutras/McLaren's *A Chairy Tale*). What I find particularly delightful is Greyson's honest and creative conjunction of self-criticism (in the interview sections that articulate a lesbian woman's complaint about racism and sexism within the AIDS activist movement) with the outrageously uplifting "melodrama" of the drug-smuggling and the funnily pornographic safer-sex ads in a video that exudes a seductively tacky and irreverent humor — or perhaps I should say camp gay humor.

At the same time, I think it would be interesting to determine to what extent the camp style is a code that can only be read by gay (insider) audiences, and to what extent the references in the video constitute a shared vocabulary originating in the gay subculture, if indeed diverse audiences will most likely exhibit a wide range of responses to the narrative styles. I think we should not presume that no one in the so-called mainstream culture can read the codes of subcultural expression, nor should we assume that the mainstream is monolithically straight. Nor can we be certain how a queer reading will mobilize an activist practice that refuses to be subjected to the interests of a culturally dominant *and* a subculturally dominant consensus. This video's political camp transgresses against the presumed etiquette of serious, "legitimate" AIDS activism/education while still remaining quite serious in its critique. It is therefore likely to polarize responses, both within and without the "professional" AIDS activist community. As a creative work, the video also resists being seen only as AIDS video or activist propaganda/documentary.

On the contrary, I would modify video maker Gregg Bordowitz's understanding of a "queer structure of feeling" insofar as the explicit relationship between video maker, subject/content, and audience is not necessarily a closed circle or feedback loop of queer self-identification but rather fluid and open to conflicting and multiple meanings over and above the position of the minority figure yet based on a critical understanding of queer camp as political, oppositional critique. And this, to my mind, also includes self-critique and a certain parody of positive representations of "politically correct" AIDS activism, drug acquisition, or sex education. The critical camp quality of *The Pink Pimpernel* lies precisely in its excessive mixing of serious and irreverent documentations of a shared vocabulary that, as the subversive antics of the Pink Panther make clear, activate "queerness" not in terms of a clear differentiation of sexual identity or behavior but as a historically evolving, discontinuous, fictionalized/narrative and performative production, which is self-consciously examined in terms of its political shortcomings, right-wing tendencies, yet also its resourceful, radically imaginative successes (e.g., smuggling treatment drugs across borders).

Given the illegal nature of drug smuggling (which has been a necessary strategy of the activist movement in fighting government inactivity or delays in releasing treatment drugs), this trickster video indeed composes a counterdiscourse, rescripting and supplying a reactionary film classic with a high-camp happy ending consisting of a long kiss in the sunset. Erotic and subversive in its transgressive knowledge of "illegal" practices, this video was actually produced several months before the drug DDI was released in Canada for limited use in clinical trials (under pressure from AIDS Action Now and ACT UP); it was therefore also intended as an organizing tool to get a new antiviral drug released. In addition to serving as a call for action, it also made visible what must remain hidden and secretive, namely, smuggling. It is rather fascinating that Percy, the Pink Pimpernel/smuggler, is portrayed as unabashedly queer (a Wildean dandy), seemingly frivolous and outrageous, whereas his Canadian lover is presented as a somber and earnest AIDS activist. The dandy's excessive behavior and performance style becomes the successful action; his character (based on a film/fiction) defies authority as a queer agent.

This defiance works on several levels, and I believe it can be decoded not only by queer but also by nongay audiences, who can enjoy the seemingly romanticized hilarity of the Pink Pimpernel persona (the Pink Panther), who embodies theatrical humor and style for effective political ends and happens to be an authentic "border crosser." As Richard Dyer has suggested in his commentaries on camp, a gay viewing sensibility, which has also intruded into the mainstream and has at times influenced mainstream visual culture, is able to hold together "qualities that are elsewhere felt as antithetical: theatricality and authenticity . . . intensity and irony, a fierce assertion of extreme feeling with a deprecating sense of its absurdity."[3] Although there are signs of self-parody written all over the video, I don't think it is self-deprecating, except in the sense that it foregrounds a highly self-conscious awareness of the emotional and stylistic tone such video work creates in reconciling conflicting emotions within an embattled context, namely, that of an official culture that has neglected or discriminated against the painful, suffering experiences in AIDS-affected—particularly gay—communities. The camp humor reflects the video maker's knowing glance at the audiences, which knows more than the police or the border guards of the disciplinary state know. Of course, the audience also understands that it is under surveillance. (This theme of police surveillance is much more forcefully explored in Greyson's later video *Urinal*, which was released in 1992.)

The Imagined Community

"Brother to brother, brother to brother, brother to brother . . ."—this is the pounding, insistent, poetic refrain at the opening of Marlon Riggs's *Tongues Untied*, voiced over the slow-motion image of a black dancer moving in and out of the soft-focus light. The video makes clear that it is made by black gay men and addressed to other black gay men, although the song can be interpreted more inclusively. In an angry defense of his work against conservative efforts of the surveillance police to ban it, the late filmmaker wrote:

> *Tongues Untied* was motivated by a singular imperative: to shatter this nation's brutalizing silence on matters of sexual and racial difference. Yet despite a concerted smear and censorship campaign, perhaps even because of it, this work is achieving its aim. The fifty-five-minute video documents a nationwide community of voices—some quietly poetic, some undeniably raw and angry—that together challenge our society's most deeply entrenched myths about what it means to be black, to be gay, to be a man, and above all, to be human.[4]

It grieves me to look back at this work with the numbing awareness that he, too, has passed on, ravaged by the epidemic that has killed so many. We need loud and angry voices like his, yet the video also says it in the most quiet, poetic way, namely, that brotherhood is above all a matter of humanity and faith in love and solidarity. This faith has been tested in recent times, and I will shortly turn to another artist and his work on the borders of the AIDS crisis. But the question of the boundaries of community in Riggs's work needs to be foregrounded, since it addresses not a "brotherhood" or "humanity" we can easily identify or know but a *demonstration* of a becoming, a vision of a movement, a revolution.

The end of the video may help to clarify this interpretation. Riggs's camera captures a series of images of (mostly white) men milling about in a joyous gay pride parade; it then cuts to a closely formed group of black men marching in the parade, carrying banners and singing or shouting slogans. The group seems intensely focused and united in its purpose and direction. One of the banners reads: BLACK MEN LOVING BLACK MEN IS A REVOLUTIONARY ACT, and these words are then repeated in intertitles at the closing fade-out, the "a" being replaced by "the." The revolution is posited as the unspeakable act that can be spoken. The gay pride parade is here used in different ways; on the one hand, it is used to project an image of self-conscious gay celebration and self-demonstration (WE'RE HERE, WE'RE QUEER, GET USED TO IT), while, on the other, it is used to imply a specific difference in the way in which the camera shows how the black men in the parade choose to march in a more militant fashion reminiscent of Malcolm X, the Black Panthers, and the civil rights movement, conjuring up a new "movement" to unite the gay brothers as a political front, perhaps congruent with the activist demonstrations and protest formations of ACT UP. This militant image is self-contradictory, since both the civil rights movement and the gay liberation movement were divided over their relationships to the Black Panthers. Riggs seems to suggest that there is no time to mourn the failures of militancy. Mourning, as Douglas Crimp has so provocatively stated, has to *become* militancy.

Most of the ACT UP demonstrations have been coalition efforts, linked to GMHC, ACT NOW, women's activist groups, and affiliated community groups from within the gay, lesbian, and bisexual communities but also inclusive of straight social workers and activists. As video maker Gregg Bordowitz has pointed out in his "manifesto," many of the videos produced during the last ten years of the AIDS crisis played a vital role in the visibility of these coalitions and the emergence of identities: "The AIDS crisis precipitated the formation of a new subjectivity—the person living with AIDS—a subject with a disease asserting his or her right to determine the conditions of his or her own health care. The formation of this identity was significant. People with a disease organized as a constituency, a political identity, questioning the ways they were positioned by authority and subjugated within the dominant culture."[5]

Video production thus became part of the demonstrations, identifications, and identity politics behind the activist movement that had formed (and reformed after the post-Stonewall gay/lesbian liberation era) under the catastrophic impact of AIDS and the need to have its concerns represented. The activist core was initially located in the middle-class white gay community, which was hit hardest by the virus, but many more rapidly unfolding stories and experiences became important subjects that needed to be articulated. Gregg Bordowitz, Jean Carlomusto, Alexandra Juhasz, and others have described the hectic activities that led up to the formation of video collectives, which produced issue-oriented tapes for distribution and programs for GMHC and its weekly "Living with AIDS" cable show. Some of the "missing stories" not covered by mainstream media were generated and disseminated, serving the specific needs of diverse communities and providing alternative viewpoints on "poverty, drug use, sexuality, homosexuality, women, people of color, prostitutes, the Third World, the inadequate health-care system, the inadequate response to AIDS from the national government, the connections between hard science and big business."[6] The diversification is particularly important in light of the demographic changes in later patterns of HIV transmission, which indicated that while transmission among gay white men had decreased slightly, growing numbers of AIDS cases were being reported among drug users, women, and African-American and Latino men.

If it engages in the political work of such representations, alternative-media production necessarily moves from within/toward its own communities—which create themselves as they represent themselves—and among different communities, for the urgency of what is being said by the oppositional groups is always directed at the dominant culture and its social institutions (including the mass media), and thus at the discursive network, which determines what might or might not be said about the spread of AIDS and people affected by it. In this sense, ACT UP or alternative media perform both distinct and inclusive strategies of "demonstration"; they have to position themselves not against but inside the rules if the mobilization of public consciousness is to foster social relations. One cannot be sure whether ACT UP interventions and the mobilization of a community around the crucial slogan "Silence = Death" are intrinsically meant to be exclusive or to support the forming of coalitions beyond the queer membership; there have been many heated discussions about this at meetings of ACT UP groups in the United States and Canada. A consensus has never really existed concerning the various tactics involved in a "demonstration" since ACT UP interventions (especially in New York) are most often confrontational, highly theatrical, and aimed at achieving gay political visibility, whereas other groups working on health care, education, AIDS service and advocacy, peer counseling, therapy, drug use and drug testing, and research have generally chosen more moderate and pragmatic strategies to achieve their goals—although they may have supported guerrilla theater on occasion. The coalition of groups organized by Body Positive in Houston, which also helps organize the annual gay pride parades, tends to be more conservatively pragmatic in its strategies, taking the local situation into account and being quite realistic about the unlikely success of guerrilla tactics in that city of skyscrapers.

As Cindy Patton has pointed out in her comprehensive study of the evolution of AIDS grassroots and "service industry" organizations, activist strategies have to be reinvented for each city because the experience of gay people and those affected by AIDS with respect to repression is unique in each location.[7] Among the public actions of ACT UP New York were symbolic and anarchist interventions, such as the interruption of mass at Saint Patrick's Cathedral, which met with disapproval both outside and inside the group; the strategy was generally recognized as a political assault on dominant institutions colluding in the silence of the legitimate discourses. ACT UP's effort to break the silence clearly signaled an unleashing of power and resistance among those marginalized and demonized by systems of social oppression, and the guerrilla tactics are certainly not unfamiliar to other resistance activities among the radical Left.

However, one must also remember that in the eighties numerous other grassroots groups and individuals became involved in nonmilitant ways of self-empowering and mobilizing local communities around health issues, AIDS-related education, agency-building, fund-raising, support programs, and so forth. Their efforts to define the operational terms for the building of AIDS service organizations revealed the enormous difficulties of linking specific service-provision and medical-treatment advocacy with the political formations of communities rooted in different forms of minority activism. Patton has pointed out that mostly white, gay, community-based groups took the initiative in AIDS organizing activities, often without knowing how to negotiate the organizing process among people of color, who were more likely to relate to cultural communities rather than a potential sexual community. She also

noted that PLWA and Body Positive movements have tended to utilize the "coming out" experience of gay people as a model for people
with AIDS in order to create a group identity/unity by claiming this
as a shared experience. As she herself has admitted, in reality everyone
cannot afford to embrace this model. Many different aspects of identity
shape the experience of living with AIDS/HIV, and both the private-
sector nonprofit organizations dedicated to AIDS work and the militant
activists cannot avoid facing the contradictions between coalition and
identity politics.

It is painfully ironic to realize that the vociferous coming out of gay
liberation—which created a challenge to social oppression by uniting
around shared, celebrated homosexuality (a gay-rights community defined chiefly in terms of sex)—witnessed the ground shifting under the
lethal impact of AIDS. It became less and less auspicious to celebrate
sex, and many AIDS service organizations felt they had to downplay
or even censure the polymorphous sexuality and promiscuity (public
sex and sex in bars and bathhouses) that was a vital part of gay life.
The promise of a sense of community gradually turned into the despair
of cumulative loss or the experience of an ephemeral social space in
which HIV antibody positivity could not positively symbolize a coherent, united kinship with gender, racial, and class identities and particular local life and community practices.

Self-preservation, fear, and the debilitating trauma of loss are not
necessarily good preconditions for coalition politics, especially given the
long-term effect of the epidemic on public policies, which, since the
Bush administration, have sought to "normalize" AIDS by treating it as
just another chronic illness that purportedly can be "managed" or monitored by transmission-halting strategies. Kobena Mercer has warned
that historical awareness of race as a central category of political antago-
nism has made us weary of official policies of risk management, but he
has defended the explosive desire and creativity of black cultural politics
in England as a sign of hope for "outernational" community-building
among radical black groups of Asian, African, and Caribbean background. In his view, the renaissance in the eighties of black politics and
artistic expression in film, literature, and the visual arts, together with
the women's and gay grassroots movements, has encouraged an evolving
black queer diaspora that could "learn from coalition-building initiatives
such as ACT UP." Mercer has admitted to the unpredictable aspects of
identification as a process both within and without redefined boundaries
of national identity. He quotes Douglas Crimp's particularly somber
reflections on the painful internal divisions of queer and AIDS activ-

ism (made on the occasion of Vito Russo's memorial service in 1990): "Political identifications remaking identities are, of course, productive of collective political struggle, but only if they result in a broadening of alliances rather than an exacerbation of antagonisms. The latter often seems to result when, from within a development toward a politics of alliance based on relational identities, old antagonisms based on fixed identities reemerge." Precisely such dynamics, Mercer adds, "have been violently inscribed in black sexual politics in the eighties in terms of black men not only refusing to *listen* to black women, but refusing to let go of old antagonisms. This is the context in which the shameful silence around AIDS in black political discourse must be transformed, and in which our understanding of mourning in black psychic life must be deepened."[8]

I believe that Isaac Julien's *Looking for Langston* and Riggs's *Tongues Untied* fall between the cracks of these dynamics and are part of the paradox of mourning. They articulate the disruptive energy of black mobilization and the desire to reinvent a revolutionary identification. Being acutely aware of the disproportionately powerful and homophobic systems of regulation and containment that operate in the dominant culture as well as in black nationalism, they have contributed to the "self-derogations" Crimp diagnosed in the name-calling by which we identify each other, rank our oppressions, and compare our moralisms. The AIDS crisis, settling more and more deeply in our subconscious, may very well have destroyed the conflation of sexuality and sociality on which the hope of the liberation movement was founded. Whatever political unity may have existed in the imagined community has been shattered as a result of our increased awareness of an activist politics that cannot simultaneously manage opposition and internal separatism.

The absent collectivity is another "missing story" that needed to be told, and Riggs has done so in the particular way in which his complex video snaps the overwhelming public phobia against black male sexuality and gay political agency. Its visual, verbal, and musical poetry dances across a wide range of filmic styles, disturbing the rules of name-calling (black/male/gay) by repositioning the *tongue*—poetic voice, oral poetry, song—as the particular medium of self-affirmation. This video is less about rendering the complex black gay experience visible to us than it is about rekindling a black revolutionary poetry intended to infuse the racial and political rhetoric of brotherhood with the diverse images of black gay subcultural life. This rhetoric carefully hints at the theme of interracial love and desire between a younger Riggs and a white boy, only to overcome the seduction by displacing it into the past tense and another location (the Castro district in San Francisco) that Riggs, as the autobiographical narrator, claims to have left behind when he moved to New York.

The movement is dramatized as one that requires the transformation of degraded self-images (largely reflective of white culture's racist depictions of black bodies) and eroticized white bodies into their opposites, which I understand to mean Riggs's slow acceptance of the power and beauty of love among black men. Several pronounced moments in the film (Riggs calls them "monologues") are deeply melancholy, and we hear Riggs's voice remembering the pain of self-derogation, exclusion, and homelessness. The narrative of these monologues focuses on an imagined "home journey" toward a community yet to be found. Yet its interpolated imagery creates a sense of strain and great effort to enact a certain wholeness, a healing between social estrangement and emotional bonding that remains out of reach. For example, there is a scene in which we see two working-class drag queens, walking and smoking in slow motion to the sentimental music of Billie Holiday and Nina Simone. They appear tragic in their isolation, and Riggs's poetic diction, incorporating the writings of five other black gay poets—in particular the oratory of Essex Hemphill and Joseph Beam ("Brothers to Brothers" is also the title of a literary anthology edited by Hemphill and dedicated to the late Beam)—strains toward overcoming this sense of isolation.

Tongues Untied yearns for the very communality it incorporates as its mode of production: the video demonstrates the collaboration of black gay poets and intellectuals. Positing its autobiographical truth, it premises itself on the more universal claim of "humanity" for the gay brotherhood. But this familial language, including its references to "home" and "house" (well-known disco star and singer Sylvester is quoted and two black gay men explain the "house" style of voguing), simultaneously appropriates the deeply ironic dimension of "We Are Family." In its conscious intertextuality with *Looking for Langston* (Essex Hemphill reads his poetry in both films and is featured by both filmmakers reciting the following haunting lines from his AIDS poem: "This night might kill us / This kiss could turn to stone"), and its reclaiming of the poetic force of words that links it with Amiri Baraka and the sixties black power movement, *Tongues Untied* gestures both at Julien's painfully reimagined Harlem Renaissance and at the very black nationalism that, in its exclusionary understanding of black masculinity, had been particularly unforgiving toward homosexuals. Riggs tries to revise this history by mixing up his visual images, merging strong, muscular bodies of militant black gays marching for the new brotherhood with soft and tender love scenes that emphasize (just as Julien's cinematographer does in *Looking for Langston*) the gentle femininity of vulnerable black bodies. The Whitney Museum gave the video a prominent place in its astonishing 1994 exhibition *Black Male: Representations of Masculinity in Contemporary American Art*, almost as if to corroborate Riggs's legitimate claim to represent black culture or, rather, his affirmation of a different, sensual, and politically active black sexuality.

A cynical queer critic might argue that the Whitney's embrace of Riggs's provocative video, which contains explicit erotic images of male bodies not unlike Robert Mapplethorpe's, gives away the game, namely, the mainstream institution's embrace of *Tongues Untied* as an avant-garde artwork. But that is not necessarily a false conclusion on the part of the Whitney, since Riggs foregrounds the video's poetic diction as "authentic" black expressionism. In so doing, however, he privileges a revolutionary rhetoric of brotherhood that introduces profound dissonances that illuminate the "old antagonisms" Mercer worries about. For example, women are nonexistent in Riggs's family except on the musical soundtrack. Straight and working-class gay black men do not speak up or compose poetry in the film, and no connection is made to other gay men of color (Asian-American, Latino, Native American). The erotic fascination with a white gay subculture (pictured in less than subtle allusions to S/M and leather-clad men) remains an unresolved subtext in a video that seems deliberately aimed at repressing all ambiguities that may reside in black nationalism (e.g., Louis Farrakhan's Nation of Islam populism or Leonard Jeffries's Afrocentrism), interracial relations, and the "poisoned relationships between black men and black women of all classes" so vehemently criticized by black feminist critics like bell hooks.[9]

In other words, in attempting to sever black gay sexuality from its burden of silence, shame, and self-derogation, his video has become potentially oppositional to all dominant nationalisms or systems of intolerance in its affirmation of a race-identified gay political eros that does not necessarily blend comfortably with other queer expressions or the turbulent spectacle of gay pride. Riggs's poetic collectivism seeks respect on its own ground, its imaginary "home." The home of brotherhood, however, occupies values of sociality (to be a man, to be human) that are already overdetermined by society or black culture. If one is to assume that Riggs's utopian revolution strives to attain a home "not at home" in the common language of nation/community, its erotic desire would have to revolutionize the very conception of what such a social home might be.

If we accept this activist premise, any notion of a collectively identified space is put into question; there is no safe space but only spaces of dissonance which our political performances engage in order to avoid the normalizing operations of dominant institutions. This is how we also need to understand Bordowitz's deliberately ironic use of the term "television," distinguishing between video as a "medium," a means of production, and television as a "situation" or a domain of mass communications whose means of production are not in the hands of the communities. Activist or community-based video production (for television) serves as a necessary intervention into the closed circuits of the dominant media. It creates "anti-homes," even though this might imply that the dominant media will perpetually try to reestablish its circuits by blocking, learning from, and, if necessary, incorporating alternative, oppositional, or camp modes of redescribing community identities and needs. It is a vicious circle, forcing activist producers constantly to shift between specific local tactics involving supporting interest constituencies and a utopian politics of identity, difference, and dispersion that refuses to be assimilated into the officially constituted nation or national culture.

However, as I have implied, the foundation of community-based media production is itself a volatile process of formation and consensus-building, and it is in the production process itself, concurrently with the demonstration of oppositional communities, that we need to locate the redefinitions or propositions that mark a project such as *Tongues Untied*. The gay community is not identical with the AIDS community; in fact, there is something in the use of the phrase "AIDS community" that I find debilitating, even though it may refer to the experience of people living with AIDS who may be existing in a different reality. Public health education as well as medical and scientific discourses can isolate and describe a virus, and they should describe HIV transmission in order to educate people and prevent the spread of the epidemic. Instead we have witnessed a history of panic and discrimination where being HIV positive has led to such a high degree of stigmatization (especially in the early years of the epidemic, when AIDS was called the "gay plague" in public discourse) that claiming a particular health status as a critical aspect of one's identity has become an arduous task, especially in light of the fact that PWAs actually find themselves living in the same reality of compounded oppression (homophobia, sexism, racism) that sustains social and political attitudes. Public health policies—which initially created the conditions of blame by seeking to police, control, and manage poor health among a wide range of marginalized people—had to be transformed, and activists in the affected communities facilitated these changes. In this sense, identifiable collectives emerged that linked the struggle for new health policies with the "speaking out" politics of minority groups. I would argue that today one can see many diverse communities, groups, and subgroups engaged in addressing the specific issues they face in local contexts of incongruous race, gender, and class relations. New political strategies are being forged that no longer emphasize personal identity but rather the multiplication of identities and social differences.

Home/Exile

I want to return to Riggs's video, since the concluding images of the demonstration of black gay men, linked to the poetic and artistic ethos of the video as whole, refer to this very complex and differentiated construction of a "home" that is, in fact, not a home but a mobile, unlocalized noncommunity whose "citizens" may live in and be affiliated with several social spaces and gay subcultures; I am thinking here of both market-mediated spheres (e.g., health clubs, discos, bars, social organizations, the print media, arts institutions, phone lines, "houses," and other businesses) and traditional nonmarket spheres (residences, schools, churches, families). The Queer Nation slogan WE'RE EVERYWHERE perhaps too exuberantly assumes that these multiple associations and the transitoriness of the queer border crossers enable a more thorough resistance to regimes representing normalcy. In such a postmodern self-understanding, there is no ontological ground for any claim to identity, only social positionalities that are strategically opposed to social integration as a whole. As Lauren Berlant and Elizabeth Freeman have stated in their theoretical manifesto for Queer Nation politics, this nonassimilationist contestation of existing cultural spaces can be a treacherous premise for revolutionary action; by rejecting the state, the new cultural activism cannot risk abandoning those civil rights that enable it publicly to make political claims. "It must be emphasized that disidentification with U.S. nationality is not, at this moment, even a theoretical option for queer citizens: as long as PWAs require state support, as long as the official nation invests its identity in the pseudoright to police nonnormative sexual representations and sexual practices, the lesbian, gay, feminist and queer communities in the United States do not have the privilege to disregard national identity." [10]

Activists and artists connected with the new social movements and gay subcultures have investigated the "official" nation's political exploitation of vulnerable subjects and bodies; their work has helped us to understand the pressures on identity constitution and the importance of gaining greater control over the rules. I want to mention briefly the work of a Californian media artist who in 1992 exhibited a series of collages and videos at the *Private/Public* group exhibition curated for the Betty Rhymer Gallery of the School of the Art Institute of Chicago.[11] Sammy Cucher's series of photo prints entitled *Blood Exile*, together with his two-year video project *Corpus* (1990–92), opened up a particularly troublesome dimension of the current debates on AIDS and AIDS activism, focusing attention on the international dimension of the epidemic and the repercussions of national health policies on the individual's experience of control, or loss of control of the body. While *Private/Public* acknowledged the powerful role the visual arts and visual documentation play in challenging both the spectacularization of a frequently stigmatized medical condition (in the media) and the privatization of medical-care management, Cucher's *Corpus* offered a series of meditations that went much further in their attack on the "private/public" dialectic. Based on personal diaries the artist kept for three years after testing HIV positive, the three videos that comprise *CORPUS* (*Meditations, CULT, -phage*) question not only the state's control over public health policy and its backhanded shifting of responsibility for health care provision to the private sector (mostly gay community-based AIDS service groups) during the Reagan administration but also interrogate the validity of generalized notions of "control," "management," and "expertise" as such. Cucher's personal meditations evoke an intense, seething cauldron of hallucinatory emotions and cool observations that mutually reinforce each other to denounce the body/mind dichotomy and any logical claims on administrative rationality, scientific discipline, and medical or political authority on the part of health organization. While *Meditations* dramatizes the apparent loss of control over his own understanding of the body, *CULT* uses a different perspective. In a sustained mode of self-observation, the camera's obsessive, repetitive voyeurism is directed at his body as if the "owner" of this body rejoiced in the voluntary abandonment of control. The heightened, microscopic proximity to his own body creates an unrelieved tension, since the policing of the skin does not provide a privileged access to dermatological or political truths of the diseased blood. The body surface is rendered esoteric.

In this video, in which we hear Cucher recite and repeat a single passage from J. G. Ballard's novel *Crash,* extreme close-ups of the body's skin create a sensuous, continuous surface texture where the bodily skin seems to merge with the TV screen and both become excitable boundaries. In *Meditations* Cucher is heard observing his states of body-mind: "For the first time, I was in physical confrontation with my body . . . My body escapes my power. . . . My body takes over the widest reaches of my consciousness." In *CULT* the personal voice-over is replaced by textual citations, but this apparent distancing effect is reversed by the intensely ambiguous, intimate surveillance of the skin's porous surface, which does not betray the dysfunctional immune system. Cucher's vision is perversely futurist, punning on Marinetti's and Ballard's obsession with the intermingling of bodies and machines; in this case the pathological camera/medium of video renders the human skin of the seropositive body as a pornographic surface experienced with an uncanny sense of autoeroticism. On another level, however, this autoeroticism is deeply ironic since it points to Cucher's implicit linking of futurism to fascism, and thus to the formation of bodily regimes and, in a larger sense, of nationality, which has historically implicated political, military, scientific, and media institutions in the conjoined regulation and "protection" of the boundaries of the state/body.

Cucher's videos thus raise the specter of state intervention and the historical trajectory of the medicalizations of homosexuality and race. In their early responses to AIDS, the U.S. government and the medical profession utilized strongly prejudicial categories that facilitated the public perception of the "gay plague," linked the epidemic negatively to poverty and drug abuse, and displaced the epidemiological focus of research onto projected sources of AIDS in Haiti and Zaire. It was only through sustained grassroots activism in the communities that AIDS and the developing health care service, education, and prevention programs became more generally socially acceptable. Public health policies remain the prerogative of the state, even though AIDS service groups and PWAs in the communities are gradually being acknowledged as valuable sources of experiential information and "esoteric" scientific knowledge. Cucher's work is about personal knowledge and about finding access to bodily reactions and survival methods during the evolving crisis. In *-phage* he depicts himself engaged in the most mundane yet significant daily rituals of following a special diet, consuming a variety of necessary drugs, and monitoring bodily reactions, in particular his digestive system. The video camera becomes a medium that asserts his own technique of medical observation to the extent that it helps him to become more aware of his body's changing physical conditions and response patterns.

Concerning the state's political control of bodies and its administration of health care policy, drug trials, and approval of certain medications, Cucher's work raises very strong objections which make it quite clear to the viewer that as an international crisis AIDS has already

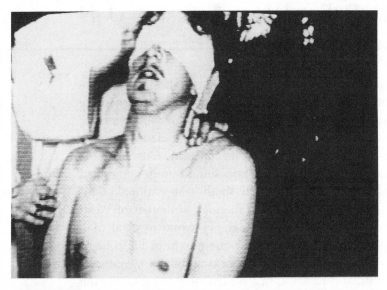

Sammy Cucher, Video still from *CULT,*
part 2 of *CORPUS,* 1990–92. Courtesy of
the artist.

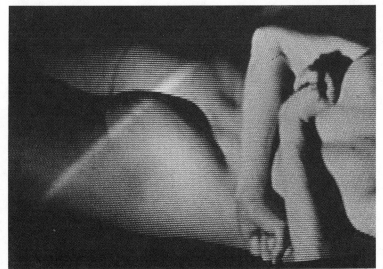

Sammy Cucher, Video still from
Meditations, 1990. Courtesy of the artist.

Sammy Cucher, *Blood Exile 2,* 1991.
Courtesy of the artist.

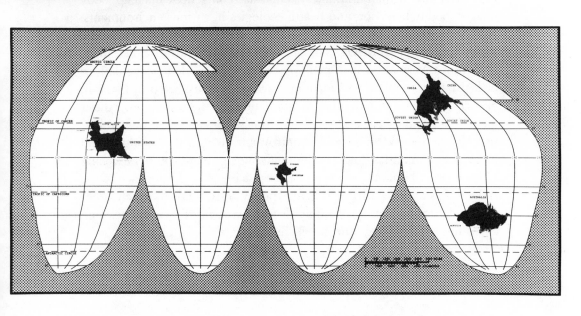

transformed the meaning of geographical national boundaries. Cucher's three collages collectively entitled *Blood Exile* (each measuring twenty by forty-eight inches, blood on photo prints) offer a striking symbolic visualization of the transnational demography of the epidemic, but the power of control is undermined in a very specific way. Cucher made black and white photo prints of flattened, horizontal representations of the globe, and then used his blood to create small, transnational continents that conjoin, in a seemingly illogical manner, a number of Western and non-Western nations. On his imaginary white tropical map ("tropic of cancer"/"tropic of capricorn" are the names of his equatorial lines), one sees several blood clots that appear to unite, for example, Iraq, Ecuador, Pakistan, and Finland. In a statement accompanying the work, Cucher has written:

> Since the beginning of the AIDS epidemic, more than 25 countries around the world, including the U.S., have established entry restrictions to travelers and immigrants based on their HIV status.
>
> Because of this continuing trend, those afflicted with the virus are relegated to a forced isolation that prevents them from accessing supportive communities, information about disease and innovative, affordable treatments.
>
> Countries that deem themselves as [*sic*] socially advanced, along with those from the so-called "Third World," are now sharing borders in an arbitrary geography originating in fear and paranoia.

Cucher's indictment of national health policies and immigration/travel restrictions raises very serious questions, not about the incontrovertible existence of different cultural and social systems or, to be more precise, different/unequal immune systems based on genetic makeup, body images, bodily behavior, and health ecologies in various environments, but about the measures that bureaucratic governments employ *against* individuals affected by AIDS or presumed to belong to so-called high-risk groups. Very often such measures, which are guided by regulations or legislation, are used to isolate or track people suspected of being ill or carrying the virus; federal or local monitoring and testing procedures inevitably produce patterns of racial, social, or economic discrimination. In the context of ongoing controversies within the scientific and medical communities, and among epidemiological researchers seeking to mark describable trajectories of the epidemic, the governance of the AIDS crisis by legislative and health policy institutions (on such issues as mandatory testing, quarantine, drug release, needle exchange, etc.) could not but challenge the state's fundamental assumptions about its role in protecting the citizenry and providing care and education based upon constitutional notions of equity. Cucher's criticism of state coercion and imposed restrictions points to complicated human rights issues that have been aggravated by cases where various foreign governments impose entry restrictions or mandatory testing in practice while officially denying that they are doing so, or where distinct government departments have conflicting policies.

We know that the existing inequities in the U.S. health care system vis-à-vis the uninsured, the poor, and the disenfranchised minorities have accelerated the crisis of confidence among citizens, who, as the epidemic has progressed during its second decade, have noticed how traditional interest-group politics has been repeated in the politics of AIDS, and how special-interest groups fighting for adequate care for marginalized populations have faced greater difficulties in locating funding and in influencing public discourse in the areas of prevention and education, as well as cultural conceptions of sexual freedom, individual rights, government intervention, and nondiscrimination in the workplace. As Cucher has suggested in his world map, without fully exploring the complexities of national policy-making, AIDS cannot be considered a national phenomenon, exemplifying instead the inescapable coupling and interdependence of countries. This interdependence cannot be disclaimed by barring visitors or testing aliens at the border, especially if such policing prevents knowledgeable activists and PWAs from exchanging their experiences and health practices with others or learning about alternative treatments or physical, emotional, and spiritual healing from others. In her critique of the bias in Western epidemiology, especially its insidious policy of conducting vaccine trials among socially devalued classes and among Africans, Cindy Patton has strongly advocated a supranational activism to achieve a better understanding of the interrelation of sexualities globally in order to "enable people to recognize the acts which allow transmission of HIV, and to sustain and re-symbolize those cultural/sexual practices which prevent transmission." Her analysis is particularly directed at the relations between first world epidemiology and colonialism, as well as at the shifting discourses of race in current AIDS prevention and health maintenance programs.

Cucher's metaphor of the "blood exile" has particular ramifications for such research on relations of domination and "othering," especially if one examines the cross-cultural exchange of sexual practices in the context of global economic transformations. In her own fieldwork, Emily Martin has succinctly pointed to readjustments in cultural ideas about bodily "flexibility" required by the new management of global corporate business, and her impressive ethnography of the "configuration of healthy bodies" illuminates the significant distinctions that exist between state or corporate education, on the one hand, and various local practices among people who resist such "training" and choose their own alternative, holistic schooling for their immune systems, on the other.

Another controversial case of internal "exiling" can be found in Cuba's quarantine policy, which was condemned abroad as a breakdown of basic human rights but was supported inside Cuba by the vast majority of the population, including PWAs, who trusted the renowned Cuban medical system. Public health and political authorities sought to contain AIDS by testing all citizens (completed by April 1991) and then isolating and treating all persons infected with the virus. Compared with other Latin American countries, the Cuban policy seemed to be successful in keeping HIV infection at a very low level. In addition to the particular care that PWAs received in the sanatorium, the Ministry of Health began an outpatient treatment and therapy program in 1994, allowing some PWAs to return to their families. There are other, more complex issues of discrimination connected with Cuba's public health and prevention strategies within the context of the culture's ongoing homophobia and suppression of open debate on sexual awareness and practices. New research has provided valuable local information that, as Patton has suggested, underscores the glaring discrepancies between different national and sociocultural economies of medical research and public health programs. But even if one considers Cuba's relative isolation during the U.S. blockade, Cucher's global map of interdependence still holds true, since Cuba's domestic economy has been so severely damaged that medical and food supplies (including the availability of condoms) are very scarce. Like many other developing nations, Cuba is in a weak position to have any influence on international science or the conceptualization of transnational policies. And since people continue to travel to and from Cuba, the transmission of HIV cannot be supervised. "HIV knows no geographical boundaries," Patton has stated.

> HIV traces a geography unrecognized by governments intent on reducing sexualities which subvert economic production, thwart social control, or merely stand as politically embarrassing reminders of richly symbolic and less rigidly conformist ways of life, once characteristic of traditional cultures, but now labelled as perverted and as a political liability by Western discourse. HIV follows the lines of transportation created by capital investment and traces a geography of bodily pleasures that defies the medical cops who police every country's border, no matter how many tests they devise.

Patton ends her analysis with a concluding statement that seems close to Cucher's artwork: "The HIV epidemic poses a unique moral challenge and will re-form both the meaning of sexuality and the meaning of local and international cooperation." [12]

I suggested earlier that claiming a health status as a critical aspect of one's identity is an arduous task, and Cucher's artwork and video production, like those of Greyson or Riggs, points to the multiple possibilities in activist work and the shifts that may occur between documentary and propagandist productions, on the one hand, and more personal or poetic evocations of subjective survival strategies, on the other. Such poetic videos can be produced by a single person or by media collectives, and Bordowitz has explained that after several years of community television and documentary/educational video productions, he preferred to focus on personal testimony and "internal dialogue" in his videos. The video screenings held during the *Private/Public* exhibition showed a similar range of progressive cultural work, including not only Cucher's personal diaries and Bill T. Jones's memorial dance but also the collective *Fear of Disclosure Project* produced by Jonathan Lee and Jeannie Pedjko. Pedjko, a Chicago-based AIDS activist, presented an inspirational tape entitled *(In)Visible Women,* a jointly created documentary on the empowered responses of three HIV-positive women of color who have become spokespersons for their communities. I felt particularly moved by Pedjko's passionate account of her work in her Latina community and her emphasis on place-bound work in the neighborhood. In the tape she urges women with AIDS to speak out, and she demonstrates the values of self-reliance, women's solidarity, and family support for the building of a local infrastructure of support and AIDS education.

I wish to conclude this chapter with the following example because I remember quite vividly a panel discussion entitled "The Aesthetics of Community-based Video" held during the 1991 Chicago Women in the Director's Chair Festival. Let me add that the festival featured Yvonne Rainer's then new film *Privilege,* Cheung Yeung-ting's *Eight Taels of Gold,* and a series of films by In Visible Colors, a Los Angeles–based volunteer collective dedicated to producing and promoting videos by African-American, Native American, Asian-American and Latina filmmakers. Numerous other short films, videos, and animations were presented at this festival, which has become an important venue for both young and inexperienced as well as more established women filmmakers and video artists.

In this context, it was particularly jarring, if not completely unexpected, that several community media activists on the panel (Maria

Dalida Benfield, Cheryl Miller, Ayana Udongo, and Saundra Johnson) were faced with the challenge of having to defend the usefulness and credibility of video works made by community organizations. The discussions were extraordinarily lively and engaging, focusing on questions of how we critique works not made by people trained in the media and how we evaluate using media as a tool of empowerment. The underlying problem, as Udongo pointed out, is the culturally prominent set of criteria that governs both the commercial film/television industry as well as the independent sphere of film/video art, which is generally curated or funded by agencies that apply formal aesthetic value criteria to projects and their development. There was general agreement that community-based video is predicated on a different politics of production aimed not at mainstream or fine-art standards of acceptability but at collective responsibility for production. Benfield argued that activist videos, shot and edited by the community for which they are intended, call into question the aesthetics of traditional video, whereupon someone in the audience responded by suggesting they should not be shown at film festivals. Alexandra Juhasz was also present at this discussion, since she had shown the video record of a community project (*We Care: A Video for Care-Providers of People Affected by AIDS*) that had developed out of her workshop with low-income women of color in Brooklyn, New York. I think Juhasz's answer was the most compelling; in times of a medical and social crisis, she said, people need a concrete project to work on in order to give purpose to their work.

In a culture where the privilege of self-expression and its public articulation generally depends on financial and social status, the voice of each black, Asian, or Latin woman—describing herself and her work in a community that needs greater access to health care and a more open dialogue about the issues—becomes a political medium. The commitment to video production generates vitally necessary languages about the experience of AIDS in communities. Such new video languages may question the formal aesthetics or production modes of film—this is why they also need to be seen and heard at festivals or on television—but this is a vital aspect of the democratic notion that in a pluralist cultural marketplace of values no established rules or criteria can remain uncontested.

Media production that is considered community-based (sometimes used disparagingly to distinguish low-end video production from video art that is presented at film/video festivals or art galleries) thus defines itself, however broadly and flexibly, in contradistinction to mainstream and commercially driven media or cable channels, as well as art-house practices, even as it seeks to infiltrate them. Deep Dish TV's satellite transmissions of independent video works became particularly important sources of information during the Gulf War and after the Rodney King verdict and the Los Angeles uprising, registering alternative perspectives on these events that were prevented or edited out by commercial television.[13] I consider the Deep Dish TV model pathbreaking and expect it to have a lasting impact on cultural production.

Such alternative or independent video production, of course, needs to negotiate with existing networks or technical production and distribution facilities, in the same manner in which we all have to face local issues and overcome institutional obstacles, such as being denied access to editing facilities at one's own workplace which I experienced at my university. However, there now exist many smaller media arts and independent production facilities. The low-end video technology, with its relatively inexpensive camera and computer-editing products, allows for wider access to, and broader implementation of, video and media-literate responses from community, grassroots, and street-level groups (e.g., the Street-Level Video collective of young Latino high school students in Chicago's West Town, which was formed in 1992).

These responses should be understood as having created a new cultural atmosphere for the low-cost media production of documentary, educational, experimental, and activist works whose immediate goal is politicized expression. In other words, the AIDS crisis as a social health crisis has been instrumental in stimulating the growth of independent video production, which performs a vital role vis-à-vis the self-identifications of communities of grassroots activism, however volatile and shifting such processes may be. Artists in all genres of the visual and performing arts have contributed to the representation as well as the critical and emotional reflection of AIDS and its effects on the body politic. In the same manner, caregivers, health care providers, support groups, religious leaders, community workers, and, of course, PWAs themselves have taken the media into their own hands and voiced their own opinions in stories and social criticism, thus enabling alternative media to contest or expand information that is broadcast and dramatized on mainstream television, in Hollywood movies, and in the print media. This cultural contesting of the discourses, interpretations, and politics of AIDS is the most significant and distinguishing dimension of the activist video production of the past decade. Its active model for the creation and intersection of new knowledge generated by divergent experiences and interests among groups affected by AIDS inspired and reinforced a local and international dialogue on behalf of the real needs and lived experience of those affected by the epidemic.

One of the most sobering experiences for me was the recognition —of which I had been relatively unaware while living in the Houston hinterland in the late eighties—of the extent to which such AIDS video production had already progressed on the East and West Coasts, and of the level of production and distribution strategies that had been achieved by Testing the Limits, WAVE, AIDSFilms, ACT UP/NY's weekly public-access program "AIDS Community TV," or the Toronto/ New York–based GMHC programs *Living With AIDS*. It was not until after I had moved to Chicago that I found the widely distributed *Video Against AIDS* set of tapes at the Chicago Video Data Bank, a compilation of more than a dozen of the most important activist, experimental, and documentary videos produced by Gregg Bordowitz, Jean Carlomusto, Maria Maggenti, Richard Fung, John Greyson, Alexandra Juhasz, Isaac Julien, Pratibha Parmar, Phil Zwickler, and others. At around the same time, I had gotten hold of the 1989 Media Network's directory of film and video on AIDS, *Seeing through AIDS,* and later I became aware of the Media Network's launching of its "Seeing through AIDS" production workshops in New York City in 1991.

From our exchanges of information and production materials at "AIDS Interfacings," we next learned how to analyze the various strategies of performance (development, participation/collaboration, shooting) and postproduction/distribution. I came to better understand some of the unresolved issues that had troubled me during the production of *Ad Mortem*. One of the most urgent lessons I learned was the focusing of production not only on the issue-oriented content and the manner of how this content is constructed, "authorized," or controlled by the partners in the video or the video producer but, even more important, on the question of its address. Unlike the mixing of metaphysical, historical/general, and local/specific images in the collage I used for *Ad Mortem,* most contemporary activist and educational AIDS video productions are highly specific in their localized approach and are targeted at a specific constituency, while clearly identifying their position from within the AIDS community.

Self-identification, however changeable, unstable, and problematic, is a vital part of the alternative self-consciousness that has contributed to the empowerment of underrepresented, silenced, or marginalized people and communities. In fact, we are still at the early stages of trying to define what we mean by community, given that the landscape and the trajectories of the epidemic are constantly evolving and changing. Yet my understanding of AIDS video/performance is primarily shaped by assumptions about its effectiveness as an *action,* and as such it is largely dependent on its localized "target" (the event or issue it addresses and the audience it tries to reach, inspire, and educate) and on the constitutive role it can play in the communal expression of concerns, needs, opinions, and visions for the ongoing struggle. The *localization* has also directly affected the manner of production as a collaborative process and the politics of self-identification and producer-audience relations, which include distribution, reception, and feedback. Perhaps more so than one would have ever dreamt in the artistic or academic arenas, activist and community-oriented work has a vital connection to constituencies and thus is directly accountable to them. The AIDS epidemic, with its devastations of human life, has brought us close to the edge, not to any paradigmatic borders of current postmodern cultural theorizing, but to a commitment to a practice of collaboration that is necessarily passionate and self-defining—if it wishes to sustain itself at all.[14]

1 DANCING WITH TECHNOLOGIES

2 IMPOSSIBLE ANATOMIES

3 CULTURE IN ACTION

4 VIRTUAL COMMUNITIES

EIGHT

EMBODIMENT: SHARING OUR WOUNDS

Body Criticism

It must be one of the more instructive ironies of the present that "the body" has become a privileged object of display in performance and in the creation of art, that it has figured prominently in recent obscenity and censorship controversies, and that it is the place where the most advanced cultural theory intersects with embattled discourses on sexual identity and orientation, subjectivity and agency, and the politics of race and class. Representations of the female body in particular have been the focus of a very sophisticated and trenchant critique, initially developed by psychoanalytic, Marxist, film, and mass-media theorists and now extending into all areas of image and commodity production within the larger feminist discourses and activisms vis-à-vis women's rights to control their bodies. As a matter of record (and radical fashion), it is now common to see university departments—and not merely the marginalized women's and gay/lesbian studies programs—turn their critical attention to the body as a "contested site" of discourses in the human and social sciences.

In her lengthy book *Body Criticism* Chicago art historian Barbara Stafford has gone so far as to envision a revolutionary, cross-disciplinary shift from an older, rationalist knowledge of the body—derived from eighteenth-century philosophical, aesthetic, and medical techniques of systematic observation—toward a new, sensory, holistic "re-embodied" and experiential method of knowing.[1] Paradoxically, we are asked to imagine the possibility of such a re-embodiment in the context of a predominantly visual culture hooked into the computer and cyberspace technologies of disembodied information-processing. It is the same culture which witnessed the prurient spectacle involving an all-male, all-white Senate Judiciary Committee trying to weigh the sexual-harassment charges raised by a black woman against her former employer (the soon-to-be-confirmed Supreme Court Justice Clarence Thomas). The body language during the hearings, brought into our homes by the new X-rated educational television, was a perverse revelation of the relations of power, race, and sexual behavior in the United States.

It is necessary to address a few other paradoxes. The first is implied by my somewhat hesitant introduction to women's bodies as sites of discursive struggle and contestation, occasioned by a 1991 exhibition entitled *Embodiment,* held at Chicago's Randolph Street Gallery, that featured the provocative work of British feminist photographer Jo Spence. Invoking the dilemmas of site/sight and the visibility/invisibility of actual women in the context of "body criticism" and its metaphors or prostheses for the body and the ongoing evidence of textual, visual, or physical exploitation of women by men, the position of a white male critic reviewing women's work is ambivalent even though he is politically committed to a shared dialogue about the subjection of bodies. My response to *Embodiment* of course involves conceptions of my own body, and I will return more directly to those in the next chapter.

What motivated me about this exhibition were the concrete and—in my own experience—very immediate concerns directed against criticism and theory within and without institutionalized feminism and art institutions. At the most basic level, then, this is not an art review. Nor can I presume to address the question raised by Mary Kelly, another British feminist artist, as to how "a radical, critical and pleasurable positioning of the woman as spectator [is] to be accomplished,"[2] even though I sensed the strong and positive reactions among the women I saw at the gallery. Rather, I want to examine how and why *Embodiment,* and the series of events growing out of the gallery's issue-oriented programing, sought to bring the art of this exhibition outside the gallery, so to speak, and into direct contact with our own lived experiences and our personal and political exploration of female/male identity and subjectivity.

The gallery's performance space was the site for these events, which included "Context Talk," "Imaging Our Selves" (a workshop facilitated by art therapist Mary Dougherty), and "Crossing Boundaries: Reinventing Our Lives" (a public discussion moderated by exhibition organizer Angela Kelly). Such recontextualizing work, which disregards the separatist and market-oriented imperatives of "art" while radically shifting its "value" toward participatory performance, goes beyond the boundaries of the art object and the traditional curatorial process itself. Indeed, *Embodiment* implies a crossing of spaces and identities both literally and symbolically. First, this was not a show by a single artist since the photo-therapy work by Spence was produced collaboratively with Rosy Martin, David Roberts, Tim Sheard, and Ya'acov Kahn, respectively (there was also a videotape entitled *Surviving Memories* that was jointly created by Spence and her brother). Moreover, it was coupled with a "Group Show" that presented the work of Heidi Kumao (in a room of her own), Andi Pihl, elin o'hara slavick, and Lisa Dianne Schwarzbek. The latter did not complement Spence's collaborative process since the U.S. women artists used very diverse means (beyond photography) of evoking their bodies and/or selves. However, in creating a dialectic between different generations and class and cultural experiences, these installations had a profound effect on our perception of how personal narrative can speak—through the ill-bodied and the embodied self—about the unspeakable or, rather, about what is hidden or made invisible through the taboos of childhood and adult sexuality, disease, and the (self-)repressions and cultural disciplining of the female body in public and private spaces.

For anyone involved in the communities of people affected by the AIDS crisis or committed to the cultural struggle for lesbian/gay/bisexual rights (in the face of public paranoia and homophobia), *Embodiment* didn't go far enough in addressing sexual and racial difference. Nor did it fully address the vexing problem of the body politics of the private self within the community at a point in time when *imaginary* identifications with "our" community (arts, AIDS activist, feminist, gay, lesbian, bisexual, queer, anticensorship, neighborhood, etc.) have been critically exposed and questioned. However, all of the works in *Embodiment* provided an intense focus on shared social experience and psychological memory precisely because they were grounded in the private and autobiographical body, and because they "came out" as dramatic testimony to women's continually changing constructions of bodies and selves within the larger history of repression and disembodiment.[3] Embodiment involves transformation and change since it disrupts the traditional models of power and authority that define who we are or teach us how to behave (e.g., within the family, at the workplace, in a museum, at school)—and how to look.

Theory, which can also be a disembodying model of power, now wants us to distrust any "natural" assumptions about bodies, identities, or biological essences. Some very influential theory has apparently given up on subjectivity/authorship, on history, and on the real (body): nothing exists that is not constructed or marked by the dominant cultural codes and disciplinary discourses. One has also witnessed an entire decade of postmodern art in the eighties that appropriated images of bodies—clothed or naked, sensationalist or abject—in order to expose and criticize the conventionality, artifice, and manipulative violence of the mediums that produce them. Each re-production of the body in art can be considered a pose that is comparable to other posings in the promotional industries of fashion, advertising, MTV, aerobics, body building, sports, and so on. There is a particular irony, therefore, in the gallery's public-service announcement that *Embodiment* "references the female body in relation to photographic means of representation," while the content of Jo Spence's work clearly invokes different processes of self-invention that are not essentially dependent on the photographic medium alone.

In the case of Spence's therapeutic work and her activism in the area of breast cancer, we are most directly confronted with the limits of the image as an aesthetic object. Her self-portraits are inseparable from their function in her personal and political life and her interactions with physicians, clients, and students. If her creative work evolves outside the art context, should her practice be discussed in pedagogical terms, inter-connecting education, psychotherapy, and community activism? Or can this crossover work also heighten our sensibilities vis-à-vis those extreme contradictions in our utterly technological and largely dysfunctional society, as revealed by other Chicago exhibitions (*The Body*, consisting of installation/video works at The Renaissance Society; *Disclosing the Myth of Family*, a photographic exhibition at the Betty Rymer Gallery of the School of the Art Institute of Chicago) or by the performances and/or writings of, say, Annie Sprinkle, Karen Finley, Tim Miller, David Woj-narowicz, or Spiderwoman Theater? What promises are embodied in the interventions and performances of these practitioners? How do we look at Spence's "Narratives of Dis-ease," "Libido Uprising," or "Unbe-coming Mothers"?

Invention/Intervention

The process of writing, composing, and creating images—and the teach-ing of this process—is performative in a sense more radical than was ever imagined by the early feminist proposition "the personal is political," which initiated women's collective consciousness-raising, peer counsel-ing, and an increasingly activist exploration of their private and public experiences and their positions in the labor market. Today's women's groups and support networks in diverse communities, together with widely publicized feminist literature, theory, and subculture magazines, have built a women's culture in which community-based activism often intersects with work created by independent media artists and film/video producers that not only records and advocates underrepresented community issues but finds its base and circulation no longer restricted to an art context and its ideologies of form. (This ongoing political process was forcefully brought to my attention at "Divided/Undivided," a conference on coalition-building organized by the Chicago Artists' Coalition and N. A.M.E. Gallery in 1991 in response to right-wing efforts to censor free expression. A quickly produced anticensorship activist video entitled *State of the Art/Art of the State?* collected testimony and critical analysis from across the country. It was available at the conference and then was distributed across the grassroots network.)

I recall being struck by the "documentary" video *History and Memory for Aikiko and Tashige* (copresented by the Randolph Street Gallery and Women in the Director's Chair), in which Rea Tajiri fashioned an autobiography of her Japanese-American family out of an extraordinary mixture of textual, visual, and aural languages, exploding the boundaries of documentary, fictional, ethnographic, and experimental codes. Her refusal to adhere to any standards of form disturbs our habits of viewing "history," undermining the power of images to linger in our memory, comparable to the way in which Vietnamese-American filmmaker Trinh T. Minh-ha has referred to her poetic writings and films as performances that approach the spaces in between, the intervals to which established rules or boundaries never quite apply.

This description of crossover work dovetails with performance art and its unpredictable, meandering history since the radical sixties. It is perhaps most significant that despite the feeling of exhaustion surrounding the political and sexual rebellions of recent years, which were influenced by the mass-market accommodations of eighties narcissism or its feebler, more desperately cynical nineties spinoffs (slacker and the "X" generation) before and after the impact of the AIDS epidemic, performance and live art have constantly reinvented themselves as embodied practices seeking to recover the body's presence and visceral physicality; they cannot be taken for granted in a society obsessed with ersatz and the cloning designs and transmutations of high technology. A nearly fascist obsession with high-tech violence and physical destruction (the so-called collateral damage on human bodies in the Gulf War) has surfaced in the militarized mainstream as well as in the underground rock-music videos or video arcades (e.g., the virtual reality "Battleship Station" at Chicago's Navy Pier), where perverse, misogynist fantasies of surgery and dismemberment are played out on women's bodies. The invasion of privacy, surveillance and policing of bodies, and appropriation of traumatized bodies (suffering from mental illness, eating disorders, drug addiction, cancer, AIDS) by medical, psychoanalytic, New Age, and fundamentalist discourses only increase the pressure on the sports fitness, health food, beauty, and entertainment industries to continually invent perfect bodies. Their investment of the biological body with fictions of self-expression, freedom of choice, and successful makeovers functions obsessively as a simultaneous denial of our psychic vulnerability, physical mortality, and also our anxiety about our potential replaceability (losing a lover, a home, a job, or a social identity).

It is in light of the phantasmatics of this denial and anxiety that one can view Spence's therapeutic "Narratives of Dis-ease" as an attempt to reconstruct herself by showing her diseased, scarred body reflecting its own history, by allowing herself to be seen as not denying the wounds of ugliness or, rather, the results of medical intervention into her body. The question of what is culturally constructed as being ugly or beautiful, "positive" or "negative," is here turned on its head and counters the false oppositions of "private" and "public." Spence's corporeal history, her aging body, is her own. By putting herself in a picture and publicly displaying her struggle with breast cancer (she had a lumpectomy in 1982 and then decided in favor of noninvasive, nonchemical treatment), she "invents" an expressive language that is and is not her own as she provocatively places herself between the iconography of the victimized and the eroticized/fetishized female nude body. It is significant that she has referred to her "Narratives of Dis-ease" as "ritualized procedures" (in the wall texts accompanying the photographs). Her procedures cannot fail to evoke memories of the female ritualized performance and body art of the seventies and eighties (e.g., Judy Chicago, Ana Mendieta, Marina Abramović, Carolee Schneemann, Yoko Ono, Suzanne Lacy, Valie Export, Mary Kelly, Leslie Labowitz, Virginia Maksymowicz, Adrian Piper, and Johanna Went). Hannah Wilke's self-portraits and portraits of her mother in the *So Help Me Hannah Series: Portrait of the Artist with Her Mother* (1978–81), Francesca Woodman's and Cindy Sherman's staged self-portraits, and Lorna Simpson's photo-textual staging of portraits of black women's bodies likewise have adopted this theatricalized mode of exploration.

The early body performances and actions seem to have passed into history following their scatological and self-abusive excesses (predominantly male performances) and deliberate risk-taking, taboo-breaking, and endurance-testing. (Abramović's work is pathbreaking in this respect; her rituals involving long duration probably gave the name to the retrospective exhibition *Endurance*, which was shown at New York City's Soho area Exit Art Gallery in the spring of 1995.) Now risk taking has returned again in the heightened rage of current autoperformances that voice the pain of the body.

I believe there is an important difference of tone and motivation in the subjective languages of, say, Karen Finley or David Wojnarowicz, on the one hand, and Annie Sprinkle, Tim Miller, or Spiderwoman Theater, on the other. Finley's performed narratives of sexual abuse, rape, incest, and male violence look and sound like rituals of exorcism in which she pushes her body to quite literal extremes of obscenity and self-degradation, repelling the male gaze and also the scopophilic look that modern medical science (e.g., Charcot's anatomical studies of women's "hystericized" body parts) directs at women's bodies. Her brutal self-debasements play havoc with the boundaries delimiting what is and is not taboo; her self-objectification must be considered a conscious strategy of critical exposure, inviting our thwarted voyeurism to participate in the rituals of complicity that constitute the scene of violent objectification. After Finley's pregnancy and the birth of her first child, her most recent installations and performance plays (written to incorporate other actors) reveal a softening of approach and a more quixotic irony. Her tone is changing, and one may or may not wish to attribute this change to her experience of motherhood or, more likely, her fatigue after the censorship battles she had to fight with the conservative defenders of "family values" and obscenity laws.

The late David Wojnarowicz's performances, more strongly than his visual and filmic works, embodied an explosive, murderous rage that unflinchingly named the violence and discrimination he suffered as a "queer in America" and a person afflicted with the AIDS virus. His "Memoir of Disintegration" (in his book *Close to the Knives*) is passionately directed outward against the silence and invisibility a homophobic society would impose on him, while some of his internal monologues about erotic longings surrealistically blend into the sordid underside of the culture he experienced as his own. Compared to Wojnarowicz's confrontational expression of his rage, some of the other performers I saw in Chicago in the early nineties made contact with their audiences in a more conciliatory and inclusive way, seeking to nurture an emotional and spiritual compassion that is often absent in the abusive world so recognizable in *Close to the Knives*.

Turning (the Body) Around

In her book on the multivocal/cultural creation of art entitled *Mixed Blessings: New Art in Multicultural America*, Lucy Lippard has dedicated her last chapter, "Turning Around," to productive strategies of playful subversion, sly infiltration, and ironic reversals of mainstream or normative stereotypes and oppressive conditions. Prior to discussing several Native American artists and their cherished use of the "trickster figure" (the wily humor of Coyote) and, correspondingly, the use of "bad taste" or sardonic kitsch humor (*rasquachismo*) in Chicano performances and visual artworks, she quotes Cherokee sculptor-performer Jimmy Durham: "As an authorized savage it is my custom and my job to attack."[4]

I find it quite thought-provoking to reflect on Durham's ironic comment and remember his or James Luna's utilization of "medicine objects" or familiar, "traditional" materials (clichés of "primitive art" in contemporary Western art circles, familiar both to indigenous and colonizing cultures yet differently so) in their installations and actions. When you experience Durham or Luna in performance, there is, of course, a sense of irony and sly humor that is everpresent in their conceptual rearrangements of the traditional signifiers, yet their most powerfully effective deployment of the trickster figure is in the disposition of their bodies. For instance, Luna's self-exhibition in a glass case during the *Artifact Piece* (1986), in which he lay sedated in an open "coffin" or museum display case, was a pathetic and sad commentary on the traditional display modalities of ethnographic and natural-history museums that exhibit the habitats and traces of extinct or endangered "Indian tribes." His glass case was surrounded by a collection of his personal belongings, accoutrements, and "medicine objects" used in ritual practice on the La Jolla reservation where he lived. Next to his body in the glass case were labels listing and explaining several of his scars resulting from drunkenness and fights on the reservation. I always remember connecting his self-deposition with the idea of the "medicine objects," interpreting his act as one of faith, in a sense, appealing to the healing force or therapeutic and spiritual dimension of such a turning of the body toward us.

Into this context of healing practices I would also place Tim Miller's work, especially the humor and tenderness of *Sex/Love/Stories* (performed at Chicago's Beacon Street Gallery, better known as the Northside Community Arts Center, which is affiliated with Hull House). In this performance he literally turned his naked and exposed body over to the members of the audience, seating himself in their laps, holding their hands, using their hands to hold and caress him, asking for their tenderness in return for his exposition of his vulnerability and anxiety over so many losses encountered, so many deaths of lovers and friends owing to AIDS and the ravages of an epidemic that had hit hardest among the gay community with which he identified, threatened as it still is with the loss of countless others.

Similarly, the highly visceral and musically affective interwoven-narrative performance of Spiderwoman Theater (held at the Chameleon Productions Theatre—a good name for trickster performances) reached out to the body of the audience without any desire to shock or alienate. On the contrary, Spiderwoman's collective storytelling in *Power Pipes,* performed ritually by a crossgenerational group of six Native American women (young and old, lesbian and heterosexual, mother, daughter, grandmother), transfers the power of compassion to the audience precisely because each of the performers wants to share her "medicine" and connect us to their communal storytelling as a source of healing and as an embodied practice comparable, perhaps, to shamanic healing rituals in Buddhist or African cultures.

Again, boundaries are breaking down if we consider Spiderwoman's cultural performance as moving between theater, dance, and oral traditions and those practices of healing, shamanism, therapy, yoga, meditation, or transformative religious experiences which are generally devalued by Western rationalist conceptions of art. In light of the serious political struggle of minorities and immigrants against exclusion from full participation in economic, social, artistic, and cultural life, we need not wax romantic over lost folkloric or native traditions but rather should recognize Spiderwoman's reinventions of the storytelling mode at the critical juncture of today's intercultural experience of living, complex, multiple identities. The stories and gestures of Spiderwoman—Native American women who grew up in New York City and name themselves after the Hopi goddess of creation—express fractures and contradictions because their physical embodiment of hybrid cultural/self-identities bespeak not stable roots but a difficult transitional process in a present in which self-knowledge, or empowerment through memory, cannot be taken for granted but must continually be reconstructed, as Spence would say. Her "Libido Uprising" consists of a series of ongoing interior dialogues about mother-daughter relationships and repressed memories; as in "Unbecoming Mothers," the photographs are staged reenactments of her mother (i.e., her imaging of herself as her mother) that seek to conjure up and transform the pain and shame of her remembered childhood and adolescence. Spiderwoman's theatrical work is based on physical improvisations directed not only at these "shame thresholds" (Spence) of remembered oppression and victimization but also at the healing power of women's (mothers') secrets, spiritual knowledge, love, and nurturance.

In one of the community workshops held in Chicago during Spiderwoman's residency, Monique Mojica described Spiderwoman's body-centered rehearsals: "Our body is our instrument. As actors on stage this is all we have, the raw material, our bodies, our voice, our memories. And we have to be able to play the instrument." Mojica is the daughter of Gloria Miguel, one of the founders of this strongly connected heterogeneous "family" of women who start their performance of *Power Pipes* in a circular, processional ritual danced to the percussive rhythms of the antiphonal pipes (traditionally used by the Cuna tribe), which they play before they tell their interwoven stories and dreams. Their performance is an invocation. I felt its spiritual and kinetic force entering my body; the incantatory sensations of eye and ear, in and out of phase, sweeping through me like a gust of air, putting things out of (my) perspective, shifting my audition away from the desire for objectification.

I stress this diffraction of the aural and visual affects (most of the opening ritual was performed in the dark) because the privilege of the visual is the stumbling block for feminist art (especially photography) and also for performance art's foregrounding of the body. Spiderwoman's audition of memory raises a slightly different problem, namely, whether the transference of memory to an audience of "foreigners" can take place insofar as my body has no calendar of ancestral events or lunar cycles, nor does it have access to a collective memory I could share with Native American women. Or, at another deep level, do we share a fractured identity? Do we, as natives, feel ourselves to be more or less "foreign" in our "own and proper" places, our improper/disappropriated bodies, cut off from our mother tongue, our mother's body, and haunted by our desire for the latter?

Our Mothers, Our Selves

In her installation entitled *Interim* (1985–90) Mary Kelly confronted the regressive and masochistic aspects of this desire to return to the body (described by feminist psychoanalysis as "maternal identification") by resolutely avoiding the female figure and the seductiveness of the feminine self-image altogether, while at the same time exploring the "subject" of feminine visual pleasure and desire. *Interim*, which was shown at the 1991 Whitney Museum Biennial in New York City, questions any essential reference or real body of gender and sexual identity. As with elin o'hara slavick's and Lisa Dianne Schwarzbek's "portraits" of surrogate bodies (dresses with embroidered confessional texts; a cabinet/music box with drawers filled with fetishes and medical instruments), we are faced with a female fetishism that does not cater to a masculine gaze.

In her performance of *Post Post Porn Modernist* at Theater Oobleck in Chicago, porn film star and former sex worker Annie Sprinkle pushed the dynamics of fetishism and the sexual commodification of the female body to its limits, flaunting her full, fleshy body and the accoutrements of her seductive (phallic) power while flirting with male and female gazes and the voyeurism of Peeping Toms or Peeping Janes in the audience. Her playing at the edges of cynical self-exploitation, masquerade, and literal objectification of the sexual body created a dangerous scene in which her matter-of-fact, documentary-lecture style of statistical display (her work in the sex industry) mingled uneasily with her mock-serious slide shows (pictures of her lovers, some of whom died of AIDS; and of ordinary-looking women who dress up to become sex goddesses) and her tacky New Age ritual of orgasmic meditation. But Sprinkle's "formal" presentation of her autobiography/labor history (the slide lectures), ostensibly constructed to show us a boundless sexual energy she celebrates in its use and exchange value, an energy she controls and now artistically deploys beyond any taboo restrictions, can also turn into hyperreal moments of intimacy (e.g., when she douches and pees on-stage or offers the audience a close-up look into her cervix). In those moments, her gentle, nonthreatening display of her sexual anatomy teases out the male gaze with her camera-ready pose. Perhaps she embarrasses and indicts that gaze (the men, with their cameras, who had shown up that night), but it is unclear how many men in the audience felt salaciously titillated and confirmed in their expectations of the porn star they had come to see. They did get their snapshots, and they gladly paid for them. Sprinkle's politics of self-display are muted, since she cannot claim to avoid the visual subjection of her vulnerable body, even though her performance proclaims her body to be hers, her treasure, property, and instrument, a source of pleasure and secrets she is willing to share. In that sense, she may claim that she is not vulnerable but in command. It is her privilege to make the dispensation, to invite us to join in communion with her flesh.

Most decidedly, however, Sprinkle's self-representation cuts both ways since she is simultaneously the subject and object of the look, while managing both to demystify the pornographic body and suggest a kind of *communal healing power of sexual practice*, which she tried to demonstrate in the concluding ritual of a self-performed orgasm achieved through her meditative concentration and the audience members' help, accompanying her motions with little percussion instruments she had passed out among us. This last suggestion, though not altogether easily comprehensible in the current age of AIDS and paranoia-induced (self-)

censorship, is the most provocative aspect of her work and worthy of further examination. It also returns us to *Embodiment* and my earlier claim that Spence's production of her self-portraits constitutes an intervention into the public sphere.

During the Randolph Street Gallery's public panel discussion on "Crossing Boundaries/Re-inventing Our Lives," exhibition organizer Angela Kelly was joined by art therapist Mary Dougherty, community activist and editor Jan Zita Grover, and movement therapist Abby Miller. Kelly immediately emphasized the interventionist role of Spence's work in order to problematize the "divisions that exist between theory and art, between mind and body, and between theoretical models within feminist discourses." All the women on the panel were boundary crossers, and the shared interests and commitments of the large and inspired audience were perhaps the surest sign that we are experiencing a vital shift in the arts toward a new social (and communal) conception of practice, embodied ecological consciousness, and the interconnectedness of cultures.

If this is a major departure from the headier days of high theory (with the eclipse of the latter perfectly symbolized in Camille Paglia's conservative postfeminism and Jean Baudrillard's nihilist celebrations of postmodern simulations), it may be the result of sheer necessity, given the fact that the economic recession has tightened its grip and many arts organizations across the country will lose their government, corporate, or private funding and go out of business. The New York *Times,* ominously reporting on the arts recession on New Year's Eve 1991, chose to address the capitalist side of the issue and why we need better "arts marketing consultant firms." Jan Grover began her comments on *Embodiment* by stating that Spence's photographic work presents only the tip of the iceberg, that many of the interventions on behalf of our ailing society have grown out of the larger, interactive field of social movements and grassroots organizations that share a wide range of therapeutic and creative techniques as well as different levels of knowledge, derived from feminist cultural theory, which they have found to be meaningful in addressing their needs.

There is an intensely democratic appeal in Spence's photo-therapy work. On one level, her rephotographing herself—a reconstruction of her "family album"—implies that anybody who wishes to exercise personal fantasies or rejected parts of our selves that don't show up in our idealized family albums or on the cover of the magazines Madonna sings about in her disturbingly superficial mimicry of "voguing" can do so. Why is it that we have no photos of the day of our divorce or the morning our lover left us? Why did we forget to photograph the moment we asserted ourselves against management at the workplace, demanding our right to obtain benefits or sick leave?

On another level, I find it interesting that Madonna's glamorous style-switching is considered provocative and shocking (to the values of the American family?), while Spence herself implies that the images of her body can shock her because they "make visible to ourselves our own tabooed inner speech" and disclose "the disturbing theatre of the many selves housed within." I should think that "shock" has become a useless term both in avant-garde performance/art and in popular culture, for we have already been numbed by the violence of experience and its ceaseless photographic documentation in the daily press. Why is the "social realism" of politically correct documentary art so ineffective? And what separation do people feel and embody when they step over the body of a dying alcoholic sprawled across their front door on their way to the newsstand, where they read about the unspeakable images of a Mapplethorpe exhibition or the quotidian slaughter of some military intervention?

The consequences of such separation, and of the ongoing techno- logical abstractions in our culture, were captured quite perfectly by the cool, ironic displacements in *The Body* (The Renaissance Society), an exhibition in which no human body as such was represented. Instead, there were abstract, self-referential objects, arranged as a kind of vir- tual reality of metaphorical biologies, forcing the viewer to deduce some prior existence of bodies now displaced by signs of medical, scientific, or industrial technology and superseded by biogenetic replications of body organisms. Tellingly, the exhibition catalogue was published after the show had already closed; instead of the usual art-historical commen- tary, it contained fiction and poetry. In an effort to put things to right, a review of *The Body* explained the works in terms of the aesthetic tradi- tion of minimalism, which presumably means the reviewer found them satisfactory on self-referential, formal grounds.[5]

This is an idea that didn't occur to me when I watched James Luna in his glass cage, looking at the traces he had placed before our eyes of a vanishing culture or a vanished people made invisible behind the fences of the reservations. The disappearance of human bodies (*los desapare- cidos*) and our astonished awareness of our own dispensibility by eco- nomic and political forces of capitalist accumulation and technocratic engineering, is another matter that is most likely not an issue of the aes- thetics of minimalism. If we look at the gallery's catalogue for *Embodi- ment*, we find subjective statements by the artists themselves as well as two brief meditations by Dougherty and Grover, the latter constructed as a dialogue with Spence's own writings about her therapeutic process. Avoiding the abstractions of aesthetic theory, the exhibition project curiously reverts back to an older discourse or paradigm of depth psychology and Jungian archetypal psychology while proposing individual transformation as the source for personal/political practice. The bourgeois implications of this return to subjectivity and interiority (with its implicit dualism of depth/surface) cannot be overlooked, and my reference to Madonna's "truth or dare" voguing was meant to question the site of the truth in both directions. Spence's "disturbing theatre of inner selves" is imaged (in "Unbecoming Mothers" and "Libido Uprising") as scenarios of phantasms and desires, in which she replays her losses and traumas, her separation from herself and her mother. Her (re)picturing of her body with her disfigured left breast subsequent to the cancer diagnosis and the lumpectomy is an extraordinarily direct and metaphorical staging of a traumatic loss and of the unrepresentable (death), remembered and unremembered as the relation to the mother's breast, which is the daughter-child's first object relation.

Spence's self-analysis of her psychic defenses and sexual desires in "Libido Uprising" (subtitled "Mother/Daughter Work") is both revealing and highly theatrical. Her hands and face smeared with (fake) blood, as she looks at the photographer/therapist (Rosy Martin) and camera/spectator, we become part of an interactive exchange in which the cause of desire—the separation—cannot be consciously recognized. "I am in the picture," Spence seems to be saying, paradoxically aware of her fractured self, which seems so corporeally present and yet so nightmarishly held in suspension by something other.

This sense of the nightmarish and phantasmatic also pervades the images of Andi Pihl (consisting of five untitled Chromogenic prints from "The Home Series"). Lacking the context of British social psychotherapy (Melanie Klein, D. W. Winnicott, R. D. Laing) in which Spence encountered sixties radical feminism, Pihl's work dramatically stages psychological scenes of abuse, abandonment, and self-inflicted pain that rely on the faintest metaphorical notions of the "home" or "family." In other words, the images of babies/Barbie dolls dangling from umbilical cords are a cultural reference to the American family, but they can hardly be called therapeutic images. Laing's influence on British feminist politics was considerable, for it helped to identify the family as the particular class-based social institution that induces psychosis, as the site in which the inferiorized psychology of women (as

wives and mothers without legal or economic independence) had been
legitimated. In the postfeminist nineties we require a different political
analysis of institutions, the fragmentation of social identities or marital
bonds, teenage pregnancy, surrogate parenthood and child abuse, health
and disease, sex education, and of the dysfunctional North American
family. I'm afraid that the School of the Art Institute of Chicago's exhibition *Disclosing the Myth of Family* was only the tip of the iceberg. The
works of Pihl, o'hara slavick, Kumao, and Schwarzbek lack any specific context of cross-institutional critique, in the sense in which we can
view Spence's photo-therapy workshops as interventions in the fields of
health and education that reflect more recent changes in patient-doctor
relations or the increasing pressure against government policies regarding clinical trials for breast cancer.

Viewed as a dialectical exhibition, *Embodiment* also embodies a contradiction: the works of the North American artists appear separate

251

Andi Pihl, "Untitled," from "The Home Series." Chromogenic print, 1990. Randolph Street Gallery, Chicago, 1991. Photo: J. Birringer.

from the communal political process implied by Spence's collaboration with her friends, students, and doctors. A fine line separates the two aspects of the exhibition, reflecting the division between the social and the aesthetic. Kumao's cinematographic shadow plays of replicated nineteenth-century photographic technology ("The Decay of Trust," "Silenced") and Schwarzbek's displacement of the pain of her facial surgery onto a beautifully crafted wooden cabinet ("A Spoonful of Sugar") draw attention to the formal qualities of their sculptural construction. At the same time, Schwarzbek's desire to reclaim authorship of her face and image is most powerful when she invokes the (almost) lost memory of early childhood's "oral sensations" (now hidden in the recesses of this Pandora's box). This invocation gains a strong visceral dimension if viewed together with o'hara slavick's "Wall of Incoherent Dresses," where haunting confessional letters are stitched into the girl's dresses saved by the mother. (A small red one reads: "I want my mother's tongue"; a long velvet gown reads: "I refused the hysterectomy of my desire.") In the photo I took of Pihl's "Untitled" (p. 251), you can see the eerie reflection of slavick's "Incoherent Dresses" mirrored in the glass frame. What ultimately links all of the works in the exhibition project is a rather difficult question to answer, at least insofar as it is formulated in terms of intrapsychic relations: How can I (re)claim what I already know?

  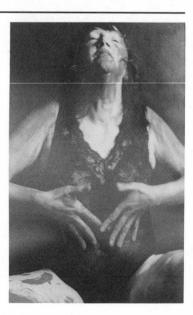

Show Your Wounds

> My wounds and my representations of them are tools that I put on the table in a classroom or workshop. The wounds that I've healed, the wound of breast cancer, or the wound of ugliness, or the wound of class shame—it is work that I've already done. Now I can release it—my raw material—as teaching material.
>
> Jo Spence, *Putting Myself in the Picture*

The question was understood differently by the participants at the public discussion. Art therapist Mary Dougherty stressed the need for women to reclaim their experience through "expressions of subjective truth [and the] authenticity of the embodied healing metaphors." In her view, the art process as a transformation of matter corresponds to the therapeutic process as a transformation of self. While the healing experience, as expressed in Spence's own words, cannot be doubted and, indeed, is reclaimable for pedagogical and interpersonal action, Dougherty tended to see Spence's photographs as images of self-transformation that validated her own "inner authority." An implicit reference was being made here to Jungian archetypal psychology and to a conception of the inner world of the body that resembles metaphors of the very dualisms (psychological and metaphysical) one ought to question in order to avoid mythical and ahistorical notions of the inner self.

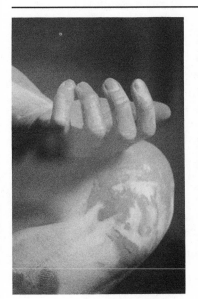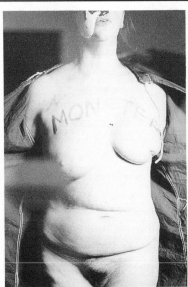

Jo Spence, "Libido Uprising," part 1, with Rosy Martin, 1989. Randolph Street Gallery, Chicago, 1991. Photo: J. Birringer.

Spence's work is not about finding her various inner selves; it is a *process* of visualization and imaginative projection that is produced within specific interactive exchanges (with therapists, doctors, friends) and power relations at a specific moment of the British feminist critique of patriarchal institutions and medical practices. The representation of her wounds transforms Spence's self-analysis into a political pedagogy; she demonstrates how she can construct her sexual or her ill body in relation to medical or mass-media images with which dominant cultural and health industries/institutions construct sexuality and health for women as consumers of such images.

For Jan Grover, who is widely known for her activism in AIDS communities, the critical relations in Spence's work between sexual politics and health reflect the urgency of an existential struggle, a struggle over living and dying, in which the creation of art can perhaps help to reconstruct the conditions of its experience. Art as therapy cannot rely on introversion, as Abby Miller suggested through her praise of women's sacred, birth-giving bodies, especially not during a time when women's freedom of choice is threatened. Although Miller very movingly described her nonvisual movement-therapy work as an ongoing process of creating positive self-awareness out of women's physical body experience (a practice that is often based on new body-mind centering techniques and a holistic approach to the sensing, loving, and attentive awareness to our experiential anatomy, the body's memory, and its imaginative and expressive powers), her emphasis on the "inner reaches of outer space" (a phrase well known to readers of Joseph Campbell) depends on a denial of the violence of experience. I don't question the importance of such denial on occasion, nor do I question denial as an unconscious process; on the other hand, such an introspective search for positive release is not necessarily helpful as a technique of self-empowerment and self-defense; a growing number of women actually prefer martial arts and self-defense workshops. The New Age culture, with its retreat into privatized therapy networks and "anonymous" self-help rituals can only create a false appearance of solidarity and community since its introverted recognition of undeniable pain is not translated into a social-action program.

When Grover asked how embodied illness can teach us how to share our wounds and the irreducible pain that threatens any and all of our metaphors, she approached the limit of Spence's "Narratives of Dis-ease," namely, the existential challenge of the body in pain. Grover informed us that night that after having been diagnosed with chronic lymphatic leukemia, Spence had not yet found a strategy to make her condition visible. Grover's comments on this personal tragedy have larger ramifications for the practices of therapy, art, and theory since she addressed the challenge of *participatory responsibility.*

In order to face the realities of the body in pain and the feelings of shame and victimization, one can neither trust artistic images (the truth and beauty of art) nor the sophisticated and dizzying elaborations of (academic) theory, since they create aesthetic distance from what we really prefer to forget. This was one of the bitter, confusing lessons I learned while growing up in Germany after the Holocaust and the war, when the healing of wounds and the expression of guilt was obligatory, being both a national and an industrial project.

I first encountered Joseph Beuys in a performance of his installation *Show Your Wound* at a time (1969) when such social action/pedagogical interventions were vital reminders not to forget and of the necessity to invent art. Back then it was a revolutionary idea to see pedagogical and political intervention as a process of participation against the status quo (including the art that was not the art Beuys had in mind when he invented the politicized concept of "social sculpture" as a democratic art form in which all could partake). It meant an opening up to a collective consciousness for social change that would lead to a more humane, artistic society. This was Beuys's trickster medicine: a therapeutic, transformative idea of active healing in the building of "social sculptures" or living organisms in which we all participated as equal citizens applying creative energies and dynamics.

The stakes are very high today since the "embodiment" of a revolutionary conscience has collapsed—and not merely in eastern Europe. The Marxist revolutionary conception needs to be reinvented, for we are without a coherent, organized international commitment to continue the process of liberation on the basis of a political and economic analysis of changing postmodern conditions. In other words, we know that we need to rebuild new critical analyses of institutions (including the system of art that is still being promoted) and institutional practices such as education, religion, government, law, medicine, the mass media, health policy, and therapeutic technologies. We also need new critical analyses of social classes, political economies and organizations, cultural productions, and social movements in order to locate ourselves, and our bodily experience in everyday life, within the fields concerned with the politics of knowledge production. It is in those fields that our "knowledge" of bodies is inscribed through the effects of "training"—the regulated training (as in classical ballet) that shapes our bodies, desires, identifications, and social behaviors, and the ways in which we respond to our illnesses and treat our wounds. Projects such as *Embodiment* forcefully remind us of the learning process we must reclaim before we forget what we already know.

Postscript

In early 1993, after completing the first draft of this chapter, I wrote a brief essay on Carolee Schneemann's work and her Chicago exhibition entitled *Cycladic Imprints*. Meeting Schneemann was a revelation, and it helped me to situate my reflections on Jo Spence in a broader context of women's body art. Writing about Schneemann's exhibition became a difficult and painful experience, however, and I want to pay tribute here to all those whose creative work and actions have heightened our critical understanding of the relations between visual representation and cultural activism at a time when our "knowledge" of bodies and sexualities is as vulnerable as our physical and moral resistance to a cumulative loss of hope. I am referring to the deaths of Jo Spence, Vito Russo, David Wojnarowicz, Hannah Wilke, Audre Lorde, Craig Owens, and many others who succumbed to the illness that attacked their bodies.

Having written about these artists or taught their work in my performance/art classes, and having shared the politics of contestation they embodied, I feel haunted by the necessity to address our losses. At the same time, we have learned so much from AIDS activism and the feminist health movement that there is an even greater need to confront the administration of research, treatment, and health care in the wider political context of those agencies and discourses that seek to control or contain bodies and sexualities. In her posthumously published book *Erotic Welfare: Sexual Theory and Politics in the Age of Epidemic* (1993), Linda Singer has argued that we are witnessing the intensification of regulatory regimes centered on phantasmatic sites of erotic danger that threaten the traditional "family values" evoked so often in the rhetoric of our governments. In Singer's view, women's sexuality occupies a crucial place within these rhetorics and regulatory regimes because of the "erotic over-investment" that is afforded the feminine. Spanning the past three decades, and springing from a (counter)culture of sexual liberation now unthinkable, the work of visual artists like Carolee Schneemann and Jo Spence has depicted sexuality and the female body in ways that have gained a new and radical significance in the struggle against disciplinary power as well as the rigid antipornography ideology within feminism that seeks to arrest or censor practices that exceed their logic and economy of values. Announcing a new video project in 1993 entitled *Imaging Her Erotics*, Schneemann started to collaborate with Maria Beatty on a "visual archeology" of her various works since her "kinesthetic environments" and performances of the early sixties. After watching the first completed segment of this video, I realized that I had seen much more than just her side of the story of what came to be known as "body art" in the seventies. Rather, the range and power of her imagery (which I discussed in my essay on *Cycladic Imprints*) affirm the role of her body in her work in ways that are absolutely pertinent to contemporary debates about sexual politics and erotics in a phobic, brutal society obsessed with a pathological fear of uncontrollable bodies. One of the major propositions in her work is to trust one's own body, including its energies, erotic impulses, dreams, and unconscious storehouse of information. Her work, as daring and unflinching as Jo Spence's, offers rich inspiration to erotic art and politically conscious cultural productions that seek to examine and subvert the conventions (and parodies) imposed upon our trust of our own bodies.[6]

NINE

DISEMBODIMENT: THE VIRTUAL REALITIES

Scene One: Cybernetic Art in the Museum of the Future

"The machine is us." Initially written as a provocative affirmation of women's experience of boundaries and of their hybrid existence, Donna Haraway's *Cyborg Manifesto* (1985) looks at science fiction stories and films about our technological future in order to analyze the stories science tells about the invention and reinvention of Nature. Her feminist critique of the scientific institutions of knowledge challenges the constructions of "humanness" at the very point at which the dominant narratives of scientific progress or evolution now converge with profound changes in late-capitalist economies and technocratic cultures. These changes in the political economy of an increasingly globalized capitalism are marked by a transformation in the nature of visuality itself. As a historian of science, Haraway has observed how the production of human knowledge encounters cybernetic technology and is increasingly determined by the operations of a new information order that disturbs the distinctions between natural and artificial, mind and body, consciousness and its simulation: "Microelectronics is the technical basis of simulacra; that is, of copies without originals. . . . Communications technologies and biotechnologies are the crucial tools recrafting our bodies. . . . We find ourselves to be cyborgs, hybrids, mosaics, chimeras . . . The machine is us, our processes, an aspect of our embodiment."[1]

Taking my cue from her interest in the science fiction of cybernetic organisms, I want to make several forays into the possible future of the late-capitalist museum and its production of knowledge, its preservation and transformation of the operations of art under the new imperatives of high technology and electronic data management. I will, of course, also venture outside the museum. What was envisioned by earlier science fiction writers has become more and more real in the sense in which we speak of everyday reality. We already inhabit a hypertechnological culture, and our speculation must address its impact on the fading "nature" of art (once understood, in its mimetic capacity, as a mirror of nature/reality) and the consumption of art's afterimages of simulacra.

Cyberspace Museum

In order to grasp our relations to technology and to late capitalist mass culture, we need to effect a *discursive* shift away from aesthetic or art-historical interpretation and toward technoscientific models of electronic reproduction, toward the abstraction of the visual effected by such models, which suggests that we must revise our understanding of the space into which the once familiar museum of the industrial era must now enter. My first intimations of this new space occurred in 1985 at the Centre Georges Pompidou in Paris. Although I have already written about it in relation to postmodernist theater, I want to recall my impressions of this spatial/conceptual experience in order to advance a new argument, moving forward into the nineties and the evolution of virtual spaces on the Internet.

Most of my visits to Paris usually include a day or two at the Louvre or at other museums that house collections of modern art. The Centre Georges Pompidou, of course, carries different connotations of a center for "popular exhibitions" (a populist version of the Kunsthalle or what is called "Temporary Contemporary" in Los Angeles, the latter being a fine name for a nonpermanent building housing short-lived fashions of new art) exploring the twentieth-century avant-garde and its mass-cultural connections, thus serving as a kind of conceptual operation probing the gradual breakdown of older aesthetic boundaries and understandings of the work of art in industrial cultures. Given the colorful and playful postmodern architecture of the physical structure itself, it is also apparent that the traditional display space of the museum and its modes of presentation have been replaced by a new emphasis on the frames of the modern art objects themselves. The Centre Georges Pompidou's self-conscious pop-architectural space is already a comment or critique of the museum as the paradigmatic institution of artistic modernism, thus contributing to the breakup of the modernist paradigm of the autonomous art object.[2]

Anticipating the emergence in the nineties of interactive galleries on the Net, French philosopher Jean-François Lyotard and his collaborators at the Centre de Création Industrielle staged their Centre Pompidou project *Les Immatériaux* as an interactive environment for conceptual explorations of our world, a "reality" no longer securely representable in perspectival or artistic terms borrowed from humanist ideology and modern aesthetics, being largely dependent on cybernetic, immaterial data flows. *Les Immatériaux* was not an exhibition that displayed artworks (least of all paintings). Rather, it was intended as a provocative response to the practice of viewing art in a museum as well as to art-historical standards of displaying unique, original art objects supported by the aesthetic discourse of individuality and tradition (as well as that of the "anxiety of influence" Harold Bloom had traced in the Western literary canon).

Moving beyond visual representation and the perceptual space, mimetic codes, and referential narratives of the modern reproductive media (film, photography), *Les Immatériaux* tried to evoke a temporal, multisensory experience of a "nervous system," a discontinuous world of invisible interfaces among heterogeneous design processes, digital codes, and theoretical constructs. Lyotard's exhibition was paradoxical, therefore, insofar as it used the actual contemporary "museum" space to present the virtual effects of mathematical data that was technically fabricated by the postmodern prostheses of immateriality, including computers, synthesizers, text processors, designer-robots, holographic and video simulation, and radar. Although no longer surprising, it should also be mentioned that Lyotard is not an art curator but rather a popular postmodern philosopher whose books invigorated transatlantic debates on the "postmodern condition." When art history no longer functions as discursive frame, its curatorial authority can no longer be assumed.

It was equally fascinating to notice Lyotard's ironic recollection of the theater as an older model of illusionistic representation that corresponded to the visual arts and to a "phenomenology of perception" (Merleau-Ponty) that now appears to be obsolete. The dark, mirrored vestibule entitled "Theatre of the Non-Body" was empty. While gazing at my reflection, I listened to a dramatic monologue from Beckett's *The Unnameable* coming through the headphones I had been given. Gradually I discovered five small dioramas of empty stage sets (models). This disembodied remainder of theater (one could also view the models as designs for a virtual theater that may or may not take a place in reality) opened onto five meandering paths that provided passages through the gigantic metallic labyrinth of *Les Immatériaux,* a labyrinth of sounds and signs, indistinctly divided by silver-gauze screens and lighting effects into sixty "sites" interpenetrated by broadcast zones and their invisible infrared signals.

Disoriented by audiovisual juxtapositions (theoretical texts by Artaud, Borges, Baudrillard, Barthes, and Virilio filled my ears yet did not refer to the technological displays), the space traveler could resort to a computerized index of the exhibition. But this index was a hypertext spreading to other scientific theories of circuits, cells, energy states, cloning processes, and biogenetic information transfers. *Les Immatériaux* thus demonstrated how contemporary technoscience might replace or advance artistic experimentation if, indeed, dematerialized digital imagery and information, dispersed and exchanged in abstract visual and linguistic codes, were to supersede older conventions of optical vision and mechanical reproduction. Claiming that the model of language replaces the model of matter, and that *material disappears as an independent entity,* Lyotard invoked a New World Order (after the so-called linguistic turn made by structuralist/poststructuralist theory) of synthetic processes or "postindustrial" productivity in the information era, that is, the passage of experiential reality into the grids, matrices, and pulses of electronic communication.[3]

Although this claim did not engage any political or economic arguments, and thus stayed within the limited arena of what Teresa L. Ebert has criticized as the "ludic" poststructuralist cultural analysis founded upon the displacement of historical materialism and economic critique, I would like to suggest that the paradigmatic site of the Pompidou installation, called "The Labyrinth of Language," had broader implications for the curatorial role of the modern museum as the guardian and collector of art and material culture.[4] By moving the hardware and software of the cybernetic systems into the Centre Georges Pompidou (already a "hyperreal" space, according to Baudrillard's theory of

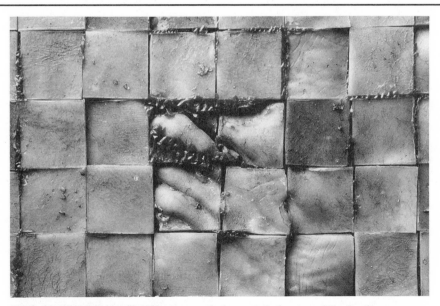

Kiki Smith, "Untitled" (detail), 1990; wax, wood, cheese cloth. Courtesy of The Renaissance Society, Chicago.

an imploding culture), Lyotard's labyrinth of technological simulation not only performed computer-generated language games in a postmodern perversion/fulfillment of earlier structuralist theory (de Saussure) or avant-garde technofuturism (Marinetti, Le Corbusier) but also foregrounded the ongoing abstraction of vision as a process of encoding/decoding in which traditional identities—the viewing subject (bodily perception, subjective reality), on the one hand, and the museum's institutional power to preserve the unique and irreplaceable embodiments of cultural knowledge, on the other—are dissolved and redefined along the vectors of a hyperexchange of the blips of "memory and data banks."[5]

Hypermedia Museum

To speak of blips of information in the context of postmodern culture and its multimedia derealization of experience is to acknowledge the correspondence between the serial reproduction of commodities, spectacles, or TV/MTV images and the cross-referenced simulations of current appropriationist art that were celebrated, for example, in the 1990 Whitney Museum exhibition *Image World: Art and Media Culture* and then reappeared, as a veritable junkyard of images and styles, in the 1991 Whitney Biennial. While museums and art galleries, not unlike shopping malls, now clearly stand in an equal and necessary relation to consumer capitalism and mass-marketing operations, it remains to be seen whether the corporate management of art products and "cultural assets" will follow the logic of accelerated technologizing and homogenization that defines other mass markets and modes of consumption predicated on simulacral experience, that is, on the inauthentic, the hybrid, the already reproduced.[6]

Individual artworks, of course, will not disappear, and museums will continue to present painting and sculpture in their objecthood and aesthetic specificity, even if such representation appears—according to Baudrillard's cynical dismissal of reified history—as so many nostalgic or archeological gestures desperately seeking to disguise the hyperreality of the fetishized "originality" of art. The historical contradictions, however, become meaningful once one thinks not of "real" art objects as such but of our technological relation to the changing modes of their presentation and emplacement, which include modes of emplotment or narrative fictionalization. The media environment does not make the museum obsolete; rather, it has already profoundly affected the way in which the new *multimedia museum* will spectacularize its art objects and their histories, and thus advertise our relation to them as knowledgeable or distinct consumers. Fine-arts museums will approximate the urban or "theme park" entertainment offered, for example, by the Cité des Sciences at La Villette (Paris) or other space and science museums around the world, or they will hype special exhibitions (the blockbuster as media event) by expanding the range of audiovisual displays, information programs, fantasy environments, and commodity tie-ins.

A fascinating example of this trend occurred at the conservative Museum of Fine Arts in Houston during the winter of 1990–91, when the IBM-sponsored exhibition *Rediscovering Pompeii* created the surreal scenario of combining the ostensible museological display of precious artifacts, frescoes, mosaics, sculptures, coins, and decorative artworks excavated from the buried city with a perplexing self-representation of IBM's state-of-the-art computer systems and software programs. Naturally, the corporate sponsor pretended to underwrite an archaeological exhibition, organized by the Italian Ministry of Cultural and Environmental Assets, which would promote the treasures of ancient Italian culture internationally and, in the words of the ministry, the "patrimony of humanity as a whole."[7]

The ministry also claimed that this exhibition, like "Columbus' discovery of America," would help America rediscover Pompeian civilization and, more important, the future management of techniques for cultural preservation. IBM's contribution to this future management is crucial, no doubt, since the exhibition was derived from a three-year research project, incorporated by IBM under the name "NEAPOLIS Consortium," during which a large team of scientists applied advanced computer technologies and hypertext languages to the study, recovery, and classification of the artistic resources of Pompeii. Rediscovering the buried site of a partially destroyed city had been a massive task for archaeologists since 1748. *Rediscovering Pompeii* became an altogether different experience for the viewer, since the exhibition was designed as a montage of "original" artworks, ripped from the context of their excavation site and displayed in the context of the NEAPOLIS Information Processing System, perversely culminating in a reconstructed garden court complete with a frescoed room filled with idyllic outdoor scenes, a mosaic fountain, and a seemingly authentic setting of flowering trees and plants.

I am fairly certain the garden was built right here in Houston by some experienced Mexican-American gardeners. While it was difficult not to notice the fabrication of this "historical site," such fabrications have, of course, always been legitimized in the name of the museum's collection and preservation of art. The reality effect, however, was completely deconstructed in this case by the simultaneous display of IBM's vast array of computer terminals and interactive "hypermedia" stations, inviting the viewer to take an electronic tour of nonexisting, simulated Pompeian houses and architecture, as well as Pompeian life itself.

Almost imperceptibly, the entire museum transformed itself into the kind of flight simulator one would expect at NASA's Ames Research Center, where pilots, wearing extraocular helmets for movement in space, can also put on wired gloves with photosensors that provide a graphic sense of tactility when touching objects in a virtual space that does not exist. Equipped with instructional handouts explaining how to use the interactive touch-screen terminals for their "journey" through electronically constructed three-dimensional territories (holographies), the viewers at the museum had not entered Pompeii but NEAPOLIS, a simulated time capsule bridging the centuries, a closed circuit within which they saw computer-generated images of frescoes rebuilt and "restored" to fit into the original historic site. In one of the museum spaces viewers could actually see a live restoration operator work from the computer model (a demonstration of the process of restoring what was computed to have been lost), or they could.log onto the dynamic

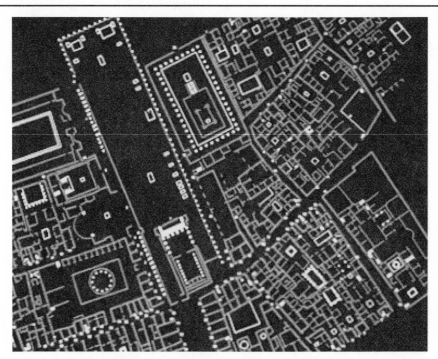

Numerical processing of the archaeological map of the Forum of Pompeii. *Rediscovering Pompeii,* **1990. Courtesy of "L'ERMA" di Brettschneider.**

"hypermedia" programs that displayed a potentially infinite database. According to the user-friendly menus, these "multidimensional" programs contained an information chain covering such diverse topics as the Pompeian home and furnishings, food, work and technology, architecture, society, religion, art, sports, and so forth, in their "logical interrelationships." I quote from the introductory menu: "The possibility of continuously making personal choices (from lists, symbols and diagrams) allows the visitor to choose and vary the depth of information, follow a whim to explore a special subject. Progressing through logical association, the visitor appears to be 'accompanied' by the objects exhibited, which 'act' at his [*sic*] request, as veritable witnesses of the past."

IBM's NEAPOLIS program thus presumes to virtually recreate a whole civilization by exploiting an awesome information-processing technology that both excites and challenges the spectator, on the one hand, and forces "him" (the gender bias in the program is hardly coincidental; it doesn't make much sense given the large number of female museum patrons who visit with their children) to surrender to the logical mapping of the journey, on the other. The new subjectivity of "personal choice" in this museum experience is an illusion, although the interactive scenario is not. Any control over these programmed images is elusive, for the time traveler merely has a kind of terminal identity that performs or acts out on a whim an immediate, touch-screen spectacle completely divorced from its historical context. The boundaries between image, simulation, subject, and reality (of the past) break down. The "witnesses of the past" are strange ghosts that have no reflection in the mirror, no texture, and would disappear instantly if the power failed. What the visitor experiences is not art or the material findings of an archaeological dig but an exhibition of the methodology of information technology applied to art, the excavation of an ancient city, and the visual/hypertextual management of "art" as cultural asset or database. The visitor takes a journey through the simulated experience of the NEAPOLIS construct.

Cyberpunk

The reinvention of Pompeii in the virtual space of NEAPOLIS reflects an apparently contradictory movement in museum culture, namely, the recycling and revival of the past within the matrix of futuristic technology.[8] Postmodern science fiction—as exemplified in the writings of William Gibson, Philip Dick, and William S. Burroughs or in the films of Ridley Scott (*Blade Runner*), David Cronenberg (*Videodrome*), James

Cameron (*The Terminator* and *Terminator 2*) or Brett Leonard (*The Lawn-mower Man*)—has already abandoned the past, especially modern culture's naive utopian fascination with technological and social progress. Rather, its representations of how the future blurs into an already dystopian present are both posthumanistic and posthistorical insofar as they imagine a global information landscape in which social and collective identities no longer exist except as permutating images or replicants that can be reprogrammed in the same manner as our photographic and televisual archives can be altered and reprocessed.

In the computer-generated world of VR technology and artificial intelligence, the space between computer and perception has mutated in such a way that human identity (history, aging, bodily reality), gendered subjectivity, and temporality are now dissolved. The proponents of hypertextual media and VR technology, like the readers of Gibson's cyberpunk fiction (*The Neuromancer*), would argue that interactive computer simulation merely extends the idea of experience beyond its empirical relationship with the material and subjective worlds. For example, laboratory research in VR technology at Jaron Lanier's Virtual Programming Languages Corporation in California or the VR lab of the University of North Carolina at Chapel Hill is partly based on science fiction ideas and, to a large extent, on recent advances in computer programming, scientific visualization, and three-dimensional modeling—already eagerly anticipated by commercial and military industries, the electronic media, and the medical field (surgery, genetic research). Forgetting the fascist dream of a future identification of man and machine (Marinetti), today's VR engineers take Gibson's hallucinogenic cyberspace (a metaphor for the corporate media world of the late twentieth century) literally, seeking to design industrial applications with a naively optimistic faith in its potential for creative play—a faith that lacks the Beckettian irony of the "Theatre of the Non-Body" at *Les Immatériaux.*

What the visual programming design of virtual reality implies, however, is precisely the play of mind or consciousness *departed from the material body,* jacked into the matrix of an electronic neurosystem and the algorithms of commutation. Dressed in VR DataSuit, EyePhones, and DataGloves, one leaves the body behind and enters into the simulated space (e.g., of a "landscape," a "city") generated by scanning and image synthesis controlled by the pixel. The electronic computation of the pixel no longer bears witness to any preexisting reality—matter, energy, light, or any figurative or abstract form of optical representation—instead visualizing purely logical and mathematical models. Image synthesis creates its own virtual reality of "images," but these are not images *of* something. Perhaps one should not call them images at all since their textures are abstractly numerical and their morphogenesis can be infinitely repeated or manipulated.

Interactive VR technologies—similar to the evolving dialectics of older and newer techniques of figuration/abstraction in painting, photography, or film—will thus have inevitable aesthetic repercussions on the visual arts and the media in terms of the challenges they will offer to (simulated) performative perception *inside* the simulated realities. To commute inside a digital world, however, abolishes the difference or distance between viewer and image, and with it the vital difference between art and the bodily reality (decay, death) with which art struggled in order to prevent our total occupation and enframement by technology, as Heidegger predicted.

At a cyberspace exhibition/symposium organized by the Deutsches Museum in Munich in April 1991, a group of scientists, computer engineers, and media artists gathered to celebrate the future of *ars electronica* and to explore the potential symbiosis of the real and the imaginary, as well as the consequences of the "interface between computer and man" in terms of our understanding of space and time. The overbearing presence of engineers and industrial designers at the conference precluded issues of political and social control, of the invasion and displacement of the body by technology, from being addressed. A more provocative dialogue between visual and media artists was offered by The Renaissance Society in Chicago during a 1991 group exhibition entitled *The Body,* which paradoxically presented a phantom show of objects, sculpture, and installations about a body that could not be seen and was not represented in any pictorial or figurative terms. Curated by Suzanne Ghez, these installations involved "virtual bodies" by forcing the viewer to deduce some prior existence of bodies now displaced by signs of medical, scientific, or industrial technology and superseded by biogenetic replications of body organisms. At the same time, the exhibition entered into a dialogic relationship with a video program selected by Carol Ann Klonarides, also entitled *The Body* (later shown at New York's Simon Watson Gallery and other venues in the United States). It featured fifteen tapes by experimental video artists who explore the dissolution of bodily identity and sexual difference, or our own death and absorption into electronic processing. Even though some of the videos record or mimic interactive simulation processes, we remain outside the screen and can observe, for example, how Barbara Hammer's *Sanctus* uses medical X-ray moving-picture techniques and digitized, sampled sound tracks to further distance us from the ghostly sign of its bodily referent. *Sanctus* reflects a profoundly ironic playing with *digital transsubstantiation,* its critical blasphemy capturing the horrific effects of medical and cybernetic invasions of the human body, whose immune system has broken down and whose sexuality and physicality have become the panic testing site for surveillance, surgery, and seduction. The technological seduction of replacing unwanted or obsolete bodies with hyperreal perfections was forcefully brought out in Aimée Morgana's extraordinary video deconstruction of Michael Jackson's protean identity in *The Man in the Mirror* and in *Cyberpunk — The Future . . . Is NOW,* a pseudopromotional "documentary" on virtual realities produced by Marianne Trench and Peter von Brandenburg.

It was already strangely disturbing to see Liz Larner's series of *Body Cultures*—nutrient agar sampled in small glass containers labeled "Somebody," "Anybody," "Nobody," "Everybody," "Your Body"—side by side with Orshi Drozdik's medical display of anesthetics and Kiki Smith's untitled wax sculpture, which arranges the total square footage of a human skin in the image of a pixel mosaic. But whereas Sean Smith's *Penetration* was a mock trade-room installation ironically showcasing the most improbable high-tech simulations of sexual organs and orgasmic experiences, there was no such comic relief in the *Cyberpunk* video. The fact that computers have come alive and that the simulations

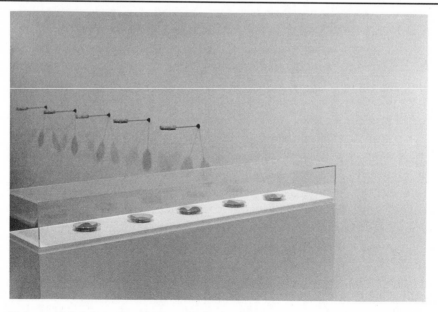

Liz Larner, *Body Cultures* (detail), 1991; nutrient agar, glass, food coloring, stainless steel.
Courtesy of The Renaissance Society, Chicago.

of geno-technology *are* becoming second nature is chillingly brought home in a fantastic series of interfaces between abstract digital images of humanoid forms and dispassionate announcements by computer engineers or plastic surgeons such as Doctor Joseph M. Rosen (Dartmouth College), who discusses his cyborgian work of reconstructing imperfect bodies and, if necessary, grafting wings onto a patient wishing to fly. When he speaks about neurosurgical implants and brain plugs, he is directly echoing Gibson's fiction of the corporate empire of cyberspace in which human sensual experience can be digitalized and cheaply produced for mass consumption through microchip implants.

The Wound of the Future

The video left me in a strangely unbalanced state of mind since it included not only such passages of futurology but others in which computer hackers, cyber cowboys, and various anarchist users proclaimed the new frontier of the information superhighway to be a test site for grassroots struggles and insurrections, a testing ground for territorial claims that would be staked by corporate industries as well as independent or activist infiltrators/saboteurs eager to expose the weak spots or hidden agendas of the software companies. I still have enormous difficulties in accepting the vision being promoted of a fully realized technological society since it avoids answering any serious questions about the power relations between technology and people, the design and distribution of information and its alternative use by different social actors or communities, and the survival of living bodies despite the violence of those final abstractions (e.g., a robotic U.S. audience was shown "entertaining" video simulations of the Gulf War air strikes).

The information science of domination exemplified in the designer's control over the simulation of war reflects back upon the controlling role museums will play in a future where art and performance are either absorbed through the techno-aesthetics of digital technology or must struggle against becoming ghosts floating in VRs.[9] The museums might become the coffins in which vampires rest during the day before they reveal themselves to the survivors at night. The ghostly vampires live on in personal fantasies of our vulnerable bodies and dysfunctional immune systems. We become addicted to vampires when they give us back what we seem to be losing.

The apparent contrasts between *The Body* and *Rediscovering Pompeii* are indicative of the struggle: both exhibitions already assume the phantom nature of their referents. But whereas the NEAPOLIS designers present a simulated environment *controlled* by information science, the lost referent of *The Body* is remembered through a negative dialectics that can activate our own memory-experience in relation to the sculptural objects. This remembrance depends on individual sense and historical perception that cannot be so easily translated into simulacra or devised through mathematical computation. In a provocative observation concerning the economics of simulacra, Pietro Bellasi suggested that such a translation was already underway in Berlin (after 1990, when Germany's reunification became a fact), where fragments of the Berlin Wall were being turned into hyperreal commodities and sold at the flea market or to museums in distant parts of the world.[10] In fact, I remember seeing a large chunk of the wall at the 1990 Houston FotoFest, but when I stepped up to touch it, it turned out to be merely a cardboard counterfeit. Perhaps it is true that one day we will see these Wall pieces as a mosaic on the computer screens or inside a VR program of an exhibition called "Rediscovering Cold War Berlin." For the time being, Berlin's symbolic history cannot be sold because its traces are written all over the body and the unconscious of the city. It remains a symbolic capital, with all the implications of what that means within a late capitalist economy. How the selling and buying, the investment management and stock market speculations, the trades and futures function would constitute another chapter in a critical analysis of the economic relations between, say, IBM or Sony and our cities and museums.

I say "our" because I grew up with the understanding that museums are nonprofit, public educational institutions open to the people. They are not in ruins yet, although their roles are changing; a growing number of private museums and commercialized public museums need to make a profit to subsidize their expensive operations and maintain their collections (i.e., buying and selling). Like the museums, the Berlin Wall has not yet disappeared, even though it is now invisible and may soon be replaced (e.g., by the new, gigantic Sony and Daimler-Benz shopping malls and office towers of the Potsdamer Platz). In the backyard, behind the parking lots, there will perhaps still exist the small "archaeological" site of the Prinz Albrecht–Strasse excavations, made in the eighties and then turned into a temporary contemporary museum documenting the evolution of Nazi terror, Gestapo tactics, and the engineering of the Holocaust by the SS. (The site, known as "Topographie des Terrors," consists of a small exhibition situated inside the excavated cellar of the Berlin Gestapo headquarters, which was destroyed during the bombing of the city in 1944–45.) Ironically, this small, documentary "museum" or memorial site lies adjacent to the beautifully preserved nineteenth-century building housing the Martin Gropius Museum and the new shopping/entertainment center that is being built. It is a thorn in the flesh of the developers and the city administration, which needs to placate its investors. But it is also already imprinted in the memory of many inhabitants and visitors who have climbed down the steps into the cellar.

In "Landscapes of Desire," the poetic conclusion to his architectural study, Alan Balfour writes about the Berlin Wall:

> The destruction of the Wall reforms all past landscapes. The Wall was the culmination of two hundred years of German culture. No other structure succeeded in slowing the passage of time. No other structure succeeded in destroying the passage of space. It was an absolute architecture, and it was the absolute contradiction of architecture—the purest monument to the divided soul of Western man. A machine that drove a passage through history, it divided a city, a nation, a culture.
>
> The Wall was an abstraction of reality from existence. . . . It was autonomous and rhetorical, and the most outrageous construction of Western civilization. . . . It was the great barricade, the supreme testament to the power of the dialectic.
>
> Reality will forever rest on the memory of this eternal division. Such essential order, once split, can never be fully restored. There will remain forever a flaw, a chronic weakness, in the foundations of all constructions in this place . . . the wound of the future.[11]

When I lived in Houston, I used to attend Alan Balfour's lectures on urban space and the historical passages of reconstruction and dialectical reformation of a "politics of order." I see him, in my mind's eye, poring over old photographs, maps, and architectural drawings. Having finished the book before the Berlin Wall was toppled in 1989, he decided to add a brief meditation on architecture and desire. Perhaps it is not inaccurate to describe the digital realities of "cybernetic art" or cyberspace communication as "landscapes of desire," territories in which the traffic in cultural assets, and in the production of knowledge and cultural values, will be carried out in the future. Having briefly discussed the abstractions from reality and historical experience that are being tested in museums today—without, however, fully addressing the commercial overdeterminations or cultural pressures that force artists and institutions to upgrade and retool their methods of display and production—I will now turn to the Internet, keeping a critical eye on the reformations of an order that is perhaps no longer explicable in terms of traditional architectural or spatial metaphors yet can still be grasped through our understanding of bodily memory, our chronic fear of losing our hold on reality, our dialectics of the wound.

Scene Two: Connections/Disconnections: Metaphors of the Network

Wall, labyrinth, construction site, real estate, museum, theater, and gallery are some of the words used to describe architectural buildings, properties, institutions, and sites. They are, of course, metaphors that function within complex narratives or conceptual arrangements to infuse our cultural, economic, and political imaginary. When I use the apparent binary opposition "embodiment" (embodied performance) and "disembodiment" (simulacrum) with reference to art, performance, material objects and material sites such as the museum or the theater, I am aware that this is a simplifying strategy, a way of getting at much larger issues. In the following pages I question the binary logic itself, yet I also continue to keep bodies and bodily practices in the foreground of my discussion, since I am particularly concerned with physical experiences and relations, interfaces with others and with the world, and thus with *border work* understood as a continuous process of movement/connections.

I need to be precise, even if the range of discourses embracing or touching upon the technoscientific imaginaries in our cultures is vast and overwhelmingly complex or stratified. As with the emergent activist critique of medical, scientific, governmental, and media discourses relating to the AIDS epidemic—especially their discriminatory, gendered accounts of the physical body, identifiable risk behavior, and HIV transmission—we are now witnessing a steady increase in the number of ethnographic, political, and cultural analyses of technoscientific ideologies. These interrogations may intensify the feminist challenges of science (biology, in the case of Donna Haraway's writings) and science fiction that were undertaken in the eighties and yielded a rich network of critical perspectives on scientific institutions and their collaborations with competitive industries of technology-driven capitalism.

In their introduction to two special issues of the film journal *camera obscura* Paula A. Treichler and Lisa Cartwright explain their increasing attention to noncinematic media by pointing to contemporary health and ecological crises and the activist context in which important critiques of science and medicine have been developed to counter

> the ascendance of visual technology as a pivotal agent in institutional management strategies—strategies ranging in scale from the computerized imaging systems that Western military forces used to chart and destroy vast territories in the Gulf War to the minute optical explorations of the body's interior channels made possible through video endoscopy. . . . Images derived from magnetic resonance imaging (MRI), computerized tomography

(CT), ultrasound, and electron microscopy, colorized and sharpened to enhance their aesthetic appeal, regularly illustrate specialized journals like *Cell*
and *Science* as well as popular magazines like *Scientific American* and *Life*.[12]

Not surprisingly, many of these imaging technologies are tested on
women in diagnostic and therapeutic applications by obstetricians, gy-
necologists, and reproductive endocrinologists (revolving around issues
of reproduction, cancer, the immune system, and other health problems), as well as by such growth industries as cosmetic/plastic surgery,
transplant and prosthetic surgery, and genetic research (e.g., the Human
Genome Project). Treichler and Cartwright have argued that these new
imaging technologies—and what is seen or unseen by science, medicine,
and the national or local health care systems—create diagnostic narratives (presently being taught to medical students and practicing physicians) that construct "new needs for women" as they create "new markets
for imaging" and popularize the "benefits" of what is being inscribed
and codified. The editors therefore have called for an interrogation and
disruption of such inscriptions, enlisting writers from such diverse fields
or positions as "film studies, cultural studies, neuroscience, obstetrics
and gynecology, medical anthropology, medical sociology, interactive
multimedia environment, history of medicine, social and cultural studies
of science, journalism, communication, women's studies, art, art history,
and activism"—a formidable team of players that now also includes the
youngest generation of theorists in performance studies.[13]

A somewhat different yet equally wide-ranging approach extending
the social studies of science has been chosen by ethnographers, who
investigate not only the production of scientific activity but its various locations, contexts, and *relations* to politics, ethics, capitalist economies, and spheres of public cultures, institutions, and communities. In
the words of Michael M. J. Fischer, this has resulted in "rewiring the
humanities and social sciences" and also popular-culture studies and
"cross-culturally juxtaposed accounts of technological sites of mediation (between law and medicine, psychiatry and computer technology;
ultrasound in Greece and in New York; law and medicine in Bhopal
and Los Angeles)."[14] Fischer is hinting both at the international dimensions of such inquiries and at the specificities of various local constraints
that condition scientific working practices and their relations to governments, institutions, and industries. Such "rewiring acts" are also at the
critical core of a few recent books and on-line journals (such as *Postmodern Culture* or *Trans >*) that seek to contest and overcome the almost
clichéd opposition between the euphoric, affirmative hype surround-

ing cyberspace and the "information superhighway" (officially named "National Information Infrastructure" by Vice President Al Gore and promoted in tandem with the "Global Information Infrastructure" he envisioned during his notorious speech in Buenos Aires in 1994), on the one hand, and technophobic or apocalyptic media criticisms, on the other. The latter has a recent legacy that could be traced back, for example, to the Frankfurt School and its pessimistic, critical aversion to media/information technologies, which it understood as a hegemonic "consciousness industry" manipulating and dominating public opinion. This technocriticism was advanced by the less fearful prophets of "post-industrial society" (Norbert Wiener, Marshall McLuhan, Buckminster Fuller, Alvin Toffler, Paul Virilio, etc.), obtaining its fullest description of technological media as vast extension/exteriorization of body sensations in McLuhan's *Understanding Media*.

Its most interesting and perverse version today is represented by Arthur Kroker's schizo-analysis of "panic postmodernism." Indebted to McLuhan, Deleuze/Guattari, Baudrillard, and especially Virilio's "aesthetics of disappearance," Kroker has published a series of books that diagnose the "disappearing body" in a declining contemporary culture riven by anxieties over a "natural body" that has been invaded by technologically constructed devices and discourses (under the paradigm of communications technologies) and fully "debased, humiliated, and inscribed to excess by all the signs of consumer culture" and commodity fetishism.[15]

What I notice in Kroker's diagnosis is a recurring, obsessive, and sensationalized emphasis on sex/fetishism, debased bodies, bodies without organs, and organs without bodies. It will hardly be surprising to feminist observers that the cultural hysteria he describes—for example, with reference to health crises (AIDS, anorexia, bulimia, and various addictions that now also include the cyberspace-interfaces)—and all the perceived or fantasized dangers to bodily safety and stable identities are inadvertently articulated as *male hysteria* vis-à-vis the "privileged female body" most persistently marked by the technological effects.[16] This marking of the female body was poignantly captured by Carolee Schneemann's video *Imaging Her Erotics,* where at one point we see a text scroll running over images of her early seventies body actions:

WE WHO ARE
ADDRESSING THE TABOOS
BECOME THE TABOO
THE SUPPRESSORS

ARE CONFUSED
THEY CANNOT
DISTINGUISH IMAGES
FROM THE IMAGE
MAKERS

This reminder serves us well in rethinking the marking or mapping of gendered bodies and images, especially in the present context of the refurbished ideologies of the global village and free-market flow of information, technological applications, and cyber cultures: these ideologies in some way or another elaborate stories of bodies and human/machine interfaces/sharewares. Beneath the globalizing rhetoric of multinational capitalism and government-driven politics of infrastructural transformation (mostly visible on the economic level and in terms of the effects of computerization on the working classes), an older story of the body politic has mutated from Hobbes's *Leviathan* and the metaphors of the machine age to the cyborg model: the automaton body and the artificial body are now reconceptualized as a cybernetic organism which, both on the individual, existential level and on that of the (formerly) sovereign state, is encapsulated by technological equipment. The prosthetic enhancements for this cyborg body today, however, are imagined under the sign of "virtuality," the huge, invisible net of information and electronic communication to which we are connected through our various lines of access. Telephone, radio, and television satellite transmission are the most common connectors; the fiber-optic, broadband digital telecommunications network opens out onto the new electronic "frontier" that is envisioned by the builders and users of the information superhighway. The frontier, however predictable as a metaphor for U.S. expansionism and millenarianism, is a strangely paradoxical metaphor, since the Internet is no place, no land, no physical space that could be conquered, but rather a new kind of architecture—and a myth—of completely bodiless and boundariless connections which the U.S. Office of Science and Technology Policy has described in terms of nodes, backbones, and lines of "network connectivity."[17] The contradictory mixing of metaphors in the official and subcultural descriptions of the Net are of interest here, for we are dealing with contemporary mythmaking that will inevitably operate as a rhetorical and ideological code that erases history and naturalizes the "truth" of the future present.

Is this concept of a noncorporeal cyberspace an essentially religious or spiritual one, as has been suggested by those who idealistically dwell on its transcendent capabilities for liberation and deregulated

democracy? Or are we to think along the lines of the rationalist, pragmatic policy planners, the new mapmakers of corporeal transformation,
who will no doubt design the information science of economic blocs and
markets, the global divisions of technological labor, and the programs
and codes of order, access, control, user-friendliness, surveillance, and
cyber-citizenship to suit their own interests?

How can we grasp this new relationship to a space that is not a
physical space, that appears to create proximity regardless of the physical or political limitations of geography, time zones, race, or social
status? How are we to understand the metaphors of the cyborg body?
What is being mediated here, and what are the implications of such a
sociocultural "territory" of cyberspace? What follows is a response that
points in three directions: the biotechnological, the media-technologi-
cal, and the transcultural-political. I conclude by positioning my own
work on the links uniting the last two.

Border Protections

The tenuous status of women's reproductive rights and the emphatic
concern shown by the New Right for the protection of the fetus correspond to a continuing reinscription of biological motherhood, paternal
authority, family values, heterosexual norms, antipornography censorship laws, anti–affirmative-action policies, regulatory testing and surveillance patterns, class and race hierarchies, and social norms of health,
beauty, fitness, acceptable behavior, and physical appearance—all of
which promote an ideological defense of the "natural" in an era of postmodern biotechnology that has already supplanted the concept of the
"natural." The logic behind the story of biotechnologies—reaching back
to Enlightenment and nineteenth-century formations in medical science, anthropology, and social Darwinism mapped onto the anatomies
and physiologies of bodies (and later explored by criminologists and
early anatomists in photography and film)—reflects evolutionary definitions of the cumulative control and power over the human organism achievable with the aid of technological prostheses or intervention.
From artificial limbs and heart or kidney transplants to reconstructive
and cosmetic surgery, the story of molecular biology, endocrinology,
plastic surgery, and recombinant DNA technologies has moved to a new
level of reprogrammable determinism that outdistances "nature" and
manipulates not only the encoding of information but also the (image
of the) physical body. The material body can be surgically altered, redesigned, or partially replaced; its organic life expectancy can be extended; its internal organs and physical boundaries (skin) can be phar-

maceutically animated, anesthetized, hormonally modified, detached, relocated, grafted, and pierced.

We are very much indebted to feminist scholarship and theory as well as to AIDS activism and politicized art of the past decade for bringing into sharper focus the role of the gendered and sexed body as material for, and limit of, descriptive and rhetorical systems, which have come under intense scrutiny as a result of the increased use of the discourse of "identity politics" in both art and political activism. Most of the theoretical "imaging" of the body remains firmly within the discursive and philosophical critique of ideology and the social construction of gender and race identities. Theory seldom pierces the body or acknowledges its organic tissue and plasticity, insisting that we don't know bodies outside of discourse and the conceptual operations that encode sex as the origin of gender by obscuring how gender roles in fact need to be "performed" in order to produce sex as the *natural* condition of its functioning as an identity. Gender identification thus serves to reproduce sexual difference as a given.[18]

A Brief Dance Rehearsal

On the other hand, if biological sex and nature are so closely aligned, any effort to redesign the physiological body might be considered transgressive against the body's "natural" identity, perhaps even crossing the borderlines of the culturally sanctioned or idealized images of embodiment. The body, in this sense, could be said to become a parasite within the cultural economy of embodiment-images constructed for its functioning. We are parasites in the house of the father.

I apply this concept in my dance workshops (from 1991 to 1995 I called them "Languages of the Body," whereas I am now calling them "Lively Bodies—Lively Machines"), and I sometimes work in response to the meditation "the body is a movement of boundaries." Working with living in the body and experiencing the lived bodyliness is a primary means of learning to comprehend our existence and movement in space, in the world, and in relation to one another. It also necessarily teaches us about human anatomy and physiology; breathing, listening to the dialogue between inner and outer experience; the relation of body and psyche; the specialized perceptions of our sense organs and bodily awareness; body (a)symmetries, postures, and axes/planes of motion; reflexes; and the sources of our inspiration and creative abilities.

When I say "primary" I don't mean technique but *process:* to move with/in one's body is always an experience over time, a time during which I bring awareness to my body and to the consciousness of my body's interaction with space. My sensory and motor areas react to stimuli and act upon my emotional awareness, my being and remembering in my body. The time of the process is also the timing of the process through which I rediscover physical sensations as well as the thoughts of the body; my timing might be off if I cannot connect physical sensations to the emotions in my body. It helps to begin gradually.

on the floor in a warm place close your eyes let your feet rest on the floor and release your legs rest your arms comfortably on the floor or across your chest relax into gravity allow yourself to be supported by the floor feel your breath and the responsiveness of your whole body allow the organs too to rest inside the skeleton the lungs the heart the digestive and reproductive organs feel the contents released within the container imagine the flow of air coming in through your nose and mouth passing down through the trachea and filling the lungs inside your ribs feel all the ribs move as you breathe feel the pulsing of your heart imagine the blood being pumped by the heart through the arteries carrying oxygen from the lungs to every cell in the body imagine the deoxygenated blood returning through the veins to the heart and the process repeating and the process repeating and place your hands on your belly and your ribs and feel them both move as you breathe imagine the flow of blood from your heart down into your belly let this continue through the hips and knees and into the ankles and feet allow the flow to return like a wave from your feet to your heart feel the movement under your hands imagine the flow of fluids moving from your heart up through the neck and into the skull to bathe the brain and back to the heart feel the flow out through your shoulders and elbows and hands pooling in your palms and fingers and returning to the center feel the continuity and constancy of flow through your whole body through your whole body imagine the fluids moving moving simultaneously from center to periphery and from periphery to center

As with all exercises that bring awareness to the body, it helps to repeat such explorations of constructive resting every day in preparation for further experiments, learning information from the body, articulating and visualizing it, and bringing attention to the body without seeking to control or manipulate it. I remember my teacher Deborah Hay once telling me that when she asks her students what brings them to her workshops, many reply, "I want to be in my body more." Dancing, she suggested, can remind us who we are. I have also put this question to some of my workshop participants, and the answers vary considerably, depending on the context and the location of the work. At the university, most students are interested in "techniques" of expression, not in experience. I sometimes have the feeling that they want to be in their body less, or that the body is instrumentalized for a particular plan of action or career choice. Many of the actors who come to such work feel uncomfortable in their bodies or confess that they don't know their bodies very well. Among students without theater and movement training one finds a tremendous self-consciousness about their bodies, to the point where they are either embarrassed about or feel intellectually condescending toward their material bodies. Unsurprisingly, most of the dance students have a different perception of the priority of their bodily understanding, and they tend to be less arrogant about the limits of the body. Perhaps at the start of such body work we are less concerned with thinking since we have to concentrate more on the perceptual awarenesses of the sentient body. The body thinks through itself, and so we try to relax it before we move again. The release of tension has a lot to do with the relinquishing of control we have been taught to practice daily in our social behavior and our entangled relations to our sexual energies. The release of tension is the first step in listening to our inner modulations and the flow of physical being.

Gradually we can begin to explore our potential for motion in space more outwardly. Our nerve ends, our skin, and our extremities make contact and react to heat, cold, touch, texture, motion, pressure, the pull of gravity, the reception of energy. We improvise with contact, move in the speed of our reflexes and the flow of our weight, extend and release weight, *share weight,* and feel the heat of movement as our breath quickens. We release tension by giving body to sensation and lightning-quick perception, and we don't question the rising temperature, the exhilaration, the merging of skin and bodies, our contact shifting with each weight change. The decision to pick another body up comes within a process, as our fear and excitement merges with trust and the seeking of limits. We don't know those limits.

Now, imagine doing such contact improvisation in the dark, feeling the space move around you without coordinates, taking advantage of pulsations and sensations not quite understandable or graspable. Later on I would ask my students: Is sex a fiction?

Up to this point, the need for such a question had not crossed our bodies. But it could be argued that the question matters since possible answers are built into the development of our bodily awareness, shape, and energy. The body shapes the fictions and is, in turn, shaped by the experience we accumulate with boundaries we touch and boundaries that are broken. Almost all the participants in the workshop tend to know intuitively when their boundaries have been crossed, although that changes in the course of the process; the boundaries are relocated and the intuitions are subjected to reflection. (Most disturbing, "intuition" has become a bad word in performance studies, its new theoretical rigor mortis. But these theories, as others apply them, don't address my intuition, and I can live with their hostility.)

The body becomes the material basis for our epistemology, but as corporeal activity our movement does not rest, and we have a certain cognitive plasticity that keeps adapting to our experiences. Our minds redraw the internal body representations and constantly react to our kinesthetic sense and emotional awareness. There is no body with organs that does not depend on its sensory interconnectedness, especially that between physical movement in space and vision/hearing. I don't know how a body without organs and sense perceptors could possibly coordinate movement and locate itself in space. It is particularly interesting, therefore, to work with eyes shut and to remember how to coordinate one's movement and how to locate one's boundary-reactions.

Our memories are inscribed in our bodies, but we may not remember all the fictions we have learned because we don't possess a stable and continuous internal self-image or conception of our sex. Such imaging always depends on our relations to the weight and gravity of our reality-experience, and thus to a continuous feedback-loop that reconnects and re-coordinates the pulsating links between our vision/hearing–understanding and our textural, emotional, and internal kinesthetic conversion of experience. We inhabit our bodies holistically and depend on the interconnectedness of our body systems and connective tissue. This material body, I think, moves at the real limit of all theorizing and terminological description, even as it provides the site for psychoanalytical speculation and for fantasy. (In this sense, cosmetic surgery comes closest to the operations of cultural codes that influence or determine what can be fantasized.) Moreover, the material body provides access to other bodies; it is a para-site, always near other bodily influences and contacts that affect it, including temperature, climate, physical environment, and the food and nurturing we treat ourselves to. In a metaphorical sense, one could say the body is always in a virtual relation with others. But a virtual body as such doesn't exist. If it crosses over into another body, such crossing takes place in the flesh, and there may be material constraints even if one wishes to be "inside another body."

Relocating the Borders

We do need our bodies to signify and understand ourselves, our sensations, and our (self-)imagings. Perhaps it is true that my body reproduces itself in relation to practices which might authenticate my social position as a sexed subject. There are specific behaviors, choices of clothes, enactments of gestures and attitudes, body languages, sexual-object choices, and so on, which might identify me within the culturally existent significations, but they have always been subject to historical change. We learn the semiotic relations connecting body, sex, and gender roles within a dominant heterosexual paradigm and the residual Christianity of Western cultural value systems, and we develop specific technologies of the self at home, in school, or at the workplace (e.g., in ballet class). But my mother's understanding of such roles differs vastly from my own, and her emotional investment in raising my oldest brother during World War II failed to produce what she would have considered natural and appropriate "gender behavior," assuming the terminology had existed then. It is the failure of her protectionism during my own upbringing in the fifties and sixties that I remember most vividly as a breakdown of the codes that were operative in our Catholic family. Interestingly, my body was never described to me as it seemed to me, and I lived out my roles in fantasies that I created for myself or adopted from various unorthodox literary and fictional sources. My initiation into same-sex orientation happened quite smoothly in the homosocial environment of our boys' school and athletic teams, and my first encounter with the heterosexual paradigm during our high school ballroom dance lessons turned out to be a marvelous fiasco. At that moment (1968) sexual liberation and student rebellions began to further impact the dysfunctional families in traumatized postwar Germany, and polymorphous sexualities were being discussed in terms of a new revolutionary rhetoric. The latter was also understood as a movement opposed to historical continuities that had permitted fascism and a compensatory liberal democracy to cover up our parents' complicity in the genocidal terror of the war and the Holocaust. At that time, the questionable idea of a "queer nation" had not yet been invented, and I was sure I did not wish to belong to any nation even as I searched for a sense of community or a communal sharing of ideas and lifestyles. This has become an ongoing search, never to be fulfilled except in the temporary, shifting coalitions we enter when we love or work with others. Since the search is primarily one of movement, I've begun to think of dance as the most precise metaphor for my practice.

In retrospect, it might be rewarding to examine these postwar breakdowns in the policing of the borders of sexual difference and normative behavior in light of those current arguments that claim "technology" as a metaphor for overdetermining institutional and social practices. The argument that institutions produce "gender identities" and thus always appropriate the body would need to be qualified by historicizing explorations of bodily experience and fantasy, which assert a certain resistance to the *conflicting* ideological systems regulating them in a particular historical era. The geographical location of my adolescence (the rural hinterland) seems significant, in this respect, since it left me unprepared for the technologically rationalized if overexposed world I would later encounter in the urban cultures of North American metropolises.

My immersion in the technological world now helps me understand more concretely the pervasive melancholia I sometimes feel about a lost world of fantasy I associate with the bodied spaces of my adolescence. I maintain a certain ironic distance to the melancholia, which helps me to create artworks that reflect on the continuing dislocations of bodily memory, of images and recollected knowledge of the past. My current techno-existence has become a familiar ground on which I can see the human body as a boundary figure belonging to two different systems of signification: on the one hand, there is the organic time of living in the body, working, dancing, creating, growing with it, and, on the other, the technocultural time of defense mechanisms against the organic body and its limits, and against the losses it cannot recover. Since there is no way to avoid a technologically determined mode of existence, I prefer to examine the blurring of borderlines, not from the hysterical or dystopian perspective of *ressentiment* (the position of apocalyptic critics whose white-male anxiety has been called "cyborg envy") but with the social and political implications of cybernetic effects on organic processes in mind.

It is in the context of this dialectic that I find Bernice Hausman's study of transsexualism and the historical evolution of the biotechnologies of sex change especially provocative. She has argued that by the fifties medical technology was able to enact what is known as sex conversion or sex reassignment, thus reconfiguring the body's sex and facilitating the disappearance of sexual difference as a "natural or original human condition."[19] She has convincingly demonstrated that twentieth-century developments in endocrinology and plastic surgery (already underway in the thirties and thus contemporaneous with the ideologically motivated eugenics experiments undertaken by Nazi surgeons) had a "discernible impact on the discourses and clinical practices of psychiatric sexology and the medical management of intersexual subjects," and that ultimately technological interventions into the body took account of the unreliability of the body's sex and, concurrently with plastic surgery, facilitated the redefinition of physiological "normality."[20]

In other words, the boundaries of what is considered *organic/natural* and *technological/cultural* have been relocated. Responding to the demand of transsexual persons to be given a "new body" they consider appropriately matched with their internally felt sense of self/sex, medical technology has complied by developing methods of operative treatment (phalloplasty, vaginoplasty, hormonal intervention) and "gender identity management" in order to reconfigure the bodies of transsexuals. In the process, plastic surgery has significantly contributed to culturally symptomatic anxieties about the conceptual fragmentation of the body and the resulting confusion over the proper order (sexual difference) or fantasized ideal of physical "normality" corresponding to anticipated or desired psychological well-being.

Plastic surgery, in an attempt to enlarge its practice and its market, most often plays along with the fantasized identifications, since modern medicine has generally sought not to comprehend the underlying causes of physical disorder and psychological distress but to intervene at the site of the physical symptoms, even as the symptomology itself is subject both to scientific and ideological description. As Hausman has shown, the description that affects therapeutic management follows a logic of reassignment that integrates conflicting physiological and anatomical sex signifiers into the dominant societal code of binary genders. One must infer that biotechnologies can manipulate the concept of sexual difference itself since they can reconstruct the physiological body more or less successfully. However, the dominant gender system became a necessary cultural formation to feed back the proper social articulation of sexed identity in order to accommodate someone suffering from gender dysphoria or discomfort (including the discomfort of being associated with transvestites and homosexuals). The technological *reproduction* of gendered identities therefore tends to suture sexually indeterminate or hermaphroditic bodies, making the material body's potential or actual "incoherence" virtually invisible. Technological intervention thus tends to stop *movement*.

If one were to listen to such experienced "incoherence" seriously, one might hear it in Kate Bornstein's performances and self-representations (e.g., in her book *Gender Outlaw: On Men, Women, and the Rest of Us*), except that Bornstein goes one step further and displays her "transgressively gendered" border-crossing (from heterosexual man to lesbian woman) triumphantly as a process that has not ended but continues its search for "third spaces," for multiplicities of genders and behaviors of playful "passing" that cannot be accommodated by the existing binary logic. In Bornstein's performances of *Hidden: A Gender* (1989) and *The Opposite Sex . . . Is Neither!* (1993), as well as in her cross-gender performance workshops, she has consistently argued against being identified as a woman who can pass as a woman, instead portraying herself as not male, not female, and not bound by the social constrictions of either gender. In interviews she has invoked the figure of the trickster, "embodying" a series of proliferating differences in *The Opposite Sex . . . Is Neither!* that plays havoc with a binary-sex system that upholds heterosexuality as the norm. Playing Maggie, a "goddess-in-training" who took a wrong turn at the moon and landed in late-twentieth-century North America, Bornstein takes on seven different personae who are "neither here nor there, and neither dead nor alive," including several pre- or postoperative transsexuals (M2F, F2M), a she-male drag queen, a hilarious religious fundamentalist who is a transgenderist, and "Billy Tipton," the passing jazz musician who "lived her life as a man because swing is for men."

Not unlike Annie Sprinkle's ritualized erotic spiritualism, Bornstein's queer idealism and her open, confessional mode of being publicly transsexual invite her audiences to explore the "choice" (she is also explicitly referring to the consensual play of S/M) of *not* passing by allowing the incoherence of nonidentity to become the unsettling, adversarial avant-garde of "outsiders" to both the mainstream and the border-guarding gay and lesbian communities. Her performances revel in the "crimes against gender" she considers a vital part of the new queer subculture that resists assimilation into a dominant ideology. After seeing the camp theatricality of her stage work (a cross between Charles Ludlam and Split Britches), I wondered at her cheerful insistence that the future "outside" is within our reach: "Cyberspace would be a doorway into the Third Space. Cyberspace frees us up from the restrictions placed on identity by our bodies. It allows us to explore more kinds of relationships. I can go on-line as anything. . . . I'd say gender is the last apparent frontier. It's the frontier that's just becoming illuminated. It's titillating. In public relations terms it's sexy. . . ."[21] There is an interesting slippage in her terminology here, since she is not only echoing the notion of a "third space"—modeled upon the call for an independent, postcolonial "third cinema" issued in Latin America in the seventies (and then adopted into the concept of a "third theatre" by Eugenio Barba in 1976)—but also freely admitting the publicity value and the fashionable sexiness of a transgenderism that eventually must deny—as she herself does in chapters in her book following "Hard Part" and the "Nuts and Bolts" (her account of the actual surgical process of technological intervention in her body)—the material realities and limits of body reconfiguration.[22] Her trust in a utopian future is deeply contradictory, for she admits that the existing political reality of economic oppression leaves the outsider class with few alternatives except "forced assimilation into a culture that would rather see them dead."[23] And yet she assumes that a new, different public space—the electronic frontier—can be freely created in which virtual reality functions as a "playing field" for imaginary constructions of the body.

At this point she insinuates a certain theory of commutation/communication or virtual free play that is deeply problematic, especially since it allows her, as I have already suggested, to disavow the organic, biological body and those tests a body cannot "pass." Biotechnological industries have staked their claims on the markets of the future in a similar disavowal of the limits of manipulation and technical control. The progressive capabilities of genetic engineering and surgical or chemical interventions into biological processes of the body tend cosmetically to hide the political/ethical relationships between technology and the cultural prejudices against the disabling, organic decay of diseased and aging bodies. It is indeed remarkable that during the past two decades the spotlight of cultural debate has not been focused on the medical sciences but on the electronic frontiers of communications technology. It is important to remember that this slant, and the fascination that the mass media self-servingly generate around new visual technologies and communications networks, does not bode well since it tends to leave medical ethics and public health policies primarily in the care of governments, courts, private corporations, and experts, while ideologies of prejudice (e.g., against aging or against people infected with disabling or stigmatizing diseases) continue to be reproduced in the popular media and in socioeconomic processes.[24]

The cultural prejudices against age, indigence, unemployment, and (I suspect) media/computer illiteracy or nonaccess are inevitably reinforced by the hype that surrounds the electronic frontier and its predominantly white middle-class scenario of a global internet of virtual free-flowing cyber commodities. This cultural discourse of network interfaces and telecommunications needs to be examined more closely in order to disentangle the sexy biopolitics that are "just becoming illuminated" in the promotional contexts of the computer and VR industry, and in the effects of such programming of a new, desirable world of technological interactivity. As our century ends, the specter of "virtual realities" has a certain ring of finality to it. But since I cannot accept the idea of leaving my body behind, I want to look/listen carefully to the proposals that are being offered to my electronically extended personal body.

The Body Incorporated

Needless to say, there is something wrong with the picture of a happy future of global vision or the "Heavenly City" of cyberspace that Michael Benedikt introduces in his "first steps" into the "ultimate computer–human interface"—a world behind the computer screen as "magical and marvelous as the one Alice discovered behind her looking glass."[25] "Alice in Cyberland" could be the name of a video game or of one of the new interactive CD-ROM movies, in which you are presented with hypertext options for the development of the plot narrative. As with the old PacMan games, the user at the console can follow the paths that have been designed, interactively racing around the corners and the loops.

As I write this, the media-industrial complex is growing constantly, and one can observe the increasingly multinational monopolistic control of all telecommunications industries (telephone, broadcast and cable television, newspapers, computer networks, software industry) by a few corporations who enter into strategic alliances (against smaller, independent media) or buy each other out. The new telecommunications act, signed by President Clinton in early 1996 and compared by him to the 1956 interstate highway legislation, promised further deregulation and increased services to "connect" the American people, revised earlier telecommunications acts and dropped federal laws requiring diversity on the airwaves and a limit to the number of media outlets a company could acquire. I had not even read the text of the new telecommunications act when I began to receive messages via e-mail from concerned activists who were alerting me to those provisions (e.g., Communications Decency Act) that purposefully restrict free speech on the Internet. When I checked into some of the on-line discussion groups on the matter, I found that the provisions make it a federal crime to transmit or display "indecent" material or language in a public forum over the Net. The deregulation favors the consolidation of media power in the hands of a few conglomerates (similar to Bill Gates's efforts to control the software production and marketing industries and his huge investment in buying out the digital rights to artworks [i.e., the license to software "content"]) while limiting the exercise of free speech.

Around the same time I received a phone call from someone who cheerfully informed me that I had been such a good customer that my phone company had decided to upgrade my long-distance service (TrueWorld Savings) so that I communicate with others even faster and more cheaply. I was surprised to hear that the upgrading was free. Then the employee asked me whether I planned to call Germany or eastern Europe more frequently. At that point I told him that I was not going to discuss my private life with him and hung up.

Earlier that day, while driving around Chicago, I listened to a commercial—whose male announcer made this sound like a very urgent matter—that I would no longer miss important phone calls because I had stepped out of the room momentarily or was in the shower. For just a few extra dollars a new service was now available that allowed you to punch in a specific number that automatically locates your last caller and calls that person back; in other words, you don't have to listen to your old-fashioned answering machine anymore. Nicholas Negroponte, director of the MIT Media Lab and author of the best-selling book *Being Digital,* has even stranger news. He writes that in the "post-information age" we will experience "true personalization" by living asynchronously, in control of our time-shifting. The old face-to-face type of communication, including direct phone conversations, will get in the way I choose to live. He suggests that answering machines should always only answer calls and allow callers to simply leave messages. E-mail thus has the enormous advantage of not interrupting my life, since I can read the messages or answer them (or not) whenever I please.

This business of upgrading has started to catch up with me, as I enter the interfaces of the computer world. Some time ago I completed my first home page on the World Wide Web with the help of a computer artist, a young student in my "Integrated Arts" class who has already started his own business selling his designs of web sites.[26] I am learning a new language which my Web handbook calls Hypertext Markup Language (HTML), a vital tool for my future experimentations on the World Wide Web, the "global, interactive, dynamic, cross-platform, distributed, graphical hypertext information system." While trying to absorb this technical terminology, I see the Net primarily as a global communications link with other artists and workers wishing to exchange information about their current projects, ideas, plans, and concerns, such as censorship on the Net. I will return to this later.

What interests me here, first of all, is the inevitability of having to upgrade one's technological equipment, as has happened in our culture and professions for centuries. After we had designed my web site—which includes texts, links, color designs, "features," and a number of images we scanned from photographs or from video footage of the performance work I have been creating with AlienNation Co. and our collaborators in other parts of the world—Giles told me that the modem in my PC was too slow for the downloading of the web site. So if I wanted to look at web sites and work on them in the future, I needed to exchange my old modem for a newer, faster one.

The question of performance or speed in connecting to the Net is only one factor that contributes to the concern I have with the imperialism of technological enhancements. Another factor is the *mode of engagement* I have with the apparatus (hardware and software), the industries, the virtual spaces of telecommunications, the codes, and the architecture of communication that is being built. Basically, I cannot deny that I appreciate the links that are established via computers: I search for ways to work with them and to be in contact with my friends and collaborators, as well as with others I do not know but who might partake of and contribute to the information disseminated on the Net. This is yet another issue I want to reflect on in future performance/media research, namely, the quality and resonance of the so-called interactivity of working on/ with the Net, since I obviously have no intention of becoming digital and losing the direct physical and kinesthetic engagement with other people and cultural workers in specific locations. But "losing one's body" might be a misconception of what it means to become digital, and such misconceptions have plagued any discussion of cyberspace. At this early stage in my digital future, I am merely offering a few critical and speculative observations about the immersive aspects of cyberspatial media, on the one hand, and the narrow distance that is created by a disidentification with the compulsory technological imperative I am subjected to. I will begin by scanning the metaphors of the transitional architecture of cyberspace and virtual reality before seeking to decouple some of the superficial linkages that are articulated in contemporary (multi)cultural slogans of *hybridity* as they are used in the promotion of the cyborg body.

I should make it clear, therefore, that I am interested in technological media and prostheses precisely because they affect my practice as a performance-worker and the relations between production and distribution. Specifically, they affect the conception of the work not only in their influence on my physical and creative relations with others but also in the way they pose political and moral questions about the boundaries that are transformed and the regulations that are reconstructed to delimit my sensorium or to force me to use my body in ways I dislike. I think a limit is reached when the implied dematerialization of human interactivity, and the actual decomposition and electronic recombination of political/public and private spaces, threaten to create redundant physical structures and human bodies, phased out because they could not log onto the new programs or incorporate the new logic of "imaginal bodies" that is envisioned by the fictional ontologies of the new virtual electronic community.

What is promised by the architects of the information superhighway is a vast new infrastructure created by video, cable, telephones, personal computers, computer networks, and bandwidth connections which can bracket the physical presence/location of the participants and allow for the transmission and reception of information with the speed of light. Electronic asynchrony will be one of the principles of the Internet's e-mail or bulletin board systems and on-demand news media, disregarding the distinctions between real-time events and arbitrarily time-shifted replays. Cyberspace, even if it is metaphorically described in spatial terms, will no longer resemble a space but be constituted by the accelerating speed of transmission and the unimaginable enormity of ephemeral on-line communications and data distributions in a borderless market. This expandable market will include information on education, art, entertainment, games, business transactions, commodities, and virtual computer-mediated environments. VR proper (i.e., virtual reality/telepresence technology) will extend the primary experience of our wired connection, which consists of graphical user-interface systems, but the connection into the electronic media is already the necessary immersive conditioning for the cyborgian inhabitation of simulated worlds.

What makes it easier for us to conceive of the information space is not its underlying mathematical or computational principles, its liquid architecture of bit design, or its exponential logic of expansion but rather the fact that it is an open-ended configuration or topology of shared collective and individual activities: news groups, chat rooms, mailing lists, bulletin boards, person-to-person interaction via e-mail, and interactive web sites indicate that cyberspace is shared by people. Indeed, more and more frequently I come across new definitions of "electronic communities" that portray the network in terms of participatory, self-regulating designs, developments, and creative activities that could enhance democratic, horizontal communication. In my copy of the *Smart-Girl Guide to the Wired World* or in the *alt.culture* guide (a guide to the nineties on-line "underground," assembled, published, and distributed by Steven Daly and Nathaniel Wice) I find numerous references to the benefits of the Net—including a wide range of resources (from health issues, recipes, and dietary or spiritual advice to sex and romance news groups and links to "alternative" discussion groups, music fan clubs, and museum or research-library files)—as well as references to web sites and software that can be downloaded.

It is becoming obvious that there is a whole range of subcultures of Internet users, web artists, and hackers, supported by iconoclastic lifestyle magazines and cyberpunk fanzines, who consider the Net space an ideal arena for freewheeling anarchist expression that contradicts the market-driven implementation of home shopping and movies-on-demand promoted by major full-service media corporations such as AT&T, IBM, Time-Warner, Viacom, Hearst, Sega, Microsoft, Bell Atlantic, Tele-Communications Inc., etc. If we are to assume that most of the major media will be owned or controlled by a dozen or so huge megacorporations that will link up mass media and the entire spectrum of entertainment and info-education with manufacturing industries and the financial sectors, then it will become all the more necessary to investigate activist theories of communications technology that take into account the social topology of the Internet and its antistructural ethos of interconnectivity.

The creative possibilities of playful invention and purposeful design were written into the early history of smaller, locally run computer networks and bulletin-board systems (BBSs). In fact, it is perhaps not surprising that Howard Rheingold (*The Virtual Community: Homesteading on the Electronic Frontier*) invoked the language of the sixties counterculture in describing the Bay Area WELL (Whole Earth 'Lectronic Link) and his participation in the building of a "grass-roots community," with its own newly developed and self-designed social contracts, friendships, shared concerns, and "gift economies." I consider this story enormously valuable because it also demonstrates the relentless speed with which the smaller, local networks were incorporated into the global network of networks. It reminds us of the technological origins of early virtual communities as well as their electronically mediated social organization, which is changing rapidly as the Internet extends the boundaries of shareable information. The WELL began in the mid-eighties as a local computer-conferencing system whose technical foundation (CMC, or computer-mediated communications) was based on the ARPANET system, a product of U.S. military research in the seventies that attempted to create a dispersed network of interlinked computers to transmit data. Computer conferencing, as developed by the WELL, emerged when home-grown programmers and hobbyists found ways to interconnect personal computers and e-mail messages or BBSs via phone lines to build social relationships or interest groups; such connections are now also known as a "handshake" (my computer with yours). Multi-User Dungeons, Internet Relay Chat systems (IRCs), and on-line discussion groups followed, and only after several years of independent, parallel, and unrelated developments and expansions (such as Usenet and Telnet) did the current fiber-optic–based Internet of the nineties, supported by the U.S. government, create the high-speed technological convergence of different types of users.

Despite the fact that the accidental history of disparate, anarchist, and experimental "homesteading" is short, Rheingold insists that it constitutes a socializing cultural formation that can potentially sustain its decentralized, democratic ethos of sharing, of both freewheeling expression and communal activism. The grassroots beginnings of virtual communities, which fostered emotional and intellectual connections through person-to-person communication, are just a legend to new users in the nineties who enter into an immense labyrinth of group-to-group communication and Net navigations where browsers/surfers from around the globe can "click-jump," with the flick of the hand, from one screenful of text to another multimedia site in seconds.

We all still operate within what is left of the small, overlapping local communities in which we live, but the concept of a virtual community may be losing its meaning if it is applied to the overarching global network where the mediating function of micro-media within the Net, such as particular discussion groups or subscriber groups (e.g., ECHO, Arts Wire, or alt.meditation), needs to be reassessed. The existence of mushrooming user and subscriber groups of all types points to the interesting possibility of "virtual cooperatives," which might consist of people from different nation-states and cultural locales relating to each other as active "web cultures" (comparable to the club subcultures). But if one wishes to draw a parallel to music or dance-club subcultures, how will a "web culture" distinguish or authenticate itself? How will it socially construe its niche aesthetic and visibility of expression or lifestyle? How will such processes carve out and fill a space and sense of "community" in the cyberspatial realm of nonphysical electronic connectivity? It doesn't seem convincing to argue that this new "web culture"—which initially attracted an elite membership consisting of university students, professors, scientists, engineers, and computer wizards and now opens its doors to commercial businesses, bookstores, museums and galleries, airlines and travel companies, the print media, and the wider consumer market—constitutes a social world or a distinct mode of social congregation. One could also think of the Internet as merely an upgraded telephone that replaced the disembodied voice with a graphic-textual dimension and enabled us to communicate with the eye and hand. I will have more to say about the eye and the hand at the end of this scene.

Except for a final chapter where he compares utopian-communitarian and technocritical thought and addresses the commodification of the informational body politic, Rheingold does not dwell on the dystopian dimensions of the colonizing convergences of the macro-media industries. He uses "dwelling" in a Heideggerian or communitarian sense of living in "micro-organisms" as being-in-the-world of integrated circuits of technological equipment. For him the "technology that makes virtual communities possible has the potential to bring enormous leverage to ordinary citizens at relatively little cost—intellectual leverage, social leverage, commercial leverage, and most important, political leverage." He first defines the Net as "loosely interconnected computer networks that use CMC technology to link people around the world into public discussions." Next he defines virtual communities as "social aggregations that emerge from the Net when enough people carry on those public discussions long enough, with sufficient human feeling, to form webs of personal relationships in cyberspace." Finally, he defines cyberspace, a term taken from William Gibson's science-fiction novel *Neuromancer,* as "the name some people use for the conceptual space where words, human relationships, data, wealth, and power are manifested by people using CMC technology."[27]

His insistence that most of the profound technological changes in the development of virtual communities have come from the fringes and subcultures raises important questions about the agency of cyborg citizens who have become digital, especially since he does not examine critically what might be meant by "sufficient human feeling" in electronic relationships, implying that the removal of physical bodies/subjects from a public social economy need not intensify the asynchronous split between the body and the CMC-producing subject but rather collapses the boundaries of the body, thus superseding older analytical categories of body/mind or biological/technological. In fact, all the descriptions he offers of grassroots and local computer conferencing networks—based on personal involvement in the WELL, his friendship with hackers and programmers (some of whom would later found the Electronic Frontier Foundation to defend civil liberties in cyberspace), and firsthand experiences of similar virtual communities in Ōita (COARA), Tokyo (TWICS), Paris (CalvaCom), and London (CIX)—emphasize the face-to-face meetings of members that evolve parallel to on-line network communication and activism. Rheingold prefers to hold on to the utopian premises by means of which all of these local micro-organisms got started and, through the initial BBSs, enabled the citizens to participate "in designing the shape of their virtual community." Referring to TWICS cofounders Joichi Ito and Jeff Shepard, he has written:

> Shepard proposed the metaphor of their place would be very important in determining what kind of place it would be, and, through a process of community design, created the metaphorical electronic island called Beejima: "Since we wanted to build a place where people would feel like they were members of something more than just another information service, we decided to use the metaphor of a community as the basic organizing principle for the new computer conferencing system we were going to install. The image of Beejima was a friendly little island community in the electronic seas of Japan, close to Tokyo but accessible from anywhere, a Japanese system modeled on Japanese context, with an international and multicultural outlook."[28]

Rheingold correctly points out that "place" in computer conferencing is a cognitive and social and not a geographical term, although he cites numerous examples of ordinary community-based RL activities and social projects sponsored by nonprofit organizations at community, city, and regional levels—feed people, provide medical care, organize disaster relief, free political prisoners, find shelter for the homeless, give counsel to battered women, deal with substance abuse—which have begun to utilize computer databases and on-line networking to enhance their outreach and efficiency despite their low operating budgets. The parallel development of social and environmental activism on the local and global levels, as we now know, would have been inconceivable without the spread of on-line networking to permit the new NGOs (nongovernmental organizations) to intervene politically in many areas of concern. EarthTrust, Greenpeace, Amnesty International, or the Red Cross are transnational organizations that link volunteer networks through global electronic mailings, bulletin boards, and BITNET or Internet communications.

It is perhaps one of the fortunate ironies of contemporary arguments about the technologically mediated "hyperreality" of our society of the spectacle that corporate industries neither control communications nor manage to make "the real" disappear. At no point in history (albeit belatedly) has there been so much actual local intervention to halt the destruction of nature and the environment. The example of *eco-linking* (on-line environmental organization) as a technology of activist coalition-building needs to be taken seriously and subjected to more rigorous testing at other levels of political importance, such as civil

and human rights violations, war, terrorism, and the appalling proliferation of rabid nationalism (reaching from xenophobia and oppression
of minorities to separatist movements and military "ethnic cleansing")
and religious fundamentalism.

International associations are virtual communities, too, as are transnational corporate bodies involved in local or overseas policy negotiations based on their actual financial power and influence on politics.
The megacorporations protect their vital interests and investments by
enlisting government/military force as an ally to deal with local or foreign disturbances at their production sites or markets. The NGOs generally select and organize their resistance or relief work reactively, and
the quantitative difference in power shows up concretely. Symbolically,
however, the NGOs have learned from and adopted media strategies
and cultural mechanisms of control, influence, and economic domination that used to belong to Hollywood and commercial television.
Greenpeace, as we have seen repeatedly, can thus enter into macrolevel
media and political struggles with Shell or with government policies
(e.g., French atomic testing in the South Pacific).

Although I am not convinced by Rheingold's argument that NGOs
and their alternate-information networks are the global equivalent of
the older nation-state institutions of civil society, I agree that civil disobedience or activism raises the very real question of how much influence the political use of virtual systems can have on the creation of non-
virtual community or solidarity, that is, to what extent the political body
—of the person living with AIDS, the black man on a California highway, the Bosnian under attack in Sarajevo, the Muslim woman raped by
marauding soldiers, or the Israeli or Palestinian killed by suicide bomb-
ers—is primarily reconfigured through physical force, relearns the codes
and networks of power and rediscovers the silence of witnesses in the
network that excludes the ailing body.

When I participated in antinuclear demonstrations, site occupa-
tions, and "die-ins" sponsored by the green movement in Germany during the late seventies, we spoke of "putting our bodies on the line," which
in the German original is "den Körper aufs Spiel setzen" or "den eige-
nen Körper einsetzen," literally, to put one's body into play, to risk or
stake one's body. Looking at the various meanings of "stake" in English,
I get closer to the German sense of "marking" the body: delimiting an
area; claiming an area (in a territory or in a new country); tying a body
to the stake—"as in earlier days, when a body was tied to a post prior
to being condemned to death by fire as punishment for heretical behavior"—or betting on or playing with the body.

More recently, during antiwar demonstrations and ACT UP interventions in the United States, the ritual of putting my body on the line, or dis-playing it in a march or a gay pride parade, assumed a multifaceted quality that it didn't have for me in the seventies. In the late eighties and early nineties, such staking of the body as a political act meant not only to protest and to take a position and assume a political stance but also to reverse the stigmatizing appellations hurled at us and to collaborate with others in building a visible, public oppositional solidarity. It meant to provoke recognition of our claims and our differences, and thus to provoke recognition of fundamental civil rights and the constitutional rights of freedom of expression and the inviolability of the body.

Demonstrating the body requires that one exaggerate it. It also entails occupying space in the proper social domain (e.g., claiming space for AIDS awareness) and rapidly shifting activity to prohibited sites such as churches, government buildings, or major city streets. In risking being arrested by the police or attacked by hostile individuals, such staking of the body highlights the very vulnerability that is supposed to be protected. Furthermore, some of the physical interventions can be pure expenditure, while others involve calculated risks: to be arrested serves as a symbolic mediation, and we can utilize civil disobedience to "capture" the event (it will be videotaped by us and perhaps even win the attention of the broadcast media, which will insert our action into their evening news programs). The bodily act creates witnesses.

One could argue that such a bodily protest connects the body to several networks; it "incorporates" itself. A staged protest, according to this configuration, enters into the power relations of filmic and political-legal interaction with the corporate structures of domination. As a participant in a larger group, I also interact with the multiplicity of experience and relative "inviolability" of our bodies (depending on each person's experience of race, gender, class, age, sexual orientation, and sero status) within the "community" of protest which we mark as a group. I *produce* my body in the event of staging its vulnerable protest; I make it visible to myself and the community we form; I also produce it for the capturing (video), the recording that can be distributed and redistributed, both through our own alternate channels of communication and through the official media, which confirms to the public at large that our protest has taken place. My relationship to the official, authorizing media is always tenuous, since I don't know how my body-action will be mediated, framed, manipulated, distorted, or silenced. I must risk accessing the official networks, trying to intercept their noncoverage or denial of my protest or political position.

Cyborgian action, in this scenario, deals with feedback loops and the conflicting interpellations by the ideological operations of media and institutions of authority. My body incorporates and plays back the logic of media technology, but it does not become an electronic out-of-body experience even if the action is "posted" in the virtual spaces of the Internet. Rather, the "posting" is only possible because the material body takes the risk to "irrupt as the real" (in Lacanian terms) into the automatism of symbolic networks of signifiers. My body does not belong to the network, but it is of consequence in the real and virtual worlds. It also may spend the night in prison. None of these processes of physical-political action, which make the actor visible in a social field of contestation during moments when the proper order is disturbed, can take place on the Internet since CMC users are logged onto the matrix and dependent on the cyberspace engineering that keeps them in programmed access modes. In order to reintroduce out-of-place movement into a nonphysical space, we need to examine how incorporation models the body or how VR may help us to reconceptualize the "incoherence" of bodies as politically necessary.

The Disillusioned Cyborg

One might argue that my physical body does belong to the network because it doesn't exist except as a representation of my body or my bodily action within the network of symbolic signifiers. This, of course, is the truth of illusion as we know it from the theater and live performance, and I would agree that an action staged to transgress against the containing power of the public order is a theatrical and social event of communication that invites targeted or accidental audiences to participate in the dis-illusionment. The baseline is not my "real body" or my organic body but my embodied action of protest, my staking a claim or posting the physical, vulnerable, and defiant body as a symbol that is literally there, in the flesh, to be beaten or arrested, vilified or recorded for video transmission as an act of dissidence, indignation, unruly behavior, or whatever interpretation may ensue. The performance simultaneously comments on placements in the social space and on the disparaged other (e.g., the government, the military, a corporation, an institution, or a social attitude like racism and homophobia as such) since it is an act of distinction. Depending on the location of the action, the distinction will be contextualized and perceived in different ways, in the same sense in which the action of our group will include differences between what we imagine subjectively and act out objectively. It is also a *movement* that deranges a clear diacritical or oppositional constitution, since the performance does not stay in place. Therefore, the idea of "othering" needs to be contested, too, so as not to end up being defined as my own otherness, my improper and alien self. One of the more distinctive moments would be while I am beaten by the police: at that point the illusion of the theatrical act breaks down and communication stops. This is when the ACT UP slogan "Silence = Death" has an immediate effect: the momentary breakdown of communication irrupts as a question put to public law-enforcement officials and spectators. The former pretend to know the answer; the impassive spectator may not grasp the question or may deny seeing it.

I feel that these distinctions and theatrical frames create the necessary distancing effect for the demystification of the performance of body-based identities. They also serve to remind us of the paradox of the actor: I presume that you are witnessing my discrete protest, and I want you to understand that this is not theatre but reality. The boundaries that seem to separate/protect us are not secure, and I refuse the logic of authority that mutually binds us into silence. The anger that sometimes spills over in protest action in fact reflects the acting out of a dangerous spilling movement. Political rage at injustice or indifference is also a defense and an overcompensation, and its most theatrical actions can point in different, punishing directions at once, including one's own feelings of recreating a lost political battle or staging one's own fantasy of impending death in "die-ins" on the street. At the same time, I invite you to witness my death and to notice how your fantasy projection (of my death) implicates another kind of paranoia.

As in other social role-playing frames, the performance of protest or of countercultural resistance to institutional power resembles the kind of "interactive role-playing environments" now advertised by VR engineers, except that generally the VR technologies neither articulate a politics nor produce a politicized body that speaks itself; rather, they promise graphic "playgrounds," as Rheingold notes in his description of the earlier IRC and Habitat on-line communities as domains in which people played with different avatars of communication and self-representation, eventually evolving rules, rituals, taboos, and communications styles that created the illusion of a shared cultural context. What is so interesting here is that on-line cooperative play, although seemingly removed from material contexts of visual codes (e.g., buildings, modes of dress and behavior, etiquette, gesture, accent, and other physical/nonverbal or contextual cues), tends to devise rules and control mechanisms in order to enforce or maintain a recognized solidarity. Rheingold has suggested that "participants react to a world stripped of nonverbal context by recreating the context that has been lost. They do this by using written words to describe how they *would* act and how the environment *would* appear in a shared mental model of a wholly constructed world." [29]

Predictably, language-based on-line communication, with its electronic avatars, reproduces the rigidifying effects of language-based behavior, often making up for the loss of movement and contact by recomposing the most familiar self-constraints, sexual and gender fantasies, transvestisms, aggressions, affections, and addictions. Some news groups or multi-user simulated environments are more controlled than others, but many of them couldn't exist without moderators, sysops, or editors who help to sustain the protocols that have evolved; there are also on-line support groups that counsel users who have become obsessively addicted to games people play. The case of "Mr Bungle's" cyber-rape of personae created by women users in a MUD created controversy along stereotypical gender lines that one would have thought irrelevant in a nonphysical fantasy world; the more interesting responses to the case surfaced on the Net and not in the print media's rhetoric of moral panic. I think we have barely begun to understand the constructions of desire in virtual bodies through externalizing technologies that seem to compose fictional scenarios in the chat rooms and *alt.sex* Usenet groups that provide the playgrounds. The issue of accountability and, more fundamental, legibility of virtual personae in political and legal terms will come back to haunt the playgrounds, since the violation of virtual personae or selves will remain part of the social interactions on the Net. And even if there are no physical bodies interacting in cyberspace, it would be foolish to think that the connection between bodies and selves, between physical experience and fictional personae, can be severed. Different or multiple constructions of "self" in virtual systems, however, raise important questions about our political understanding of subjectivity. The relations between body and identity cannot be taken for granted, nor are the social meanings and identifications of a particular physical body guaranteed or produced in a self-evident way under any circumstances, real or virtual, in which mediation occurs.

To cross a police line means putting my body on the line by daring to be arrested. I identify myself through my action, which spreads and moves across containments and against the inaction or oppression it protests. To cross over into the virtual playground presumably means to "navigate" without the corporeal shackles that Plato had described in his allegory of the mental logic of ideas. VR environments are supposedly "beyond" the body, replacing its empirical, spatiotemporal reality with computerized information and simulated space. Consequently, in the metaphysical logic of virtual reality the body is supplanted, that is, both conceptually and materially repressed, by the token simulations of cyberspace. One of the crucial paradoxes here is the tokenism. Cyberspace literature may indeed imagine the transformation of body-based sexual identities or human personalities, dismissing the supplanted body as dead "meat" (*Neuromancer*), but such dismissals are actually not possible in the interfaces of VR technology. The computerized (in)formation that is simulated will still use descriptive codes for the body, and it will depend on the imperfectly wired paradigm of scopic viewing that is constructed in the VR bioapparatus.

The Virtual Performer

I will try to relive my first electronic dance by remembering the phenomenological experience of virtual performance in the VR gear. As with certain sports or artistic genres, I am prepared to wear a costume or outfit that protects me, facilitates my activities, or supports the creation of my persona. Unlike my actual dance practice, my first virtual dance seems to require no warm-up or concentration period; all the preparation is spent on fitting the head-mounted display, which consists of stereoscopic "eyephones" and earphones, and then slipping into the DataSuit and the DataGlove (a kind of power glove worn on my right hand). I am literally being wired to the computer, preparing to interact with the stored data and the 3-D graphic environments created by the program and my "movement" into it. I will not look at a computer screen but rather dive into an inclusive environment. The program will simulate my motion or the movement of my wired hand and body, and it will make me see, via the LCD screens in my eyephones, what appears to be the movement of whatever it is that is me *inside* the scenes projected on my eyephones. I am told that I will get *inside the information;* I therefore imagine that I will be inside my dance, experiencing movement without actually moving. However, I am also told that I need to remain in a vertical position, at least initially, in order to begin to orient myself inside the design of the cyberspace. I am reminded that my flesh-and-blood body, which wears the apparatus, is used to gravity and vertical motion. This is a disappointing reminder, since I was hoping to leave gravity behind.

The engineer at the SIGGRAPH convention where I took my first steps is like a patient gym teacher. He shows me how to hold myself and how to avoid too many perceptual conflicts between the real and virtual worlds. I begin to notice the extended ground plane and horizon inside my computer-designed world; apparently it is designed with perspectival and peripheral vision in mind. What a relief! I can relax and reassure myself by looking at my virtual fingers, which appear in the blueish red and orange field that is constituted like an animation in the acoustigraphic scene that is my dance space. I have animated fingers. I hear faint gurgling noises that could be caused by the stretching of my wired hand, or perhaps it is sound sampled by the computer and meant to represent the flow of blood in my arteries. I remember reading that this is a haptic feedback device, and that the more complex virtual environments operate with software designed to create the illusion of touch and sound. These design applications are "coupled" with my location or navigation inside the virtual world, and they will be cued by my traveling through the matrix and my manipulation of point of view or of virtual objects. I am told that I can manipulate these objects with my hand, my eyes, or my voice commands. I can move with variable speed in any direction and can select any perspective I want, including sudden changes of location, since such relocation is independent of space and time. I am independent of space and time and can fly—or, rather, my points of view can fly.

So I close my eyes and take a deep breath. I am vaguely familiar with cartoons and animation, and I pretend that my virtual dance will not be a cartoon but unlike anything I have tried before in physical space. I want to be inside the dance of flight and experience the dislocations of a motion unconstrained by gravity or the body symmetries I have come to know. I imagine being transformed into a protoplasmic shape-shifting water lily or sea horse or a girl-turned-mermaid, floating in and out of invertebrate forms and exploring radical and unexplored asymmetries. I imagine becoming an undulating movement of sound touching space in many locations at the same time, sliding across an airy ocean of colors like algae, and then drifting apart into single cells and reforming again as a sponge with nine legs and fourteen arms. Perhaps I can dance as a spine without head or tail, forgetting my solar plexus, merging my skin with the landscape of greens and browns. My neuromuscular reflexes will not be needed since I require no sense of balance. I don't need to integrate, unalignment is everywhere, and I don't need to know how long it takes to sense the momentum of my floating nerves. I am not moving into space; rather, space moves through me.

When I open my eyes I see a cartoon version of what looks like Houston or any other city with tall buildings and wide streets and things on the ground. It is a cartoon version of Houston, not the city I remember. I seem to be cruising inside a vaguely abstract urban landscape with bright and colorful walls and glass windows. My perspective is that of a camera eye moving forward during a tracking shot, and this bodiless eye appears to create a "realistic" sense of a movement forward that my eye-level perspective makes. I realize this when I turn my head (my real head) to the right, since the change of angle in the scene projected onto my stereographic screen indicates, with a very tiny time lag, a perspectival change to the right of the landscape as I would have experienced it in the real world. I turn my head to the left, and I see the world going by and changing to the other side. I worry for a moment about the time lag. What if I turn my head display more quickly? I decide not to worry about gaps and zoom forward, my camera eye flying slowly into a building and a golden room full of bright blue tables. I have landed in a restaurant or a dining hall, and I try to dance across the tables by making a hopping movement. Somehow I must be losing my center of gravity, and my normal point of view goes out of whack. Before I can realign my camera-eye, its tracking motion scans pictures or maneuvers me in directions I can barely interpret. Perhaps I'm now flying through the ceiling or the floor, or I'm inside the tabletop and merging with it like being flattened against the wing of an airplane. I try not to think, and without noticing that I didn't feel my legs or feet hit any obstacle, I tumble outward, become aware of my failed perception of gravitational pull, and begin to worry.

I try to look down and see blue. A windlike sound blows into my ears and I imagine falling into trees like a rookie parachutist. However, these brown things are not branches but a liquid something I don't know, and I am losing control and wish to enjoy it but worry about my face. I seem to be tumbling or rolling sideways through a fence, and before I can make an instinctive gesture of grasping or holding, my camera-eye shoots images of a vertiginous whirl of lines blurring into a massive wall of polygons that bumps into me. It's a formless wall or container and I am trying to locate myself, but the syntax of this space is unknown to me and I get even more anxious. My pulse quickens and I feel my mouth going dry. The images no longer cohere and I don't know where I am and what happened to gravity and my body. I feel that I am sweating but I have hardly moved—at least I don't remember actually moving my legs or turning a lot or shifting my weight. I don't feel my weight and I am scared.

I want to instruct my feet and legs to move more slowly, but my camera-eye is now grabbing a bunch of seaweed and the eye floats with the blue water down deeper and deeper in areas of purple and red and ocher, trying to taste the waves in amazement of curving rhythms upon the surface of empty momentum dropping off out of the picture and . . . The cues are not interacting and I dimly feel that my geometry has gone astray and my mind can't draw the picture. Then I remember that I have forgotten my hand. Perhaps I could have pointed into the right direction or given myself more time to reconstruct my internal body or my proprioception, but my camera-eye did not meet the expectations that my body is used to expect in perceiving the things outside of the body. The perceiving or tracking was done with a disembodied eye hurtling along without the timing of physical touch and sensation. The "penetrating" or forward motion mimics the macho trope of mastering space so common in VR games. Since my eyephones did not represent a full body to myself, apparently my force-feedback failed or I traveled in virtual space without kinesthetic and internal body senses. Was I imagining feeling both orientation and disorientation, or did my visual, stereoscopic environment generate a partially coordinated representation of what the body might experience while moving through antigravitational space? Could I have moved in cyberspace without the body I possess in physical reality? And how would I have known how to do that?

The dance broke off before it seemed to have started, and I was too startled to continue the experiment. I was not ready to fly with my eyes, unhindered by my body and my expectations of the pull of gravity; my explorations of hands and feet; my sensory knowledge of textures, scale, proximity, and distance; my awareness of my inner ear. Navigating in virtual reality, propelled by the gaze of the eyephones and lulled by the ambient sound of earphones, would imply composing a new sense of body, a sense of kinesthesia simulated electronically, or perhaps even amputated. In other words, the navigation might imply the amputation or forgetting of the actual body if the interactive graphic construction and information matrix could generate a new cognitive mapping of a different reality (i.e., not one that represents the known world).

At this moment in history, the limited development of the gadgets of VR technology prohibits speculation about the encoding of a new logic of reconfigured sensory perception and hallucinatory consciousness. My VR trip may have been an interesting experiment in disorientation inside the VR environment, and I am sure the software design can improve that experience in either direction, enhancing the hallucinatory effect or constraining the movement of the disembodied eye. But however real and coordinated virtual reality might become, my corporeal body remains pathetically stuck, donning the apparatus and doing a weird tap dance on the other side of the senses. My wired body must have looked like a cartoon in the real world. For the virtual dance my biological organism is inadequate.

HAVE YOU EVER FELT
EMBARRASSED BY YOUR
POOR ESCAPE VELOCITY?

YOU WILL.

I am writing about this experience because I want to record the failure of VR's ideology of a bodiless cyberspace, which is, by implication, also genderless, classless, and boundariless. If VR technology wishes to make such claims for the design of simulated worlds, in which floating perspectives create a dizzying sense of freedom, it must do so by hiding the fact that my real participating body, wired to the apparatus, cannot be eliminated: its history and knowledge of movement and sensory perception, its intimate and emotional subjectivity, cannot be effaced. The technology seeks to exploit my imaginary relations to my body, to the images I have (had) of my body and of others, by constructing tokens and body data that cue me into virtual interaction with recognizable or inexplicable (dis)appearances in cyberspace. The floating perspectives are meant to seduce me into an exhilarating loss of control over the body, but they actually traumatize my consciousness of inhabiting my body because the visual cues in the cyberspace scenes do not connect to direct physical sensations. A *virtual body* does not exist, and cognitive disorientation in cyberspace thus becomes a calculated effect of the apparatus, forcing me to adjust to a different processing of information.

Ultimately, what is at stake here is the political and ethical role of VR design in the engineering of constructed "worlds" in which floating, bodiless perspectives or flights are being tested. Such tests have significant ideological and aesthetic dimensions since they administer deeply ambivalent, even schizophrenic, illusions of control (and loss of control) over the real world, our corporeal sensorium, and our social experience of identifications. VR technology is based upon the cybernetic science of control and communications systems; the wiring of the cyborg body politically connects the user-participant to a computer-mediated environment programmed, controlled, and animated by information that is fed to the user. My hybrid role as a machine-organism is to rehearse my freedom to explore flights of the eye, hallucination, and cognitive dissonance, but the digitally enhanced freedom is always overdetermined by programmers' modeling of attributes based on their assumptions of bodies, gender, space, desire, power, and a set of abstract variables. VR technology, like the Net, presupposes an interactive user, which permits me to resituate my position vis-à-vis the cybernetic system of control: the hybrid role allows me to reinterpret and intervene politically into the technological, quasidisembodied relations and sets of variables that are created.

In other words, the cyborgian dissonance I have described allows me to think through the social changes and the new relations of production that have been put into place by the information-glutted societies in the West. The machine-organisms of wired communities and networks, and the discourses of popular culture and critical theory that float around them, become the active agents of new practices being tested, which will influence the economic, political, and cultural processes of negotiation. If the global arena of capital—with its mechanisms of control and its transnational flow of information, goods, and persons—produces "virtual realities," it is crucial to explore the conceptual space of VR applications in terms of its economic and geopolitical effects if we are to oppose its aggression and utilize its potential to achieve a new understanding of the actual dissonances of experienced cyber-citizenship in the locales we inhabit.

Imagined Communities

The aggression I have in mind is an effect of VR technology's deliberate denial of the body and implicit hostility toward uncontrollable organic life. The psychedelic effects of computer animation and the fantasy scenarios of computer games seem to promise excitement, pleasure, and even omnipotence to users who prefer to be relieved of the social experience of interaction. In this sense, virtual realities are both hallucinogenic and reductive, since they simulate a freedom that is delusional. Quite often the life of simulated freedom also has a rather low resolution on the screen; this has been used, paradoxically, as a low-end video effect to imbue realist fiction with cinema verité quality, as in recent Oliver Stone and Spike Lee movies, whereas the low-resolution, cartoonlike quality of virtual reality is a problem of program design which will surely be corrected in the near future.

Whatever the quality of such resolution, there is no pure freedom, just as there is no technological solution to unemployment, illness, war, death, alienation, and the daily struggles we see in our economically and racially divided societies. We have barely begun to grapple with the dynamics of the densely multicultural and heterogeneous space of urban life in the age of transnational capitalism, which downsizes or displaces labor and constantly shifts skilled and unskilled immigrants into new situations where they are forced to relocate themselves, alter their life-styles, and sacrifice their civil, political, and cultural rights. We still have not found any answers to such problems as life-threatening diseases; the lack of an adequate health care system; rising unemployment and the impoverishment of the unskilled; substance abuse, homelessness, and street crime; and the decay of the public school system.

The permanent crisis that we are facing today is monitored by economists and sociologists, banks, insurance companies, therapists, governments, and promoters of religious faith, yet the aggressiveness of late-capitalist accumulation plays itself out in a vast arena of extortion in which worker-consumers and the corporate class are all jacked into the bioinformational assemblage—the networks of files, codes, and data transmissions. The information superhighway, as Marx might have predicted, is a technology that converts labor, objects, people, and events into information. What is so troublesome about VR technology is not the dissonant fantasy of programmable scenes of simulation it asks me to assimilate but the fact that it already takes my cyborgian existence for granted. Even if I didn't play this particular game, or refrained from computer games altogether, I would have to function inside the arena in which my labor is being consumed by electronic machines, which carefully collect vast amounts of information about me: my income as reflected in tax returns, insurance, health treatments, money transactions, telephone calls, debts, school and arrest records, arts grants, and my credit history, along with my travel (my movement) and lifestyle preferences. In exchange—if one can call it that—I am sold entertainment, consumer products, and more information, some of which I need but most of which I don't. I am also reminded that I will be upgraded.

Collectively, we not only live in urban zones of conflict and anxiety, spatial segregation, and social inequality or degradation; we also participate in the late capitalist conversion of computerized prosthetics into a vast system of imperatives, surveillances, and controls. Foucault's analysis of the disciplinary and panoptic society, which persuasively describes the general model of the organizational management of control over the deepest layers of the social body, reframes Marx's critique of Capital and the commodification of labor in modern industrial societies. Foucault's analysis itself needs to be reframed and linked to the VR discourse of cyberspace technologies, where knowledge/power is hyperrealized to the extent that data interconnectedness operates on a new level of "informated" control that circles back on itself like a Möbius strip: it is a self-participatory and self-regulatory mode, just as the proponents of virtual, on-line communities have argued. The more such human prac-

VIRTUAL COMMUNITIES

tices as communicating, socializing, decision-making, working, thinking, seeing, and playing go on-line, the more they become *agents* of the information science of virtual systems. The fantasy-fulfillment is paradoxical: we participate in the informational control systems and become our own observers. We are "on-line" all the time, so to speak, written into the program, plugged into the software that produces/simulates the virtual community that we believe we inhabit with our connections. The utopian-communitarian dream of an alternative community is just that: a digital dream.

This is a very peculiar performance of "imagined community" if we think of Benedikt Anderson's original theory of nations (and national discourses of domination) as historical constructs and ideological fictions, especially his thesis that the function of the print media (which we can extend to telecommunications) is to help people imagine themselves as a collective nation among others they have never seen.[30] The history of wars, immigrations, and postcolonial struggles for independence has demonstrated the unresolved contradictions in the disastrous process of nation building, and the current wave of crude neonationalism and corporate warfare blatantly operates according to retro-cyborg principles of "ethnic cleansing," possession of territory and market shares, and the right to dominate. There are several botched "peace processes" going on in the world as I write, all of them fragile and liable to break down after the next bombing or hostage crisis. The dead and traumatized "meat" of people killed or relocated doesn't show up in the equations of cyberculture, except as short horror-movie film clips on the evening news, edited for sensationalist consumption. The ideology of the global information superhighway operates on a level of fantasy that is perplexingly disenchanting since its logic of accumulation/virtualization upgrades televisual media, which is based on the hyperexpansion of the relays and flows of information irrespective of the different or overlapping oppressions that affect people in various locations.

I have yet to find, among the proponents and critics of cyberspace, a critical reference to the utopian imaginary of "data interconnectedness." From the point of view of network operations and virtual systems, human history or human rights do not matter at all. What matters is the operational management and perfection of the communications interface between cyborg workers and information systems, which from a historical perspective has always been the major task of bureaucratic organization in industrial societies. If one adopted Yevgeny Zamyatin's vision of OneState (in his early and instantly banned dystopian novel *We*), one would have to consider virtual systems a final revolutionary stage in the perfection of supersurveillance on a transinstitutional level of communication. The "benefactors" of super-vision—the industries and bureaucracies in communications, data collecting, profiling, testing, credentialing, consumer targeting, encoding, cloning, and cosmetic and genetic modeling—already seem to inhabit practically every aspect of everyday life, affecting my performance as citizen, worker, and consumer, my sense of privacy and leisure, and the manner in which I apprehend issues of risk concerning political expression, health, sexuality, and the body.

Descriptions of such virtual systems of control and influence approach the pathological; it is almost as if my connection to computerized culture is subject to epidemiology and its predictive detection of my location (as carrier of information) and vectorial movement. In fact, as we have learned during the AIDS crisis, epidemiology is precisely about policing and securing the public space by defining boundaries or visualizing body-subjects (risk groups) that are hypothesized as imagined communities of risk behavior. The same mechanism operates in governmental or populist-political processes of pathologizing unwanted carriers of information, such as illegal immigrants, refugees, ethnic minorities, religious sects, outspoken and queer artists, black male rappers, street gangs, radical feminists, single mothers, and so on. The populist hype surrounding cyberculture needs to be examined in the light of the inclusionary and exclusionary rhetoric of "community" if we are to probe the depths of "informated" closed-circuitry imagined by both multinational corporations (the military-industrial-entertainment complex) and the "cyberdelic" underground.

In his examination of capitalism and the reemergence of fascism, John Simmons has observed that

> with cyberspace—and virtual reality—come new combinations of media that are psychologically invasive. Cyberspace no longer merely offers to bear information that must be fitted into a personally created context; it provides context, however primitive. Cyberspace infantilizes even while it enlightens, appealing to the senses with speed and power and exploiting receptors of human emotion with vivid new colors and kinaesthetic awareness. In doing so, it provokes confusion over the means by which we—in the limited sense in which we are *we*—conceptualize experience, examine self and others, and generate and perceive beauty.[31]

If the influences on our imaginary have profound social effects, the context provided by virtual systems can hardly be called primitive, since it already involves a far-reaching and motley mix of techno-transcendentalist ideologies coupled with hyperbolic science research, corporate marketing, and mainstream service providers, on the one hand, and fringe cybercultures rehearsing subversive hacker experiments and industrial junk art, on the other. If one understands the matrix of data interconnectedness as the context for virtual communities composed of user groups, corporate communications industries, and "cyberdelic" subcultures, then it is all the more important to isolate the political questions skirted by cybernetic operationality from the *aesthetics* of imaginary scenes threaded by virtual machines. Simmons speaks of generating and perceiving "beauty," and his atypical question about human emotions takes him outside the matrix of the techno-fetishistic strategies of the virtual theater. But it seems unavoidable to address human emotions, needs, and creative expressions in order to gain a better understanding of the kind of imagined communities that are being constructed. We need to talk about tools when looking at computer-mediated communications, about who constructs them and how they are implemented and used, and whether they can be retooled and refunctioned from the bottom up. (The cyberpunk motto "The street finds its own uses for things" is more viscerally understandable than older leftist or postmodern notions of "subversive resistance.")

Sampling current writings on the Net—including publications about science fiction, media, film, MTV, and rock music—as the shared historical subtexts for the emergent technological formation of virtual communities, I find numerous references to the entanglement of diverse cultural milieus that produced the current generation of on-liners. Those who write as insiders (e.g., Rheingold, Sandy Stone, Brenda Laurel, Terence McKenna, Mark Dery, Douglas Rushkoff, and the contributors to *Mondo 2000* and *Wired*) often emphasize that the roots of the techno-cultural zeitgeist of the eighties and nineties lie in the sixties counterculture of rock 'n' roll and drugs. Those roots include the diverse strands of anarchist, romantic, and esoteric hippie cultures, as well as the West Coast human potential, techno-pagan, and New Age movements, that intersect with acid rebellion and political protest before drifting off into the various offshoots of punk and postpunk youth cultures, hacker and programmer communities, research labs, and the "cyberdelic" generation of ravers, university techno-kids, music groups, and artists.

Although ethnographies of the new cyberculture are now beginning to appear in the United States and Britain (owing to a growing interest in "cultural studies" in these countries), one should realize that Western self-expressive lifestyle options and consumerism in the nineties are vastly different from both the political radicalism (including the civil rights, antiwar, black power, Chicano, and feminist movements) and the psychedelic Woodstock generation of the sixties. This difference has considerable consequences for political concepts of "community," since it also reflects the demise of the radical Left, while the newer social movements are still in the process of inventing themselves. Moreover, a sociological study of global Internet "communities" will prove exceedingly difficult, especially since the user populations worldwide are growing constantly, and postings, groups, web sites, and events surrounding Net culture are just as ephemeral as performance art. It would make more sense to investigate how particular social groups are, in fact, using technologies for social and cultural change, how they are integrating new equipment into their futures.

The phenomenon of virtual communities, therefore, is subject to unwarranted speculation, and I am not prepared to equate on-line chat rooms and electronic micro-niches, plugged into corporate lifestyle marketing and recording industries or the vapid myths of Slackers and Generation X, with community building. The hypertextual configuration of the Internet sends us in potentially infinite directions, and many users have already experienced the overwhelming feeling of being a tiny floating island in an ocean of data, even as they confess their desire to "be connected." At the same time, as Sherry Turkle has argued, people desperately want to interact, and they "explicitly turn to computers for experiences that they hope will affect their social and emotional lives. When people explore simulation games and fantasy worlds or log on to a community where they have virtual friends and lovers, they are not thinking of the computer as . . . an analytical machine. They are seeking out the computer as an intimate machine," an evocative screen onto which they can project their dreams and build intense, anonymous relationships.[32] Sometimes Turkle sounds like a queer theorist of the fin de siècle, but I don't know that many folks who enjoy cruising "intimate machines."

The fragmentation of social and cultural milieus at the ground level is likely to be intensified in such an apparently endless, seductive dreamworld of cyberspace, and it worries me that we have started to speak of virtual communities without even examining the extent to which older political meanings of organized struggle, solidarity, kinship, intimacy, class consciousness, and coalition building seem to have melted into thin air. The expression of lifestyles in the here and now (or in the future) becomes profoundly cynical if it is touted, by the promoters of cool cyberpunk rebellion-as-"social irresponsibility" (the catchphrase of the *Mondo 2000* editors) with a dismissive attitude toward old-fashioned political struggle and activism. Listening to the excessive, adolescent rhetoric of cyberculture in magazines and fanzines, and observing the entrepreneurial savviness of the cybercultural producers and computer experts, I find the posturing of subversive hedonism—including the guerrilla concept of "Temporary Autonomous Zones" (a utopian manifesto published by Hakim Bey in *Mondo 2000*)—rather unimpressive. The posturing goes along with privileged access to the Net, and it is hardly surprising that most of the *Mondo 2000* and *Wired* readers are either students, suburban, college-educated business people, or young urban professionals who work in the communications industry.[33] The tool makers, users, and promoters are well connected and appear to be unaffected by the more dire social and economic realities at the ground level and in the inner-city war zones in the first world or on other continents. They also seem to forget that computers, robots, and automation inevitably displace human labor, and that if the working populations in industry no longer have jobs and money to spend, they won't be able to afford the new personalized and seductive hardware/software.

The rhetorical radicalism of alternate low-bandwidth culture also needs to ask itself how it will sustain its own open access and the utopian imaginary of "free-flowing" information exchange and interactive cyberart in the face of emerging censorship debates and regulatory-control mechanisms that will inevitably haunt the virtual systems once the megacorporations begin to streamline their producer services or once local governments set up legal roadblocks (e.g., the notorious case of the Munich district attorney who compelled CompuServe and AOL to restrict access to their servers). The intertwined operation of computer-controlled manufacture, capital, and consumption is so obvious that it strikes me as disingenuous to claim cyberspace as a reservoir of empowerment and creative tinkering, especially if the content providers will tailor their services and images to meet your need for playfully derivative "tinkering."

However, in order to distinguish among hardcore hackers, creative tinkerers, and everyday users, I wish to return to the notion of experienced incoherence by asking whether it has become necessary to interpret the creative experience of multiple/virtual or role-playing selves from different political and aesthetic perspectives that are enabled by the culture of simulation and not only contribute to new constructions of identities, communities, and bodies but also to the ways in which we make sense of meaning and fight over the social application of our technologies. One of these struggles, I believe, will involve the application of "interactivity" and its potential for new forms of intersubjectivity, that is, the political effects of the deconstruction of a unitary, bounded subject and the concomitant loss of the integrity of the material body. If interaction and the partial "life on the screen" (as Sherry Turkle has documented it in hundreds of interviews with users) is connected in social or performance terms to a politics of community and communal experience, one will have to distinguish not only between corporate commodity-content providers and grassroots, individual negotiators of interactive technology, on the one hand, but also between the competitive vanguard of hackers, programmers, or research labs and the various noncompetitive, creative, and social applications explored by alternative cooperatives, on the other.

I want to cite a few examples of the latter as well as convey some of the cautious optimism expressed by activists, interactive-media artists, and young Web artists such as my Web collaborator Giles Hendrix. First, one can observe that the phenomenon of the cyberspace museum, with which I began this chapter, is quickly becoming an everyday practice of museums, galleries, community centers, and educational arts organizations actively seeking to expand their local infrastructures of information. While local bookstores, music stores, and alternative galleries in Chicago are becoming more user-friendly by adding coffee bars and cyberstations for browsers, our libraries and museums are going on-line and developing micro-galleries, web sites, and CD-ROMs as a teaching and information outreach strategy for the local public. They are also designing exhibitions with the Internet in mind, utilizing the World Wide Web—which supports graphics, images, and sound as well as hypertext links to other sites—to distribute their artwork and scholarship, thereby making them available to all those who might not be able to travel to Chicago. Pioneering efforts to place exhibitions and collections on-line had already been made by London's National Gallery (whose "MicroGallery" is available on CD-ROM), the San Francisco Museum of Modern Art, the National Museum of American Art, the Whitney Museum, the University Art Museum at Berkeley, the J. Paul Getty Museum's Art History Information Program, and—more interesting—the Contemporary Art Institute of New York, which launched on-line art projects and interactive multimedia installations during its 1995 SoHo Arts Festival.

Alternative galleries lacking the budgets of major museums have tended to be more inventive in their "site-specific" Web art experiments, and many alternative art spaces around the United States are now interlinked through the Web and through specific events, such as concerts or discussion forums, that take place in a physical site (e.g., The Kitchen's

Electronic Café network) and are simultaneously uploaded into the Net. Both at Chicago's Cultural Center and at the Randolph Street Gallery Spanish artist Antonio Muntadas created interactive installations in 1994 that utilized access to the Web to create a "public-information project" entitled *The File Room,* where cases involving cultural censorship were stored in an electronic archive that will remain on-line and continue to grow as new cases are added. Muntadas has called the project a "public artwork" in the political sense of Joseph Beuys's social sculptures or democracy/education actions, deliberately extending and blurring the conventional meaning of art in public spaces by making the censorship archive available to the global network and receptive to inputs by individuals or groups (http://fileroom.aaup.uic.edu/). The physical installation of the archive subsequently traveled to Leipzig and Bucharest, suggesting to contributors from these former Eastern bloc countries the possibility of documenting offenses committed by former regimes. Other on-line Web sites (e.g., ArtNetWeb, äda 'web, ArtsLink, The Thing), BBSs and services such as Arts Wire, American Arts Alliance, or CultureNet publish work or provide information and links, set up collaborative projects and discussions, and advocate support of public-arts funding or other political issues.

As a new system of "broadcasting" art, cultural projects, and advocacy, this use of the Net raises very significant issues of public space and public communication, especially since Web sites can be created by any individual or group with access to the Net, circumventing the institutional mechanisms of approval, funding, and legitimation that restrict who can exhibit what and where. In this sense, the low start-up cost of the Net and its global outreach has produced a new phenomenon of potential democratic empowerment: anyone with a computer and a modem can create, install, and broadcast *public media.* This mode of production also drastically alters the relations between context, production, and distribution, for within the Net production and distribution are equivalent and synchronous. Moreover, interactive Web sites and art galleries reshape the relations between art and audience since the viewer is also a participant who can recompose and alter the work-in-progress as well as scan and download particular images. In a survey essay Mark Dery quotes VR pioneer Jaron Lanier's claim that "computers pose a direct threat to the economic basis of the art world." By implication this claim touches on proprietary concerns and digital copyright issues extending to all other media markets involving images, sound, and text that can be scanned, digitized, altered, and rebroadcast in electronic networks that exceed Andy Warhol's wildest dreams. In response to Dery's question as to whether Web artists are concerned about other Net users downloading their art, Remo Campopiano (the founder of ArtNetWeb) answers: "You're talking about art as commodity. I'm talking about art as a social movement." [34]

It remains to be seen what, exactly, is meant by "social movement." In Chicago all of the social or cultural activism and political advocacy I am familiar with occurs in a person-to-person manner and in real time, involving people coming together in neighborhood committees, community groups, and support networks which thrive because each meeting helps to build tangible relationships and continuities. These intersubjective continuities are vital since they also generate the sustaining energy of, and faith in, collective action as a means of identifying and addressing a grievance or creating a policy to improve housing or health care conditions, playgrounds for children, nursing homes for seniors, employment or educational opportunities, coalitions between ethnic or political groups, and so forth.

Every social worker I have spoken with confirms the intrinsic vitality of face-to-face communication, exchange, and dialogue in order to locate and resolve misunderstandings, share experiences, and foster cooperation. None of this would happen without community meeting spaces for such gatherings, I am told, since the diversity within urban communities often leads to isolation and segregation among groups and generations, whose sense of alienation or prejudice exists largely because they don't know each other. Organizing and activating group projects that emerge from cooperative meetings generally means using older channels of communication (phone, mail, fliers, word-of-mouth). Whereas such relationships, based on recognition and trust in the context of community building, cannot be adequately performed in the anonymous space of BBS and Internet chat rooms, it is conceivable that on-line communication can complement the transmission of information and the much-needed increase of individual participation in the formation of public policy.

Two of Chicago's largest alternative weekly newspapers (*The Reader; New City*) went on-line to facilitate reader input. In Evanston several aldermen asked Northwestern University to provide free Internet access, through its network, to public libraries so that individuals could connect to the city hall web site and post opinions or learn about meetings and read city council minutes. (As of this writing, the local government was still dragging its feet and a home page had not even been designed.)

Within the nonprofit arts organizations I have noticed a sense both of excitement and fear. Some believe that electronic art on the Net will create an equitable public-access space, open to collaborative improvisations unavailable on this scale in any other medium. Others worry that such interactivity will depend on advanced hardware and software, and that social communication and meaningful transcultural cooperation in electronic-media projects will soon be curtailed by legal and economic battles over the ownership of content and the rights of digital reproduction. In fact, the economic battles have already begun, and cuts in public funding of the arts and social services may further divide media artists who work in the real world and in cyberspace. At a recent panel discussion held during the 1996 Women in the Director's Chair Film/Video Festival, Kate Horsfield (of the Chicago Video Data Bank) pointed out that many women video makers already lose funding support to those who have moved into cost-intensive but fashionable CD-ROM production.

The distribution of resources also affects one's understanding of those social processes of electronic public art that involve free and unlimited reproducibility and parasitic proliferation, to the point where on-line "collaboration" may become indistinguishable from white noise: If one is no longer able to determine the authorship or subjectivity of a voice, an image, or a message, how can one hope to discriminate between valuable and insignificant information in the seamless, contextless flow of pixels? How can one reimagine the need for ethical consensus on the question of accountability and responsibility in a particular work situation—as is traditional in collaborative rehearsals for a performance or video production—and apply such ground rules to cultural production in the electronic forum? The discussion at present tends to center on the question of accessibility and "audience" participation or recomposition; even more important, there is little agreement as to what constitutes art/content and creative or perceptual *interactivity* in cyberspace.

She Loves It, She Loves It Not

I want to compare two projects. A good example of the new interactive CD-ROM work that makes use of multimedia technology in order to account for the author's critical interest in technology is Christine Tamblyn's *She Loves It, She Loves It Not: Women and Technology*. Presented during the group exhibition *ADA: Women and Information Technology* organized by Chicago's Artemisia Gallery in early 1996, Tamblyn's work achieved a humorous, poignant, and instructive synthesis of personal and historical narratives in the context of a feminist project dedicated to women's influence on the development of digital media arts and on alternative "feminine interfaces," as curator Andrea Polli has described it. (I should add that Artemisia is a nonprofit women's cooperative dedicated to the nurturing of women's creative art endeavors and its productive relationship to local communities.) All the artists in the exhibition showed interactive, hypertextual, or on-line work that in many cases was developed collaboratively; for example, Abbe Don's *We Make Memories II* represented a visual-narrative piece composed of stories by the older women in her family; Judy Malloy and Cathy Marshall's *Forward Anywhere* was an intimate composite text based upon women's diaries reflecting their long-distance, on-line relationship during a PAIR collaboration (an artist/scientist "coupling" sponsored by the Xerox Palo Alto Research Center in 1993). Tamblyn's CD-ROM had a similarly intimate and meditative quality since it appeared to evolve as an autobiographical story addressed to the imaginary, private reader. From the very beginning she placed her image and voice up front, recording her motivation to do multimedia work and sending the following "letter" to me (all the "letters" are accessed through envelope icons):

> Dear Reader,
>
> Creating artificial life is tantamount to usurping the function of God. If interpreted in Judeo-Christian terms it entails a certain element of Satanic hubris. I initially started working in multimedia because recording and editing magnetic or chemical traces of light seemed to impart alchemical powers. I could enact the life of an alternative persona with different characteristics than the "real" me on film and video.
>
> Regards,
> Christine

Translating the "letter" (language, writing) into performance of personal narrative or autobiography is a well-known strategy of performance art or video poetry, and Tamblyn here shifts her voice/persona into the hypertextual domain of the multimedia graphical interface: I am "personally" addressed and invited to follow her point of view into the various layers of the unfolding stories, which are assembled as collages of photo-text and filmic "histories." Her provocative intentions become clearer once I have accepted her opening introduction (a Quick-Time video clip): "Hello, my name is Christine. Welcome to my mind. I want to interact with you. I am a woman who is now appearing to you as a virtual subject. I have prepared some performance loops about women in relation to technology."

On the screen before me the home page appears with her face and open mouth—speaking and then frozen in mid-speech (screen text: "if you want to move, please click on my mouth")—followed by the main interface screen with a circle of daisy petals I can pluck to find out whether or not she loves me. Each petal is given a subject heading: Control, Memory, Power, Violence, The Other, and so forth. This unusual and disconcerting opening invitation to interaction with her open mouth already hints at the underlying ironies of her history. The petal-paths lead to stories not of love, sex, or romance but to the rather more violent dominant history of technology and industrialization monopolized by patriarchal teleologies of progress based on the expropriation of cheap labor, here represented primarily as a feminist revision of labor history that depicts women as domestics and factory workers, office assistants, typists, mothers, wives, nurses, and movie icons (Hollywood's versions of the beautiful, docile, mysterious and eroticized love object). Her critical history–hypertext creates a collage of many scenes in a kaleidoscopic "labyrinth" (another title of a petal) which threads its way through different and interrelated chapters of a book on male domination, power, and surveillance. In a poignantly ironic yet gentle manner, Tamblyn's historical genealogy of History and the technological mastery of knowledge and bodies teaches a lesson about the sources of power over women, both socially and politically, within the hierarchical matrix of industrial capitalism. The artist manages to convey this genealogy primarily through the screen constellations or tableaux of critical commentaries, explanations, and documentary photos, as well as video clips from movies showing women interacting with technology. In other words, Tamblyn has created a montage in the Eisensteinian sense of assembling her tableaux to recompose an obvious and not so obvious composition reflecting historical images that function like a *gestus*. For example, an entire social and economic arrangement can be read in the photo-scene where the male surgeon "repairs" the female worker's body (depicted as half human, half machine), while a brief text appears in the lower-left corner:

> One of the reasons that women are in an economically powerless position is that they possess a fraction of the world's technological expertise. Knowledge about making or using tools or machines makes it possible for those who have it to dominate both matter and other people.

In the upper-right corner we simultaneously see a video clip from a science-fiction movie (*Star Trek*), the major North American genre reflecting anxiety and impending horror at the maintenance/loss of privilege and control over space, bodies, and aliens. Tamblyn here manages to connect the industrial and medical technologies of power to the role

of women's eroticized and victimized bodies in many science-fiction scenarios, which seek to exorcise male fantasies of dissolution or emascu-
lation through a hyperbolic violence that seems to underlie the colonial
imaginary of Western technoculture. Tamblyn's knowledge of this history is here applied as a gesture of re-appropriation; she recombines
fragments of media images lifted from the data banks of economic realities and popular fiction. Her CD-ROM is an engaging tour de force,
and I spent about an hour moving through the paths until I seemed to
have completed the circle of petals reflecting my menu of choices. I felt
drawn into the narrative, as if Tamblyn's composition had enabled me
to make my own connections and draw my own conclusions in the sensory palette created for the reader.

At the same time, the main weakness of CD-ROM multimedia
remains its very limited application of *interactivity;* its hypertextual arrangement consists of a performance loop that precludes any input from
my end. It does not allow any back-and-forth exchange, intervention, or
recomposition; therefore Tamblyn's letters cannot be returned. Moreover, the work is not only constrained by this conventional unidirec-
tional mode of address but also enacts a political performance narrative
that may work particularly well only in the specific local context of the
feminist group exhibition that grounds Tamblyn's archive in a web of
interrelated counternarratives. If the content of the CD-ROM were uploaded into the Net and open to random surfing, the function of its
address to anonymous browsers would be politically diluted, given that
there would be no context of mutual recognition in the exchange of
critical ideas.[35]

What I am hinting at is the problem of understanding the new role
of "audience" in a public cyberforum, especially if one thinks of the
strong emphasis in contemporary political art and activism on acknowledging and knowing the audience or community one is addressing. As
I suggested in the previous chapter on video art, community-directed
activism or media art takes the idea of "interface" literally, insofar as
the contested zone of cultural activism is itself marked by concrete interactions through which community is reciprocally constituted, first during the participatory media-production process itself and then in the
contextual feedback to the production. However provisional and strategic, the communal-action-as-production creates the political dimension
in which we can test and interrogate ourselves and our reimagining of
community in the process. This process initially remains separate from
the distribution of the work to a larger audience or targeted politi-

cal institution. With the absorption of production and distribution into simulated interface or synchrony, "interactivity" no longer involves any mutual or reciprocal process *toward* a shared dimension. Such process is virtually dislocated.

Synergies

Were I to extend the notion of art "process" and communal action to include the production's political and ethical dimension as a public practice, and thus to redefine the creative, community-building process itself as a site-specific artwork or sited performance, I would be able to subsume the more conventional aesthetic or technical assumptions about the creation of art under the new alternative paradigm of community activism. Before I offer an example of this paradigm, I will point out that Giles Hendrix and other Web artists may indeed see the public dimension of shared production/distribution on the Net as a manifestation of the successful dislocation of "site-specificity" into a new mode of "universal exhibition."

In his research on visual art sites on the Web, Giles found a number of new venues for artists to gather, create, and display art. In particular, he examined the modes of operation in OTIS (Operative Term Is Stimulate), an on-line forum/gallery for collaborative projects. (It was begun by Ed Stastny in 1993 as a small File Transfer Protocol [FTP] and then was offered free space with SunSITE, the largest experimental information server on the Web, owned by Sun Microsystems and connected to the Net through the University of North Carolina.) Giles noticed the enormous growth and success of OTIS and contacted the "curator." According to Stastny, in 1995 the site received more than ten thousand hits each day. He has described its operational philosophy as follows:

> OTIS, at its most basic interpretation and intention, is a place for image-makers and image-lovers to exchange ideas, collaborate and, in a loose sense of the word, meet. OTIS is a collection of images and information accessible mainly via Internet that is open for public perusal and participation. The quickest analogy drawn is that OTIS is like an "art gallery." Not only because it's a place to see art, but also because of its social reverbs. People do meet "on OTIS." Ideas are exchanged. Conversations are had via electronic mail. Influential works do "hang" on OTIS. People have been inspired. But this "art gallery" is open 24 hours and serves an ever-increasing "community," the Net. This art gallery is hardly exclusive; it's fairly easy to get your work displayed on OTIS.[36]

Disembodiment: The Virtual Realities

After monitoring some of the ongoing projects on OTIS, Giles concluded that it "functions in many different ways for many different people. Furthermore, it functions for tens of thousands of people a day. It allows the universal exhibition of all artwork that is submitted. It coordinates several fascinating and complex collaborative art projects. It functions as a catalyst so that people meet and interact. It creates numerous cultural issues and administrative experiences for those that maintain the site, and it may even be used to generate possible revenue."

Giles is always excited when he speaks about his findings, and he is particularly stimulated by the open accessibility of the site and its egalitarian approach to the creation and sharing of images. In our regular meetings at Northwestern University's Media Development Library, I have observed the inexhaustible energy and curiosity with which he probes interactivity on the Net, combined with his intimate knowledge of the newest Adobe and Macromedia applications provided by image- and sound-editing software. He has shown me his latest projects, the first of which is called *Brodie's Interpretations,* a "site on a long-lost server, allowing users of the newsgroup *alt.dreams* to view their own dreams as quick-time movies," for which he combined selected dreams to create a script and then videotaped the performance. The other is an animated film about Dante's *Inferno* that he has created as a graphic interface, with Virgil guiding the navigation. I asked him how he defines "visual art" and the notion of "site" on the Web.

GH: Every artist is as close as their [*sic*] computer. It is a matter of digital creativity and ingenuity. For example, OTIS does not physically exist anywhere; the administrators reside throughout the United States, and the artists reside around the entire globe. Every day they discuss Net art and the future of art itself.

JB: Are you not talking about computer-generated images, or a kind of computer graffiti, or copies of copies that someone scanned and then modified?

GH: I see this new web art as a living entity, still evolving. Everyone is able to try it out and create something unique. You can configure your own images or you can scan your physical artworks into the pages. Ranjit Bhatnagar, who developed the Web-Crawling and Page Integration at OTIS, told me that it can take a lot of thought to express what you want in as few pixels as possible, and that one learns to design for the strengths and work around the weaknesses of the medium, just like in any other medium.

JB: How does one contribute work to OTIS if one doesn't have the advanced software to scan images or create animated and acoustic art?

GH: OTIS recognizes the problem of access and high-end equipment, and they have offered solutions. They have announced on-line that they encourage teachers, students, graphic designers, gallery owners, 'zine publishers and other people dealing with the visual arts to expose people to OTIS and to help those who don't know how to scan pictures or get them on the Net. Such local interaction could be a learning experience for all involved. OTIS also offered to accept disks or actual pieces of art and scan them in themselves. Ed Stastny admits being aware that many people, perhaps especially people in other cultures without access to electronic equipment, are excluded from the site, but he doesn't have the time to address the practical side of it, since he already works up to 45 hours a week administering OTIS without pay. More volunteer work would be needed to get more artwork online.

JB: How does collaboration work on OTIS? (I expected him to explain the virtual mode of artistic interfaces, but he cited a local example that took me by surprise.)

GH: In fact, there was a collaborative project in 1994 called SYNERGY: CORPSE which got started here in Chicago and culminated in a six-week exhibition at the Kopi Café. Harlan Wallach, an active OTIS participant and independent artist, organized the event on-line and off. Participants created body parts for templates that were eventually put together as different corpses, printed, framed, and exhibited physically. This exhibit actually proves that Internet art is not just for the Internet anymore, but that the virtual site can also exist on a successful level in the tangible art world. If museums can go on-line, why cannot on-line museums become real exhibits? Ironically enough, however, the virtual counterpart of this SYNERGY project exhibits the work to a much greater number of people.

This idea of "counterparts" has interesting implications. If I were creating a process with collaborators here in Chicago, and if for some reason our exhibit were interrupted, closed, or censored, I could then use video footage of the work and scan and upload it to OTIS, where it would be posted on the Net instantly. The work could also theoretically be shown the next day in Finland or Australia, in a physical site, where collaborating organizers would only have to scan and print out the images for display in their space. In a sense, this mode of transmission replicates the global reach of television, except that independent media would not be subject to the control and delivery systems of the broadcast corporations. This crucial difference needs to be kept in mind when exploring the rescheduling potentialities of independent video and Net art across borders and monopolized markets.

Still unclear about the prospect of on-line interactivity, I ask Giles about his experience on OTIS. Accessing the site, he shows me some of the artwork that was created collaboratively. Most of it consists of abstract, brightly colored, richly textured computer imagery, but there are also figurative "paintings" and pop-art collages that show the various complex results of digital matting, masking, shading effects, filtering, surface manipulations, thresholding, posterization, and so on. The project he has logged onto is called THE INFINITE GRID.

GH: THE INFINITE GRID takes the concept of gridding into the netherland of the beyond. By constructing multiple pieces for each piece of grid, the grid has nearly infinite proportions. The construction of fragments from common templates ensures that any one piece will fit with any neighboring fragment. This project began in June of 1994, is ongoing, and there's no end in sight. In a similar manner, the various SYNERGY projects generally begin with one person's starter image, and then another person would manipulate the image, and another would continue or complete the image for final display. Earlier versions such as REVOLT or CROSSWIRE have now been developed further, allowing more continuous evolutions of image works. This is a media form that is really about evolution and experimentation.

JB: How do the artists communicate with each other about the content or the purpose of what they are manipulating together?

GH: Well, there was a particular event that helped to inspire more substantial interaction. In January of 1994, an entertainment organization called Cyberplex called OTIS and asked for help in creating an interactive art-gallery exhibit for a two-day event referred to as smartBOMB 1.0. Because of smartBOMB's attempt to show the power and usage of the Internet, Ed Stastny helped to set up a live collaboration project called SYNERGY: PANIC. This project would gather artists in real-time to manipulate images grabbed at the Rogue Nightclub [where smartBOMB was taking place]. Things turned out far from perfectly hardware-wise at the club, and far fewer images than expected were generated from the event itself.

JB: So the equipments didn't quite match. Isn't this a problem of compatibility that plagues the entire technoculture? [I wanted to suggest that the equipment mentality is disorienting, in a social sense, since it obscures the fact that the HTML language for the Web does not make direct connections between users, reflecting a fatal dependency on the newest technological connections that promise solutions when, in fact, the failed prosthesis is much more indicative of the reality of our social relations. I smiled at Giles.] The nightclub people must have been frustrated. Was there an actual panic?

GH: Not at all. [His face became animated. He was clearly irritated by my skepticism.] It didn't stop the artists at all. They quickly took the initiative and began exchanging images with each other [à la REVOLT and CROSS-WIRE] via IRC and FTP, generating over 480 manipulations over the weekend of January 28–30. The results of that powerful weekend are still being sorted out. Every week since that original PANIC, participants have been meeting on weekends via IRC [channel #OTIS] and collaborating, socializing, and making art history. They've also developed several interesting new forms of collaboration and interaction for computer/network artists, including Grids, exquisite corpses, ZygOtes, and Masks. It was around the same time that Wallach started his CORPSE project in Chicago, revamping the classic "exquisite corpse" drawing exercise in which participants all draw parts of a body which is, in the end, put together or unfolded into a vision of often very bizarre disjunction.

I can't help feeling the impact of this narration, since it conjures up images of necrophilia and science-fiction horror scenes of mutilated or disfigured bodies. These "corpses" are drawn together: Is this a remote-controlled rehearsal in composite fantasy, an illusionistic theater of sadism, or simply an exercise in the computer art of virtual figure painting freed of any threatening boundaries of abjection or trauma? Like the rituals of ecstatic nightclub dancing amid the wild sampling of techno and acid rock music, the SYNERGY simulations reflecting the ritual explosion of the body's form are perhaps symptomatic rituals of cyberculture, narrating a history different from the one Christine Tamblyn is telling. I notice the emphasis, in Giles's account, on improvisation and the sustained manipulation of the emergent VR fantasy (the aftermath of smartBOMB, or smart composition of the exploding cyborg corpse), but nowhere do I get a sense of critical feedback to the configuration. The OTIS operation continues its recombinant, surrealist fantasies apparently without interruption or objection, which immediately renders any facile assumptions about the interactive virtual gallery as a "universal" exhibition quite problematic.

The "exquisite corpse" is only a computer-generated display. But it is also a playful fantasy enacted by SYNERGY participants, who are morphing virtual body parts as if the imaging technology no longer had any relation to the organic world and the specific limitations or vulnerabilities of human bodies. The critical feedback that is missing is the reflection on content or on the stated personal/political expression (e.g., as was done by the body artists who worked with their living bodies). A reflection on interactive technology itself is also absent, with respect to an ethical evaluation of the objects or processes that are posted "universally." There is a chilling lack of concern, as far as I can tell, about the (techno)logic behind the presumably infinite modifications of the body images, this at a time in our culture when political, economic, and moral pressures directly conflict with the individual's right to control his or her body.

Perhaps I can also explain my position with reference to the example of the nightclub or disco. There were times when I frequently went to the clubs alone, feeling the desire to let go and immerse myself in the darkness, the flashing lights, luminous video screens, and throbbing rhythms of the music, surrounded by all those dancing bodies and the sonic eroticism of the scene, feeling both visible and invisible in the energy of the space. I always felt that the sense of community created in the scene was exhilarating, fragile, and tentative; it was an erotic fantasy with which I could momentarily identify. I would enjoy the anonymous cruising but would often leave with a profound sense of isolation or emptiness. I recount this experience not because I agree with the pseudopuritanism of a Larry Kramer or a Randy Shilts, which condemns anonymous sex or ostentatious promiscuity. Rather, the participation in the event of dancing and intermingling with others seemed precisely to pose the question of how we imagine community as a performance of bodies or selves in a particular location or ambience. Identifying ourselves in the context of deviant desire and dance, our claiming of the scene contained all the ironies of such claims, and I could never quite grasp the logic of anonymity that seemed to give pleasure without reciprocation. Basically, one's own personal history and one's desire get entangled in the pride of shame and the knowledge of not belonging (not wanting to belong). It was as if I needed a very healthy narcissism to enjoy the pleasure of looking/listening, sweating during the dance and closing my eyes when the trance started to set in. There were other nights, too, when I would go out with friends to dance together to "our" music, singing or screaming along, enacting the gestures of bonding that connect the autoerotic with the intersubjective, thus merging with the shared movement of the "scene" of the club, the scene that is the club. Perhaps this is the closest image I have of a "temporary autonomous zone," but I remain skeptical of such autonomy because it depends on the melodramatic denial of deadly realities, of the transformation of cruising and desire after the deadly impact of AIDS.

The impulse to want to connect is perhaps as strong as the lingering awareness of disconnection and dispersal following the exhilaration of momentarily belonging to the fantasized community. The contradictory emotions I am describing also underscore the differences in the process of working together with others during and after rehearsals for a new performance or film project, or collaborating on a political action that requires a similar continuity and commitment. I always have to come to terms again with the painful experience of reintegrating myself and my life after an intense period of working together with others. The workshop experience allows for the heightened sociability and the intensity by means of which we open ourselves up by taking risks, embracing each other's uniqueness, coordinating our different ideas and shared beliefs, and expanding traditional boundaries. The synergies I trust happen to be based on such an unfolding of creative intercourse, which is localized, specific, and most likely unstable and temporal yet predicated on *being there*. I mistrust the notion of synergetic communities that are universally or equally accessible, mediated by graphically unified screen-sites, composed by the operations of machines whose algorithms don't know the scene.

While I consider the premise of imagined communities built upon not being there and the reductive aesthetics of an "interactivity" that relies exclusively on surface manipulation of pixel-texts as dangerous, I am also convinced that Giles and other web artists view their computer-generated art as a form of communication, a new medium that is much more than a tool, a lifestyle and an expansion of the boundaries of agency that will necessarily lead to critical questions about the reframing of public space and politics, including the issue of who gets compensated for the creative ideas that we upload into cyberspace. Even if the new communications systems succeed in shaping and sustaining the global-information economy, they have also become a significant factor in local economies, where place-bound production sites, material facilities, and specialized services are needed, and where the new local/global performances are politically and socially constituted. Before turning to this local struggle, I want to conclude my conversation with Giles. I asked him whether computer/Web artists see themselves as a subculture and, if so, how they position themselves vis-à-vis the corporate mass media.

GH: Well, my initial thoughts are that the subculture, specifically identified as low-capital individuals who work independently or in small groups for both personal and commercial ventures on-line, view themselves as children of a new age of civilization where communication, business, art, and life itself is conducted in a dramatically new way. We view ourselves as all small players who can do anything a corporation can, only faster, more efficiently, cheaper, and, of course, better. We stay informed on as many issues as possible, we know where to get any information we may need, and we use each other as resources to meet these ends. This is what Alvin Toffler describes as third wave, whereas corporations are second wave. They are tied up in capital investments, that is, real estate, manufacturing, textiles. They are involved in the complex work of financial bureaucracy that is a giant political game. The "subculture" is not national, it's a global union that is bridged every time in seconds. Our interests are not in the stock market or the U.S. trade deficit, but in admitting these things have taken the world as far as it can go under such systems. We want to make information, and thus power, available to everyone—inherently changing the patterns of culture as we know it.

JB: That's a rather comprehensive vision, if you are indeed assuming that information, and the power connected to it, is transforming culture and the economic relations of production. But how are the relations transformed, and what will this new information culture look like? Who is served by these immense information flows, who takes advantage of them, and who is paying for the deficits? How can you possibly speak for all the "children of a new age"? What about the children on Chicago's South Side or in Nicaragua? Or let me ask the question differently. How do the elite of knowledgeable Net users you describe pursue "personal ventures," and how are the media that surround the Web instrumental in the congregation of a certain subculture of Net users and the formation of that subculture (I mention fanzines, *Wired, Mondo 2000,* chat rooms, sites). Or are you arguing that web artists/ Internet users are no longer a subculture?

GH: The media plays two parts. Those who are capitalizing on this culture for second wave corporations and those who genuinely believe in fostering the change. This can be simply ascertained by finding out who ultimately owns what one is watching. *Wired* is huge, but it is an independent company in debt to no company. This is very important. The articles on TV and in the paper are just their way of reflecting the hype to get an audience. Newspapers know that they are information services and must get on-line or die. The paper they are printed on costs twice as much every year as trees become more valuable.

JB: Oh, you think cyberspace is more ecologically sound?

GH: Of course. Furthermore, just being on-line does not make anyone part of the subculture. To be a part of the subculture you must first "lurk." This means reading newsgroups, surfing sites, learning the social traditions that have been established. There are very strict rules that exist in cyberspace. They exist for very important reasons: to enable the most efficient use of resources. I could talk about these forever. When someone just posts a stupid question to a newsgroup, it creates more flames and endless bandwidth waste. If they had read the "read me" for that particular area, the question would have been answered. Otherwise we would spend all of our time just answering the same question every hour. This is just one example. Therefore "lurk" and gain the information. Knowledge in this area truly becomes status and power. You can be black, white, 6 or 66, it is all still just about knowledge. The other key factor is contribution. You must not just take what you need, but you must also contribute your work, your experience, your opinions, your papers, etcetera, to be considered a part of the culture. If you do both of these things, contribute and respect the smart rules, then the Internet and the world itself will repay you infinitely.

The library is closing and we are forced to leave. Giles wanders off to his apartment to work on his "Art Manifesto for the End of the Millennium," and I take a stroll along the lake. I feel tired and my body tells me that I am reading the wrong information. The efficient knowledge Giles spoke about is very abstract to me, and most of the situations in which I felt myself entangled in the crosswires of politics and power did not necessarily pay me back in the manner he suggested. I have not learned the smart rules yet.

Scene Three: Street-Level Media/Action

My last example therefore points in a different direction, namely, back to the grassroots level of local activism. After we had completed the workshops and joint dance-theater productions for the Grenzland festival in Eisenhüttenstadt in 1994 (see chapter 4), Imma Sarries-Zgonc and I returned to East Germany in the summer of 1995 to participate in a new project we had proposed to some of the dancers and cultural workers in this border town located in the state of Brandenburg. During our previous visits and work periods we had noticed that the nearly total transformation of the political and socioeconomic infrastructure of East Germany after unification had thrown the steel workers' town into a state of limbo, or, if you prefer, a kind of Dantean purgatory, severely crippling local efforts to effect a smooth transition to free-market capitalism, which was more generously supported by West German investments in other cities or regions. The undecided fate of the EKO steel factory and its ten thousand plus laid-off workers created a near standstill in industrial production that affected all the other economic sectors of the town, including its profit-making ventures, tax revenues, and the spending allowances of households and the city government. Federal support helped to get the institutional transformations under way—new roads were paved and new telephone lines laid; small businesses stuttered into existence, schoolteachers went through remedial training to learn the new "content"—but the cultural domains suffered from an almost total downsizing and the closing of many of the venues of local cultural activity under socialism.

It was this experience of the evacuation and closing of cultural spaces that motivated us to propose to our friends and former collaborators a workshop scenario for the summer of 1995. We envisioned it as an urban "archaeology" of *closed spaces,* focusing not only on the particular memories/histories connected with specific sites but also on their present function in the urban topography of frustrated expectations. Furthermore, this scenario would implicitly include the topography of interrelationships among the partly closed steel factory, the ruins or abandoned sites of cultural production, and the high-security former police-training barracks. In 1991 the latter had been turned into a shelter for refugees, which was subject to frequent neo-Nazi attacks against those who were housed there.

After receiving a small grant from the labor union of German Media Workers for my conceptual sketch of a fictive scenario for urban actions, we approached the female director of a small youth club called Marchwitza, which had recently reopened under the name Klub Vielfarben (Club of Many Colors) as a nonprofit organization that catered luncheons and sponsored social activities and music concerts for the local youth and senior citizens alike. Anett Schauermann allowed us to rent space there and use the club—including its office computer, telephone, and copy machine—and its grounds as our base, which proved ideal since it was located on a hill directly adjoining the small, emergent community-access television station. We agreed to announce our idea as a free workshop open to any participants interested in a summer project on "urban fantasies." I also decided not to formulate a research/action plan but simply to act mainly as a facilitator.

Under the fictive name Tomaz Grenzländer, and with the collaboration of Catalan choreographer Imma Sarries-Zgonc (who had worked extensively with the young amateur dancers from Eisenhüttenstadt and knew the small women's network in town), I designed the ad for the newspaper and sent letters to some of the local artists, teachers, and steel workers I knew. I then began to draw up some contingency plans and compiled a list of equipment we would need, since the workshop would potentially involve a wide range of media (photography, video, radio, posters, print media, music, etc.). When we started up, a group of fifteen (later expanded to twenty-eight) young and old people joined the workshop; several of the female participants brought their small and adolescent children, and we also enjoyed the presence of several workers from the EKO plant, a librarian, a psychologist, several high school students and young artists, and a young man who claimed to be a bodyguard-in-training. At our first meeting we constituted ourselves as an anonymous ensemble under the name "Fantasielabor" (Fantasy Laboratory) and spent the first week getting to know each other by exploring the neighborhoods together and compiling a sketchbook of ideas, memories, discoveries, and collective efforts that became our slowly growing database.

It would take far too long to explain the psychological and physical process involved in creating a sense of mutual understanding and respect and of easing initial tensions. The latter arose primarily because Imma and I were perceived as outsiders and as people from "the West," conjuring up all the understandable emotional resentments and projections with which many East Germans grappled after the imposition of the new political economy, which destroyed the social cohesiveness of the highly regulated organism of collectivity. This earlier regime was now being remembered in a highly conflicted and often unreflective manner mixed with feelings of nostalgia, pride, and guilt. We tried to understand this climate of psychological disorientation, anxiety, longing, and frustration within the specific peripheral situation of this town, which was once considered a model city and now lay, forgotten and abandoned, on the Polish border, aware of its second-world status within the first world. This self-perception of the townspeople may have appeared unreasonable to the Polish neighbors living across the border river that served as a natural border, since the material conditions in Eisenhüttenstadt (i.e., the level of consumption of goods and services) were already higher than at any point under socialism. But the border itself, perceived as the boundary with eastern Europe, has remained a constant reminder of a past shared with the Eastern bloc, which is now denied by many unified East Germans.

The self-perceived marginalization can be understood as a psychological effect of the dissonances, the failed political harmony or sense of mutual respect, following national unification. Many townspeople saw their current crisis of unemployment and dysfunctionality as an undeserved and wholly unexpected setback, a humiliating and sobering wake-up call after the initial joy over newly gained freedom achieved through the revolutionary democracy movement. I never found hard evidence that the democracy movement had any roots in Eisenhüttenstadt, and the tightly organized life (the steel workers performed three shifts in succession) and sociocultural organization of this workers' community had now been replaced by an ostensibly new value system and free space for individual initiatives for which most of the inhabitants were not prepared. What the local people I talked with had expected from the unification were the promised "blooming landscapes" (Chancellor Kohl), which they translated into political stability, financial security, growth of opportunity, greater freedom, and access to Western standards of consumption. What actually happened is a very different story, elements of which I have just sketched here from my notebook jottings and the observations that became part of my documentary film *Border-Land*.

At the point where our project touched upon the evolving historical trajectory of Eisenhüttenstadt's identity crisis, the city seemed to have entered a second phase, following the traumatic aftermath of unification. The resurgence of neofascist subcultures (especially among skinhead cliques) and the more widely symptomatic xenophobia against foreigners and refugees had slightly subsided, partly because the regional government reduced the number of refugees housed in the shelter and did everything to minimize their visibility. Local businesses and restaurants were beginning to establish themselves, and two new supermarkets (modeled upon the American mall) had opened up, one located right next to the entrance to the EKO steel plant, which was in final negotiations with a Belgian investor who had promised to keep it afloat, albeit with the currently reduced number of jobs offered there (roughly 3,500). The city's inhabitants had decreased from 71,000 to 64,000; many families had left and graduating high school students feared the prospect of unemployment.

Accepting this volatile situation as the context for our work, we began to improvise a series of site-specific interventions and interactions with local citizens and the public media, culminating in the occupation of the closed and decaying former dance/music hall Der Aktivist (The Activist) and its symbolic reopening on 10–11 August 1995. Our decision to choose the centrally located hall was a strategic one both because the building was very visible and accessible and had achieved mythical status as the main meeting space for workers' festivities—including weddings, graduation parties, and balls—and had showcased many of the local music bands during its thirty-three-year history. It became a coveted object of real estate speculation, even though buyers shied away from the enormous costs of renovation (the building is protected by federal law as an architectural landmark, representing one of the first collective efforts of the young socialist model city in 1955 to build a cultural center for workers). Now boarded up and in a state of utter dilapidation, the two-storey building, with its peeling yellow ocher facade and ornamented columns, is a visible reminder to the community of a past era, replaced by the current period of profit-driven venture capitalism, with its synthetic malls parading as "city centers."

Our group located a number of vacant and abandoned sites during our fieldwork, and we collected stories and memories of these buildings and their original uses in the local culture. We worked openly, with cameras, sketchbooks, and other assorted and fantastical instruments; we were variously looked upon as a film crew, a team of restorers or architects, or a museum or high school group out on a field trip. When passersby inquired, we would sometimes explain that we were gathering information about all the places that were closed, or we would spread the rumor that we were working on a tourist film exploring a new and attractive dimension of the town's ruins that could be marketed to foreign tourists interested in an "adventure holiday" on the border, drawing attention to Eisenhüttenstadt's "central European location between Moscow and Paris." This idea only emerged by accident, so to speak, because we were experiencing such fun and excitement cruising the streets and discovering the dramatic potential of some of the sites we examined during our shoots with the video cameras, including the river itself (we staged an illegal swim across to the Polish side), the old municipal outdoor swimming pool (now empty and overgrown with strange weeds), and the colossal, gutted ruin of a power plant built by the Nazis in 1944 but destroyed by Russian aircraft the day after it went into operation in 1945. Next to the train station we also found an old building, the former Hotel Aufbau, which was in complete shambles after having been boarded up and abandoned in 1989.

These scenarios, along with several other inner-city buildings—such as the *Aktivist*, the former home for senior citizens, the former discotheque Huckel, and several cafés that used to house literary and cultural events—practically invited performative actions, but at that point we were only beginning to understand the role of our physical presence and seemingly incongruent activity in front of and around these closed spaces. It was a role that was totally undefined and open to all kinds of interpretations, and our playful demeanor made us look utterly harmless until the day we participated in an "official" graffiti competition sponsored by a local meat-processing company that wished to have its gray walls decorated by local artists. Each graffiti artist was allotted eight square feet of wall space, so we showed up with eight people and received sixty-four square feet, allowing us to paint a huge conceptual mural depicting the future of urban planning under capitalism, which was signed with a modified quotation from a popular Communist hymn ("Out of the ruins, forward we march"). We then issued our first press release to the provincial newspaper covering all local events, announcing our ongoing work as a "Fantasy Laboratory."

Overnight the large mural was defaced by skinheads (they were observed by the company's guards, who didn't intervene), and by the end of the day we were already being interviewed by newspaper and radio reporters. We began to realize that every step from now on would potentially be a public action mediated by the local communications systems, and we held a strategy session to determine how we could create situationist *détournements* to distract the media and involve more people from the neighborhoods, who might have direct physical and emotional connections to some of the sites and their histories.

Our group debated the feasibility of such a larger community-based project. At that point I also realized that the concept of urban action or performance art was unfamiliar to the local participants. Such cultural projects had not been possible under socialism, and the few local artists who had lived here for years were all trained in specific disciplines (painting, photography, music, dance) institutionally administered and controlled from the top down. An independent or "freie Szene" (alternative scene) did not exist. At this point the whole process of collaboration entered its most critical phase, since some of us didn't share the same perspectives or political opinions on the nature of public space and our relationship to it or to the urban communities, media, and institutions. We realized that some of the group members might compromise themselves (as city employees) or feel uncomfortable about the political and legal implications of direct action, even if such action might be "performed" as a theatrical act or simulation.

Since we all agreed that we wanted to emphasize the social dimension of the loss of cultural meeting grounds and art spaces, some of us began work on a political manifesto to draw attention to the need for such places of sociocultural communication, while others prepared materials for a site-specific exhibition of our findings, photographs, films, and conversations with citizens. We formed smaller action groups that visited people's workplaces—the steel factory, the shelter, the schools, and the neighborhood housing projects—and we also opened an information stand in front of the "City Center" shopping mall, soliciting citizens' opinions on their perceptions of the cultural future of Eisenhüttenstadt.

Our work was structured around the practical needs required by these interactions; we listened to the members of the community, especially their concerns about the local economy and the survival of the town as such. These ventures into everyday existence—discussing old buildings, making contact, and holding conversations in the street—illuminated the dimension of such involvement in real time and space for the composition of a community-based project. We had started a process that would take months to evolve, one which laid the groundwork for a larger network of citizens to assume greater responsibility and commit themselves to creating cultural policy. We had already noticed that a number of laid-off workers or people in early retirement seemed willing to help in the restoration of a cultural site they cared for, such as the Aktivist. On the other hand, most people said they didn't think they had the right to take such action, preferring to delegate responsibility to the elected city council. Our group knew that we were stretching to the limit, working long hours on the project and shooting film scenes in the evenings. Since most of us had allotted our vacation time to the workshop and needed to return to regular jobs, we felt we had to create a specific ritual action that would bring into sharper focus our exploration of cultural action *as* political process in order to demonstrate how public effect (spatial reconfiguration/urban planning, media/publicity, intervention into bureaucratic procedure and economic/legal policy) might be constituted.

We assumed that such a ritual event would focus attention on a perceived lack or gap in the infrastructural changes manufactured by capital and city hall's dependence on capital interests. We wanted our performance action to be both nonthreatening, surprising, and inspirational, allowing citizens to feel inspired by a civic initiative that was a little fanciful (*fantasievoll*) yet contributed to a new understanding of the relations between performance, media production, urban research, the democratic political process, and the site-specific struggle for cultural space. The performative process of the group work initially consisted of an exploration of our understanding of community-based, site-specific cultural action (*Aktionskunst*), as well as of the parameters of participatory methodologies for the creation of "public art," especially in the context of a city where no independent art scene existed and where the involvement of "outsiders" was often greeted with suspicion. Devoting ourselves to a culture-in-action project meant feeling the discomfort of irresolution and lack of experience, yet allowing them to become a condition while our responses evolved. The primary content of *interaction* could then unfold in relation to specific cultural objects and sites to which attention had been drawn and which were significant in the memory of the local residents.

In retrospect, I would say that we began to *act upon* these sites, resulting in a twofold process. First, fieldwork activities sprung up at several abandoned cultural spaces that had existed during the socialist era of the GDR and were now either left in a state of decay or were the object of unresolved investment speculation. (In many cases the federal state is the nominal proprietor, but the agency that handled the sale of former collective property was dismantled in 1995, and the current legal situation is often unclear, with property rights reverting to the community or city.) These included the production of photographs, testimonies, and a fictional documentary film on the urban scenario of ruins. Second, there was a discursive production of theses and ideas on infrastructural transformation or economic change (in the larger context of Eisenhüttenstadt's monocultural dependency on the survival of its EKO steel plant) and its negative effects on living culture and the potential of independent cultural production under the new political regime.

Since our field description was both critical of the new venture capitalism establishing itself in the city and shaping new territories of commodity consumption (e.g., "the City Center" shopping mall) and concerned about the future of the severely impaired production of local culture—with its lack of alternative options and venues for artists, students, youth and the worker population (including the unusually high percentage of un- and underemployed or laid-off workers in Eisenhüttenstadt)—our project was committed to a double focus: (1) creating an awareness of the need for a nonadministered, independent culture and, most important, for the reopening of spaces for cultural production not subject to the market-driven imperatives of the commodity-culture industry; and (2) inventing strategies for direct action, including the production of our own media and the tactical use of existing local and regional print and broadcast media (press, radio, television).

Near the end of our workshop and during the occupation of the Aktivist, the visibility of our actions had reached an unexpectedly high level, for the small staff at the community television station had "adopted" us. (The Oder-Spree Fernsehen [OSF] channel is adored locally because it reports on the town's problems in a decidedly funky and "unprofessional" manner, in the sense that it avoids all the pretensions and slickness of the national/West German broadcast media and reports mostly in an improvised fashion, repeating certain feature stories during the weekend as a kind of "local highlights" program.) They began to consider us a kind of outlaw political theater company and followed us around, shooting some of our activities and broadcasting them "live" or as a series of short stories featured in their evening program. During the day of the occupation they also interviewed citizens and thus "copied" or doubled our own documentation, even inviting us to share our footage with them.

The radio stations tried to report on events more objectively and sent reporters with microphones, but we were also able to infiltrate the stations by placing "listener calls" to the DJs demanding live broadcast from the occupied site. One station complied and broadcast excerpts of the public speeches and music from the women's band Shacopay, which played on the evening of the squat. Providing a proper mix of glee and irony, the newspapers depicted the occupation as a daring stunt and a long-overdue challenge to the city's passivity and negligence, following up their initial coverage with a series of investigatory reports on the building's history, present condition, and contested status within the city's urban planning, public order, and finance departments.

Our own publicity campaign mostly consisted of word-of-mouth communications and fliers distributed citywide three hours before the occupation, as well as "squatting bulletins" published during the two-day event and the group's postproduction activities. In addition, we knew that a lot of people had to drive by the site on their way home and would therefore see the "reopening" and hear the music of our outdoor bands.

We had also sent the bulletins and our manifesto to the members of the city council, the cultural department, and the mayor's office. Surprisingly, the police didn't show up until two hours into the evening outdoor concert/exhibition we were staging on the beautiful terrace of the Aktivist, and by the time they arrived a local children's dance group was performing in front of excited parents (a folk concert prepared by Harald Selle, one of our group members who is the local dance teacher for the grade schools). Increasingly, neighbors seated themselves on the chairs we had provided and ordered beers, dazed and happily confused by the inconceivable "reopening" of their favorite dance hall. The police decided not to make a scene and—apparently without orders or experience in such matters—cautiously congratulated us on such a fine cultural event while reminding us that the loudspeakers would have to be shut off after ten o'clock.

Disembodiment: The Virtual Realities

We had cleaned up the large terrace area of the building during our "gardening action" in the morning, and when darkness fell and the band was playing, we illuminated the photo exhibit we had hung on the outsides of the boarded-up windows, while a large, transparent banner affixed to the top-floor balcony of the building, displayed our logo for everyone to see (AKTIVE FANTASIE). Later that night we premiered the first tourist film ever made in Eisenhüttenstadt, projecting it onto the peeling facade. The young and old that had assembled for the event were clearly pleased, holding their breaths as they realized that the tourist-actors in the scenes were their own sons and daughters, enacting a strangely adventurous dance among the ruins of cultural community.

Fantasielabor, "Dancing in the Ruins,"
Old power plant, Eisenhüttenstadt, 1995.
Photo: J. Birringer.

VIRTUAL COMMUNITIES

After the Scene

> I had learned to function quite well, believing in the great Idea of communism . . . just as I was taught to. We were simply educated to be schizophrenic. If you are not disturbed by gaining too much insight through painful experience, you can live quite well in this manner. In general, the discrepancy between television and daily life, between that which was required by the teachers to get an A and what we saw, had become so normal and mundane that the game of simulation was really easy.
>
> Cornelia Geißler[37]

In conclusion, I want to offer some reflections on the relations between the production and postproduction of the scene I have just described, especially in light of the "Fantasy Laboratory's" micropolitical role—its body politics—in relation to the virtual realities discussed in this chapter. Our performance process recognizes its interpenetration with technology and translocal communications systems, but it also exemplifies the insistent value of grassroots collaborative action, on those sites where we negotiate with power and surveillance systems and have to reimagine not some kind of utopian alternative or organic community but self-empowering political participation that fosters social change translocally instead of confirming existing relations and institutions.[38] The translocal, in this case, refers to the opening of closed spaces that are local yet also symptomatic and representative of much larger issues encountered in the struggle against neonationalism or provincial resentment, vital issues in the current discussion of Europe's imagined collective identity.

I think it should be clear by now that I am neither accommodating to technological teleologies that insist on the inevitability of "being digital" nor assuming to know the answer to the cyborg politics envisioned by Donna Haraway's manifesto, which deconstructs the apparent dichotomy of embodiment/disembodiment. The irony of the scene we produced in Eisenhüttenstadt lies not in the process of the mediatization of the event, which may have "disembodied" the actual labor we accomplished, but has to do with the fact that we were negotiating with a specific local site and the town in which it is situated. Our own group is a good example of the transitional, nonessential relations of culture (the Aktivist) to geographical territory or to an imaginary, homogeneous "community." Even in the nonstratified, proletarian steel town of Eisenhüttenstadt—which had experienced decades guided by a collectivized, close-knit, social concentration of purpose (an entire civic life had been organized around the pulse of the steel factory and the leisure or sociocultural activities mediated by the "Kombinat" and the party)—it is now apparent that cultural communication has increasingly and irrevocably been delocalized. Mass-media entertainment (radio, television, videocassettes) has transformed public space into private consumption of publicity, thereby reducing social interaction and replacing previous leisure-time relationships.

Furthermore, several members of our group do not even live there (anymore), while others have told me that they no longer feel part of a closed community. Our performance itself reflected the transitions now under way in East Germany and the European Union—transitions into transcultural relations marked primarily by the multiple, fluid links among individuals, social groups, denationalized economies, and symbolic systems. The predominance of the media and conspicuous consumption, coupled with the delocalization and diffusion of cultural products, has transformed the meaning of and need for public space. In this sense it is perhaps logical that after the collapse of socialism the traditional, popular meetings grounds for cultural activities closed down. The Aktivist is a relic that is no longer needed for the staging of a sense of collectivist community since collectivism itself has been replaced by capital's postmodern logic of deterritorialization.

The different narratives we tried to set in motion during our work process—the folkloric and the touristic, the industrial and the migrational—were, in fact, intersecting at the very conjunctions of local memory (the nostalgic defense against capitalism's new "City Center" mall) and intermedia fiction (i.e., the cosmopolitan fantasy of Eisenhüttenstadt's future role as a "border town" depicted in our tourist film). Conceptually our goal was not to reclaim a site that once played a central role in the culture of this town but rather to open it symbolically in order to draw attention to the transformation of culture at this stage of Eisenhüttenstadt's transition to the transnational economy of capitalism. The site would have to be imagined differently, with the new temporalities in mind.

On the other hand, the relations of *performance* and media are always site-specific, bearing in mind the asymmetries and inequalities among political classes and countries. The border relations and transactions between the cultural and political fields in postmodern cities such as Houston or Chicago are different from those in postsocialist cities such as Ljubljana, where liberal-capitalist economies have become entangled with authoritarian neonationalisms or pseudonationalisms. The situation in Cuba is entirely different because the social and cultural spheres are overwhelmingly determined by scarcity and the imminent danger of political collapse. The radical democratization of the former East Germany was played out politically as a process of annexation, whereas economically the rapid transition to free-market capitalism meant overnight deregulation and privatization, precipitating the sale and closure of so-called inefficient state-managed enterprises. The consequences for a town like Eisenhüttenstadt were devastating; the sharp rise in unemployment and social unrest coincided with the heavy influx of eastern and southern European immigrants and refugees after the opening of the borders in 1989 and the outbreak of fighting in Yugoslavia in 1991. When we started the "Fantasy Laboratory," the closing down of local cultural production (the small music school and crafts center for children survived, but there was no theater, no cinema, no orchestra, no literary cafés, no professional dance company, no alternative culture, and no institute of higher education) had reached a frightening level, and to my knowledge there was not even a single modem in town. Cyborg politics was frustrated by industrial stagnation and by the concomitant rise in retrograde right-wing and neo-Nazi ideologies. The latter were mediated on the national political level by new antiimmigration policies, which led to the closing of borders and to local resentment against Polish neighbors or any foreigners perceived as a threat to the newly imagined community and its social services.

Our group action therefore introduced the question of the "imagined community" and posed it in our manifestos for the squat, asking whether the economic crisis in Eisenhüttenstadt had created a "virtual reality." We claimed that the future of the town could no longer depend on the single industrial mode of steel production, and that a newly diversified economic infrastructure would also necessitate (and depend on) varied and innovative cultural production. We conjured up a vision of the shared communal interest in creative production, appealing to the citizens' sense that each local community is inevitably part of the current evolution of the European Union and therefore needs to ask itself how it conceives of cultural regionalism, new forms of narrowcasting (i.e., cultural projects aimed at specific target audiences; specialized media-arts productions for differentiated audiences), and new, integrative models of production that prepare people for the pan-European communications networks, as was done in the neighboring city of Frankfurt, where the new Europa University opened in 1993 and where joint German-French-Polish cultural/educational projects are under way.

However limited the symbolic effectiveness of our squatting manifesto may have been, it did represent a concrete material intervention into the "closed space," the closet of passivity in the cultural scene as well as into the normative bureaucratic reality of the local administration. Our multimedia performances during the squat, as well as the deviant networking we accomplished through our use of local media to put pressure on city hall, showed the potential "intermediality" of several discrete sites. Our photo and film montages directly linked economic, social, and cultural locations—the steel plant, the "City Center," the abandoned home for senior citizens, the Aktivist and other cultural ruins, and the refugee shelter—thereby pointing toward the shared space in which community organizing could take place if the various sites were no longer perceived as separate or "other" but as mutually informing and interactive.

Our film about illegal border crossing caused a lot of discussion. Audience members initially thought it was illogical to want to swim to the other (Polish) side. Similarly, a dance-drama sequence we filmed on the bombed-out rooftop of the nineteen-storey ruin of the old power plant (which is fenced in and off limits) caused moments of tense silence, for we had revived the suppressed memory of the plant's history (after the war the terrain had been used by local militia for "civil defense" exercises), as well as the present rumor that the gutted building was a favorite hangout for lovers and also for neo-Nazis.

We broke through the silence with our next film, which extended the theme of "adventure-filled tourism" in Eisenhüttenstadt by offering a gentle parody of local hospitality toward foreign visitors. This scene involved the partly destroyed and decaying Hotel Aufbau, considered an eyesore by most of the citizens since it is the first thing one sees when stepping off the train upon arrival. We staged such an arrival, and the local TV station picked it up for their broadcast. By chance, it so happened that two of my artistic collaborators (Mariko Ventura, a Japanese-American visual artist, and Craig Roberts, a photographer from Albuquerque, New Mexico) were working in Berlin at the time, and I invited them to visit us in Eisenhüttenstadt. When they arrived at the station, still ignorant of our film, the cameras were rolling. We had cordoned off an area outside the entrance, causing a small traffic jam, and then had rolled out a red carpet upon which the "tourists" were greeted by a reception committee sent from the mayor's office (impersonated by our actors). Our guests, whom we honored as the 100th and 101st arriving in Eisenhüttenstadt, received flowers, a golden key to the town, and a free night in the best hotel (the Aufbau). A local taxi driver volunteered to drive them once around the block and back to the rundown hotel, where a parade of flag-waving children created the proper ceremonial ambience while our tourists checked in and were received by the hotel director, champagne bottle in hand. Our flattered tourists were then asked to make a small donation to aid the reconstruction of local ruins, followed by interviews with several camera teams who posed questions in German, Spanish, and English. The local TV station went along with the parody and broadcast the English-language version of the interview.

When we showed the film the night of the squat, we noticed that many people in the audience considered the scene to be very funny, and we used the relaxed moment to announce that this scene was only the first in a series in which we would be interviewing local residents, legal nonresidents from "the other side," and refugees in the shelter, hoping to collect impressions, memories, and emotional experiences of life on the border that could later be shared and exchanged. I will never forget the stunned look on the faces of the dozen or so refugees who had accepted our invitation to join the squat and have a beer with the locals. They had been sitting quietly around the tables, and it was as if the larger audience only now recognized the friendly "foreigners" in their midst. The evening—held together by creative improvisation, the music of the local bands, and the general spirit of excited disbelief among all the young and old participants—harbored a tremendous sense of transformative power, and even if the performance was ephemeral and actually constituted illegal trespassing, we felt that the positive feedback we received from the people on the streets and from the local media was uplifting and encouraging in many ways. The absence of police force and the embarrassed silence of the city administration made it very clear to the participants that they had carried this event: they had given a new meaning to the old Aktivist site without even using the ramshackle interior of the building.

We continued the squatting during the night vigil and the "restorative performance" the next day. Neighbors offered to help with gardening and cleanup activities, while members of our group solicited public testimonies and citizens' opinions on the possible future utilization of the Aktivist. All of these commentaries were carefully documented as a steady stream of visitors who had heard about us on the radio or read the news stories dropped by. Later that day a few individual members of the city council showed up to add their comments to our book or to ask us who had covered our expenses. We answered that all the equipment, tools, and food were donated by citizens, and that we could probably hold out for weeks if the feedback loop continued in the same way. An elderly man who visited us composed a long story, which he entered into our book, about his memories of past festivities held in the building. He was crying and visibly moved when he left. He returned the next day to add a story he had forgotten. A group of young women came by to inquire whether the new Aktivist would house a women's center. The band members asked whether there would be rehearsal space for them. Imma was already drawing up sketches for a dance studio that could host international summer schools, and I contributed a sketch of a multimedia studio for the development of a media-arts outreach project that could be linked up with local schools and the children's music center. Finally, just before we declared the symbolic squat concluded, we were visited by Andreas Ludwig, director of a private local museum (Dokumentationszentrum Alltagskultur der DDR) dedicated to collecting material objects and cultural artifacts from everyday life under socialism. He seemed enthusiastic about our project and asked whether we had thought about drawing up a new plan for the building, and whether we might consider including a gallery space for a future exhibition devoted to the cultural recollections of the community.

Reflecting on these suggestions, I realized that although our actual performance was over, it had not really ended, and that our real/fictive occupation was not only acceptable to the community but had already led to a promising series of political and cultural negotiations about new initiatives and diverse visions concerning the future use of the building/monument. The Aktivist, in this sense, had already become an imaginary site, a nodal space traversed by different desires and speculations; it had thus become "interactive" with local cultural knowledge and the dynamics of change. Coupled and recoupled with memories and new visions, it therefore could be considered an interactive site similar to the composite work of SYNERGY. The crucial difference here is that the Aktivist has a history; it has a virtual presence only to the extent that it is open to intervention from various sides. It remains a physical site that has property value and legal status. We were told the next day that the only reason we were not arrested was the fact that the city, which controls the property, was caught off guard by the "artistic" nature of our embodied action. The city officials made comments to others implying that we obviously were dreamers who had no sense of economic and legal reality.

Postproduction

After such official feedback, there was only one logical answer, namely, a "legal" performance. The first phase of our action was completed on 17 August 1995, when the group submitted a formal proposal to the city administration outlining a communal initiative for the restoration and reopening of the Aktivist, in cooperation with city and regional or federal agencies (e.g., building-preservation agencies, European cultural funding agencies), as a not-for-profit arts organization. We formally handed over a detailed script of the proposition to transform the Aktivist into a "kommunales Baukunstwerk" (communal artwork-in-progress) whose future role could evolve, through community participation, into a multifunctional and multicultural media-arts center, inclusive of a wide range of applications by various users, groups, schools, and international residency programs and projects.

With this proposal the "Fantasy Laboratory" had progressed beyond its original intention of staging a series of actions to draw attention to the lack of communal cultural spaces for production and exhibition purposes. It was only because of the empowering experience of the theatricalized actions in the urban scenario, and the positive feedback and

Fantasielabor, The closed space of the Aktivist before the squatting action, Eisenhüttenstadt, 1995. Photo: J. Birringer.

Fantasielabor, "Squatting Action," the Aktivist, Eisenhüttenstadt, 1995. Photo: Craig Roberts.

support received by the population, that members of the local ensemble decided to enter into negotiations with the political institutions and into a legitimating process to demand access to and use of the property, based on citizens' requests and community interest as well as on a draft resolution to build a cooperative for the shared reconstruction of a cultural space for public/communal art.

A first series of negotiations with the Department of Culture, the Office of City Planning, and the mayor's office took place in October and November 1995. At the time of this writing the process was ongoing and would continue through 1996 and 1997. After the first production phase, the project entered a postproduction phase (to use the language of film editing) involving both legal and administrative/political dimensions. It has continued to evolve as a grassroots cultural action dependent on local consensus, lobbying, and fund-raising, thus constructing further narratives and images of an independent movement for community art and the recognition of the role and the space of performative identities/relations.

For my future research and performance collaborations, I will need to scan the methodological, analytic, and interpretive issues involved in such a community process and participatory cultural action in order to develop a thick description of the concrete and symbolic effects, symptoms, and choreographies of cultural performance. There were many physical/emotional experiences involved during the action, including a dangerous dance we rehearsed, which I have not described here. But in this performance, a spontaneous site-specific action *initiated* the theoretical reflections that can now be further explored in order to obtain a broader perspective on the political, rhetorical, and aesthetic issues involved in the reconfiguration of social space in a transitional society (in this case the former German Democratic Republic [GDR], but there are obvious connections with the workshops we held in Dresden, Ljubljana, and Havana).

I would argue that the economic, political, and cultural spaces can no longer be integrated by governmental agencies; furthermore, the articulation of community needs or disaffections takes place through discursive and spatial engagements among political factions (and minorities) despite and in opposition to the apparently democratic, cohesive discourse of the state. Especially in transitional economic and political arenas such as the former GDR or eastern Europe, governmentalized or "subjugated bodies" (Foucault) are transforming authorized discourses and practices of subject formation as part of an effort to reinvent themselves as political actors. I am interested in looking at the differences

between the identity movements in the United States and the "identity formations" in the former GDR (and in eastern Europe, especially
Slovenia and the Czech Republic, where I have worked on several occasions), organizing my writing and filmic postproduction research around
the case of the conflicted rhetoric of identity among local actors in
Eisenhüttenstadt, where, for example, our "occupation" of the Aktivist,
and the effort toward building a new cultural alternative center, could
be misconstrued as an act of nostalgia or sentimental recuperation of a
collectivist-proletarian culture. I propose to pay special attention to this
phantasmatic relation to a lost and discredited past. A unique opportunity may arise through our proposed integration of the Dokumentationszentrum Alltagskultur der DDR into the newly reconfigured Aktivist.

A very important dimension of this work will therefore involve the
question of the deconstruction of political or national/local identities in
a process of cultural transformation, which also problematizes the community's relationship to its *disengaged* or *disidentified past* (viz. the culture
of the former socialist regime). Recovering a grassroots space for cultural action at a time when the new capitalist market imperatives and
conservative government (promoting corporate interests and the hyper-
development of consumption) are deconstructing and dismantling the
social space which our identities require means that we need to understand the *territories* in which performative identities/relations are played
out and to examine how individuals and communities are situated in
fields of power.

This understanding also requires that the role of institutions and
media and the significance of government (state or local administrations) all need to be reevaluated in order to introduce new ideas for
performance or social theory and the fields they posit (the social actors
and bodies that struggle on behalf of themselves or their communities,
perhaps supported by the solidarity of transnational affiliations and the
informational and logistical help provided by NGOs). In conjunction
with Foucault's genealogies of governmentalized bodies/subjectivities
and Althusser's theory of ideological state apparatuses, it will be necessary to develop further the notion of "spatial practices" (de Certeau)
as informed by more recent (i.e., post–civil rights) feminist, liberation-
ist/postcolonial, postcommunist, minority, and queer struggles to secure
body-space, safe space, and communal space, which in many cases has
produced political subjectivities that are relatively autonomous of the
state/state apparatuses. I am particularly interested in the question of
securing social space through identity (national, ethnic, sexual) or communal needs (cf., in this context, Slavoy Žižek's and Renata Salecl's cri-

tique of identity movements based on their explorations of the *function of fantasy* in structuring power relations and psychic realities).

The notion of "spatial practices" and "unruly practices" can be extended by utilizing Pierre Bourdieu's concept of fields, which distinguishes among different performances by defining a field as constituted through and constitutive of a value (cultural capital) that organizes benefits and the struggles for them.[39] Such capital, possessed by performers within a field, is distinguishable and sustained as a value by virtue of the rules of an ongoing struggle in a field. One would have to evaluate what role activism and *Aktionskunst* play within such a field, how they can create deviant roles, or how practices of experimental ethnography relate to such deviancy and enter into processes of shared "evocation" that shift the relations of power in a given field. Possession of capital and control over the rules of its evaluation together constitute power (or "distinction"), that is to say, power is performative and a function of the value and rules of struggle within fields. Distinct accumulation of capital conveys specific material power. There are different forms of power, and its visibility is dependent on apprehending the fields in which it operates or the languages it uses. The forms of capital (symbolic, cultural, educational, political, social) and dimension of power are sustained through institutions that claim to possess the rules and the grammar within a field. However, as my example of the occupation-performance has shown, power always runs the risk of dispossession if the rules for distinguishing "capital" (and thus the fantasy of power) change. Artistic work, especially in its use of a range of media, functions precisely on the *imaging sites* of such fantasies of power, thereby disturbing the accumulated myths. It can contribute to the production of change since it has transformative strength. This is where the filmic term "postproduction" becomes wonderfully paradoxical. Each film we made in Eisenhüttenstadt generated a new chapter in the process and helped us to create our own countersurveillance of city hall.

My contribution to a field theory of performative relations (contra disembodiment and technological transcendentalism) therefore consists in shifting attention to the performative/local praxis of collaborative or communal struggle. The struggle is undertaken to increase the value and visibility of needs or desires—and its network of recognition—by imposing its actors' social capital (even though underrepresented, marginalized, or dispossessed) onto the political field, that is, *squatting* the field and its governing conditions (its property) in order to change or modify the rules of subject formation. This process, which I have described as a *real/fictive squatting* (creating publicity and public support in the unfolding) of a significant, symbolic "closed space" in the urban/ cultural fabric of the city, can succeed in bending the rules, appropriating the power of mediation/self-representation on the path to a more *legible claim*. In our case, the claiming of a building for culture is also the claiming of a space of expression for the hitherto nonexistent, nonlegible "freie Szene" in the city. The performance constituted a "freie Szene," and we forced the city administration to acknowledge this fact by sending their letters to our anonymous group. The action/project is constitutive of real subject-bodies and their communal cultural interests in future "urban planning," which produce conditions for making a previously impossible or unimagined claim.

Our media work is unending. We are now involved in monitoring the ongoing process of negotiations between the (semifictional) cultural cooperative and the city administration, as well as the mediating functions of press or community articulation. We are developing a "postproduction" script that analyzes the culture-in-action project (*Verschlossene Räume,* or *Closed Spaces*) and interprets the choreographies of the performative relations among the actors in the political field. We are therefore also ethnographers of our own constitutive and evolving reality as a performance group.

During 1996–97 we worked toward the completion of a documentary film on the events and the political process of negotiation in Eisenhüttenstadt. Additional on-site fieldwork was necessary in order to investigate the particular role and symptomology of the emergent Dokumentationszentrum Alltagskultur der DDR in the current context of ersatz nostalgia for the former GDR with special emphasis on the relations between memory and popular culture. This project of finding sites and modes of collecting memories, at a time when electronic media function precisely as "decollecting" technologies of simulation, could be discussed transculturally on the Net; a fruitful debate on these issues of local contests might be of interest to cultural workers elsewhere. As I have suggested throughout this book, the question of the future of utopia and our visions for future cultural "meeting grounds" and joint rehearsals of physical/virtual performance are at stake in any discussion of virtual realities.[40] Being a theory of performative relations, culture-in-action is first and foremost a physical project, a dance of being there, even if it occurs in transitional states, countries, territories, and always appears on the border of the technological media that serve as our extensions. We are not a world unto ourselves, but each of us can inform the practices of collaboration needed to sustain our claims that we exist and that our differences matter in terms of our recognition of others.

Parsifal-Epilogue

The reader, having opened this book and perused its cover image of a manipulated theater façade, may not be surprised to discover that my final remarks refer to an ethnographic project that succeeded the action in Eisenhüttenstadt. Inspired and disturbed by the Peruvian Grupo Chaclacayo's *Parsifal Prolog* in 1994, I entered into an exchange of letters, sketches, discussions, and meetings with this group, which gradually evolved into workshops and various plans for an extended collaborative experiment with local artists in Dresden to investigate the mythic material of Wagner's opera indirectly by confronting the ruined utopian architecture of what is left of the Hellerau colony itself.

In the fall of 1995 I traveled to Hellerau with Imma Sarries-Zgonc to live in the colony for two months and work with members of the Dresden-based Gruppe RU-IN on a fieldwork project we called "irritations." The idea of irritating the mythic content and cultural weight of the Wagner opera overlapped with our own intersubjective process of discovering differences among our aesthetic and political approaches and working methods. Increasingly tense and contentious communication with Grupo Chaclacayo led to the withdrawal of the Peruvian group. The disagreement was over the aesthetic direction of the collaboration, and the members of Grupo Chaclacayo decided that they didn't want to relinquish aesthetic control over their visual performance methodology. Our East German collaborators insisted on a nonstructured and more anarchic confrontation with the site itself, proposing to abandon conceptual grids and any formal method that might predetermine our ways of entering the field.

Our initial plan to displace the system of Wagner's sacred music drama through an investigation of the differences in our unconscious relationship to cultural constructions of utopian myth shifted toward the more disturbing realization of the ruptures in the stories we tell each other during the false rituals of rehearsal. Some rehearsals cannot cover what is not shared, while others will not reveal what happens to each of us in our experience of a spatial, historically burdened, and politically contaminated context, as the closed system of art locks us into its limited parameter. Stepping outside the parameter, we also need to recognize the preconceptions and fantasies we have of each other's working methods and the unconscious assumptions we form of the other.

However, the difficult period of living in the devastated colony, meeting and working each day in empty and damp rooms under the fallen-in roof, stumbling into the debris of objects and associations, expanded our sense of an overly full emptiness and brought us closer together in our patient listening to the silence, the rain, the birds on the roof, the falling plaster, the rumbling and screeching sounds of the found objects we dragged in and out of the dark halls. Before long we ran out of theories and concepts, and some of the objects we found seemed to remain uninterpretable. So each night we dispersed—examining the floors, cellars, walls, doors, and the paved gray square and overgrown gardens outside—before returning to the insides to begin our sound rehearsals, which consisted of movement and interactions with the space. How does one interact with a space that does not act? We began to treat the building as a kind of "score" or, rather, a broken instrument or echo chamber that we tried to empty of its echoes and semantic structures. We soon lost all interest in Wagner's opera, although some of us kept stumbling into the perverse ironies of excavated bones, monumental Red Army victory murals, bird droppings, jealous shadows, the sound of steel mesh, wires dangling from rotting ceilings in an abandoned building. The wound would heal, tired of its symbolism in the service of unlikely redemption.

Parsifal, an installation, is a work-in-progress developed in a specific site. It also triggers other engagements with the implications of our LBLM experiments with "interfaces" and the movement of memory in the era of the digital, when degeneration will have no place in the fantasies of technoscience. *Parsifal*, an installation, is an analog project, derived from degeneration and the back-and-forth movement of our failures to remain in sync. It makes less sense to speak of creation or performance; therefore let's say we have been working in the crumbling architecture of the empty theater at Hellerau, listening to the decomposition of corpses. The work insists on the redundancy of any theatrical gesture or representation; the architecture takes place as an acoustic choreography in fourteen different rooms of the dilapidated east wing of the Festspielhaus. Surveillance cameras are installed in every room so that viewers who don't wish to walk inside can watch the monitors on the threshold. They are silent. While the doors to the building remain locked, the "opening" is a movement solo by Imma Sarries-Zgonc in front of the Festspielhaus facade, modified with video stills applied by Jo Siamon Salich. The stills seem to capture moments from the ordinary late-night horror and science-fiction movies broadcast on German television, while Imma's movement is so slow that it is practically imperceptible. Lasting as long as Wagner's overture to the opera (sixteen minutes), it could resemble a white balancing, a weight balancing, a protracted silent dialogue with the huge, round saw blade discovered in the backyard. Its surface is smooth, its edges dangerously sharp. It is growing dark now, and the rain keeps splitting the focus. Eventually the doors open, and a cycle of fourteen actions is in process while the audience tries to locate itself among the fourteen rooms of the east wing and among the surveillance cameras. The main auditorium itself remains empty, closed and inaccessible, although the visitors can look into it from two second-storey windows.

The performers are unaware of each other's actions, although we have become attuned to each other's preoccupations and sensibilities, having learned to listen to every sound. The cycles of the installation-performance begin the slow and deliberate fragmentation of the Wagnerian myth of the grail/redemption in the modified architectural ruins of an abandoned German modernist utopia. How are we connected to such abandonment in our cultural unconscious? While working in the collective process, the performers individually act out their associations with the contaminated site and the terminal condition of a dead myth and its psychopathology. As a result, many of the simultaneous actions might appear accidental or circumstantial, severed from any allegiance to Wagner's score and libretto, removed from the "system" of a self-sufficient musical performance. No music from the opera is heard. All acoustic and electric sounds audible in the installation are produced by the performers interacting with the building. The only clearly marked interactions between performers occur during the three physical alterations of the interior "design" (suspended iron grids normally used for construction work) in the largest of the fourteen rooms. Otherwise, the individual actions are movement stills of "reconstruction." Some are based on acoustic "samplings" of the ruin, others on biographical stories and symptoms of the body, and still others on "leitmotifs" that explore the dangerous implications of dissonant resemblances with the racial ideology of blood sacrifice and purification that underlies Wagner's mysterious depiction of communion among the knights of the grail.[41] The installation-performance thus touches intimately on the concrete resonances of the ruined site: the perversion of utopian aspirations is everywhere visible, and Wagner's final opera is transformed into an empty shell, remembered as a failure precisely of its will to metaphysical and total power (the totality of the *Gesamtkunstwerk*), a lingering trauma of the epiphany of necessary bloodshed, the castrations and exclusions that consecrate the rites of purification.

When I leave the building later that night, I notice that the surveillance cameras are still on, as they always are, and some people are standing around watching the gray-blue light of the control monitors. **351** Being accustomed to seeing our images appear on screens during the editing process, I stay for a while, too, waiting for our images to appear. Then I realize that I have left for good, or that they have left, and my performance is no longer necessary. The cameras will transmit the spaces where we might have met.

Imma Sarries-Zgonc in *Parsifal,* opera installation/performance, Festspielhaus Hellerau, Dresden, Ninth Dresden Festival of Contemporary Music, Germany, 1995. Photo: J. Birringer.

N O T E S

1   This is the Theater That Was to Be Expected and Foreseen

1. See Mark Dery, *Escape Velocity: Cyberculture at the End of the Century* (New York: Grove, 1996), 153–69. For a computer engineer's view on optimal interfaces, see Brenda Laurel, *Computers as Theatre* (Reading, Mass.: Addison-Wesley, 1993).

2. Goran Stefanovski, *Sarajevo (Tales from a City)*, rpt. in *Performing Arts Journal* 47 (1994), 53.

3. See Susan Leigh Foster, *Choreographing History* (Bloomington: Indiana University Press, 1995), 18ff.

4. Marko Košnik, "Ples z jeziki razkosanih teles/Dance with Tongues of Severed Bodies," *Maska* 4, nos. 1–2 (1994), xix.

5. Walter Benjamin, "The Author as Producer," in *Reflections*, ed. Peter Demetz (New York: Harcourt Brace Jovanovich, 1978), 229.

6. Avital Ronell, *Finitude's Score: Essays for the End of the Millennium* (Lincoln: University of Nebraska Press, 1994), 1.

2   Corporealities and Digital Bodies

1. See Susan Leigh Foster, *Reading Dancing: Bodies and Subjects in Contemporary American Dance* (Berkeley: University of California Press, 1986), and Anna Halprin, *Moving Towards Life: Five Decades of Transformational Dance* (Hanover, N.H.: Wesleyan University Press/University Press of New England, 1995). For my earlier essay, see "Pina Bausch: Dancing across Borders," *Drama Review* 30, no. 2 (1986), 85–97.

2. Jacques Derrida's deconstruction of phenomenology and his interest in Mallarmé's "Mimique" and in Artaud have been noted in the field of poststructuralist theory. Julia Kristeva and Hélène Cixous were instrumental, among French feminists, in addressing bodily writing and dancing bodies. But the most provocative revision of dance history and criticism has emerged from dance and performance studies, especially the group of scholars invited by Susan Foster (University of California–Riverside) to participate in the 1992 research project "Choreographing History." A small flood of books has now emerged, claiming, almost in the style of manifestos, the creation of a complex new critical repertoire of interdisciplinary "dialogues" with bodily discourses and promoting "choreography" as a central metaphor for the temporal, spatial, and political dynamics of cultural theory. The work that has thus far been published is truly exciting and wide-ranging, even though the self-congratulatory tone of the complex academic performances occasionally reminds me of Robert Wilson's or Martha Graham's late work. See, for example, Susan Leigh Foster, ed., *Choreographing History* (Bloomington: Indiana University Press, 1995) and her *Corporealities: Dancing Knowledge, Culture and Power* (London: Routledge, 1996); Marta E. Savigliano, *Tango and the Political Economy of Passion* (Boulder, Colo.: Westview Press, 1995); Mark Franco, *Dancing Modernism/Performing Politics* (Bloomington: Indiana University Press, 1995); Ellen W. Goellner and Jacqueline Shea Murphy, eds., *Bodies of*

354

the Text: Dance as Theory, Literature as Dance (New Brunswick, N.J.: Rutgers University Press, 1995); Barbara Downing, *Samba: Resistance in Motion* (Bloomington: Indiana University Press, 1995); Andrew J. Strathern, *Body Thoughts* (Ann Arbor: University of Michigan Press, 1996); Sally Ann Ness, *Body, Movement and Culture: Kinesthetic and Visual Symbolism in a Philippine Community* (Philadelphia: University of Pennsylvania Press, 1992); Ramsay Burt, *The Male Dancer: Bodies, Spectacle, Sexualities* (London: Routledge, 1995); Michèle Febvre, *Danse contemporaine et théâtralité* (Paris: Editions Chiron, 1995); Helen Thomas, *Dance, Modernity and Culture: Explorations in the Sociology of Dance* (London: Routledge, 1995), and Randy Martin, *Performance as Political Act: The Embodied Self* (New York: Bergin and Harvey, 1990). There is also a growing number of important revisionary dance histories. See Susan Manning, *Ecstasy and the Demon: Feminism and Nationalism in the Dances of Mary Wigman* (Berkeley: University of California Press, 1993); Ann Daly, *Done into Dance: Isadora Duncan in America* (Bloomington: Indiana University Press, 1995); and Christy Adair, *Women and Dance* (New York: New York University Press, 1992).

3. For the "mattering" of bodies and the volatile debate surrounding poststructuralist or semiotic and phenomenological accounts of bodily reality, see: Judith Butler, *Bodies that Matter: On the Discursive Limits of "Sex"* (New York: Routledge, 1993); Elizabeth Grosz, *Volatile Bodies: Toward a Corporeal Feminism* (Bloomington: Indiana University Press, 1994); Rosalyn Diprose and Robyn Ferrell, eds., *Cartographies: Poststructuralism and the Mapping of Bodies and Spaces* (Sydney: Allen and Unwin, 1991); Chris Shilling, *The Body and Social Theory* (London: Sage Publications, 1993); Juliet Flower MacCannell and Laura Zakarin, eds., *Thinking Bodies* (Stanford, Calif.: Stanford University Press, 1994); Moira Gatens, *Ethics, Power and Corporeality* (New York: Routledge, 1996); Robyn Wiegman, *American Anatomies: Theorizing Race and Gender* (Durham, N.C.: Duke University Press, 1995); and Stanton B. Garner Jr., *Bodied Spaces: Phenomenology and Performance in Contemporary Drama* (Ithaca, N.Y.: Cornell University Press, 1994). For additional bibliographic references to current theories of bodies, see the notes accompanying chapter 9.

4. Sarah Thornton, *Club Cultures: Music, Media and Subcultural Capital* (Hanover, N.H.: Wesleyan University Press/University Press of New England, 1996), 4. For an important study on the relations between music, popular culture, and technology, see Simon Frith, *Performing Rites: On the Value of Popular Music* (Cambridge: Harvard University Press, 1996).

5. Here I want to emphasize the international dimension that was clearly built into the vision of the utopian community as a whole. Visitors to Hellerau in 1912–13 included Stanislavski, Stravinsky, Kokoschka, Pavlova, Diaghilev, Nijinsky, Rilke, Le Corbusier, Shaw, Granville-Barker, Zweig, Claudel, Pitoeff, Tzara, Kropotkin, and many others. My narrative relies on documents, photos, and architectural designs I was shown during my residencies in 1994–96 at Hellerau and its newly constituted independent Förderverein für die Europäische Werkstatt für Kunst und Kultur, which has successfully tried to rescue the ruined site from further neglect. On Hellerau, see Karl Lorenz, *Wege nach Hellerau* (Dresden: Hellerau Verlag, 1994); Hans-Jürgen Sarfert, *Hellerau: Die Gartenstadt und Künstlerkolonie* (Dresden: Hellerau Verlag, 1993); and Richard C. Beacham, "Appia, Jaques-Dalcroze, and Hellerau," *New Theatre Quarterly* 2 (1964), 154–64 (Part 1) and 245–61 (Part 2).

6. Daly, *Done into Dance*, 127.

7. Ibid., 138–39. For a more politicized, revisionist interpretation of Duncan's ex-

pressionism and staging of feminine subjectivity, see Franko, *Dancing Modernism/Performing Politics*, 1–24.

8. Isadora Duncan's essay "The Dancer of the Future" was written in 1902 and first published in 1928. It is collected in *The Twentieth-Century Performance Reader*, ed. Michael Huxley and Noel Witts (London: Routledge, 1996); quote on p. 161.

9. I am carefully echoing the feminist and *völkisch* terms Susan Manning has introduced in her elaborate and often fascinating critical study of Wigman's dances, including her extension and subversion of expressionism and her ambivalent complicity with fascist projections of essentialized national identity. Obviously the term *Gemeinschaft* has connotations in the Hellerau context that are vastly different from those of the Nazi era. The dream of Hellerau's art community was already over by the end of World War I. For Manning's views on Hellerau and Wigman's feminist emancipation in the 1920s, see her *Ecstasy and the Demon*, 47–130.

10. Manning is critical of the ideology of modernist theories of "absolute dance" and scrutinizes the changing cultural spaces in which such ideologies become associated with forms and practices of dance. Instead of "absolute dance" Manning uses the German phrase "Gestalt im Raum," which she translates as "configuration of energy in space" based on reviews that described Wigman in performance, not as a character or persona but as a "design in space." This may be an interesting miscomprehension of the metaphysical connotations of the German words *Gestalt* and *Figur* used by the reviewers. See Manning, *Ecstasy and the Demon*, 15–84.

11. Hillel Schwartz, "Torque: The New Kinaesthetic of the Twentieth Century," *Zone 6 (Incorporations)*, ed. Jonathan Crary and Sanford Kwintner (Cambridge: MIT Press, 1992), 71–127; quotes on pp. 73–77 et passim.

12. Wassily Kandinsky, *Concerning the Spiritual in Art* (New York: Wittenborn, Schultz, 1947), 66.

13. Herbert Blau's fascinating critique of bodily disciplines and the history of acting techniques starts out with a rereading of Trotzky's *Literature and Revolution* and spirals its way forward through the corporeal self-dismemberments of recent body art. See the chapter "The Surpassing Body," in his book *To All Appearances: Ideology and Performance* (New York: Routledge, 1992), 87–126. My reflections on Hellerau/Laban are supported by Ana Sanchez-Colberg's inspiring critical interpretation of physical theater and its roots in dance; see her article "Altered States and Subliminal Spaces: Charting the Road towards a Physical Theatre," *Performance Research* 1, no. 2 (1996), 40–56.

14. See Rudolf Laban, *A Life for Dance*, trans. Lisa Ullmann (New York: Theatre Arts Books, 1975), 87ff; quote on p. 89.

15. See Beacham, "Appia, Jaques-Dalcroze, and Hellerau—Part 1," 154–64; the Salzmann quote appears in Part 2, p. 251.

16. Adolphe Appia, "Acteur, espace, lumière, peinture" [1919], *Théâtre populaire* 5 (1954), 40 (my translation).

17. Appia's commentary on the mise-en-scène of *Orpheus and Eurydice* is quoted in Part 2 of Beacham's article, pp. 256–58.

18. Manning, *Ecstasy and the Demon*, 41.

19. Walter Gropius, *The New Architecture and the Bauhaus*, trans. P. Morton Shand (New York: Museum of Modern Art, 1937), 65–66. See also Walter Gropius, ed., *The Theater of the Bauhaus* (Middletown, Conn.: Wesleyan University Press, 1961), which includes "Man

and Art Figure," Oskar Schlemmer's most significant description of his conception of the *Kunstfigur*. For Kandinsky's role, see Clark V. Poling, *Kandinsky's Teaching at the Bauhaus: Color Theory and Analytical Drawing* (New York: Rizzoli, 1986). For a discussion of the overlapping concepts of technological art in Russia and the West, see Christina Lodder, "The VKhUTEMAS and the Bauhaus," in *The Avant-Garde Frontier: Russia Meets the West, 1910–1930*, ed. Gail Harrison Roman and Virginia Hagelstein Marquardt (Gainesville: University Press of Florida, 1992), 196–237. For a critique of indirectly protofascist/Stalinist visions of aesthetic totalities, see Boris Groys, *The Total Art of Stalinism: Avant-Garde, Aesthetic Dictatorship, and Beyond*, trans. Charles Rougle (Princeton, N.J.: Princeton University Press, 1992), esp. 3–74.

20. Schlemmer, "Man and Art Figure," 25–28. I should note that the masculine pronouns throughout Schlemmer's text refer to the German masculine noun *der Mensch;* it is also obvious that Schlemmer is not concerned or conscious about his gender assumptions, preferring to think in abstract terms about the "human form," translating two-dimensional shapes on canvas into three-dimensional space.

21. Ibid., 29.

22. For a more extensive description of the context of my encounter with Slovenian artists, see my article "The Utopia of Postutopia," *Theatre Topics* 6, no. 2 (1996), 143–66.

23. This manifesto is quoted from a CD text leaflet accompanying *Krst pod Triglavom*.

24. Unless otherwise noted, all references are to recorded/videotaped interviews with Slovene artists made during my visits.

25. The use of German in the titles and references to Slovene artists is significant; nor should Živadinov's obsession with Potočnik's research be underestimated. Laibach, an NSK band referred to earlier in this chapter, is in fact the German name for Ljubljana and was used during the Nazi occupation in the forties. The NSK design department has now republished Potočnik's original book in German, which appeared in Slovenia in 1993.

26. Malevich referred to his pictorial experimentations as "alogical" or "transrational," and a similar transrationalism has been attributed to his friend Velimir Khlebnikov's futurist prose poems. Slovene theater director Marko Peljhan has adapted Khlebnikov's writing conceptually in several of his projects, especially his current *LADOMIR FAKTURA* surfaces; see my article "The Utopia of Postutopia." The First Surface is an extraordinary electronic re-composition of Kandinsky's 1928 paintings for Mussorgsky's musical portrait *Pictures at an Exhibition*, and thus functions as a contemporary simulation of the "spiritual in art" in the late age of technological reproducibility. For the context of Peljhan's work, see Velimir Khlebnikov, *The King of Time: Selected Writings of the Russian Futurist*, trans. Paul Schmidt and ed. Charlotte Douglas (Cambridge: Harvard University Press, 1985). For a critical discussion of futurism and suprematism that illuminates some of these connections, see the essay by Magdalena Dabrowski, "Malevich and Mondrian: Nonobjective Form as the Expression of the 'Absolute,'" in *The Avant-Garde Frontier*, 145–68.

3 Dance Screens

1. Stelarc, Home Page <http://www.merlin.com.au/stelarc/>. The version I downloaded was shown on the Web on October 14, 1996. Used with permission.

2. See Brenda Laurel, *Computers as Theatre* (New York: Addison-Wesley, 1993). For the

most extensive critical reading of Stelarc's performances, see Mark Dery, *Escape Velocity:*   **357**
Cyberculture at the End of the Century (New York: Grove, 1996), 153–69. For earlier statements
on Stelarc's performance aesthetics, see the catalogue *Obsolete Body/Suspensions/Stelarc,* ed.
James D. Paffrath with Stelarc (Davis, Calif.: JP Publications, 1984).

3. See William Gibson, *Neuromancer* (New York: Dell, 1984). For a feminist critique of
sexual connotations in cyberspace fictions, see Claudia Springer, *Electronic Eros: Bodies and
Desire in the Postindustrial Age* (Austin: University of Texas Press, 1996).

4. Simon Frith, *Performing Rites: On the Value of Popular Music* (Cambridge: Harvard
University Press, 1996), 239–40. For a pathbreaking musical analysis of Anderson's per-
formances, see Susan McClary's brilliant essay "This Is Not a Story My People Tell:
Musical Time and Space According to Laurie Anderson," in her book *Feminine Endings:
Music, Gender, and Sexuality* (Minneapolis: University of Minnesota Press, 1991), 132–47.

5. Quotations from Anderson's songs refer to the recording of *United States* (Warner
Brothers Records, 9 25192–1, 1984) and the film of *Home of the Brave* (recorded during a
concert tour in Japan and released with Japanese subtitles).

6. Sally Banes has commented on the collectivism of the group in a chapter of her
book entitled "The Reinvention of Community": "The second striking aspect of the Judson Dance Theater . . . is that the JDT seemed to supply a work life indissolubly woven
together with a social life. . . . The Judson dance workshops were rich in community
feeling, deeply linking work and play. This utopian feeling of unalienated, socially rooted
labor attracted artists from various other disciplines. . . . That is, Judson Dance Theater became a metacommunity of sorts where the different communities revolving around
single arts disciplines coalesced and where interdisciplinary imagination flourished."
Greenwich Village 1963 (Durham, N.C.: Duke University Press, 1993), 72–73.

7. Bianca van Dillen and Mari-Jan Boer, the directors of the Dutch "Stamina Choreographic Computer Atelier," kindly gave me hands-on training with LifeForms during
the 1996 "Connecting Bodies" Conference at Amsterdam's School for New Dance Development (SNDO). I quote from their descriptive manual:

> LifeForms allows you to create movement for multiple articulated figures, particu-
> larly realistic movement for human figures. Movement sequences may be used in
> animations, dance choreography, games, multimedia titles, sports, movement edu-
> cation, space visualization and various uses in human motion studies. For the dance
> maker, it provides the opportunity to work on his or her own to prepare new or
> modify existing choreography without dancers. LifeForms includes all the tools you
> need to create and design movement on a computer for human figure and character
> animation. You can position and move individual body parts using the mouse and
> joint-specific potentiometers. . . . LifeForms facilitates the composition of complex
> movement through its intuitive and powerful interface. There are three distinctive
> views: the spatial view, the sequence editor and the temporal view. With these views,
> the animator can construct an animation conceptually in terms of time, space and
> interactions between figures. The figure in LifeForms is not liable to gravitation, you
> can jump, fly, etc., so you have to simulate gravity using the program. The animator
> has access to stored libraries of predefined sequences for walking, dance, sports and
> others. To reduce time and effort, these motions can be inserted directly into your
> animation sequence or modified as needed.

8. See John Belton, "Looking Through Video: The Psychology of Video and Film," in *Resolutions,* ed. Michael Renov and Erika Suderburg (Minneapolis: University of Minnesota Press, 1996), 61–72. Belton offers a good critical introduction to these issues of technology and perception. I am also indebted to Ron Burnett's wide-ranging critical investigation of video images and the indeterminate relations between film/video projection and the *viewer's projection* of meanings into the event. See his *Cultures of Vision: Images, Media, and the Imaginary* (Bloomington: Indiana University Press, 1995).

9. Susan Sontag, "For Available Light: A Brief Lexicon," *Art in America* 71 (December 1983), 102. I want to thank Henry Sayre for drawing my attention to Sontag's response. See his highly perceptive interpretation of postmodern dance in *The Object of Performance: The American Avant-Garde Since 1970* (Chicago: University of Chicago Press, 1989), 101–44.

10. Paul Virilio, *The Aesthetics of Disappearance,* trans. Philip Beitchman (New York: semiotext(e), 1991), 104. Jean Baudrillard and Arthur Kroker have intensified such projections of disappearing subjectivity and the implosion between simulation and reality. For a critique of Baudrillard's "cyberpunk" sociology, see Douglas Kellner, *Media Culture* (London: Routledge, 1995), 297–330, and Verena Andermatt Conley, ed., *Re-Thinking Technologies* (Minneapolis: University of Minnesota Press, 1993), esp. 173–90.

11. Unless noted otherwise, all references to Wim Vandekeybus are drawn from the transcriptions I made of his remarks in *The Power of Dance,* the first segment of a PBS-produced series (1993) directed by Geoff Dunlop and narrated by Raoul Trujillo. Quoted with the permission of Thirteen/WNET New York.

12. André Lepecki, "Breaking the Rules of Presence: Thoughts on the New York Dance," *tanz aktuell/ballett international* 7 (July 1994), 28. See also Lepecki's wonderful and moving essay "Embracing the Stain: Notes on the Time of Dance," *Performance Research* 1, no. 1 (1996), 103–7, which delineates a closely shared concern with a new ethics of time.

13. See Mary Russo, *The Female Grotesque* (New York: Routledge, 1994). In the West, more recent discussions of the grotesque body are indebted to Bakhtin's concept of grotesqueness as elaborated in *Rabelais and His World.* It would be fruitful to compare his views with Latino and Chicano cultural expressions of death, the body, and bodily humor. See, e.g., Tomás Ybarra-Frausto, "Rasquachismo: A Chicano Sensibility," in *Chicano Art: Resistance and Affirmation* (Los Angeles, Calif.: Wight Art Gallery, 1991), 155–62.

14. Pina Bausch, "Not How People Move but What Moves Them," interview by the author, 9 November 1978, in Norbert Servos, *Pina Bausch Wuppertal Dance Theater, or, The Art of Training a Goldfish* (Cologne: Ballett-Bühnenverlag, 1984), 230.

15. Pina Bausch, interview in *Bilder . . . aus Stücken der Pina Bausch,* dir. Kay Kirchmann. Metrovision Film, 1990.

16. See N. Katherine Hayles, "Embodied Virtuality: Or How to Put Bodies back into the Picture," in *Immersions in Technology: Art and Virtual Environments,* ed. Mary Ann Moser with Douglas MacLeod (Cambridge: MIT Press, 1996), 1–28. Hayles and her colleagues write about a three-year Art and Virtual Environments Project at the Banff Center in Canada which resulted in nine large-scale exhibition-installations.

17. Heidi Gilpin, "Digital Dynamism: Technologies of Movement Performance," lecture-demonstration held 16 June 1996 at the "Connecting Bodies" conference, School of New Dance Development, Amsterdam. I had seen the CD-ROM before I met with Gilpin, but I am very grateful for her many insightful and provocative explications. I also want to acknowledge the work of Canadian dance researcher Susan Kozel, who has been

at the forefront of opening dance practice and theory to VR technologies. See her articles **359**
"Choreographing Cyberspace: An Assessment of the Possibility for Dance in Virtual Re-
ality," *Dance Theatre Journal* 11, no. 2 (1994), and "Space Making: Experiences of a Virtual
Body," *Dance Theatre Journal* 11, no. 3 (1994). She also gave an eloquent lecture on "The
Virtual World: New Frontiers for Dance and Philosophy" at the 1995 "Border Tensions"
dance conference at the University of Surrey, England.

18. Quoted from William Forsythe's program notes to *Eidos: Telos*, published by the
Frankfurt Ballet, 1995.

4 Lively Bodies–Lively Machines: A Workshop

1. The "Connected Body?" workshop/conference took place 21–28 August 1994. Organized by Scott deLahunta and Ric Allsopp, who represent an international partnership
(Writing Research Associates) in creative work, consultancy, and education, the event
was hosted by SNDO in Amsterdam. The main ideas, concepts, and workshop discussions were published; see *The Connected Body?* (Amsterdam: Amsterdam School of the Arts,
1996).

2. For a more comprehensive description of Deborah Hay's dance philosophy, see
her profoundly inspiring book *Lamb at the Altar: The Story of a Dance* (Durham, N.C.: Duke
University Press, 1994).

3. The "Bodies of Influence/Connecting Bodies" conference/workshop was held 9–
21 June 1996, again organized by Allsopp and deLahunta, with Suzanne Epstein and
Dennis Gillanders, and held at SNDO. Text references are to the weekend conference
on the connections between dance and technology. Direct quotations are from my video
transcription and from additional transcripts kindly provided by Scott deLahunta. I wish
to thank the authors for permission to quote them. I especially want to thank Diana Theodores for her incisive and challenging synopsis of the various media demonstrations and
theoretical premises she focused on under the rubric "technography," the term she coined
to address the mutually informing processes of technology and choreography.

4. References to *Dancing with the Virtual Dervish: Virtual Body* are drawn from *Immersed in Technology: Art and Virtual Environments*, ed. Mary Ann Moser (Cambridge: MIT
Press, 1996).

5. References to "The Cave" and the work of David Rokeby are based on my on-
site visits to the Electronic Visualization Laboratory (University of Illinois) and Gallery
2 (Chicago Art Institute). Paul Sermon and Rokeby were featured in the exhibit "The
Presence of Touch," organized by the Department of Fiber, 20 Sept.–1 Nov. 1996. Other
important video and digital art exhibitions include "Rites of Passage: Art for the End
of the Century" (London: Tate Gallery, 1995), "Sonambiente" (Berlin: 1996), "Being &
Time: The Emergence of Video Projection" (Buffalo: Albright-Knox Art Gallery, 1996),
and "Mediascape" (New York: Guggenheim Museum, 1996).

6. The "Lively Bodies–Lively Machines" (LBLM) workshop took place 10–19 July
1996, merging with "Split Screen," an interdisciplinary international arts conference exploring the relationship between the arts and technology. Organized by Chris Butler, the
event was held at the Chichester Institute of Higher Education in Chichester, England.
For our resource text on cyborgs, we utilized Margaret Morse's essay "What Do Cyborgs
Eat? Oral Logic in an Information Society," in *Technologies on the Brink*, ed. Gretchen Ben-

der and Timothy Druckrey (Seattle: Bay Press, 1994), 157–89. The proceedings of the workshop/conference were edited and published by Butler (forthcoming). A video of the LBLM proceedings can be purchased directly from AlienNation Co. The workshop will be taught in Dresden each summer, as well as in other locations.

5   Performance/Video Art

1. See Roberto Aparici, Manuel Mandivia, and Augustín García Matilla, *La imagen,* 2 vols. (Madrid: UNED, 1987); Roberto Aparici, *Lectura de imágenes* (Madrid: UNED, 1989), idem, ed., *La revolución de los medios audiovisuales* (Madrid: Ediciones de la Torre, 1993). The video *La imagen* (1988) was produced in conjunction with the book Aparici coauthored.

2. Walter Benjamin, *Das Passagen-Werk,* in *Gesammelte Schriften,* vol. V.2, ed. Rolf Tiedemann (Frankfurt: Suhrkamp, 1982), 1026 (my translation). For an introduction to Benjamin's "materialist pedagogy," see Susan Buck-Morss's comprehensive study *The Dialects of Seeing* (Cambridge: MIT Press, 1989), 287–330. Gregory Ulmer has written the most provocative Benjaminian theory of video pedagogy to date; see his *Teletheory: Grammatology in the Age of Video* (New York: Routledge, 1989), esp. chapter 3 on "Mystory," 82–112. For teachers and artists interested in the current "critical pedagogy" movement, I recommend the following: Henry Giroux, *Border Crossings: Cultural Workers and the Politics of Education* (New York: Routledge, 1992) and *Disturbing Pleasures: Learning Popular Culture* (New York: Routledge, 1994); Henry Giroux and Peter McLaren, eds., *Between Borders: Pedagogy and the Politics of Cultural Studies* (New York: Routledge, 1994); and Becky W. Thompson and Sangeeta Tyagi, eds., *Beyond a Dream Deferred* (Minneapolis: University of Minnesota Press, 1993). My friend and video teacher, Deborah Leveranz—who invited Aparici to Houston and was artistic director of the Southwest Alternate Media Project—was involved in developing media-literacy outreach programs in Texas high schools and has written the most significant blueprints for such video pedagogy in the United States to date. In a special issue dedicated to "Media in the Schools," Leveranz and West Coast media activist Kathleen Tyner coauthored the programmatic essay "Inquiring Minds Want to Know: What Is Media Literacy?" *The Independent* 16, no. 7 (1993), 20–25. See also Matthew Sommerville, "Whether Maps: Pedagogic Strategies in Recent Video," *Afterimage* 18, no. 5 (1990), 10–13; and David Trend, "To Tell the Truth: Strategies of Media Literacy," *Afterimage* 18, no. 8 (1991), 12–14.

3. For critical discussions on the globalization of media and the emerging "video culture," see Sean Cubitt, *Timeshift: On Video Culture* (London: Routledge, 1991); Roy Armes, *On Video* (New York: Routledge, 1988); Cynthia Schneider and Brian Wallis, eds., *Global Television* (New York: Wedge Press, 1988); E. Ann Kaplan, *Rocking around the Clock: Music Television, Postmodernism and Consumer Culture* (New York: Routledge, 1987); and Armand Mattelart, Xavier Delcourt, and Michelle Mattelart, *International Image Markets* (London: Comedia, 1984).

4. References to the theories of Vostell, Paik, and Acconci are drawn from interviews and catalogue texts cited by John G. Hanhardt in his essay "Décollage/Collage: Anmerkungen zu einer Neuuntersuchung der Ursprünge der Videokunst." This essay, together with extensive biographies and "videographies" of the artists featured at the

Cologne exhibition, appeared in the exhibition catalogue *Video-Skulptur: retrospektiv und ak-*   **361**
tuell 1963-1989, ed. Wulf Herzogenrath and Edith Decker (Cologne: DuMont, 1989).

5. Carolee Schneemann, *More than "Meat Joy": Complete Performance Works & Selected Writings,* ed. Bruce McPherson (New Paltz, N.Y.: Documentext, 1979), 21.

6. Increasingly, book-length catalogues on the works of some of the more well-known video artists are now being published in conjunction with exhibitions. See, for example, *Paik-Video,* ed. Edith Decker (Cologne: DuMont, 1988); *Muntadas: trabajos recentes* (Valencia, Spain: IVAM Centre del Carme, 1992); *Bill Viola,* ed. Alexander Pühringer (Salzburg: Salzburger Kunstverein, 1993); *Gary Hill* (Seattle: Henry Art Gallery, 1994); *Francesc Torres: Belchite/South Bronx* (Amherst, Mass.: University Gallery, 1988); *Francesc Torres: Plus Ultra* (Berlin: DAAD, 1988); *Klaus vom Bruch: Arbeiten 1987-89* (Düsseldorf: Städtische Kunsthalle, 1989); *Resolution: A Critique of Video Art* (Los Angeles: LACE, 1986); *Image World: Art and Media Culture* (New York: Whitney Museum of American Art, 1989); *Video Spaces: Eight Installations* (New York: MoMA, 1995). See also Roswitha Mueller, *Valie Export: Fragments of the Imagination* (Bloomington: Indiana University Press, 1994). Given the ephemeral nature of video exhibitions and the relatively short life expectancy of tapes, these exhibition catalogues have become a vital documentary source for historical scholarship on video art.

7. Margot Lovejoy, *Postmodern Currents: Art and Artists in the Age of Electronic Media* (Ann Arbor, Mich.: UMI Research Press, 1989), 243. Having seen most of the work she describes, I continue to be impressed by her critical intuition and her comprehensive scholarship. I have used her book in my media/art classes, where students found it extremely helpful.

8. See Bonnie Marranca, "The Century Turning: International Events," *PAJ* 35-36 (1990), 66-74.

9. Simon Watney, *Policing Desire: Pornography, AIDS and the Media* (Minneapolis: University of Minnesota Press, 1987).

10. The radio workshop, held at Lou Mallozzi's Experimental Sound Studio, was a component of Guillermo Gómez-Peña/Coco Fusco's three-month residency in Chicago during their *Year of the White Bear* multimedia project, which I describe in my forthcoming book *Border-Work.* We composed a series of idiosyncratic multicultural and multilingual "public service announcements" commenting on white paranoia about "aliens" and other social issues such as AIDS, "English Only," racism, and homophobia. The PSAs were later recorded onto a cassette and privately distributed to friends and friendly radio stations. In the summer of 1993 the soundtrack was also installed as background music in public elevators at the Chicago Cultural Center.

11. My interpretive synopsis of the S-LV activities is based on the following: personal conversations; my own viewing of some of the tapes and their sitings; a talk given by Iñigo Manglano-Ovalle at the "National Symposium on Integrated Arts and Curricular Innovation," Northwestern University, 7 October 1995; and a summary of the project by curator Mary Jane Jacob published in *Culture in Action/Sculpture Chicago* (Seattle: Bay Press, 1995), 76-87. I have described my personal relations with another youth group, Ojos del Pueblo, in my forthcoming book *Border-Work.* I am grateful to the community artists in Chicago for sharing their work experience with me. I am also indebted to a follow-up report on the continuing and expanding life of the S-LV collective; see Melissa Bargar-Hughes's interview with the young members, "Smells like Teen Spirit: Getting it Straight

from Street-Level Video," *New Art Examiner* 23, no. 6 (1996), 34–37. During my research for this chapter, I also participated in events organized by another community arts alliance, "Insight Arts/End of the Ladder," in the Rogers Park neighborhood. I am grateful to Craig Harshaw for inviting me; for a provocative insider manifesto on the obstacles faced by community artists and activists, see his "Dissolving into Everything: A Personal Look at Art and Community," *P-FORM* 27 (1993), 5–7.

6 *Ad Mortem:* An AIDS Performance Project

1. Documentation is based on my notes and video recordings assembled during 1990–91. Some of the references I cite are examples of the broad range of critical, activist, and artistic responses to AIDS and its representation in the dominant media and political/medical institutions. Much of the social work done by church, support, and community groups still remains underreported. For the role of video within the contemporary context of AIDS, as a sociocultural and sociopolitical communication and intervention tool, see the special issue of *Video Guide* (10, nos. 3–4 [1989]) and various issues of *Afterimage* and *The Independent* published in 1989–90. Many of the videos that document alternative-media interventions are available under the title *Video against AIDS* (a series curated by John Greyson and Bill Horrigan, produced by Kate Horsfield) from the Video Data Bank in Chicago and New York and from V/Tape in Toronto; most other currently available videos can be obtained from ACT UP/NY and GMHC (New York) or through other alternative-media centers across the country. For information on the exhibitions and activities organized by VISUAL AIDS for the annual AIDS Awareness Day, write to: VISUAL AIDS, 108 Leonard Street (13th Floor), New York, NY 10013. For the *Seeing through AIDS* video guide, write to Media Network, 39 West 14th Street (Suite 403), New York, NY 10011.

2. For a self-description of the trajectory of Deborah Hay's dance practice, see her article "Playing Awake: Letters to My Daughter," *Drama Review* 33, no. 4 (1989), 70–74. A more expansive meditation and reflection on "practicing the perception of dying" and "inviting being seen" can be found in Hay's extraordinary dance book *Lamb at the Altar: The Story of a Dance* (Durham, N.C.: Duke University Press, 1994).

3. See, e.g., William Alexander, "Clearing Space: AIDS Theatre in Atlanta," *TDR* 34, no. 3 (1990), 109–28; Douglas Crimp, ed., *AIDS: Cultural Analysis, Cultural Activism* (Cambridge: MIT Press, 1988); Brian Wallis, ed., *Democracy: A Project by Group Material* (Seattle: Bay Press, 1990); Simon Watney, *Policing Desire: Pornography, AIDS, and the Media* (Minneapolis: University of Minnesota Press, 1987); David Wojnarowicz, *Tongues of Flame* (Normal: University Galleries of Illinois State University, 1990).

4. See Crimp, *AIDS,* 73.

5. Wojnarowicz, *Tongues of Flame,* 106, 89.

6. Examining whether and how communities are mobilized around the AIDS issue as a health crisis, one quickly discovers the kinds of discrepancies on the microlevel described by Jan Zita Grover in her comparison of New York and San Francisco:

> In any meaningful terms, I don't think there is such a thing as *the* AIDS epidemic in the United States. It's a useful fiction for the federal government, the politicians, and the media, who so radically simplify everything, but in point of fact, there is no trans-

national AIDS epidemic except at the levels of federal policy, funding, and national media. Instead there is a series of local epidemics that are very different in terms of who is affected, what is funded, and whether official and voluntary responses are just stonewalling or something positive and effective." (quoted in Wallis, *Democracy,* 248)

7. In the fall of 1991, the interactive exhibition was also shown at Atlanta's Peachtree Center during a conference of communications scholars, and sections subsequently traveled to other sites or entered into exchanges with teachers and activists on other campuses in the United States. The process also involved duplicating and disseminating materials and advocating the use of these tools in the classroom.

The following books were utilized in our *AIDS Interfacings* workshop/exhibition and consulted during subsequent analysis and research. These titles are part of a growing and invigorating production of social, cultural, and artistic analysis of AIDS representations and varieties of activism; I have focused more directly on studies that engage media production and criticism, excluding local publications, newspapers of the alternative and gay press, leaflets, pamphlets, and 'zines that have most certainly contributed to or even facilitated the gradual emergence of critical media theory in the fields of gay/lesbian studies, social studies, and cultural and performance studies: Cindy Patton, *Sex and Germs: The Politics of AIDS* (Boston: South End Press, 1985); Mary Catherine Bateson and Richard Goldsby, *Thinking AIDS* (Reading, Mass.: Addison-Wesley, 1988); Elizabeth Fee and Daniel M. Fox, eds., *AIDS: The Burdens of History* (Berkeley: University of California Press, 1988); Sander L. Gilman, *Disease and Representation* (Ithaca, N.Y.: Cornell University Press, 1988); Chris Jennings, *Understanding and Preventing AIDS* (Cambridge: Health Alert Press, 1988); Ines Rider and Patricia Ruppelt, *AIDS: The Women* (San Francisco: Cleis Press, 1988); Erica Carter and Simon Watney, eds. *Taking Liberties* (London: Serpent's Tail, 1989); Larry Kramer, *Reports from the Holocaust: The Making of an AIDS Activist* (New York: St. Martin's, 1989); Panos Dossier, *AIDS and the Third World* (Philadelphia: New Society Publishers, 1989); Monroe E. Price, *Shattered Mirrors: Our Search for Identity and Community in the AIDS Era* (Cambridge: Harvard University Press, 1989); ACT UP/NY Women and AIDS Book Group, eds., *Women, AIDS, and Activism* (Boston: South End Press, 1990); Tessa Boffin and Sunil Gupta, eds., *Ecstatic Antibodies: Resisting the AIDS Mythology* (London: Rivers Oram Press, 1990); Douglas Crimp, with Adam Rolston, *AIDS Demographics* (Seattle: Bay Press, 1990); Lawrence O. Gostin, ed., *AIDS and the Health Care System* (New Haven: Yale University Press, 1990); Stephen R. Graubard, ed., *Living with AIDS* (Cambridge: MIT Press, 1990); Mirko D. Grmek, *History of AIDS* (Princeton: Princeton University Press, 1990); Elizabeth M. Osborn, *The Way We Live Now: American Plays and the AIDS Crisis* (New York: Theater Communications Group, 1990); Cindy Patton, *Inventing AIDS* (New York: Routledge, 1990); Charles Perrow and Mauro F. Guillén, *The AIDS Disaster* (New Haven: Yale University Press, 1990); Stephen Schecter, *The AIDS Notebooks* (Albany: State University of New York Press, 1990); Jane M. Gaines, *Contested Culture: The Image, the Voice, and the Law* (Chapel Hill: University of North Carolina Press, 1991); James Miller, ed., *Fluid Exchanges: Artists and Critics in the AIDS Crisis* (Toronto: University of Toronto Press, 1992); Frank Browning, *The Culture of Desire* (New York: Vintage, 1993); Frederick C. Cory, ed., *HIV Education: Performing Personal Narratives.* Proceedings of a conference held in Arizona State University, 1993; Larry Gross, *Contested Closets* (Minneapolis: University of Minnesota Press, 1993); Linda Singer, *Erotic Welfare: Sexual*

364

Theory and Politics in the Age of Epidemic (New York: Routledge, 1993); Richard Dellamora, *Apocalyptic Overtures: Sexual Politics and the Sense of an Ending* (New Brunswick, N.J.: Rutgers University Press, 1994); Lee Edelman, *Homographies: Essays in Gay Literary and Cultural Theory* (New York: Routledge, 1994); Michael Ryan and Avery Gordon, eds., *Body Politics: Disease, Desire, and the Family* (Boulder, Colo.: Westview Press, 1994); Terry Wolverton, ed., *Blood Whispers: L.A. Writers on AIDS* (Los Angeles: Silverton, 1994); Nina Felshin, ed., *But Is It Art? The Spirit of Art as Activism* (Seattle: Bay Press, 1995); Suzanne Lacy, ed., *Mapping the Terrain: New Genre Public Art* (Seattle: Bay Press, 1995); David Van Leer, *The Queening of America* (New York: Routledge, 1995).

8. It is also clear that the particular constituency of a private institution of higher learning with very weak links to the urban communities offers a sociopolitical context that is vastly different from local working-class and immigrant populations on the South and West sides of Chicago. In the winter of 1991 a musician friend asked me to produce a video of a benefit performance on the South Side, where The Spell Group and The Kupona Network ("Kupona" is a Swahili word meaning "to get well") had begun to create a support network to address AIDS in the African-American community. As had happened in numerous cases elsewhere in the country, this network had been created by concerned members of a particular local community. It was committed to teaching, sharing information, support services, advocacy, counseling, and residential services provided by Ashanti House, a temporary residence for African-American men infected with HIV/AIDS. Mara Adelman introduced me to another hospice, the Bonaventura House, which offered similar health-care services and spiritual counseling to indigent men and women in a North Side neighborhood. CALOR is another nonprofit organization in Chicago that assists Latinos with AIDS, and David Hish, a member of our workshop, introduced me to TPAN (Test Positive Aware Network) and its support network. The dedication of staff and volunteer workers in these underfunded and struggling support groups has to be seen to be believed. It is through the daily battle with illness, destitution, and death carried on by these health-care support networks that one must come to terms with one's trust in image-making and one's feeble hold on reality. Video production cannot save lives, even if it contributes to the sharing of information and provides inspiration that may prolong the physical and emotional work of bonding that has to be done. AIDS videos, one might argue, have become a part of this bonding, and they thus function as an activist tool or longtime companion for the struggle and a therapeutic medium for "getting well," sustaining the hope that there will be a cure.

7 Media Activism

1. Gregg Bordowitz, "The AIDS Crisis Is Ridiculous," in *Queer Looks: Perspectives on Lesbian and Gay Film and Video*, ed. Martha Gever, John Greyson, and Pratibha Parmar (New York: Routledge, 1993), 211.

2. John Greyson, one of the most important activist filmmakers in the alternative field, admits to "strategic compromises" yet distinguishes nine different types of alternative AIDS media, ranging from independently produced cable programs (such as *Living with AIDS*), documentaries of AIDS plays, portraits of persons living with AIDS (PLWAs), and educational or safe-sex tapes to experimental and activist works that criticize mainstream representations or take on a particular issue. Actually, since 1986 Greyson's work

has embraced almost all of these alternative modes, including their multilayered com-**365**
bination in a single work, such as *The Pink Pimpernel* (1989). See Greyson, "Strategic
Compromises: AIDS and Alternative Video Practices," in *Reimaging America,* ed. Mark
O'Brien and Craig Little (Philadelphia: New Society Publishers, 1990), 60–74.

3. See Richard Dyer, "It's Being So Camp that Keeps Us Going," *Body Politic* 10
(1977), 11–13. See also his book *The Matter of Images* (New York: Routledge, 1993), 19–51.

4. Marlon Riggs, "Tongues Re-Tied," in *Resolutions,* ed. Michael Renov and Erika
Suderburg (Minneapolis: University of Minnesota Press, 1996), 185. *Tongues Untied* was directed by Marlon Riggs and produced by Signifyin' Works in 1989. The distribution rights
rest with Frameline's Lesbian and Gay Cinema Collection. References to the poetry in the
film are drawn from my transcriptions and the published version in the anthology *Brother
to Brother,* ed. Essex Hemphill (Boston: Alyson Publications, 1991).

5. Gregg Bordowitz, "Operative Assumptions Concerning Community-Based Production of Television," in *Resolutions,* 175.

6. Alexandra Juhasz, *AIDS TV* (Durham, N.C.: Duke University Press, 1995), 10.
See also Jean Carlomusto, "Making It: AIDS Activist Television," *Video Guide* 10, nos. 3–4
(1989), 18, as well as her collaborative writings in the same issue of *Video Guide.*

7. Cindy Patton, *Inventing AIDS* (New York: Routledge, 1990), 1–23; 121–32.

8. Kobena Mercer, *Welcome to the Jungle* (London: Routledge, 1994), 312n. See also
Douglas Crimp's well-known essays "Mourning and Militancy," *October* 51 (1989), 3–18,
and "Right On, Girlfriend!" *Social Text* 33 (1992), 2–18.

9. bell hooks, "Feminist Transformation," *Transition* (special issue) 66 (1995), 93–98.
For further reference to hooks's thinking about the antifeminist backlash and misogyny in
black culture, see her book *Outlaw Culture: Resisting Representations* (New York: Routledge,
1994). For a subdued essay on Riggs (reprinted in the Whitney Museum catalogue accompanying the *Black Male* exhibition, see her book *Art on My Mind: Visual Politics* (New York:
New Press, 1995), 202–12.

10. Lauren Berlant and Elizabeth Freeman, "Queer Nationality," in *Fear of a Queer
Planet,* ed. Michael Warner (Minneapolis: University of Minnesota Press, 1993), 197.

11. The exhibition, curated by Park Chambers, Tim Doud, and Lawrence Steger,
presented a wide range of works in all media by artists who identify themselves as PWA/
HIV and whose work is informed by their diagnosis. The project specifically addressed
the issue of the public status of people's diverse experiences of living with HIV/AIDS,
in particular their right to participate in public discourse and health education generally
controlled by media and institutions. Cucher's work was shown alongside that of Larry
Jens Anderson, Anne Becka, Robert Blancheon, Robert Farber, Edward A. Hochschild,
The Infected Faggots, David Keating, Khalid McClung, Frank Moore, Philip Pirolo, High
Steers, Michael Tidmus, and Glenn Traer. Video screenings accompanying the exhibit
also included the work of Cucher, Randy Esslinger, Michael Kearns, Zack Stiglicz as well
as Marlon Riggs's well-known *Anthem* and Bill T. Jones's powerful dedicatory dance video
Untitled (for Arnie Zane).

12. Quotes are from Cindy Patton's chapter on "Inventing 'African AIDS,'" in *Inventing AIDS,* 36. See also Emily Martin, *Flexible Bodies* (Boston: Beacon Press, 1994),
especially part IV, "Configurations of Healthy Bodies," 113–59. For a cautious and comprehensive analysis of Cuba's AIDS politics, see Marvin Leiner, *Sexual Politics in Cuba:
Machismo, Homosexuality, and AIDS* (Boulder, Colo.: Westview Press, 1994). See also Ian

Lumsden, *Machos, Maricones, and Gays: Cuba and Homosexuality* (Philadelphia: Temple University Press, 1996).

13. For an illuminating discussion of the role of video and media in the Rodney King verdict and its aftermath, see Robert Gooding-Williams, ed., *Reading Rodney King/Reading Urban Uprising* (New York: Routledge, 1993), and John Fiske, *Media Matters: Everyday Culture and Political Change* (Minneapolis: University of Minnesota Press, 1994). For an excellent collection of essays on the politics of AIDS media activism, published following the Fifth International Conference on AIDS held in Montreal (1989), see Allan Klusacek and Ken Morrison, eds., *A Leap in the Dark: AIDS, Art, and Contemporary Cultures* (Montreal: Véhicule Press, 1992).

14. While revising this chapter, I was inspired by two books in particular. The first, by the influential feminist sociologist and activist Cindy Patton, is entitled *Inventing AIDS* and offers a brilliant and challenging analysis of the emergent discourses of the "AIDS service industries" and the ways in which public policies and political strategies, as well as our own notions of identity and community, are constructed. I was particularly impressed by her exposition of the "hidden voices" among affected communities and volunteer workers, and the conflicts between scientific expediency and the immediate emotional and practical needs of people affected by HIV/AIDS. Her critical discussion of the "limits of community" represents a major contribution to our thinking about activist politics. The second book, Alexandra Juhasz's *AIDS TV,* had just been published and has remained crucially significant for our validation of video activism. A video producer and member of WAVE since its inception in 1988, Juhasz writes from the perspective of her intimate engagement in the ACT UP and women's activist video movement, contributing a detailed critical theory of alternative video production in conjunction with a moving and eye-opening case study of the WAVE productions she participated in. Her stunning book incisively portrays the (New York–based) political arena of media activism as a form of community-building, which I have only managed to sketch briefly here. Together with the writings by John Greyson, Gregg Bordowitz, Paula Treichler, and Jean Carlomusto, it has become a major resource for a new video theory/practice.

8   Embodiment: Sharing Our Wounds

1. Barbara M. Stafford, *Body Criticism: Imaging the Unseen in Enlightenment Art and Medicine* (Cambridge: MIT Press, 1991). Her comprehensive study of modern attempts to visualize metaphors of the human body might be read in conjunction with Emily Martin's ethnography of more recent changes in the configuration of body images, especially under the impact of AIDS and new "corporate" policies of flexible management. See her *Flexible Bodies: Tracking Immunity in American Culture: From the Days of Polio to the Age of AIDS* (Boston: Beacon Press, 1994). For a historical critique of the modernization of vision and visualizing metaphors, see Jonathan Crary, *Techniques of the Observer* (Cambridge: MIT Press, 1990).

2. Mary Kelly, "Desiring Images/Imaging Desire," *Wedge* 6 (1984), 7.

3. For a sample of Jo Spence's writings and documentation of her own practice, see her *Putting Myself in the Picture: A Political, Personal and Photographic Autobiography* (Seattle: Real Comet Press, 1988). For critical studies of the construction of bodies and embodiment, see Boston Women's Health Collective, *Our Bodies, Our Selves* (New York: Simon and Schuster, 1971); Nancy Chodorow, *The Reproduction of Mothering: Psychoanalysis and the Soci-*

ology of Gender (Berkeley: University of California Press, 1978); Carol S. Vance, ed., *Pleasure and Danger: Exploring Female Sexuality* (Boston: Routledge and Kegan Paul, 1984); Luce Irigaray, *This Sex Which Is Not One* (Ithaca, N.Y.: Cornell University Press, 1985); Kate Linker and Jane Weinstock, eds., *Difference: On Representation and Sexuality* (New York: New Museum of Contemporary Art, 1985); Elaine Scarry, *The Body in Pain: The Making and Remaking of the World* (New York: Oxford University Press, 1985); Susan Rubin Suleiman, ed., *The Female Body in Western Culture: Contemporary Perspectives* (Cambridge: Harvard University Press, 1986); Teresa de Lauretis, *Technologies of Gender: Essays on Theory, Film, and Fiction* (Bloomington: Indiana University Press, 1987); Emily Martin, *The Woman in the Body: A Cultural Analysis of Reproduction* (Boston: Beacon Press, 1987); Jane Gallop, *Thinking through the Body* (New York: Columbia University Press, 1988); Michel Feher, Ramona Naddaff, and Nadia Tazi, eds., *Fragments for a History of the Human Body*, 3 vols. (New York: Zone Books, 1989); Jane Gaines and Charlotte Herzog, eds., *Fabrications: Costume and the Female Body* (New York: Routledge, 1990); Elisabeth Bronfen, *Over Her Dead Body: Death, Femininity, and the Aesthetic* (New York: Routledge, 1992); Chris Shilling, *The Body and Social Theory* (London: Sage, 1993); Rosalyn Diprose, *The Bodies of Women: Ethics, Embodiment and Sexual Difference* (London: Routledge, 1994); Elizabeth Grosz, *Volatile Bodies: Toward a Corporeal Feminism* (Bloomington: Indiana University Press, 1994); Andrea Maihofer, *Geschlecht als Existenzweise* (Frankfurt: Ulrike Helmer, 1995); and Moira Gatens, *Imaginary Bodies: Ethics, Power and Corporeality* (New York: Routledge, 1996). For the ways in which the constitution of the body and embodiment are being reconfigured in transitional societies of the former Eastern bloc countries under the new pressures of capitalist modernization, see Cynthia Enloe, *The Morning After: Sexual Politics at the End of the Cold War* (Berkeley: University of California Press, 1993); Nanette Funk and Magda Mueller, *Gender Politics and Post-Communism* (London: Routledge, 1993); and Ellen E. Berry, ed., *Postcommunism and the Body Politic* (New York: New York University Press, 1995).

4. Lucy R. Lippard, *Mixed Blessings: New Art in a Multicultural America* (New York: Pantheon, 1990), 199.

5. Kathryn Hixson, ". . . and the object is the body," *New Art Examiner* 19, no. 2 (October 1991), 20–24.

6. See my article "Imprints and Re-Visions: Carolee Schneemann's Visual Archeology," *PAJ* 44 (1993), 31–46.

9 Disembodiment: The Virtual Realities

1. Donna J. Haraway's "Cyborg Manifesto" first appeared in *Socialist Review* 80 (1985) and has been reprinted in her *Simians, Cyborgs, and Women: The Reinvention of Nature* (New York: Routledge, 1991), 164–65, 177, 180. For an earlier version of my argument here, see the chapter "Overexposure: Sites of Postmodern Media," in my book *Theatre, Theory, Postmodernism* (Bloomington: Indiana University Press, 1991), 113–31.

2. The argument underlying this observation was the focus of the late Douglas Crimp's collaboration with photographer/conceptual artist Louise Lawler in their book *On the Museum's Ruins* (Cambridge: MIT Press, 1993). Emphasizing the role of photography, Crimp traces the historical shifts from the so-called autonomous modernist art object to the postmodernist critique of institutions and the new discursive contexts of poststructuralism/deconstruction within which the shifts are interpreted. What is remarkable,

however, is Crimp's strictly "high-cultural" and aesthetic or, one might say, art-historical framework of discursive argument, which leads him to the somewhat predictable and melancholy conclusion that the museum has served its time and is now "in ruins," a diagnosis that leaves out most of the popular and mass-cultural contexts in which the museum—like any other institution that wants to educate and/or entertain—is constantly readjusting and upgrading its display technologies.

3. See Jean Baudrillard's early work *L'Effet Beaubourg: Implosion et dissuasion* (Paris: Editions Galilée, 1977) and his later books on simulation and hyperreality, especially *Simulations,* trans. Paul Foss, Paul Patton, and Philip Zeitchman (New York: semiotext(e), 1983), *In the Shadow of the Silent Majorities,* trans. Paul Foss, Paul Patton, and John Johnston (New York: semiotext(e), 1983), *The Ecstasy of Communication,* trans. Bernard and Caroline Schutze (New York: Semiotext(e), 1988), and *Seduction,* tr. Brian Singer (London: Macmillan, 1990). Lyotard's comments appeared in several interviews in German and French newspapers, as well as in the exhibition catalogue for *Les Immatériaux* (Paris: Centre Georges Pompidou, 1985), which is structured like a conceptual index.

4. See Teresa L. Ebert, *Ludic Feminism and After: Postmodernism, Desire, and Labor in Late Capitalism* (Ann Arbor: University of Michigan Press, 1996). Ebert's forceful criticism of contemporary feminist discourse/text theories and cultural theories traces the apolitical tendencies in current theories of performativity back to the anti-Marxist writings of French postmodern philosophers (Derrida, Lacan, Foucault, Lyotard, Virilio), who, I suggest, constituted the immediate conceptual context of the Pompidou exhibition.

5. Jean-François Lyotard, *The Postmodern Condition: A Report on Knowledge,* trans. Geoff Bennington and Brian Massumi (Minneapolis: University of Minnesota Press, 1984), 67.

6. In discussing the postmodern afterlife of minimalism and the waning of the "authentic" art object, Rosalind Krauss anticipates that the technological museum, like Disneyland, will promote "simulacral experience rather than aesthetic immediacy." See her "The Cultural Logic of the Late Capitalist Museum," *October* 54 (1990), 3–17.

7. Quoted from the promotional literature and the exhibition catalogue accompanying *Rediscovering Pompeii* (Rome: "L'ERMA" di Brettschneider, 1990). The catalogue, subtitled "Exhibition by IBM-Italia," lists more than forty members of the organizational/curatorial staff.

8. See Robert Lumley, ed., *The Museum Time Machine* (London: Routledge, 1988). For a provocative analysis of the current cultural discourses on "hybridity," see Néstor García Canclini's *Culturas híbridas: Estrategias para entrar y salir de la modernidad* (Mexico: Grijalbo, 1990), published as *Hybrid Cultures,* trans. Christopher L. Chiappari and Silvia L. López (Minneapolis: University of Minnesota Press, 1996).

9. In the past few years, an increasing number of books have appeared that seek to promote and affirm our cyborg relations to technoculture; they compete in a vast market of popular consumer and industrial magazines, handbooks, and fanzines that address the computer-literate populations and the aficionados of cyberspace communication. There are relatively few critical studies of the economics, politics, and social implications of VR and Internet applications, and almost none that address cybernetic art or the new Web art, its interactive design aesthetic, or the whole arena of Internet communications and performative collaborations. Since the academic-book market tends to remain separate from the popular consumer markets, it is interesting to see which discourses or performance styles cross over (e.g., Arthur Kroker interviewed by *Mondo 2000;* Gregory Whitehead act-

ing as interviewer for *Mondo 2000,* or Kate Bornstein and Orlan doing lunch with the Fun City MegaMedia mag), which specialized techno idioms are formed in the computer and Internet magazines and 'zines and in the on-line news groups and multiuser dimensions (MUDs) themselves, and which discrepancies result in the much larger political context of the economic power relations that are being retranslated into relations of access, control, and creative leadership among the dispossessed and the engineers, technical specialists, "theorists" of digital reality, and corporate owners (such as Bill Gates). I can only offer a small, eclectic list of references (see n. 17), some of which may be helpful in building a critical vocabulary for analysis. It is at least as important to experience and participate in the on-line discussions, postings, and World Wide Web interactive communications in order to gain a sense of the consciousness or the imaginary of the spaced-out space of the Net's life.

10. Pietro Bellasi, "Berlin: A Metropolis at the Flea Market," *Tema Celeste* 31 (May–June 1991), 24–25.

11. Alan Balfour, *Berlin: The Politics of Order, 1737–1989* (New York: Rizzoli, 1990), 253.

12. Paula A. Treichler and Lisa Cartwright, introduction to "Imaging Technologies, Inscribing Science" (special issues) *camera obscura* 28 and 29 (1992), 5.

13. Ibid., 6. In the context of feminist critiques of science and technology, see Karen Knorr-Cetina, *The Manufacture of Knowledge: An Essay on the Constructivist and Contextual Nature of Science* (Oxford: Pergamon, 1981); Joan Rothschild, ed., *Machina Ex Dea: Feminist Perspectives on Technology* (New York: Pergamon, 1983); Ruth Bleier, *Science and Gender: A Critique of Biology and Its Theories of Women* (New York: Pergamon, 1984); Evelyn Fox Keller, *Reflections on Gender and Science* (New Haven: Yale University Press, 1985); Susan Suleiman, ed., *The Female Body in Western Culture: Contemporary Perspectives* (Cambridge: Harvard University Press, 1986); Ann Oakley, *The Captured Womb: A History of Medical Care of Pregnant Women* (New York: Basil Blackwell, 1986); Emily Martin, *The Woman in the Body* (Boston: Beacon Press, 1987); Michelle Stanworth, ed., *Reproductive Technologies: Gender, Motherhood and Medicine* (Minneapolis: University of Minnesota Press, 1987); Donna J. Haraway, *Primate Visions: Gender, Race, and Nature in the World of Modern Science* (New York: Routledge, 1989); Rosalind Petchesky, *Abortion and Woman's Choice: The State, Sexuality, and Reproductive Freedom* (Boston: Northeastern University Press, 1990); Judy Wajcman, *Feminism Confronts Technology* (University Park: Pennsylvania State University Press, 1991); Constance Penley and Andrew Ross, eds., *Technoculture* (Minneapolis: University of Minnesota Press, 1991); Judith Keegan Gardiner, ed., *Provoking Agents: Theorizing Gender and Agency* (Minneapolis: University of Minnesota Press, 1993); Susan Bordo, *Unbearable Weight: Feminism, Western Culture, and the Body* (Berkeley: University of California Press, 1993); Elizabeth Grosz, *Volatile Bodies: Toward a Corporeal Feminism* (Bloomington: Indiana University Press, 1994); Judith Flower MacCannell and Laura Zakarin, eds., *Thinking Bodies* (Stanford, Calif.: Stanford University Press, 1994); Judith Halberstam and Ira Livingston, eds., *Posthuman Bodies* (Bloomington: Indiana University Press, 1995); Bernice L. Hausman, *Changing Sex: Transsexualism, Technology, and the Idea of Gender* (Durham, N.C.: Duke University Press, 1995). See also numerous articles that have appeared over the years in feminist journals such as *Signs, Feminist Review, Feminist Studies, Hypatia, Journal of Women's History, Genders, differences, Heresies, Off Our Backs,* and *Ms.* For new critical studies of technologies of visualization, see Jonathan Crary, *Techniques of the Observer* (Cambridge: MIT Press, 1990), Barbara Maria Stafford, *Body Criticism: Imaging the Unseen in Enlightenment Art and Medicine* (Cambridge: MIT Press, 1991), and William J. Mitchell, *The Reconfigured Eye: Visual*

Truth in the Post-Photographic Era (Cambridge: MIT Press, 1992). For an excellent example of the critique of scientific/medical "performance" practice, see Terri C. Kapsalis, *Public Privates: Performing Gynecology from Both Ends of the Speculum* (Durham, N.C.: Duke University Press, 1997).

14. Michael M. J. Fischer, "Eye(I)ing the Sciences and Their Signifiers (Language, Tropes, Autobiographers): Interviewing for a Cultural Studies of Science and Technology," in *Technoscientific Imaginaries,* ed. George E. Marcus (Chicago: University of Chicago Press, 1995), 47. For a programmatic introduction to the goals of this second volume in the Late Editions series, see the essay by series editor George E. Marcus, 1–10.

15. See the introductory chapter by Arthur Kroker and Marielouise Kroker, "Panic Sex in America," in *Body Invaders,* ed. Arthur Kroker and Marielouise Kroker (New York: St. Martin's Press, 1987), 10–33. Most of these essays first appeared in the *Canadian Journal of Political and Social Theory* 11, nos. 1–2 (1987). Arthur Kroker's rhetoric of the "panic body," and his trenchant post-Foucauldian and Nietzschean symptomology of the dissolution and dematerialization of bodies in the new cyber/data trash culture, runs through the ever-widening circuits of his books, including *The Postmodern Scene: Excremental Culture and Hyper-Aesthetics* (New York: St. Martin's Press, 1986), coauthored with David Cook; *The Hysterical Male: New Feminist Theory* (New York: St. Martin's Press, 1991), with Marielouise Kroker; *The Possessed Individual* (New York: St. Martin's Press, 1992); *The Last Sex* (New York: St. Martin's Press, 1993), with Marielouise Kroker; *Spasm: Virtual Reality, Android Music, Electric Flesh* (New York: St. Martin's Press, 1993); and *Data Trash: The Theory of the Virtual Class* (New York: St. Martin's Press, 1995), with Michael A. Weinstein.

16. Kroker, "Panic Sex in America," 24f. Kroker calls women's bodies the "privileged objects of [a] domination," extending McLuhan's analysis in *The Mechanical Bride* into the postmodern arena of advertising and health care industries; his discussion of commodity fetishism constructs a female, gendered body as the postmodern paradigm of "disappearance" (the last sex?).

17. See Chris H. Gray and Steven Mentor, "The Cyborg Body Politic and the New World Order," in *Prosthetic Territories: Politics and Hypertechnologies,* ed. Gabriel Brahm Jr. and Mark Driscoll (Boulder, Colo.: Westview Press, 1995), 219–47. I am indebted to Gray and Mentor's exploration of cyber politics. My reflections represent an attempt to interface their critique of the construction of "virtual communities" with my readings of "hyper-smart" magazines such as *Wired, Mondo 2000, bOING bOING, Future Sex, Mediamatic, Now Time, RE/SEARCH, Computer Life, Axcess, Fusion, Virtual City, Cybersurfer, Presence, Deadline,* as well as other newsgroups and web sites, the whole filtered through my samplings of a few published books that try to dance with the new cybertechniques. My dance guides include: Klaus Theweleit, *Male Fantasies,* vol. 1, *Women, Floods, Bodies, History* (Minneapolis: University of Minnesota Press, 1987); Mark Poster, *The Mode of Information: Poststructuralism and Social Context* (Cambridge: Polity Press, 1990); Michael Benedikt, ed., *Cyberspace: First Steps* (Cambridge: MIT Press, 1991); Howard Rheingold, *Virtual Reality* (New York: Simon and Schuster, 1991); Scott Bukatman, *Terminal Identity: The Virtual Subject in Postmodern Science Fiction* (Durham, N.C.: Duke University Press, 1993); Verena Andermatt Conley, ed., *Re-thinking Technologies* (Minneapolis: University of Minnesota Press, 1993); Howard Rheingold, *The Virtual Community: Homesteading on the Electronic Frontier* (Reading, Mass.: Addison-Wesley, 1993); Bob Cotton and Richard Oliver, *Understanding Hypermedia:*

From Multimedia to Virtual Reality (London: Phaidon, 1993); Sunil Gupta, ed., *Disrupted Borders* (London: Rivers Oram Press, 1993); Gretchen Bender and Timothy Druckrey, eds., *Culture on the Brink: Ideologies of Technology* (Seattle, Wash.: Bay Press, 1994); Mark C. Taylor and Esa Saarinen, *Imagologies: Media Philosophy* (London: Routledge, 1994); Sherry Turkle, *Life on the Screen: Identity in the Age of the Internet* (New York: Simon and Schuster, 1995); William J. Mitchell, *City of Bits: Space, Place, and the Infobahn* (Cambridge: MIT Press, 1995); and James Brook and Iain A. Boal, eds., *Resisting the Virtual Life* (San Francisco: City Lights, 1995). Carla Sinclair's *Net Chicks: A Smart-Girl Guide to the Wired World* (New York: Henry Holt, 1996), which appeared after I had completed this chapter, provides an inspiring well of hot links.

18. See Judith Butler, *Gender Trouble: Feminism and the Subversion of Identity* (New York: Routledge, 1990). Butler's gender theory of "performativity," understood as a critique of the fictive category of gender identity which does not exist but is continually constituted by performative acts of repetition conforming to the norms of cultural intelligibility, has become notorious and remains a favorite model for adaptation by queer performance theorists who cherish her chapter on "Subversive Bodily Acts" (79–141) as a rehearsal technique for "parodic subversions" and transgressive redeployments of gender identities. The rehearsals showed up in numerous essays on drag performance and gender bending, applied to actual performance art or popular and gay/lesbian subcultures. Butler has subsequently tried to criticize her fans by pointing out that "performativity" is not to be understood as volitional choice nor as necessarily transgressive of the sex/gender system that regulates the available categories. See her *Bodies That Matter: On the Discursive Limits of "Sex"* (New York: Routledge, 1993), a somewhat disappointing book that remains firmly encapsulated by the constraining discursive operations of a virtually totally dominated "matter," encoded figures of "bodies" whose ("outside") reality she cannot imagine except in the case of the unanswered question of physical violence and bodily injury (see 53–55).

19. Bernice L. Hausman, *Changing Sex: Transsexualism, Technology, and the Idea of Gender* (Durham, N.C.: Duke University Press, 1995), 192.

20. Ibid., 70–71.

21. Kate Bornstein, "Puttin' on the Titz: An Entr'acte with Kate Bornstein," interview by Trish Thomas, *Mondo 2000* 13 (1995), 116–17. Ironically, the interview with Bornstein appears next to a rather sensationalist photo-text interview with French performance artist Orlan, who explains her latest self-directed/programmed surgical body-alteration experiment, by means of which she intends to change her face into a composite mix of features bit-mapped in a computer-generated model of the chin of Botticelli's Venus, the lips of Boucher's Europa, the nose of Gérôme's Psyche, and the forehead of da Vinci's Mona Lisa. The Orlan text is preceded by references to Frankenstein, de Sade, and Artaud's Theater of Cruelty, and the discussion then instantly takes up questions about "techno-art" and virtual reality, before returning to Orlan's claim that her skin surgery allows her literally "to bring the exterior image back into relation with the interior image," the body under the skin. See Orlan, "The Doyenne of Divasection," interview with Miryam Sas, *Mondo 2000* 13 (1995), 106–11. Orlan was one of the few featured artists at the first Performance Studies Conference held at New York University in 1995, appearing on a panel entitled "Gendering the Medical Body." She showed a video of her operations and mostly remained silent, causing a predictable commotion at the conference, which spilled

over into a drawn-out, heated e-mail discussion on the Internet (published in excerpts in *Drama Review* 39, no. 4 (1995), 142–63).

22. The first gathering of the "third theatre" initiative was led by Eugenio Barba in 1976 as part of the Theatre of Nations event in Belgrade, sponsored by UNESCO. Barba later published the "third theatre" manifesto and proclaimed the actors' groups that develop comparative cultural research "floating islands," neither belonging to the "first theatre" (classical/traditional) nor the "second theatre" (avant-garde), but rather connected by an intercultural network. See Eugenio Barba, *Beyond the Floating Islands* (New York: PAJ, 1986).

23. Kate Bornstein, *Gender Outlaw: On Men, Women, and the Rest of Us* (New York: Vintage Books, 1995), 121.

24. I am indebted to Kathleen Woodward for an instructive research seminar she taught in Chicago, and to her critical examination of the discriminatory effects of high-tech reproductive technologies on women, particularly in the disavowal of aging women's bodies, which seem to be disproportionately targeted for cosmetic reconstruction in a force field of highly mediated images of youth and feminine beauty. See Woodward's "From Virtual Cyborgs to Biological Time Bombs: Technocriticism and the Material Body," in *Culture on the Brink,* 47–64.

25. See Michael Benedikt, introduction to *Cyberspace,* 1–25. The book's tone is a very confusing blend of upbeat, visionary, "insider" descriptions of the scientific architecture of cyberspace and critical, philosophical, and anthropological speculations on the technological consequences for the human bodies and communities as objects of power relationships. Benedikt, who works in the field of architecture, design, and "mental technologies," is to be commended for assembling such a jarring collage of viewpoints.

26. I am indebted to Giles Hendrix for his wonderful design work and his helpful instructions. We worked together on an Internet research project in the winter/spring of 1996; his Web-art survey can be reached via: <http://www.webslingerz.com/ghendrix/manifesto>. The web site of AlienNation Co. can be reached via: <http://www.ruf.rice.edu/~orpheus/>.

27. Rheingold, *The Virtual Community,* 4–5.

28. Ibid., 215–16. For a full discussion of grassroots activism and eco-linking, see Rheingold's chapter on "Electronic Frontiers and Online Activists," 241–75.

29. Ibid., 180–81. Rheingold's description is based on Elizabeth M. Reid's graduate research on user behavior in Internet Relay Chat systems.

30. Benedikt Anderson, *Imagined Communities: Reflections on the Origin and Spread of Nationalism,* rev. ed. (London: Verso, 1991). See also Partha Chatterjee, *Nationalist Thought and the Colonial World: A Derivative Discourse?* (London: Zed Books, 1986) and Homi K. Bhabha, ed., *Nation and Narration* (London: Routledge, 1990).

31. John Simmons, "Sade and Cyberspace," in *Resisting the Virtual Life,* 157.

32. Turkle, *Life on the Screen,* 26.

33. A 1991 advertising flyer for *Mondo 2000* reported that 80 percent of the readership worked in information or communications fields and had a yearly median income of about sixty-five thousand dollars. See Mark Dery's comprehensive and provocative diagnosis of high-tech subcultures in *Escape Velocity: Cyberculture at the End of the Century* (New York: Grove Press, 1996), esp. 21–72.

34. Mark Dery, "Art and the Computer," *ARTnews* 95, no. 3 (March 1996), 99.

35. I should also mention that the *ADA* exhibition as a whole, with its eight work-stations, or computer/screen consoles, had a remarkably cold and perfunctory look, reducing the sensory and tactile experience of artworks almost entirely to the mechanical interfaces (clicking the mouse, moving the cursor) and readings of the screens. No attempt was made to create a different ambience or kinesthetic experience of "feminine" or artistic interfaces that might involve a more conscious, self-reflective framing of the disembodied logic of screen gazing.

36. All quotations are drawn from conversations with Giles Hendrix and are based on his paper "OTIS: A Case Study of Visual Art on the WWW," presented at the Theory of Integrated Arts Seminar, Northwestern University, 1995. Excerpts are quoted with permission.

37. Cornelia Geißler, "Kampfreserve der Partei," *Kursbuch* 111 (1993), 38 (my translation).

38. After completing the final draft for this last section, I realized I had entered into an overlapping discussion of some of the same issues analyzed in Néstor García Canclini's poignant chapter "Hybrid Cultures, Oblique Powers" in his *Culturas híbridas*. I am delighted about this convergence and empathize with his argument, although he mostly focuses on (Latin American) metropolitan urban culture, whereas my case study in East Germany happens to take place in an underdeveloped town or region within the first world.

39. See Michel de Certeau, *The Practice of Everyday Life,* trans. Steven Rendall (Berkeley: University of California Press, 1988); Nancy Fraser, *Unruly Practices: Power, Discourse and Gender in Contemporary Social Theory* (Minneapolis: University of Minnesota Press, 1989); and Pierre Bourdieu, *Entwurf einer Theorie der Praxis* (Frankfurt: Suhrkamp, 1976) and *Distinction: A Social Critique of the Judgement of Taste,* trans. Richard Nice (Cambridge: Harvard University Press, 1984). For the conceptual links between activism and social-field theory, I am particularly indebted to Cindy Patton's essay "Refiguring Social Space," in *Social Postmodernism,* ed. Linda Nicholson and Steven Seidman (Cambridge: Cambridge University Press, 1995), 216–49. Subsequent references to contemporary ethnography and "evocation" are motivated by my interaction with Cuban artist/ethnographer Abdel Hernández and the "artists in trance" workshop he and Surpik Angelini conducted in Houston (January–March 1997) alongside the campus of Rice University's anthropology department. One of the most poignant provocations for a new, creative ethnography had been written in the mid-eighties by Houston ethnographer Stephen A. Tyler; see *The Unspeakable: Discourse, Dialogue, and Rhetoric in the Postmodern World* (Madison: University of Wisconsin Press, 1987), esp. 199–216. Hernández's still unpublished and untranslated writings include a book of essays entitled *Bordes y Desbordes del Arte: crisis de frontera y apertura al transarte.* I wish to dedicate the following epilogue on Parsifal to him and his inspirational fieldwork.

40. In my forthcoming book "Border-Work: Performances/Collaborations," I write about "meetings grounds" in a chapter on the "transcultural imaginary." The entire book is organized more performatively and dialogically as a series of encounters, workshops, conversations, and rehearsals. Again, it needs to be emphasized that such encounters take (a) place and are carried out in a site-specific manner, thereby dislocating the aesthetic

parameters within which performance/art has been perceived, interpreted, and evaluated. Collaboration, in the sense in which I understand it, is not a process that depends on aesthetic criteria or fulfills itself in a production (an object on display for an audience), although it is, of course, a vital dimension of our social, creative, and productive lives. The publication of a collaborative effort is always a sad epilogue, a bit grainy, like the dubs of our videotapes.

41. Speaking of grainy dubs, our installation-film/documentation of the dark soundings of Hellerau has been reviewed and analyzed by performance-studies and music scholar Norma M. Darr (who has carried out research projects on the theatricality of rock music and the Doors). Interestingly, her strongest and most visceral response was to Imma Sarries-Zgonc's dangerous, intimate dance with the sharp saw blade and to the parodies of blood-letting in our installation. See her "Reading the Body and Blood of *Parsifal:* A Performance at Hellerau," *The Musical Quarterly* 80: 4 (1996), 629–47.

I N D E X

Abdoh, Reza, 20–22; and Dar a Luz, 12, 20
absolute dance, 43, 53. See also *Ausdruckstanz;*
    Wigman
abstraction, 30, 32, 43–46, 59, 61, 262, 269. *See*
    also expressionism
Abramović, Marina, 109, 156–57, 242
Acconci, Vito, 156–57
acting theory, 10
ACT UP, xv, 15, 174, 201, 204–6, 212, 214–16,
    295, 297
Ad Mortem, 189–203, 232
AIDS, xv, 13, 15, 174, 189–203, 204–6, 212,
    214–17, 232–33, 239, 241, 243–44, 254, 256,
    272, 274, 277, 307, 323; and activism, 190,
    195–96, 198–200, 204–33, 239, 294–95, 310,
    313, 317–18; *Interfacings,* 201–3, 232; and
    performance, 189–203; and video, 201–3,
    204–33
AlienNation, 112–16
AlienNation Co., xxv, 105, 110–18, 287, 348–51
Althusser, Louis, 345
Anderson, Benedikt, 306
Anderson, Laurie, xv, 9, 64–68; *Home of the*
    Brave, 64–67, 72, 74; *United States,* 64–67
Appia, Adolphe, 4–41, 43, 71
architecture, 32, 36–42, 44–50, 98, 259, 270–71
Arcos, Guillermo, 183
Arp, Hans, 42
ars electronica, 5, 267
art, 258–69, 311–14; on CD-ROM, 311–18; on
    Internet, 319–26
Artaud, Antonin, 3, 37, 260
artificial intelligence, 266–67
Athey, Ron, 16
Atlas, Charles, 68
Ausdruckstanz, 28, 32, 35–46, 87–88. *See also*
    expressionism

Balfour, Alan, 271
Ballard, J. G., 223–24
ballet, 50–58, 95–101; and biomechanics, 38, 50,
    52, 58; and Cosmokinetic Kabinet, 20, 50, 54.
    See also dance; physical theater
Barba, Eugenio, 284
Barry, Judith, 9
Barthes, Roland, 9
Baudrillard, Jean, 4, 248, 260–62, 274
Bauhaus, 32, 44–46, 88, 163. *See also* Schlemmer
Bausch, Pina, xv, 9, 13–14, 21, 27–31, 39, 71,

82, 86–95; *Café Müller,* 90, 92, 94; and
    Fellini, 30; *1980,* 90, 93–94; *Nur Du,* 30, 93;
    Palermo, Palermo, 89, 93; *Walzer,* 93–94. *See*
    also Wuppertaler Tanztheater
Beckett, Samuel, 6, 260, 266
Bellasi, Pietro, 270
Bender, Gretchen, 9, 158–59, 163
Benedikt, Michael, 286
Benfield, Maria Dalida, 230
Benjamin, Walter, 18, 148
Berber, Anita, 42
Berkowitz, Terry, 170–71
Berlant, Lauren, 222
Berlin Wall, xvi–xvii, 4, 112, 270–71
Bernhard, Sandra, 68
Betontanc, 73–75
Beuys, Joseph, 154, 164, 168, 180, 255, 313; *Show*
    Your Wound, 255
biotechnology, 258, 276–77, 280, 282–85
Birnbaum, Dara, 9, 166, 168–69
bisexual, 190–203, 206–33, 237, 239, 243, 284,
    307
Black Planet Productions, 16
Blau, Herbert, 355n
blood exile, 277
Boán, Marianela, 20
body, the, 27–63, 66–67, 86–101, 105–43, 155,
    237–58, 267–69, 274–80, 294–95, 299–303,
    307, 311, 316–18, 322–23; and computer
    technology, 106, 118–30, 299–304; and dis-
    embodiment, 258–326 passim; and fetishism,
    67, 82, 150–52; and healing, 101, 117, 241;
    and illness, 189–203, 223–29, 239, 250–56,
    274; and new dance, 107–18; reproduction
    in art, 239–40, 255, 259; on screen, 59–101;
    and technology, 28, 45, 59–101; therapy, 240,
    244, 248–57; and transsubstantiation, 196,
    268; virtual, 260, 267, 274–75. *See also* cyborg;
    dance
body art, 8–10, 61, 109, 128–29, 155–56, 164,
    237–43, 248, 258–69, 322–23; *The Body,* 240,
    249, 267–70; *Embodiment,* 237–56; *Endurance,*
    242–43
body building, 240
Body-Mind Centering, 107, 117, 254
Bogdanović, Zoran, 110–11
border, xvi–xvii, 110–17, 145–47, 209, 212–13,
    272, 276–77, 280–85, 326–47
Bordowitz, Gregg, 211, 214–15, 221, 229, 232

376

Bornstein, Kate, 17, 283–85
Bourdieu, Pierre, 346
Bread and Puppet Theater, 10
Brecht, Bertolt, 3, 27, 30, 44, 77, 148, 165; and
  theatrical *gestus*, 27, 165
Brisley, Stuart, 156
Brith Gof, 12
Brook, Peter, 10, 19
Brown, Trisha, 67, 69–70
Brus, Günter, 156
Burden, Chris, 156
Burman, Chila Kumari, 9
Bustamante, Nao, 17
Butler, Judith, 30, 260
butoh, 87–89, 95

Cage, John, 7–8, 10, 67, 142, 153
camp, 17, 68, 87–88, 128–29, 150, 211–12, 221,
  284
capitalism, 5, 7, 18, 30, 258, 305, 325–29
Carbonne 14, 12
Carlomusto, Jean, 215, 232
Cave, the, 125–26
Chaclacayo, Grupo, 49, 348
Chekhov, Anton, 3
Childs, Lucinda, xv, 10, 19, 67, 69–71
Chong, Ping, 10
choreography, 20–22, 29, 34–58, 63, 67–77,
  87–101, 105–43; and technography, 118–19,
  127–30. *See also* technology
Cixous, Hélène, 9
Cobb, Portia, 16
Cochrane, Lisa, 76
communications, 5, 204, 261, 274–75, 286–326,
  336–47
communism, 49–52
community, 16, 24, 176–85, 189–93, 204–5, 210,
  229–33, 306–7, 309, 311, 323–24, 329–47; and
  communications, 204–5; electronic, 288–326;
  and identity politics, 210–18, 221–22, 229,
  277, 284; and national identity, 213–23, 226–
  27, 336, 344–47; organization, 24, 215–19,
  229–33, 326–47. *See also* AIDS activism
community-based art, 24, 175–85, 204–13,
  229–33, 240, 326–47
computer, 28, 95–101, 132–42, 167–72; and
  cyberspace, 5, 61, 86, 95, 99–101, 259–
  69, 271, 274–77, 288–304, 324; and digital
  communication, 261, 274–75, 286–326
constructivism, 32, 44–46, 49, 52–58, 60, 63, 65,
  73, 95
contact improvisation, 67–68, 131
corporeality, 37–43, 45, 66, 78, 108. *See also* body
Craig, Gordon, 41, 43
Crimp, Douglas, 214, 217–18

cross-cultural performance, 18–23, 47–49,
  78–79, 86–94, 107–18
cross-dressing, 16–17, 128–29, 219
Cuba, xvi, 111–12, 228, 337–38
Cucher, Sammy, 223–29
culture-in-action, xv, 175–85, 333
Cunningham, Merce, xiv, 8, 27, 67–68, 95, 118
cybernetics, 119, 123, 258–66, 271, 275, 286,
  304–33, 349
cyberspace, 5, 61, 86, 95, 99–101, 107, 130, 133,
  139–44, 172, 237
cyborg, 60–64, 76, 130, 135, 258–69, 275–77,
  282, 288–89, 296, 303, 306, 322, 336, 338

Dada, 32, 153
Dalcroze, Emile Jacques, 33–38. *See also*
  Hellerau
dance, 6–23, 27–144, 277–82, 296–303, 331,
  347; and expressionism, 36, 50, 72–75; on
  film, 68–72; and hyperdance, 12, 19–23,
  76–86, 88, 128; modern, 27–29, 35, 78–79,
  154; non-western, 19–20, 28, 78–79, 245–46;
  postmodern, 67–101; scholarship, 353n. *See
  also* ballet; constructivism; *Tanztheater*
Dar a Luz, 12
De Certeau, Michel, 345–46
De Keersmaeker, Anne Teresa, 76
De Lauretis, Theresa, 9
Deleuze, Gilles, 274
Delsarte, Francois, 33–34
Derrida, Jacques, 8, 30, 98
Dery, Mark, 60–61, 212–13
design, 37–38, 40–46, 53–58, 70–72, 94–101,
  136–44
Diaghilev, Sergei Pavlovich, 32
digital, 5, 28–101 passim, 117
disappearance, 128, 249, 274; and escape
  velocity, 59–63, 303
Disclosure, 5
Dougherty, Mary, 248, 253
drag, 16–17, 128–29, 219
Dresden, 33–44, 46, 348–51
Drozdik, Orshi, 268
Dubois, Kitsou, 119–21
Duchamp, Marcel, 18, 153
Duncan, Isadora, 32, 34
Durham Jimmy, 244
DV8, 12, 76, 87–88
Dyer, Richard, 212–13

Eisenstein, Sergei, 51
electronic art, 258, 267–69, 284–85, 311–26,
  349; and digital imaging, 261, 321–22. *See also*
  cybernetics; technology; virtual reality
English, Paul, 190, 194, 198

Index

Eno, Brian, 163
erotic art, 212, 220, 256–57, 284
ethnography, 10, 273, 336–47
eurhythmics, 33–41
Eurocentrism, 10
Export, Valie, 156, 242
expressionism, 32, 35–36, 50, 59; in art, 36, 40, 45–46. *See also* dance

Fabre, Jan, 10, 12, 19–20, 51
Fantasielabor, 328–47
Farabough, Laura, 159
fascism, 46–51, 77, 281
Fassbinder, Rainer Werner, 211
feminism, 237–57, 277; and medical technologies, 266, 268–69, 272–85; and performance, 238–57 passim; and technology, 267–69, 314–18; and theory, 272–85
fetishism, 242, 246–47
Fiadeiro, João, 19–20; *Recentes desejos mutiladas,* 20
film, 5, 36–37, 68–70, 83–86, 106–7, 115, 130, 133, 139–44, 145–46, 151, 209, 217, 229–30, 237, 259–60, 265–67, 272, 276, 286, 304, 308, 314, 316, 330; as dance, 69–72; as "third cinema," 284
Finley, Karen, 240, 243
Fischer, Michael M. J., 273
Fleck, John, 17
Fluxus, 7–8, 152–54, 164
folklore, 165, 334
Folkwang School, 39, 88
Foreman, Richard, 159
formalism, 27, 43, 45–46; in dance, 27, 71
Forsythe, William, xv, 95–101, 106, 118, 126; *ALIEN/A(C)TION,* 95; *Artifact,* 98; *Eidos: Telos,* 95; *Enemy in the Figure,* 97; and Frankfurt Ballet, 95–100; *Impressing the Czar,* 98; and "Improvisation Technologies," 95–101, 106; *Limb's Theorem,* 97; *Self Meant to Govern,* 96; *Six Counter Points,* 100
Forti, Simone, 67
Foster, Susan, 9, 27
Foucault, Michel, 9, 169, 210, 305, 341–45
Franko, Mark, 355n
Freeman, Elizabeth, 222
Freyer, Achim, 9
Frith, Simon, 64–65
From the Border, 113–14
Fuller, Loïe, 32
Fura dels Baus, La, 12, 23
Fusco, Coco, 16
futurism, 4, 32, 262, 266

Gaines, Jane, 207

Galás, Diamanda, 10, 66
Galotta, Jean-Claude, 76–77
Ganz, Isabelle, 190, 194
gay, 16–19, 50, 128, 190–203, 206–33, 237, 239, 243, 284, 307, 345; and Queer Nation, 210, 222, 281. *See also* bisexual; lesbian; queer
gaze, the, 9, 81–82
gender, 16–17, 113, 277, 281–84; and sexuality, 277–79, 282–85, 295
Genet, Jean, 211
Gert, Valeska, 42
Gibson, William, 61, 265–66, 292, 299
Gillette, Frank, 158
Gilpin, Heidi, 97–101, 119–20
Glass, Philip, 71
Gómez, Marga, 17
Gómez-Peña, Guillermo, 16, 176
Gordon, David, 67
Graham, Martha, 31, 129
Gran Fury, 204
Green, Renée, 9
Greenberg, Clement
Greyson, John, 211–13, 229, 232
Gropius, Walter, 37, 44
Grosz, George, 42
Grotowski, Jerzy, 3
Group Material, 204
Grover, Jan Zita, 248, 250, 254–55
Gržinić, Marina, 50
Guattari, Felix, 274
Gulf war, 205–6, 269, 272

Halprin, Anna, xxv, 25, 61, 86
Hammer, Barbara, 267–68
Haraway, Donna, 259, 272, 336
Hausman, Bernice, 282–83
Hay, Deborah, 8, 15, 67, 109, 190, 193–95, 197, 200, 202–3, 209, 278
health, 175, 237–56; policy, 221–29, 273
Hellerau, 33–49, 348–51; *Parsifal* Project at, 49, 348–51
Hendrix, Giles, 311, 318–26
Hernández, Abdel, 373n
heterosexuality, 17, 189–203 passim, 208–13, 276
Hijikata, Tatsumi, 87
Hill, Gary, 9, 158
history: and memory, 281,-82, 326–51; in "post-histoire" debates, 270
Hoffmann, Reinhild, 88
Hofmannsthal, Hugo, 30
Holocaust, 77, 255, 270
homophobia, 178, 190–91, 194, 218
homosexuality, 18, 217, 219
hooks, bell, 220
hybridity, 31, 258

hypermedia, 262–65
hyperreality, 5, 262, 293

Ibsen, Henrik, 3
ideology, 7, 12, 16, 209, 281
images: and dance, 27–58, 139–44, 296–303; movement of, 59–101, 105–44, 146–47, 274–75, 321–23; and music, 64–67. *See also* technology; video; virtual reality
Immatériaux, Les, 259–62
improvisation, xxii, 106–11, 118
incorporation, 286–96
Indian dance, 113
information processing, 259–65, 269, 274
information superhighway, 269, 274–76
interactivity, 108, 120–30, 135, 140–44, 165; and immersion, 124–26, 133, 136, 143, 155, 288, 299–303, 323
Internet, 59–61, 185, 259, 271–76, 286–326
Iwai, Toshio, 9

Jackson, Michael, 64, 268
Jesurun, John, 159
Jonas, Joan, 156
Jones, Bill T., and Arnie Zane Dance Company, 13–15, 229; *Still/Here*, 13–15
Jones, Rhodessa, 16
Joos, Kurt, 39, 88, 91
Judson Dance Theater, xv, 8, 67–70
Juhasz, Alexandra, 215, 230, 232
Julien, Isaac, 209, 218–20, 232

Kandinsky, Wassily, 36, 40, 46
Kelly, Angela, 238, 248
Kelly, Mary, 237, 242, 246
kinesthesia, 29, 33, 81–85, 269–80, 296–304
King, Rodney, 16, 209
Košnik, Marko, 12
Kozel, Susan, 127
Kresnik, Johann, 23, 88, 94
Kreutzberg, Harald, 87
Kristeva, Julia, 8
Kroker, Arthur, 274
Kumao, Heidi, 239, 251–52
Kushner, Tony, 18; *Angels in America*, 18, 21

Laban, Rudolf von, 35–43, 91, 96, 100, 142
Labowitz, Leslie, 242
Lacan, Jacques, 8, 296
Lacy, Suzanne, 242
Lafontaine, Marie Jo, 9, 166, 169–70
Laibach, 49–51, 73, 75
LaLaLa Human Steps, 76, 168
Lanier, Jaron, 266
Larner, Liz, 268

Laurel, Brenda, 60, 308
LBLM, xv, 126, 130–43, 277, 349
lesbian, 16–19, 50, 128, 190–203, 206–33, 237, 243, 284, 307, 309, 345. *See also* bisexual; gay; queer
LifeForms, xv, 41, 69
Lin, Hsin-Wei, 20
Linke, Susanne, 88, 90
Lippard, Lucy, 243–44
Living Theatre, 46
Llibre Vermell, 194–95
Lock, Edouard, 76
Lorde, Audre, 256
Lovejoy, Margot, 159
Lovers Fragments, 70
Ludlam, Charles, 284
Ludwig, Carsten, 48
Lyotard, Jean-François, 259–62

machine aesthetic, 32, 46
Madonna, 64, 149–52, 248–50
Maksymowicz, Virginia, 242
Malevich, Kasimir, 36–37, 51–52, 56–57
Mallarmé, Stéphane, 30
Manglano-Ovalle, Iñigo, 176–83
Manning, Susan, 42–43
Mapplethorpe, Robert, 220, 249
Marinetti, Filippo Tommaso, 75, 224, 262, 266
Marranca, Bonnie, 168
Martin, Emily, 227–28
Martínez, Daniel, 16
Marx, Karl, 305
masculinity, 16, 214, 220
masks, 43, 197
mass culture, 28, 149, 237, 259, 337
McCaulie, Robbie, 16
McClary, Susan, 357n
McLuhan, Marshall, 61, 274
media, 5–6, 28–31, 61, 76–86, 204–33, 304–24, 326–47; alternative, 190, 208–22; arts, 153, 176–85; and guerilla theater, 216; technologies, 6, 105, 107–8, 118–30, 146, 148–49, 166–68, 266. *See also* activism; performance; video art
medical technology, 266, 268–69, 272–85, 316
Mendieta, Ana, 242
Mercer, Kobena, 217
Meyerhold, Vsevelod, 36, 38, 51
Miller, Abby, 248, 254
Miller, Tim, 17, 240, 243–45
Minarik, Jan, 90–92
minimalism, 71, 249
Mnouchkine, Ariane, and Théâtre du Soleil, 10–11
modernism, 3, 18, 28–50

Index

Moholy-Nagy, Lázló, 37, 44, 163
Monk, Meredith, 10, 69
Montano, Linda,
movement, xiv, 27–29
multiculturalism, 11, 16, 18–19, 21, 243, 245, 293
Mulvey, Laura, 9
Murray, Alison, 76
museums, 258–69, 311–12; Cleveland Center of
  Contemporary Art, 9; Cologne Kunstverein,
  167; Contemporary Arts Museum, Houston,
  171; Deutsches Museum, Munich, 267; MFA,
  Houston, 263–66, 269–70; MoMA, New
  York, 166, 170; Renaissance Society, the, 240,
  249; School of the Art Institute of Chicago,
  251; "Topographie des Terrors," 270–71;
  Whitney, 166–68, 220, 246, 262
music, 28–29, 50, 64, 68, 71, 76, 146, 163, 291,
  308, 322–23, 331; electronic, 64–68, 76, 153;
  and eurhythmics, 33–41; harmony, 33; and
  opera, 34, 40–41, 348–51; and trance, 77–86,
  323
Mussorgsky, Modest, 45

nationalism, 52, 57, 336–37, 345–47
Native American art, 244–47
Nauman, Bruce, 158
Neshat, Shirin, 9
Neue Slowenische Kunst (NSK), 49–58
new dance, 72–101. See also dance
Newson, Lloyd, 87–88. See also DV8
Nitsch, Herrmann, 8, 156
Nunemaker, Richard, 190, 197

Odenbach, Marcel, 9, 164, 171–72
Ohno, Kazuo, 87–88
Ono, Yoko, 242
opera, 23, 40–41, 46, 48, 347–51
Oppenheim, Dennis, 156
Orpheus and Eyridice, 34, 40–41
Oursler, Tony, 9

Paik, Nam June, 9, 151–54, 157–58, 163, 166–68,
  170
painting, 29, 258–62
Pane, Gina, 156
Parsifal, 348–51
Patton, Cindy, 216, 227–29
Paxton, Steve, 76
Pedjko, Jeannie, 229
Peljhan, Marko, 356n
performance, 6–23, 154–55, 159–62, 165–66,
  184, 190–203, 205, 221, 232–33, 237–38,
  240–43, 246–49, 256–57, 267, 269, 272–73,
  296–304, 309, 311, 314–15, 318–19, 323–24,
  330–47; art, 145, 152, 154, 157, 190, 202, 241,
  309; and collaboration, 105–20, 130–44, 151,
  176–85, 205–8, 218–21, 230–33, 326–47;
  multimedia, 106–44, 159; and site-specificity,
  326–47; technology, 49, 105–43, 252, 336;
  video, 155, 157, 165, 191–215. See also activism
Pfeiffer, Travis Christopher, 197, 200
phenomenology, 29, 72, 260, 277–80
photography, 29, 106, 145, 147, 238–40, 242–57,
  260, 267, 276, 316, 331
physical culture movement, 28, 34–39, 115
Pihl, Andi, 239, 250–51
Piper, Adrian, 9, 242
Piscator, Erwin, 37, 44
Platou, Per, 118
Pograjc, Matjaž, 73–75
Pomo Afro Homos, 17
pornography, 21, 81, 211
postmodernism, 8–10, 259, 265, 274; and art,
  23, 258–71; and performance, 9, 6–8, 51; and
  science fiction, 258, 265–69, 292; and theory,
  8, 63, 260–62. See also dance
poststructuralism, 8–9, 261
Potočnic, Herrman, 53–58
Prince, 64
public art, 170–85, 204, 326–47

queer, 19, 206–33, 237, 239, 243, 284, 307, 345.
  See also bisexual; gay; lesbian

R.A.M.M. Theater, 12
race, 18, 196, 200, 213–18, 220, 238, 242
Rainer, Yvonne, 67, 69, 229
Rauschenberg, Robert, 68, 71
Rediscovering Pompeii, 263–65
Reich, Steve, 10
revolution, 32, 111–12, 329
Riggs, Marlon, 208, 213–14, 218–22, 229; Tongues
  Untied, 218–22
ritual, 9, 16, 242, 245–47, 297
Rokeby, David, 118
Ronell, Avital, 24
Rosenbach, Ulrike, 164–65
Russo, Vito, 256
Ryan, Joel, 118

Said, Edward W., 8
Salecl, Renata, 345–46
Salich, Jo Siamon, 348–51
Salzmann, Alexander von, 40
sampling, 30, 64, 133
Sarajevo, 3–6, 21, 58, 75, 110–11
Sarries-Zgonc, Imma, xxv, 116, 130–43, 326–27,
  335, 349–50
Schiele, Egon, 36

Schiphorst, Thecla, 118, 120

Schlemmer, Oskar, 32, 44–46, 50, 59, 63; *Figural Cabinet I,* 45; "Man and Art Figure," 44–45; *Triadic Ballet,* 32, 43

Schmidt, Beverly, 69

Schneemann, Carolee, 8–9, 155, 256–57, 274–75

Schneider, Ira, 158

Schwartz, Hillel, 36

Schwarzbek, Lisa Dianne, 239, 246, 251–52

Schwarzkogler, Rudolf, 156

science, 53–55, 243, 258–64, 266–85

sculpture, 29, 44–46. *See also* video

Sellars, Peter, 19

Sermon, Paul, 119. 121–23, 26

sexuality, 279–85; and transsexuals, 283–84. *See also* biotechnology

Sharir, Yacov, 124–25

Sherman, Cindy, 242

Simmons, John, 307–8

Simpson, Lorna, 242

simulation, 159, 172, 258, 262–67, 269–70, 298–305, 309, 322

Singer, Linda, 256

situationism, 176–85, 331–47

slavick, elin o'hara, 239, 246, 251–52

Smith, Anna Deavere, 68

Smith, Kiki, 268

Smith, Sean, 268

Snajder, Slobodan, 4

social dance, 28, 30–31, 78–79, 323

socialism, 49–52, 326–47 passim

social psychotherapy, 250

Sorokin, Vladimir, 48

space, 11, 28–47, 50–55, 170, 272–77, 296–304; and architecture, 46–49; of bodies, 33–46, 50–58; movement as production of, 29–31, 37, 294–97; social, 175–85, 221, 309, 326–47; urban, 270–71. *See also* cyberspace

spectacle, 4–5

Spence, Jo, 237, 240, 242, 245–56

Spiderwoman Theater, 17, 240, 243, 245–46

Split Britches, 17, 284

Sprinkle, Annie, 17, 240, 243, 247–48, 284

Squat Theatre, 10

Stefanofski, Goran, 5–6, 22

Steggell, Amanda, 118, 128–30

Stelarc, xv, 5, 59–65, 72, 129, 138, 156; *Actuate/Rotate,* 63

Stone, Allucquere Rosanne, 308

Street-Level Video, 174–85, 231

Stuart, Meg, 20, 22, 87–88, 128

suprematism, 32

surrealism, 32

Syberberg, Hans-Jürgen, 48

Tabori, George, 48

Tajiri, Rea, 241

Tamblyn, Christine, 314–17, 322

Tanztheater, xiv, 3, 27–31, 86–95, 99, 165. See also *Ausdruckstanz*

Tatlin, Vladimir, 37, 51–52

technology, xiv, 75, 94–101, 118–44, 145–47, 258–347 passim; in art, 45, 61; as disembodiment, 258–326; and science, 258–70, 272–347. *See also* dance; machine aesthetic; video

television, 5, 21, 145–47, 149, 152–53, 170–72, 178, 221, 229, 231, 234, 294, 320, 333, 349; and MTV, 10, 149–52, 240, 262, 308; and neighborhood, 178–85

Tessenow, Heinrich, 39

Thater, Diana, 9

theater, 3–37, 49, 51–58, 70–73, 240–46, 260, 296–97, 334–37; and avant-garde, 4, 8–10, 12; Next Wave Festival at BAM, 13; as "physical theater," 12–13, 20–24, 28, 47, 53, 72–86. See also *Tanztheater*

Théâtre du Soleil, Le. *See* Mnouchkine, Ariane

Theodores, Diana, 119, 127–28

Thornton, Sarah, 30

Torres, Francesc, 172–74

transavanguardia, 10

transculturation, 17, 285–99, 304–11

Treichler, Paula A., 272–73

Trinh, T. Minh-ha, 165–66, 241

Tropicana, Carmelita, 17

Trotzky, Leon, 38

Turkle, Sherry, 309, 311

Udongo, Ayana, 230

Ullmann, Victor, 48

utopia, 33–47, 284, 292, 350

Vandekeybus, Wim, xiv, 12, 20, 23, 76–86; *Mountains Made of Barking,* 77, 79–86; in *The Power of Dance,* 79–86; *Roseland,* 77, 79; and Ultima Vez, 76–77; *What the Body Does Not Remember,* 80

Vertov, Dziga, 38

Victory over the Sun, 56

video, 13, 70, 75–86, 108, 110–18, 190–203, 260, 267–69, 295, 304, 314–17, 319, 321; art, 8–10, 145, 152–85; and grassroots activism, 163, 174–85, 205–33, 248, 256–57, 269, 277, 336–47; conferencing, 121–23; documentary, 190–203; and history, 170–85; installation, 9, 154–65; "In Visible Colors," 163, 165–66; and the museum, 166–72; performance, 9, 110–18, 155, 157, 165, 191–215; projection, 136–38, 155, 170–72; sculpture, 9, 154–65; telematics, 127. *See also* AIDS

Index

videodance, 69, 79–86, 115, 165
Viola, Bill, 9, 166
Virilio, Paul, 260, 274
virtual reality, xvi, 5, 60–65, 75, 86, 95–101, 105,
    121–24, 130, 133–35, 138–39, 241, 263–70, 275,
    285, 289–326, 336, 338, 347
virtual space, 259, 263–64, 288–326, 328
VKhUTEMAS, 32, 46
voguing, 150–52, 219, 248, 250
Vostell, Wolf, 153–54, 164
voyeurism, 82, 151, 164, 223, 243, 247

Wagner, Richard, 42–43, 49, 348–51
Warhol, Andy, 151, 154, 211, 312
Watney, Simon, 174, 196
web art, 287, 319–26
Webb, David, 197
web cultures, 291–92
Weidt, Jean, 87
Went, Johanna, 242

Wigman, Mary, 33, 35–43, 50, 53, 58, 77–78,
    88–90, 92; *Ekstatische Tänze,* 42; at Hellerau,
    32–44; *Hexentanz,* 42–43
Wilke, Hannah, 242, 256
Wilson, Robert, 10–13, 19, 37, 46, 51, 71, 159;
    Einstein on the Beach, 71
Witnesses of Existence, 111
Wittgenstein, Ludwig, 98
Woodman, Francesca, 242
Wooster Group, 159
World Wide Web, 287–326 passim
Woynarowicz, David, 198, 200, 240, 243
Wuppertaler Tanztheater, xiv, 27, 86–94. *See also*
    Bausch

Zamyatin, Yevgeny, 306–7
Zapp, Andrea, 119, 127–28
Živadinov, Dragan, 20, 50–58; *Krst pod Triglavom,*
    51; *Noordung,* 54–58; *Warttenberg,* 54–58
Žižek, Slavoj, 51, 345

Library of Congress Cataloging-in-Publication Data

Birringer, Johannes H.
    Media & performance : along the border / Johannes Birringer.
        p.   cm. — (PAJ books)
    Includes bibliographical references and index.
    ISBN 0-8018-5851-8 (hardcover : alk. paper). — ISBN 0-8018-5852-6 (pbk. : alk. paper)
        1. Arts, Modern—20th century. 2. Performance. 3. Postmodernism. I. Title. II. Title:
    Media and performance. III. Series.
    NX212.B57   1998
    700'.9'04—DC21   98-12702 CIP